ROADS TO QUOZ

To Jim

Heatmoon

11/9/08

Also by William Least Heat-Moon

Blue Highways: A Journey into America

PrairyErth (a deep map)

River-Horse: A Voyage Across America

Columbus in the Americas

WILLIAM LEAST HEAT-MOON

ROADS TO QUOZ

An American Mosey

LITTLE, BROWN AND COMPANY

NEW YORK   BOSTON   LONDON

Little, Brown and Company
Hachette Book Group
237 Park Avenue, New York, NY 10017

Visit our Web site at www.HachetteBookGroup.com

First Edition: October 2008

Little, Brown and Company is a division of Hachette Book Group, Inc.
The Little, Brown name and logo are trademarks of Hachette Book Group, Inc.

Photo restorations by Ailor Fine Art Photography. Illustrations are by the author.

Library of Congress Cataloging-in-Publicaton Data
Heat-Moon, William Least.
  Roads to Quoz : an American mosey / William Least Heat-Moon — 1st ed.
    p. cm.
  ISBN 978-0-316-11025-9
  1. United States — Description and travel. 2. Heat-Moon, William Least —
Travel — United States. I. Title.
  E169.Z83H43 2008
  917.3 — dc22   2008019375

10 9 8 7 6 5 4 3 2 1

RRD-IN

DESIGNED BY LAURA LINDGREN

Printed in the United States of America

Para Quintana

CONTENTS

By Way of Explanation

"Upon my honour," cried Lynmere, piqued, "the quoz of the present season are beyond what a man could have hoped to see!"

"Quoz! What's quoz, nephew?"

"Why, it's a thing there's no explaining to you sort of gentlemen."

— Frances Burney,
Camilla,
1796

I.
Down an Ancient Valley

The Ouachita River Country

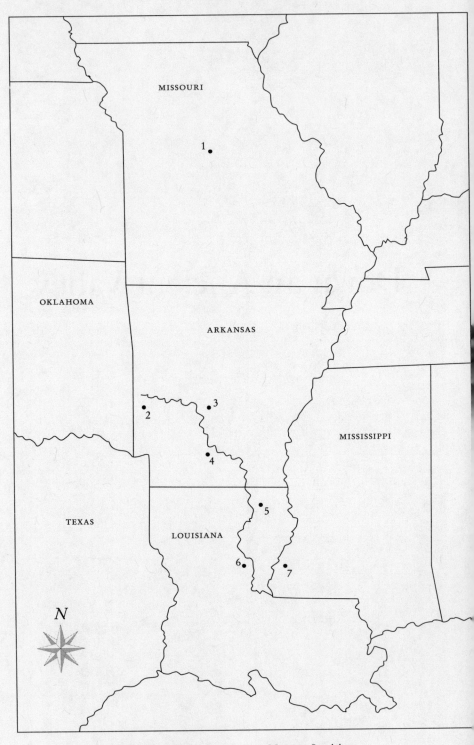

MISSOURI

OKLAHOMA

ARKANSAS

MISSISSIPPI

TEXAS

LOUISIANA

N

1 Columbia, Missouri   5 Monroe, Louisiana
2 Rich Mountain, Arkansas   6 Jonesville, Lousiana
3 Hot Springs, Arkansas   7 Natchez, Mississippi
4 Camden, Arkansas

Down an Ancient Valley

Before It Shall All Be Disenchanted

Alexandria, Louisiana, April 21, 1835

Dear Sir —

You remember the promise you exacted from me last summer in Philadelphia to visit the Maison Rouge Grant on the Ouachita. You see I adopt the good old French orthography of that river. I know not whether your motive was to give me pleasure or to inflict a salutary discipline. If the latter, should you take the trouble to read this, I shall have my revenge. In any view, I cannot doubt that it originated in a benevolent wish in some way to confer a benefit. I am now seated to give you a sketch of my mode of performing that promise. I spin this long yarn with the more confidence, being aware that you cannot but take an interest in reading surveys, however inadequate, of a region so extensive, so fertile, so identfied with your name as its possessor, into the alluvial swamps of which, in your bygone days, you too have plunged.

The Ouachita is a beautiful river, of interesting character and capabilities; and, although unknown to song, classical in forest narrative and tradition, as having been the locale of the pastoral experiments of the Marquess Maison Rouge and Baron de Bastrop, as well as many other adventurers, Spanish, French, and American, not to mention its relation to American history as the point where Aaron Burr masked his ultimate plans of ambition and conquest. I wish to seize some of its present fresh and forest features, before it shall all be disenchanted by being transformed into a counting-room flower-garden or cotton plantation. I will even hope that this sketch will awaken pleasant reminiscences of your own extensive journeys and stirring incidents in these remote central forests. You may, therefore, christen this prelude to my Ouachita trip a preface or an apology, at your choice.

— *Journal of the Rev. Timothy Flint,*
From the Red River to the Ouachita,
or Washita, in Louisiana in 1835

❥ 1 ❧

The Letter Q Embodied

As travelers age, we carry along ever more journeys, especially when we cross through a remembered terrain where we become wayfarers in time as well as space, where physical landscapes get infused with temporal ones. We roll along a road, into a town, past a café, a hotel, and we may hear stories and rising memories. Then our past is got with feet, and it comes forth: *There, I met her there.* Or, *That's the place, that's where he told me about the accident.* Since each day lived gets subtracted from our allotted total, recollections may be our highest recompense: to live one moment a score of times.

For me, having now become an elder of the road, these risings of memory from a specific topography can almost lead me to believe all previous miles have gone to create some single moment, and then I can see how meaning begins in and proceeds from memory. Backseated children able to find only boredom beyond car windows — *if they're looking out* — are nevertheless laying a foundation for meaning to arise one day when they'll need significance far more than experience.

My occasional stories to Q, which some particular landscape happens to evoke, serve to pass a stretch of slow miles as the tales also fortify my memory. I think she doesn't mind my rambles now and then, perhaps because in a "previous Administration" (an earlier marriage) she once crossed the length of Kansas in silence — unless you deem as conversation that quondam husband's "We gotta stop for gas."

7

Q is my wife, Jo Ann, a moniker for which she's never felt much kinship. In fact, with nomenclature she's not been lucky, even in her church. When it came time for confirmation, her elder sister convinced six-year-old Jo Ann every female saint's name was taken except one: Dorothy. That name, linked to the pluck of the *Wizard of Oz* heroine she admired, contributed to her deciding she possessed the power to fly *if* her belief was firm enough: she straddled a kitchen broom, her toy cat strapped to the bristles, and from the top of the basement stairs, leaped. She broke no bones, and if you consider falling in a slightly horizontal pattern to be flight, she flew. But she no longer trusted in half-reasoned faith.

But as Jo Ann grew up to become Jan (her tomboyishness would have made Joe not inaccurate), she learned to speak Spanish and visited Mexico, and found herself intrigued by a Yucatán place-name taken from a Mexican revolutionary hero, all the better that he was male: Quintana Roo. Quintana Roo — the state, not the man — is the territory of the quetzal, the plumed serpent sacred to the indigenous Maya, especially to the Quiché, and perhaps the most stunning bird in the Western Hemisphere north of the equator; to her, it's a creature of fascination.

Not long after our meeting, she told me about her delight in things beginning with the letter *Q,* a revelation at a restaurant-supper one night that struck a note within me — someone who has always loved the seventeenth letter for its rarity: a mere seven pages in my desk dictionary, while neighbor *P* gets 120. I like to think sinuous *Q* (only *O* has a more purely geometric form) makes up for its paucity in entries by its peculiarities of meanings, by its pictographic capital-shape (a serpent curling out of its den, a tethered balloon floating away, a hatchling with one foot out of the egg), and by its unbreakable bond with its beloved *U.* Of greater import are those quirky words we'd not have without *Q:* quark, quack, quadrillion, quantum, quidnunc, quoits, quench, quisling, quilt, quipster, quince, quincunx, and that most universal *nonword* on the planet, QWERTY. And, should I not mention that recondite Christian holy day, Quinquagesima, Shrove Sunday?

Is there another letter with such a high percentage of words both jolly and curious, so many having to do with quests and questions and quintessences? Is it not a letter of signal q-riousness? How could a fellow of the quill not love the letter Q? How could a defender of the underdog not love a letter that's the least used on a keyboard, the one that never takes on finger-shine?

Nonetheless Q, alphabetically superfluous, has tricks: For the tongue there's *quick* and *quiche;* for meaning there's *queer* and *queen;* and there's *quell* (put down) and *quell* (well up). And to enhance its mystery, Q has a dark side, words to give you qualms: queasy, quagmire, quarantine, quarrel, quibble, quinsy, quash, quackery, quietus, quake, quicksand, quadratic equation.

It's a letter that has suffered loss, thinning our language as we went about minding our p's while forgetting our q's; if Shakespeare possessed those lost words, why can't we? Here's a quorum of such quatches ripe for revival, ready for your quaintance: quaddle (grumble), quizzity (oddity), querken (stifle), quiddle (dawdle), querimony (complaint), queme (pleasant), quetch (go), queeve (twist in a road). And there's the handy *quisquilious:* in one sense it refers to something composed — like a life, a book — of odds and ends, and in another import it means rubbish.

I can see now the letter one of you will write me:

Dear Mister Fancy Author,
I'd like to querken your quiddles on the quizzities of the letter Q
because they aren't queme and leave me quaddling and full of
querimony. Stick to the queeves and get quetching on your way
to your quisquilious Quoz.

Querulously yours,
Ace Reeder

So that brings us to *quoz:* a noun, both singular and plural, referring to anything strange, incongruous, or peculiar; at its heart is the unknown, the mysterious. It rhymes with *Oz.* To a traveler, it's often the highest quaesitum. For me, everything — whether object, person, or event — when seen clearly in the depths of its existence, in its quiddity, is quoz, and every road, every alley, the hall to your parlor, the course of a creek, the track of a comet, all are a route to quoz for any traveler, any querist willing to question, to go in quest, to ask the cosmic question of medieval church drama: *Quem quaeritis?* Whom do you seek, O pilgrim?

Forgive me, quick-witted reader, if this quodlibet to Q has made you querimonious; I'll leave the letter and return to Q, the woman, after I tax you with one more notion. The vocabulary of our language is an abundant — and often untapped — storehouse of concepts neatly embodied in a few squiggles of ink or in a column of air vibrated by vocal cords. To fail to embrace and thereby honor a rich vocabulary is a sacrilege advocated by those who would reduce the expanse of our lexicon to fit their own limited expression; these are often novices and drudges and certain book reviewers who ought to be confined to the exposition of instructions for installing a water heater. A genuine roadbook should open unknown realms in its words as it does in its miles. If you leave a journey exactly who you were before you departed, the trip has been much wasted, even if it's just to the Quickee-Mart.

During that restaurant-supper, I admitted to Q — call it a quid pro quo — that since my boyhood, when my favorite number was five (I could handle it mathematically easier than, say, seven or nine), I've longed to be not William but five-lettered Quint. Its Roman version, Quintus, helped lead me in high school to enroll in Miss Nell Adams's Latin I and II. How different my life might have turned out with Spanish or French, I don't know, other than to say that somewhere among the ancient declensions of Rome and the Etruscan *qu*-words, I was becharmed by a girl seated in front of me, and for the next five years I discovered all that goes with infatuation. So you see, the letter Q has shaped me in ways beyond my comprehending, even now as I write these words.

While this recital of our pasts came forth, I think Q and I began to recognize a fellow traveler sitting across the table. There we were, our imagined names revealing more about us than could ever those strapped onto us by others. For me she was Quintana, only later becoming simply Q.

But I've become neither Quint nor Quintus. Because we met through a forgotten manuscript of William Clark — the William of the great 1804 to 1806 western expedition, he who is buried not far from where Q grew up along the Missouri River, he whom she was then writing a book about (the very undertaking that introduced us), he whom I am named after — Q has not been willing to yield up my William, and so to her, Will I am and remain.

She is a historian who left the practice of law not long after she discovered Clark's logbook of his 1798 trip down the Ohio and Mississippi rivers to New Orleans, a voyage — virtually unknown and totally unexamined until her research — he made six years before his ascent with Meriwether Lewis up the Missouri River and on to the Pacific. It was a journey I had made and written a book about just before I met Q. Over the course of the travels we were about to undertake, she would tell me from time to time of her surprising discoveries about William Clark descending the Mississippi into Spanish territory. So, along with my stories triggered by our passing a place I'd visited before, we began traveling miles overlaid with several dimensions of time. During these travels, Q was a quinquagenarian, and it was sheer chance we began them in the old lands of the Quapaw, and not far from the ancient Tunica "town" Quizquiz [Kees-Kees].

Because she's important to these roads to quoz, I'll try to set her before you now and then, but not by physical description except to say she is slender, with straw-colored corkscrew hair that can draw from men long glances that amuse me. No husband should undertake to describe his wife in detail, especially a wife who practices law and knows something of libel, invasion of privacy, and, when pressed, can even explain the Rule Against Perpetuities. It's unwise to monkey — in print, at least — with such professional counsel. I think she will emerge from her own words and doings which I hope will catch her quintessence and maybe even a touch of her mystery emanating from her quietness.

For now, let one incident reveal something of Q, an event in her eleventh year. Walking home from her parochial school with her friend Deborah, the pretty girls in their perky uniforms — white blouse, navy-blue pleated skirt, matching kneesocks — Q saw two lads from the public school approaching. As the children passed, one of the impious Protestant boys said, "You girls are sluts." Never breaking slide, Q gave him a raspberry. Deborah whispered, "What's a slut?" Young Q had no idea, but it sounded intriguing, so the girls went to the town library only a block away and opened the fat dictionary on a pedestal under the tapestry of George Washington. There, in the greatest single volume of American lexicography — *Webster's New International Dictionary of the English Language,* 2nd edition — they found the word. Narrowing the definitions meant looking up several other terms, but it was the illustrative citations from esteemed sources that shed light:

· "Sluts are good enough to make a sloven's porridge" (old proverb).
· "Such wicked sluts cannot be too severely punished" (Fielding).
· "Our little girl Susan is a most admirable slut" (Pepys).

Q said to her friend, "I have a feeling those twerps didn't mean this last definition."

Her capability to listen so intently to one of my stories may cause her to ask, well after the story is finished, "Did you say somebody tried to shoot you down like a dirty dog?" This happens because, while I'm getting a tale down its road, she takes a turn bending off in a promising way but not on the route of my narrative. I've learned to watch her face for indications her mind is heading for Texas when the story is on its way to Tennessee.

I'll mention now, in all of our miles over neglected and strange routes, she never once has complained of even the most twisted of intimidating roads. If she gets uneasy at one of my route decisions, she expresses it only with silence and a certain slant to her lower lip. But her nether lip can also betoken an odd idea or a different track coming on, sometimes resulting in a new route, including her idea of going to Arkansas to follow the Ouachita River.

In 1849, J. Quinn Thornton published a guide to westward emigration called *Oregon and California in 1848.* He said of the people setting out for the Far West that "some were activated by a mere love of change; more by a spirit of enterprise and adventure; and a few, I believe, knew not exactly why they were thus upon the road." If you will grant the writing of books as an enterprise, then of the other reasons J. Quinn enumerates, I could be convicted on all counts. But for me it is that last reason which underlies all the others, for to go out not quite knowing why is the very reason for going out at all, and to discover the *why* is the most promising and potentially fulfilling of outcomes. I'm speaking about a quest for quoz, of which I'll say more as we go along, but until then, you might want to see Quoz as a realm filled with itself as a cosmos is with all that's there, not just suns and planets and comets but dust and gas, darkness and light, and all we don't know, and only a fraction of what we can imagine.

I've spent so many years rambling alone and not knowing exactly the reason, I now believe the answer to why we "were thus upon the road" lies in both the *why* and the *how* I became a writer in the first place: to break those long silent miles, I must stop and hunt stories and only later set down my gatherings in order to release them one day to wander on their own. A few years ago, a friend traveling in Nepal was lying on a pallet in a dormitory; atop a small shelf he saw a book dust-jacket and my face watching him. He said to me later, "You've traveled where you've never been." To write is to have a reason for hoboing through one's life and sometimes through those of others, whether or not you've met them. It's for this reason you will find me now and again addressing you, the good reader. What the deuce, I might see you someday at that bookshop in Oshkosh or maybe we've already met at that lunch counter in Yazoo City.

13

These days, when Q and I take off down some two-lane where I begin to wander into a tale about that very road in another time, my recital is not just to pass uneventful miles; even more it's my try at recollecting and reclaiming what once occurred. After all, for each of us, at our finale — if we're lucky — we end up with only memory. As long as it lasts, memory — upon which love is utterly dependent — is the lone, truly portable outcome of our days. It's a snare for the transitory happenings that have been our life. Everything you will remember in your last days probably will come from encounters on your own roads to quoz. When one's past can no longer be summoned forth (even if elided and distorted as it must be through our frailties in perfect recall), that's the day we become a former person, a cypher with the rim rubbed out.

My first book ends with this fragment from a Navajo wind chant: "Remember what you have seen, because everything forgotten returns to the circling winds." Through those ancient words, and the others preceding them, Q first knew me and thereby set in motion our path to that supper conversation about the seventeenth letter of the alphabet.

As best I can figure it, my job is to go out and get stories and to pass them along as far as they can carry themselves. You can see what I'm saying: A search for quoz gives me a reason to get out of bed and step into the shower and wake up and once again take up a quest. That some particular quoz I find might one day later find you is not a requisite to my travels, but it surely is nice.

So then, quizzical reader, you who are yourself an infinity of quoz bound temporarily as one, it is now *you whom I seek* in hopes you're ready for the quest and ready with a second question: *Quo vadis?*

❧ 2 ❧

Mrs. Weatherford's Story

O N THE SECOND DAY of spring 2004, Q and I headed for the Ouachita Mountains, she at the wheel. I told her this story soon after we crossed the border of northern Arkansas not far from a road that triggered my recollection. I spoke of Mrs. Weatherford — as I'll call her here — and a tale she passed on to me some years earlier.

Traveling alone, I met her aboard the steamboat *Delta Queen* on a voyage down the Mississippi from St. Louis to New Orleans. By chance I got seated next to her at the supper table the first evening. Despite her age — barely shy of eighty — she was attractive, slender, and quick, and she was a widow. Although she had little formal education, Mrs. Weatherford was a reader and articulate and happy to let her two companions — rich ladies, as was she now — do most of the talking, yakking really. In their fifties, her friends were overweight, mirthful women from Houston whose husbands gladly set them up in expensive sun-deck cabins for long boat-trips. The two companions talked often about money but not in dollars. Rather, their terms were the chattel of a well-heeled suburban life: "Why, the ring he gave that girl!" or "That man has never known a mortgage!" or "The First Lady said my gown was to die for!" And so on. The pair fell silent only when Mrs. Weatherford told a story from a time none of us had seen; although she never spoke of money or the life attached to it, despite being wealthier than her shipmates.

After each supper, I would follow Mrs. Weatherford and her friends to a quiet deck near their cabins where they would pour a nightcap. Then was the time she would pull up a story. My dedicated attention must have been encouragement because she kept telling things the other two had never heard. Mrs. Weatherford's clear recollections made me wish her a relative or a neighbor, someone I could drop in on just to listen to what were really prose georgics from an era seemingly more distant than her years would allow. When she had finished a story, told in her soft Ozark cadence, I'd ask questions — the first night just to keep the others silent for a while longer but afterward to learn more details. She was pleased when I wrote some of them into my shirt-pocket memo book.

One evening we were sitting topside with our various nightcaps — mine was two fingers of a Kentucky straight Bourbon distilled not far to the east of where the boat was just then. We were watching a kind of alpenglow on the horizon behind a dark mass of big cottonwoods having the silhouette of low mountains. I said the sunset must be radiating all across Arkansas, and Mrs. Weatherford straightened in her chair as she did when something stirred her memory.

The version I set down now is from my notes:

"None of you know I grew up in north Arkansas," she said. "The western side, in the hills. It was mostly rocks, soil no thicker than worn-out muslin. Everything, except our chickens, we had to get out of a creek-bottom field so small Poppa could plow it with a mule in a day. The hills were good for firewood and some walnuts and a squirrel or two. We didn't eat coon. Usually, dessert was a half-dozen verses from the Bible. King James Version."

She paused and picked up my tumbler of whiskey and held it up against the dusky western sky to make the liquor gleam in a deepened hue. She put the glass down again and said, "My mother would call that 'the color of sin.' To her it was 'the distillation of damnation.'" (Mrs. Weatherford, for her part, took an occasional vodka, neat.) She said, "Poppa made a clear, corn whiskey that would burn the gallstones out of your uncle's brother."

"You're talking moonshine?" one of her friends asked.

"White lightning, bottled-in-the-barn booze. Ozark nose paint. Field whiskey. By whatever name you want, Momma knew it as sin, and she knew it was only a question of time before the Lord was going to settle up with Poppa. Now, at her insistence, he would read the evening Bible verses to us, but he could just as well have been reading the labels on a feed sack, and when it came to his still, there wasn't anyone — man or woman or wife — going to argue him out of that. And the Sunday-school teacher didn't help because he was known to accept on the q.t. a quart every holiday, including his birthday. He drank in his cellar and never showed himself until he'd finished it all and slept it off. The congregation said his wife was usually down there with him. And sometimes, so we heard, they'd get 'plumb nekkid.' Otherwise, he was vociferous against alcohol, and Momma accepted him because she thought his words might work on somebody. He liked to say, 'I have known the jeopardous sin of liquor,' as if those days were past.

"And of course Momma knew that without the money from Poppa's still, she'd be hard-pressed to set the table three times a day for four of us. I'm talking now of the early thirties. Even our church dresses had mendings over the mendings. Poppa wasn't above nipping into some of his finishings but never in front of us children. Even on a cold night, if he had a couple of nips, he'd stay down in the shed where the works were, curled up near the fire. He called it 'the works.' I think he drank mostly because of our poverty. He was ashamed of not providing more for us."

Mrs. Weatherford, once she had our attention, would take long pauses, holding them like a concert master just to the right moment, then she'd follow on with her memory as if it were a score she knew well but hadn't conducted in years.

Nodding toward the sunset, she said, "Over there, it's almost like the northern lights. They call them the northern lights because they don't shine in the South, or at least not very often down this way. In northwest Arkansas they hadn't shone ever as far as anyone back then could recall. Nobody had any idea what they were.

"Well" — and here she took her first long pause — "they did shine one night, and they did it with a glory as if they were making up for all those years of dark skies. One evening Momma came out of the kitchen onto the porch to sit a spell before bed. My older sister, Maylene, and I were there waiting for her. It was late in the year, and she had her shawl on. She sat there humming a hymn, collecting herself, always wanting to be ready for salvation. She stopped in the middle of her hymn and said, 'Why, girls, look over in that corner of the sky!' and she pointed to the north toward a long ridge that sort of shut us in. 'The Atgoods' barn must be on fire!' It was well past sundown, but the sky was rosy like dusk, except that bright sky was in the north. We went round the house to the front to see better, and there it was — the whole north was a pale curve of light rising from the tree line. We stood and watched it until we were certain it was truly getting brighter. Momma went to the window to holler up Poppa to come outside. He stepped out on the front stoop in his union suit he slept in when the weather cooled.

"By now there were rays like searchlights shooting up. Then the bottom part started turning orange and flickering just like fire. Poppa said, 'That ain't the Atgoods',' and Momma said, 'Oh dear Jesus!' I thought this was all good fun until I saw her face. She was alarmed. Alarmed bad. And I looked at Poppa. It was the same expression when he saw Maylene fall off the mule.

"I'm vowing to you the sky was like the old picture-show curtain in Fort Smith. I mean the sky was moving the way folds in the curtain swung when it got pulled open or closed. We just stood there watching until lower down the sky started getting even brighter, and rays seemed to kind of clump up and form into a big, flickering crown just like a king would wear.

"At the sight of that, Momma stepped back so sharply she banged her head against the house and didn't even know it. She said, 'It's here! It's here! It's happening tonight! *This is the night!*' And she grabbed me and Maylene and started pulling us toward the house. 'What's here?' Maylene said. 'What's happening tonight, Momma?' 'The Lord, child! The Lord! The Lord's a-coming!'

"Now, she was a practical woman, more clearheaded under pressure than Poppa who was still standing there in his droopy union suit and his mouth hanging open. I was starting to cry. Maylene said, 'Should we get under the bed?' 'No, child! You don't hide from the Lord! You girls go inside and put on your church dresses and lay out straight on the bed! And I mean straight.' She shoved us toward the house, then called out like an afterthought, 'And wash your feet!'

"We did it fast, but we didn't get in bed. We went to the window. Now the sky had flashes coming up from below like gigantic flames. Momma had hold of Poppa's arm and was shaking it and talking fast. All I heard was 'And, Cloyd, I mean now!'

"The whole sky seemed to be on fire. Momma saw us in the window and yelled, 'Get into bed and get R-E-A-D-Y! Ready! The Gates of Hades have been opened, girls!' She and Poppa disappeared around the back and headed down into the hollow toward where the still was. But we didn't get into bed — we went to the back porch and hid in the shadows. There were terrible sounds, Momma shouting, something smashing into wood and metal, glass breaking, and every so often a shower of sparks rose up. That went on for maybe twenty minutes, and then we smelled smoke, and then we saw a glow in the treetops down in the hollow. Maylene said, 'Poppa's burning the works.'

"It didn't take long. We saw Momma coming toward the house. We ran back to the bed and got ourselves all laid out like we'd been told. She came to the door and looked in on us. I said, 'I'm scared, Momma.' She stepped into the room and stood over us. 'This is Judgment Day, girls. If you've done right, you'll be ascending. Graves all over the county are opening. The Arising has begun! The Glory has come!' and she left the room. Then Maylene started crying. She was afraid Resurrection zombies were going to come forth and reach through the window and carry us off to damnation.

"Then Poppa came back. He wasn't scared anymore. We heard him say to Momma — his voice was so weary, so defeated — 'It's gone. Every last quart of it. Gone.' And Momma said, 'Our need for money is gone too, Cloyd. This is all dross now. Wash yourself and come in and pray with us.'

"Momma called us into the front room and told us to get down on our knees. Maylene said, 'Are we going to die now?' And Momma said, 'Girls, I can't tell you. I've never been through one of these before.'

"Poppa came in with his church shirt on. I don't know whether his face was red from the fire or from crying. Momma commenced praying, pointing out how we little ones were too young to have much sin attached to us. Then she took up Poppa's cause, a more complicated one, given the liquor and his occasional cussing. I don't remember much of it because I was watching the window. The sky had faded, but there was still enough light to see Jesus when he appeared to call us Home. After a while we went back to bed to wait, and the next thing I remember is the window was white with light and Maylene was asleep, her mouth open. I poked her to see if her soul had ascended yet. 'Quit it!' she said. Apparently it hadn't.

"It was dawn. I got up. My Sunday dress was a muss of wrinkles. I went down to the hollow to where the works had been. It was just a heap of ashes and some twisted and scorched metal and broken glass everwhere.

"Everbody was up when I got back. Poppa was at the kitchen table with his head in his hands. He wouldn't talk. Momma said, 'We'll just go about our affairs until the Lord or one of his angels comes for us. But first, get down on your knees.' And she went to praying again, pointing out the innocence of children, making specific comment about her responsibility for the time in the schoolyard when the elastic in my underpants broke and let them fall to the ground. Then she called on Poppa to ask forgiveness, but he just kept his head on the table. So she tried to intercede for his 'Sin in the Hollow,' emphasizing that the liquor he made was to provide for his family and, besides, he'd now renounced 'Distilled Damnation' by destroying the 'Machinery of the Devil' and pouring the 'Liquid Hellfire' into the ground. At that, Poppa raised his head as if to say something, but only a little moan came out, and he just put his weary head back down.

"Momma went on, working her way into her sins — leaving a few out, like judgmentalism — but before she could finish, we heard the sound of some old flivver come sputtering up toward the house. Maylene ran to the front porch and said, 'Is Jesus coming for us in a Ford car?' I went to the window and peeked from behind the curtain. I told them I didn't think it was Jesus unless Jesus wore baggy seersucker pants and a slouch hat.

"We were all frozen. Even Poppa had his head up. There was a rap at the door that might as well have been a rifle shot, we all jumped so. Nobody moved. I'd never seen Momma so fixed. There was another rapping, and a voice said, 'Hey in there! Lampkin!' Poppa, maybe figuring he had nothing more to lose, slowly went to the door. 'Lampkin!' the voice called again. Like a summons.

"Poppa opened the door, opened it real cautious. The voice spoke again, too low for us to understand, and Poppa turned to us inside and said, 'Tain't Jesus. It's a feller from Ioway.' Aware that it might be Jesus in disguise to test her charity, Momma ordered Poppa to let him in. The stranger stepped in, removed his hat, and turned it nervously in his hands. Nobody said a word. We were waiting for him to tell us how to proceed to Heaven, or perhaps Hades, in Poppa's case. The man just twiddled his hat. Maylene whispered to me Jesus hadn't shined his shoes. Finally, to break the silence, he said, 'That was some show in the sky last night.'

"Poppa said, 'Tell my missus why you're here.' Can you imagine it? Momma was about to hear Jesus address her with his instructions for her salvation. If you could see her face! It was saying, 'Yes, Lord? Yes, Lord? Show me The Way, Lord Jesus! O, the glory!'

"The stranger, still fiddling with his hat, turned to Poppa to make sure he was to divulge his mission. 'Tell her,' Poppa said. 'Go ahead on.'

" 'Well, ma'am, I'm passing through, you see, and I got directed out here to your place.' Momma, so excited, interrupted him, 'And you've come for us!' and he said, 'Ma'am, I just come for a couple of quarts.' "

Here Mrs. Weatherford conducted a long pause. The longest yet, and she punctuated it with a sip of her vodka.

"Poor Momma!" she said. "Why, that stranger didn't come to carry away her soul! He came to carry away a couple of quarts of Arkansas nose paint."

And again Mrs. Weatherford performed a pause before her baton of words moved again.

"But then Momma recovered. Fast recovery was one of her strengths. It was a test! And she and Poppa had passed it! In triumph she said, 'Gone! All of it gone! Cleansed with Righteous Fire! Gone!' It was too much for Poppa. He went back to his chair and buried his head in his hands again. The stranger didn't quite understand, but he knew something was wrong. He said, 'Did you folks have a fire last night? I'm smelling smoke or something.'

"Momma said, 'A Righteous Fire, right here on Earth, right here last night. One to match that glorious one of Yours in the sky.' The man, who was stepping toward the door to leave, said, 'It was a glory for certain last night. It was as good as we used to see them up in north Iowa, but I never seen so much flickering orange before.'

"At that, Poppa raised his head. 'What's it you're talkin about?' and the stranger said, 'Them lights last night. That oral borlis or whatever they call it. You know, them northern lights.'

"Poppa got up real slow and went up to the stranger and said, 'That's what northern lights is? All them movin colors?'

" 'That's them,' the man said, and excused himself. He could smell trouble. Poppa told us to go to our room and close the door. We heard him yelling, then there was a terrible thud, and we came rushing out. Jesus must be throwing Poppa like he did the moneylenders! But there Poppa was, standing over Momma who was sprawled on the floor with a bloody lip. He was saying, 'I just hope you didn't know all the time, because if you did —' Then he hurried out to catch the stranger before he got away. Loud enough for Momma to hear, he said to the stranger, 'Give me ten days. You'll have to bring your own jugs.' "

Mrs. Weatherford stopped and drained her little glass. One of her friends said, "And your mother?" Mrs. Weatherford thought about it. "Momma took that as final proof that some men can't ever, by any force, be healed. Her time with Poppa would be in this world and only in this world."

Then, cradling the empty glass, Mrs. Weatherford closed her eyes and seemed to be gathering herself. There was something more. The last lines of her recollections were always something more.

"My mother," she said quietly, "was so locked into her notion of an afterlife of one kind or other she just didn't put much value on their final years together here on Earth."

3

Rivers and Dominoes

THE ARKANSAS JUNKET was to be the first leg of a long trip that would become a continuing but not continuous journey. Q and I would set forth for several weeks, loop about, return home to pick up the mail and water the wilted begonia, then strike out again. A circuit more of directions than destinations. This pattern, I confess, had something to do with my becoming a high-mileage, back-route geezer who loves his travels but has come in his seniority to want them in smaller portions. Nothing sharpens a traveler for the road better than the grindstone of home, and never have I arrived home but with great relief nor have I ever set out except with eager expectation. The English writer William Hazlitt said in 1825, "I should like well enough to spend the whole of my life in traveling abroad, if I could anywhere borrow another life to spend afterward at home." Circling in and out of our place would be a compromised solution to such a wish.

On the third day of spring, Q and I found ourselves in the Ouachita Mountains of Arkansas, a couple of hours west of Little Rock, traveling through the Ouachita National Forest that is largely contiguous with the rumpled belt of those untypically latitudinal mountains. We were there in search of the highest and most distant water of the Ouachita River so that we could follow it for its six-hundred miles from top to bottom, source to mouth. I've traveled rivers before — upstream, downstream — but usually atop them, *on* them. This time I wanted to follow *the valley* of a long river to see how it and its humanity fill the shape it has cut for itself. A river fits

its vale as a seed its fruit, but to know the pit is not also to know the peach. Could an artist who has never seen a pomegranate paint the fruit from studying its seeds?

If the name Ouachita is one you've seen on a map but never heard pronounced, you might want to hear it correctly in your mind: WASH-uh-taw or, more locally, WASH-taw. The people along it take some merriment in a visitor who asks a question about the Ooo-uh-CHITT-uh. No need to divulge how I learned that.

Ouachita is also spelled in a more English fashion as Washita — especially in Oklahoma, where lies the western end of its mountains — but that version can lead people to confuse it with the smaller Wichita Mountains near the Texas Panhandle. The French set down the name in their orthography with reference to a group of indigenous folk and their territory. Although distantly related, the Ouachita people, like the mountains, should not be confused with the Wichita tribe farther west where it maintains a noteworthy presence in western Oklahoma; as for the current whereabouts of the Ouachita, that's something of a mystery. My guess is that they live on in the blood of several extant tribes more broadly known as Caddo.

Q and I were in the Ouachita Mountains because she had begun talking some months earlier about a "Forgotten Expedition," one that two centuries ago had the potential to be in significance second only to the Lewis and Clark exploration. Of the numerous words in the English language that will disrupt whatever else I'm thinking about, *forgotten* and *expedition* are two of them. Put them together, and I'll listen with an interest beyond reason.

Having purchased the unimaginably large tract of land called the Louisiana Territory, Thomas Jefferson knew the first requirement for it was to establish dominion, and to do so Americans had to understand the territory and fix a military and economic presence in it. Lewis and Clark were to perform those functions in the northwest portion of the great purchase and on westward (when they crossed the Rockies at Lemhi Pass on the present-day Montana-Idaho border, they left the United States). For the southwest section — and beyond — Jefferson called upon a Scottish immigrant, William Dunbar, who asked assistance from another Scot, George Hunter.

I've not done so, of course, but were I to stand on a downtown corner of Toledo or Boston or San Jose or any other city you might name and wait for *just one* passerby to tell me *just one* thing about the Dunbar-Hunter Expedition, I'd likely be standing there among the citizens weeks later. Such an unawareness, though, is not really their fault; rather it's the result of historians themselves generally overlooking early explorations into the near Southwest, a situation slowly changing. For myself, I can't profess to have known much about the two Scots until Q revealed my ignorance; in defense of all of us, I can only say, to find a copy of either explorer's account was, until not long ago, difficult. Still, a copy of Hunter's *Journal of an Excursion from Natchez on the Mississippi up the River Ouachita* had been sitting unread on my shelves for several years. The Dunbar-Hunter exploration — the "Forgotten Expedition" undertaken in 1804, exactly two centuries before our arrival in the mountains — seemed to me a useful hook to pull us toward the resident quoz of the Ouachita Valley.

So there we were in the mountains. That morning we followed on a topographic map a narrow blue line, one we assumed to represent the nascent river, a streamlet through a pinched, forested declivity where U.S. Highway 59 keeps close to what we took for the infant Ouachita. It was but six or seven feet wide and narrowing rapidly as we ascended what was no longer a valley but more a broad cleavage in the mountains. As the creek neared the crest of the two-lane, its continuance at last became so indeterminable, we stopped so I could climb a small signal-tower along the tracks of the Kansas City Southern Railway paralleling both creek and blacktop. Oklahoma lay six miles west. I called down to Q we were running out of water. What was now scarcely more than a runnel disappeared under a tangle of wiry brush, and beyond were only seeps and dribbles. She said the map gave no name to the blue squiggles delineating creeklets.

I climbed down and took a taste of the Ouachita without swallowing, and we crossed the road and headed toward a building, a general merchandise set among scraggly pines and still-leafless oaks. I said the name on the store, Rich Fountain, was probably a confirmation we were indeed at the headwaters. Q looked at me with something between compassion and amusement and said, "You might want to reread that sign." I did: RICH MOUNTAIN SNACKS, CRAFTS, GROCERIES. My frequent wishful thinking sometimes allows Q to outsleuth me.

Inside, the wooden place was older than its new facade suggested, and its happy clutter exhaled the classic scent of an old grocery, making me forget the question I came in with, not just because of the smell of food but also because the place was not quaint — it was simply genuine, a quality ever more uncommon these days along the American road.

Q ordered up two cheese sandwiches, a MoonPie, and a couple of "sodas," despite my earlier advisement that we were now in the land of *pop*, where *soda* could refer to a carbonated ice-cream drink, seltzer, a baking substance, or a bicarbonate of. She, who has her moments of sauciness, said, "That particular usage will never pass my lips." This is what happens when one grows up near St. Louis where folks insist on pronouncing the state name Muh-zoo-ree, when those of us on the western side know it's Muh-zoo-rah — just as it's soda *pop*. We like onomatopoeia. My old friend Gus Kubitzki, of whom you will hear more later, used to insist the term should be spelled *sodaPOP!* and be pronounced with a click of the tongue as if we were Hottentots. Step into an old soda fountain in Kansas City — should you be determined enough to search out one — and order up a "soda," and you'll be asked, "What flavor?" If you then name, say, a cola, you'll be considered insane, for sodas are made usually with vanilla, chocolate, or strawberry ice cream. Our marriage, thus far, has been able to surmount such linguistic variances, much as a number of marriages in Cincinnati have survived the local pronunciations of the final vowel of their city.

I was standing among the shelves of "crafts" and looking at the slow blinks of the resident reptile required in these places, this particular critter an iguana. A lanky man whose dark hair belied his nearly seventy years came up to converse: "He's direct from Mexico. Won't eat a bug without pepper sauce and a side of tortillas." The fellow, dentureless, spoke in deep Ozarkian but said he hailed, years past, from Minnesota. He'd been a long-haul trucker who drew good pay, but the work didn't allow him to put to use his professed master's degree in archaeology. He asked me, "Got yourself a skull?" I started to say *No, just sawdust up there.* Then I noticed he was displaying for me a cow skull painted with a desert scene in colors unknown to nature but available on the hood of a stock car or in a peyote-induced dream.

I said I didn't need any wall art but I could use some information an archaeologist might know. He changed from clerk to professor when I asked if the creek across the road was the Ouachita River. "That's her," he said, "and right here's where she heads up." He waved toward the front window. "You go a few steps on west, and the water there runs down the other side of the mountain plumb into Oklahoma. This here's a pass."

Curious how far his knowledge reached, I asked where the Ouachita went to. "Down the mountain," he said. How far? "I know she gets over to Hot Springs, but after that I cain't say. Maybe she just gets soaked up in them springs, and that's all she wrote."

We conducted this conversation while he trailed me around the store. In walking from the east-side shelves of cedar boxes and onyx ashtrays to the lima-bean shelf on the west, we'd walked halfway across town: the store and a couple of attendant buildings *are* Rich Mountain, Arkansas. Just beyond the bean cans, effectively the town line, was a domino game where a trio of elders — each accoutred with a mug of cold coffee, a butt-filled ashtray, and an abacus to tally points — sat at an old, rough-sawn wooden table with one chair empty for whoever might turn up next. Over the years, the sliding of the tiles into play at the center of the table had worn through the yellowed enamel-paint and into the wood to create a shadow of a Celtic cross or, to change cultures, the figure of the Zia on the flag of New Mexico, an emblem of light and friendship. I pointed it out to Q who saw the cruciform in the table as a quilt-block design. And it was that too.

The room, with its shelved goods and artless crafts, was turned into an authentic country-store — that abused term of our time — by the domino game, for without it you would have an auto without an engine, a pen without ink, a torso without a heart.

Sometimes a good journey is like stepping into an empty chamber of blank walls, which the traveler is free to make into his own space by appointing it with representative furniture and accent pieces found en route. For my Ouachita room, I'd come upon a graven table. It is just such a quoz that a traveler can carry away into subsequent years, a transport allowing us for a time to snatch a small something from the maw of impending mortality and to have a sound answer to a disturbing question: Was I really present that day if, a few weeks later, it left me with nothing other than a little more sag here, more droop there, and one less day to be alive?

4

The Wandering Foot

MOTHERS, FATHERS, GIVE FORETHOUGHT to what you allow your children to sleep under. I don't mean roofs and rafters; I mean something closer to their skin, their heartbeats, their souls, if you will. My parents, early, put me under a quilt hand-stitched by a paternal great-grandmother, a woman who saw Abraham Lincoln at Gettysburg and a few years later packed her things into a covered wagon near Reading, Pennsylvania, and walked beside it all the way to the western Ozarks of Missouri. She knew something of hard travel, and that could be why she especially liked a quilt pat-

 tern commonly known as "wandering foot" or "turkey tracks." It has at least two other names: "flying swallows" and "flying corners." You can readily see all those images in the pattern.

For each of her first three grandchildren, she made quilts of wandering feet until the death of the youngest, a World War II airman whose plane was brought down over Holland by Third Reich flak — what one could call fly-ing corners of steel. Thereafter, she changed to "snail" or "basket" patterns for the last three grandchildren, her designs becoming ever more ones of security and stasis.

Some years ago I came upon a batch of my father's photographs in an old two-drawer, wooden cigar box that still smelled of tobacco. The pictures were curling up as they used to do before synthetic backings. One of them showed a child in a white dress making a wobbly pursuit after a flock of semidomesticated turkeys, a breed feathered in their fine natural colors. On the back was penciled, "Bill's First Steps." My father had snapped the picture in 1940 on his grandmother's farm in the Missouri Ozarks. She was the maker of the quilts, the woman who, thirteen years later at age ninety-four, picked my fourteenth birthday to die on. If you will imagine a kind of spiritual mitochondrial DNA, she is my key link with the nineteenth century for reasons that go beyond the story here, but relevant now are her quilts which to me serve as further evidence of ways the peculiar and the seemingly random — the quoz of a human life — can shape it. We can't choose our ancestors, but they, often in ways never to be guessed, can select pieces of *our* future.

I asked my parents what was going on in that photo and why I was wearing a dress. My mother quickly said, before my father could concoct a tale about boys dressed like girls, "All little children at that age wore dresses then. It was easier." She was talking of diaper changes. He said, "You saw those turkeys, and you got up off your hands and knees for the first time, and you went staggering after them. I didn't see you until I heard the women hollering. Your mother was saying, 'Look! He's walking!' and your aunt was shouting at me, 'Get holt of that boy before those turkeys flog him!' They'd flogged your little cousin Marlene the year before, and Uncle Charley took a stick and killed one of them."

I got snatched up short of any avian confrontation, but once I was set down again, my days of hands-and-knees locomotion were finished (except for an evening in Penzance, England, in 1969 when I took too literally the phrase *pub crawl*). Today I believe bedding me down under a cotton quilt covered by 120 turkey tracks created in trapunto is the likely reason my mind chose a pursuit of fowl as the moment to put feet under itself for better exploration. That the maker of the quilt was the very woman who daily fed those dozen bipedal-gobblers confirms it all in my mind.

But it doesn't stop there. I continued to use the quilt; in fact, I napped under it the day before Q and

I headed toward the Ouachita Mountains, and I offer now the possibility that its influence gravitated from turkey tracks to wandering feet.

After we left the store atop Rich Mountain and I'd said something about memory and how the domino table was the first furnishing in my Ouachita room, she, whose interest in quilts goes beyond mere curiosity in Q things, said, "My memory is like a quilt, a crazy quilt. Happenings come back to me in recall so haphazardly." As we drove toward a quiet spot in the forest to eat our sack lunch, she picked up the topic again. "My memory is a quilt wearing thin with time. It has holes in it." She paused to reason her trope. "But if I don't unfold it and spread it out and use it, the fabric itself begins to vanish." She saw me writing down her words, and she said in a resonant voice as if she were onstage, "Eaten away by the moths of time." And a mile farther along, she said, "By the way, there's a boy in my family who slept many nights in a Teenage Mutant Ninja Turtle sleepingbag. Except for his martial-arts class, he's growing up inside an invisible shell."

Several weeks later, looking in a book to verify the names I used for the design on my coverlet, she came across a couple of sentences in *Quilts in America:* "A pattern called 'Wandering Foot' was thought to convey wanderlust. As such, it was never used on a young person's bed for fear he or she would travel west and never be heard from again; eventually the block was renamed 'Turkey Tracks' to break the jinx." It's a peculiar sensation to see one's life reflecting folklore, even if it reverses, well, the pattern. For me, the design is an emblem of anyone's quest for quoz, a graphic reminder of an ancient notion found in Asian thought: *Wandering can help restore one's humanity and reestablish the harmony once existing between us and the cosmos.* I add that even if such harmony is only imagined, a longing for it can humanize.

I'm indebted to my westering, quilting great-grandmother and to my unsuperstitious father — who taught me how to read both books and maps — for bedding me down under a welter of turkey tracks across a field of blue and for sending me out wandering westward and to every other point of the compass which he also taught me to read. So far, it's been a pretty good life, pieced together as if a quilt, from books, maps, and an old puritanical jinx.

Greene County, Missouri, 1940.

✎ 5 ✎

A Planetary Washboard

THE OUACHITAS TOO HAVE WANDERING FEET — around, up, down. That is to say they've been transported and translocated by plate tectonics, orogeny, and erosion, and those forces make them a fit metaphor for a human life and the way we're born from a uterine sea, carried about until we become self-locomoting and find our elevation rising before sometime later we begin to see the erosions of time on our bodily substance.

Four-hundred-million years ago, the Ouachitas were sediments. A hundred-million years later, having become shales and sandstones, yet still submerged on the globe far distant from where they are today, they began heading westerly on a collision course that would assist in raising them above the ocean. Once risen, they began moving back down again flinder by flinder toward the sea from whence they came, for nature aboveground seems to abhor a mountain or even a hill: wind and rain and gravity make certain all which rises will fall. Dame Nature is an acrophobe. On Rich Mountain — the name comes from pockets of fecund soil created out of the hard mountain by erosive elements — you can see one proof of that natural abhorrence for height in the so-called rock glaciers, massive swaths of sandstone boulders slipping down the mountain not tokus over teakettle but like a quilt drawn off a bed, sliding down as if pulled, as in fact they are.

I should mention here a local notion that certain fertile basins on Rich Mountain — places especially good for raising vegetables — are the result of years of feculence left by millions of roosting passenger pigeons (this, of course, before humanity exterminated the last of the species within living memory). Once, the number of wood, or wild, pigeons (think not of a dismal city-bird but a mourning dove decorating itself in handsome red feathering) may have been greater than all other American species combined, and the sizes of their roosting grounds defy easy comprehension. In Kentucky, John James Audubon wrote about one that was three miles wide and forty miles long, and said the excreta covered the ground like snow. He described the arrival of the birds at sundown as sounding "like a gale passing through the rigging of a close-reefed vessel" and causing a mighty air current as they passed.

The Ouachitas are unusual in America because their trend lies latitudinally in forested ridges, striking a course east and west to create a lateral topography like the Uintas of Colorado and Utah and unlike the great longitudinals of the Appalachians and Rockies on the interior and the Cascade and the Coastal mountains farther west. At two-hundred miles, the length of the Ouachitas makes them the largest latitudinal range in the Lower 48.

A half-billion years ago, when northern Arkansas lay beneath a shallow sea, a deeper basin to the south, called the Ouachita Trough, accumulated sand and clay sediments almost six miles thick. Even farther south, creeping ominously north, was Llanoria, a mass of land that would eventually collide with the trough and compress 120 miles of sea sediments into only sixty, creating the Ouachita Mountains. Imagine a bulldozer pushing a 1960s Buick up against a huge and unyielding stone-wall until the long hood crumples into lateral folds. If you drive road-cuts through the Ouachitas, you often can see the tortured crumplings of that terrific compression. The rate of uplift, however, has been more or less commensurate with erosion, so the height of the Ouachitas today is similar to much of the Appalachians but modest compared to that of the younger Rockies.

From the air, these foldings appear like the half-drawn bellows of an accordion and are the major reason that Interstate 35, on its course directly south from the western shore of Lake Superior, shies off halfway down at Kansas City to make for the gentler eastern edge of the Great Plains to end up not in New Orleans, where it rightfully should — given its original bearing — but five-hundred miles farther west in Laredo, Texas. The resulting broad gap between the big bend of the Missouri River at Kansas City and the Red River at Shreveport, Louisiana, is by far the largest area lacking a longitudinal interstate highway in the eastern half of the United States. Thank you, Ouachitas.

You might suppose, then, they are mighty mountains, and perhaps they are, although their greatest elevation, Mount Magazine, said to be the highest point between the Appalachians and the Rockies, rises only a couple of thousand feet above its valley floor. Still, a few physiographers, seeing them as mere outliers of the larger Ozark Plateau, talk as if they are not truly mountains at all. How many of those professors have hiked them north to south or driven *across* them in snow season, I don't know, but I'm sure such an undertaking would rid the debate of a certain fussy academicism, as would a reading not of a textbook but of an Arkansas FAA aeronautical chart: because the top of Rich Mountain can become veiled in clouds, it carries the label HIGH FATALITY AREA. The Ouachitas are mountains enough.

In years past, I've always come into that planetary washboard athwart, and on two of those occasions I've had to stop along one of the twisting, transverse routes for a passenger to leave her breakfast along the roadside for the possums, a consequence of transit not unlike that in a boat sailing a short sea. It's as if the undulated rocks remember their oceanic days and wish to prove it with a gift of motion sickness.

There is certainly a cause and result in the presence of the Ouachitas and the subsequent absence in them of the deleterious domestication of lands lying east, west, and south. Despite some logging and mining, their roughness has kept humanity thinned to a sensible — that is, sustainable — number, and it has been more difficult here for predatory American economics, with its watchword not of thrift or care or prudence but of avarice, to dislodge the natives from their links with the land.

The trucker-archaeologist in the Rich Mountain store knew where the Ouachita rose, and he understood how the domino table rested at the top of a watershed, even if he knew not the other end of the river six-hundred miles distant. I said as much to Q, and she mentioned a young waitress we'd met at lunch several months earlier near Norfolk, Virginia. The café sat with its backside nearly hanging over the Great Dismal Swamp Canal, yet our waitress knew neither the name of the channel nor its purpose and certainly not its long history; worse, she had no notion of the ways, however obvious or subtle, the canal shaped her life even though a year previous she'd been "stung" there by a mosquito and required testing for West Nile virus. (It proved negative.)

When we're on the road, it's always a risk for Q, in whatever context, to mention lunch — or breakfast or supper — because roads exist for me, claims she, mainly to furnish reasonably direct connections between cafés and chili parlors, taco wagons and beaneries, eat shacks and confectioneries, burger joints and frozen-custard stands, barbecue sheds and fish camps. In other words, roads are there to tie one reason for living to another.

Such places are not bountiful in the Ouachitas, and the best I could do then at her mention of food was to pull out dessert. One of the joys of age is watching the young and inexperienced get introduced to life, life in this instance being a MoonPie, of which no true Southerner (Q is a Yankee) can live long without forming an opinion. In Dixie, to be ignorant of a MoonPie is akin to being ignorant of Stonewall Jackson or a boll weevil or a boiled peanut. As evidence of such a claim, I offer exhibit A: *The Great American MoonPie Handbook*. If you've not happened upon the cookie, originally an Appalachian snack for deep-shaft coal miners, it's a pair of circular wafers sandwiching a marshmallow filling, the whole coated with chocolate or vanilla.

I unwrapped the little confection and watched her nip into it. Never have I seen her twist her face around when trying a new food, even after that sushi of raw sea-urchin, nor did she just then with her MoonPie. After a second bite for confirmation, she said, "The best part of it is the name." Some people, I said, consider it a veritable artifact of Southern life. "It tasted like a veritable artifact." I read aloud the ingredients on the label to reveal the compounded miracle of corn syrups a MoonPie is. "It sounds" — she nodded — "as if it were made by a chemist instead of a chef." Indeed, such products of our time come not from recipes but from formulas; they are concoctions of crucible and test tube, with nary a sifter or rolling pin near; they smack not of a baking oven but of a Bunsen burner. My long-time friend Gus Kubitzki, whose pronouncements over the years have been companions on my travels, believed ingredient labels on packaged foods should begin WARNING: IF YOU WISH TO ENJOY THIS PRODUCT, READ NO FURTHER. But then, comfortable in his old-school notions, Gus believed that between harvesting and cooking there should be only seasoning — anything else was adulterating.

❥ 6 ❥

Inscribing the Land

ARKANSAS TOPONYMS HAVE SOME NATIONAL RECOGNITION —
preeminently Hope, Flippin, Yellville, and Smackover — but
outsiders have not been especially heedful of other names even more
worthy of eccentric distinction: Greasy Corner, Chanticleer, Figure
Five, Number Nine, Whisp, Twist, Wild Cherry, Possum Grape, Oil
Trough, Seaton Dump. In a state where alcoholically "dry" counties
abound, there's Beverage Town and Gin City, neither name referring
to ardent spirits. Since the state university mascot is a boar, you'll
not be surprised to find there Hogeye and Hog Jaw, communities (so
the names suggest) apparently lacking a chamber of commerce. Elsewhere, you can imagine the waggery proceeding from a certain con-
catenation of towns along a northern slope of the Ouachitas between
Needmore and Blue Ball, near Nella and Nola, with Harvey lying
between them (all these south of Kingdoodle Knob).

On its official road-map, the Arkansas Highway Department
shows almost fifteen hundred "cities, towns, and communities," and
on that list, Ouachita stands out because it is one of a few Indian
names in a place with a human presence reaching back thousands of
years before the arrival of McDougals, Delaneys, and Ludwigs. An
Arkansas gazetteer index reveals no towns named Quapaw (from
which the name Arkansas likely descends) or Tula or Tunica. To the
founders of the state, it seems, those peoples never were.

The Ouachita River contributed to that erasure when steamboats
brought hundreds of tribal Americans upriver as far as a vessel could
ascend and put them ashore to follow the valleys on westward into

39

the "permanent Indian Country." That's a tale not of wandering feet but of the forced relocation proposed by Andrew Jackson (Jefferson and Monroe had considered it also) and approved by Congress with the Indian Removal Act of 1830. The Quapaw went no farther west than required and settled across the Arkansas line in the northeast corner of the Indian Territory on land holding unknown mineral resources that eventually yielded them significant wealth.

As Q and I followed the descent of the Ouachita off its generating mountain, we came into a valley open enough to push the ridges to the horizon. In places, trees growing close to the highway removed the hills from sight altogether, and there the flow of the river slackened as it widened from a creek to braided shallows a hundred yards across. To the north rose broad-backed mountains, but on the south they were serrations seeming to betoken a different territory.

State Route 88 was a road I'd for years wanted to travel, not because of the river but because along it, in an orderly spacing like words on a page, are the settlements of Ink, Pencil Bluff, and Story; and to the north in the Ouachitas is Magazine, and southward in the river valley is Reader. Considering my method of writing, driving through that territory gave new meaning to *auto*biography: I write a first draft in pencil, the second in ink from a fountain pen, and only thereafter do I enter the realm of binary digits (although six drafts — three-thousand pages — of my first book came *tickity-tick-tick* out of a typewriter). From that archaic process, this pencil pusher, this ink dribbler, hopes to leave you, the reader, with a story or two.

To me, the Ouachita Valley was a writer's paragon of a riverine course as it lured us on with a quoz here and there that became memoranda-book entries to turn into full texts to send on to you in your easy chair so that one of you somewhere, sometime may write me and point out my overlooking something like Scribblers Corner or Oghamville or Wordmonger City.

The river changed from a pellucid mountain-stream to wide water the color of faded olive-drab Army fatigues, but we saw more of the tributary creeks crossing under Route 88 than the tree-fringed

Ouachita itself, and that was acceptable since we were not in pursuit of it but rather its valley. At Ink, where we stopped so I could take a snapshot of the "town" sign, even before I could push the shutter button, a man pulled up to offer a ride, a gesture reminding me of a sentence with inarguable logic I'd heard on the mountain about the lower valley: "People are people down there."

In 1887, citizens at the Ink crossroads gathered to petition for a post office, requesting their settlement be officially named Melon only to be turned down, for reasons unknown to me, although I suggest the possibility someone just might have found the name too silly; after all, wasn't Tomato, Arkansas, enough? A tale I like but am skeptical of holds that the second ballot to select a name contained the direction to WRITE IN INK, so residents did, and they got their PO, one that closed eighty years later. The fellow who offered me the ride said, "They must've wrote in disappearing ink."

The afternoon Q and I were there, Ink was a few houses scattered around a road intersection and a church cemetery with a solidly squat pyramid of native rock seeming to mark more the presence of Ink than any particular former citizen's grave. Unlike their post office, the pyramid, as inextirpable as they could make it, was intended for the ages.

The officialdom of Arkansas calls such settlements "communities," but the few residents of Ink, even more loosely, will use the word *town* which it surely is not, any more than "Y" City — nine miles north — is a city. (Is there another American hamlet or town with a single letter and quotation marks in its name? Incidentally, given the half-dozen scattered houses near the three-way intersection, a more accurate name would be T "City." While I'm asking, is there another American town with two hyphens besides Ho-Ho-Kus, New Jersey?)

Except for New Englanders, Americans have largely turned away from the apt and pleasant words *village* and *hamlet* and are today more likely to call these unincorporations *hick towns* or *hoosiervilles* or *jerkwaters* or, more kindly, *whistle-stops* (there is, in fact, a

Whistleville, Arkansas), all descriptions not likely to endear an out-sider to the natives. My word for such settlements, when they are free of charm or attractiveness, is *unincorptons*, a term lacking, as they do, any allure. Not long ago in Opolis, Kansas, where anything metro was clearly missing, Q suggested that very name could be a useful generic term, and she especially liked it in the plural — rhym-ing with Thermopylae — as in "The opoli of Arkansas are many, but few are quaint." I've come to like it myself.

We passed a pole sign salvaged, it appeared, from an abandoned gas station and repainted with an arrow pointing toward the river: LITTLE HOPE BAPTIST CHURCH. (Q: "Our Lady of the Holy Negativity.") A year earlier in eastern Arkansas, as I was photo-graphing a sign for the HOLY GHOST DISTURBED CHURCH, the pastor came out, disturbed by my snapshooting, and made clear he had scant interest in explaining whether any other local disturbances lay in the Ghost, the church, or his brain.

On a recent visit to my boyhood hometown of Kansas City, Mis-souri, Q was taken with the name Country Club Christian Church. I mentioned to her the proposal by Gus Kubitzki (whose name you now recognize, a man known more for professions of sarcasm than faith) that the CCCC folk, in their posh area, were on to something: Why not organize congregations by avocations? The First Church of Latter-Day Duck Hunters? The Reorganized Assembly of United Numismatists? The Full Gospel Guiding Fellowship of Gossips? Sharing divinity among people of like interests would surely be more communal than having the golfer praying next to the skier, the teetotalist beside the oenophile. Gus held that shoulder-to-shoulder prayers focused toward similar wishes would be more fervid and — hence — efficacious: give us this day our daily duck.*

---

* Contextual footnote for those offended: Gus Kubitzki said he once visited the opolis of Halfway, Missouri, to see about joining the Halfway Christian Church, figuring it accurately described him, but his aged mother (who forbade him to use the word *Devil* in her presence lest evil be called forth) told him he'd be better off in Peculiar where maybe they had a Christian church for his kind. I have all this on his authority.

Arkansas 88 rolled through an area formerly cotton fields and moonshine hollows until the Depression and poor agricultural practices in the pale-orange soil took their tolls. Many residents sold their land to the federal government and moved to California, so that today nearly two-thirds of Montgomery County is national forest, and top-of-the-chain wildlife — black bears and pumas — have returned.

A few years earlier, in one of my rambles through hinterland America, I began noting an increasing number of gravel roads and dead-end lanes, even rural driveways, marked with "street" signs; the day before, I'd seen a two-lane track into a pasture with a sign: *WHODATHOTIT ROAD.* I interpreted it as commentary on the arrival of 911 emergency service and its requirement to provide identification useful to a fire truck, ambulance, or sheriff. Undoubtedly, some of these names will survive in the sprawling of the nation, as pasture paths get turned into avenues of subdivisions named Highland Heights or Forest Woods and as dead ends get opened and paved into some new Asian auto-plant. Your descendants may one day drive a vehicle assembled on Whodathotit Expressway.

Since public forums can be difficult for an individual citizen to enter, these road names are an opportunity for expression along state rights-of-way, one second only to vanity license-plates. Two days earlier, we came up behind an overpriced, overpraised, overpowered, oversized, Teutonic vehicle with an overweening license-plate: 4U2NV. I wished ours was 4GETIT. Or better, that one I saw a few years ago: IDGAF (my interpretation begins with "I Don't Give"). And what about that front plate of 3M-TA3, a message taking on new meaning in a rearview mirror?

At Pencil Bluff, a T intersection with a cluster of homes and a scatter of businesses — propane distributor, church, gas station, highway-department depot — we pulled up at Hop's Store, a new building where any character of place had to come from a character walking through the door. I did my part. Inside was a man exceptional in his blandness, a fellow more of shrugs than sentences, who answered a couple of my questions by only raising his shoulders. I asked — my fourth question — why the hamlet was called Pencil Bluff. At that, he actually spoke: "I don't have any idea." His interest in the question likely matched his curiosity about counted cross-stitch or bookbinding or linear algebra. Then he shrugged *and* spoke: "Before my time," he mumbled, as if a man can be expected to know only what occurs during his life.

My practice on the road when I ask such questions is to present them resoundingly so that others may hear; in piscatorial terms, it's the difference between casting a dry fly and throwing a net — the chances of hauling in *something* increase. On occasion it works, and it did then in Pencil Bluff (once Sock City; why, I didn't learn). A smiling customer standing to the side whom I'd not noticed before, an oldster so long exposed to the sky he wasn't tanned so much as simply discolored, offered an answer, his solution corrected and expanded on by the cook making sandwiches at the grill. "Out on the river," she said, "that's the bluff, and it's all slate rock where people here used to get their writing stuff for school. Back in the *Deepression*." Communal memory now primed, a woman whose face lighted at the chance to inform said, "It's out there at the preacher's hole. The old baptism pool." And that aroused the shrugging man to speak yet again, his memory opening at last: "There's big catfish and brim out there in that hole. Durin Lula Jo Parson's baptism, a catfish swum plumb between her legs, and she took a-hollerin, 'Hallelujah! Hallelujah! The hand of the Lord's full on me!'"

I asked where the bluff was, but the directions needed enough clarification that the sunned man said, "It's easier if I just show you." He took his sack of sandwiches, and we followed him to his pickup; on the tailgate was one of those little chromed-plastic icthyoidal emblems evangelicals stick to the back end of their vehicles, those fundamentalist fishes so often swimming — however inappropriately — forever leftward across the trunk lids of America.

As we fell in behind him, I said something about catfish holes and baptismal pools, and to the tune of the old hymn, Q sang, "He will make us fishers of quoz if we'll follow him." He led us into trees and brush along the north bank of the Ouachita where we came upon a beautifully fractured ledge of dark shale crumbling down to the river. The rock laminations were of some regularity in thickness and broke free into both smooth tablets and slender pencil-like strips. While the slate was of ready cleavage, it wasn't possessed of enough integrity to serve as a schoolroom blackboard any more than it could as the bed of a billiard table or even as roof tiles, yet it was too hard to function as a good pencil except when scratched against itself, and to that end it served well. Its economic inutility had kept it from being quarried, thereby preserving a splendid riverside outcrop along a section beloved by canoeists. Q turned to me. "Do we have a quoz here?"

Thinking of baptisms and Route 88 place-names, I picked up a small tabletlike piece and, with a sliver for a pencil, scratched, "In the beginning was the Word," and tucked the slate back into the bluff to await the next freshet that would wash it down to the river. I was thinking not just of John's gospel but also of Mark Twain's: "The face of the water, in time, became a wonderful book."

Who now can say whether any past citizens here toyed with the notion of the river absorbing their words or considered their pencilings from the bluff being made from seawater and sediment transubstantiated by the ancient compressions of the rising Ouachita Mountains? If some few did think along those lines, they might dispute John's "No man hath seen God at any time" — provided they could see deity at work through the grand mechanisms of plate tectonics. I suppose it all comes down to where one seeks his thaumaturgy.

This theological wandering had been brought on by the beauty of the old baptismal pool and furthered by an explanation we'd heard that morning for an opolis on down the road: Washita, sitting at the west end of Lake Ouachita, behind the dammed river. Back on the mountain, a man said (in different terms) Washita was an anagram from "*wash*ed *i*n *t*he blood of the Lamb."

Q thought Wablodlam would more accurately carry the message. "But then," she added, "maybe it's too close to Bedlam." I thought it bold for businesspeople in Washita to offer an opposing etymology in their contention the name has no religious significance, deriving as it does from an Indian word meaning "good hunting and fishing." Considering the village economy depended in no small way on hunters and fishermen, I found the claim as suspect as the first, but the intrinsic nature of their views was fully Bible Belt where down-home, supersaturated religion faces off with local cash registers. Profitable is the place when they meld: "Let's build," says the mayor, "the World's Largest Observation-Deck Cross. Light it up at night. Install an elevator and charge three bucks a hoist. By God, we'll be knee-deep in tourists!"

What we do know about the word *Ouachita* is that French trappers met a tribe or perhaps just a moiety who apparently referred to themselves or their territory along the lower river with sounds the Frenchmen imitated as *wah-shee-tah*, the stressed syllables unknown today. I've come upon a pocketful of spellings for *Ouachita* but no unquestionable interpretation of its meaning, and that, to me, allows a traveler to infuse it with his own associations; after all, such personal interpretation is a central purpose for traveling: to visit Bogalusa or Chugwater or Pinetucky and to return home with your own definitions.

During their exploration of the river in 1804, William Dunbar consistently spelled it *Washita* while partner George Hunter, almost as insistently, wrote *Ouachita*, neither man yielding to the other's orthography despite a certain sharing of journal entries. As for the Ouachita people themselves, they apparently moved away from the European newcomers — and any troubles with orthography — to join Caddoan relatives, the Natchitoches, farther west.

Among forsythia shrubs just opening into puffs of bright yellow, the road turned northward to skirt the coves and inundated tributaries of the drowned river, its original bed now lying six miles distant, and we entered low hills that wrenched the asphalt around for some way east of Story, another T intersection opolis, a place incapable of catching our fancy any more than the explanation of its name, one (if you will) without much of a story: the first postmaster was Mrs. James Story. And so ended the string of writerly opoli — except for the one farther downriver, the one belonging to you, Reader.

Along our route was an occasional front yard with a tree swing cut from a tire (two of them shaped most artfully into sea horses) or a lawn full of trestle tables offering for sale 165-million-year-old quartz crystals broken out of nearby quarries. The stunning clarity of the polyhedrons turned sunlight into all its visible colors and cast little spectral lights over the grass so that ruptured rainbows danced across lawns.

In the early spring sky, vultures wheeled in their distinctive tilting flight, their earthbound clumsiness transformed into a grace surpassing that of an eagle. Those black eaters-of-the-dead made me think of mortality. "Again?" said Q. To her, they were transformers of decay into life, and she was right, for what was the engendering Ouachita soil itself but moldered mountains and decomposed vegetation feeding the leaf feeding the rabbit feeding the vulture?

The way mortality kept popping up that afternoon, I'm not at all surprised I began to see it in the nomenclature of the upper valley. To name a place is not simply to confirm its existence, even if it subsists only in an imagined land — Erewhon, Quivira, Yoknapatawpha County — with no more actuality than a high-tailed wampus cat. Bestowing a name also extends longevity when a corporeal presence vanishes, when a town (or a human) gets deincorporated. To read an old American road atlas is to travel a land no longer existent except on its pages; names, like bestowers of names and their buildings, come and go. When the last brick dissolves in a ghost town, the place can survive for a while longer, if it is to survive at all, only in the word. The surest refuge, the most certain habitat for a ghost, lies in stories, and perhaps that's the reason ancient Egyptians, enwrapped as they were with immortality — a meaningless notion unless coupled with mortality — considered the tongue the seat of their eternal souls.

The pyramids of Egypt crumble a little more each year as they work their way back into the desert, but to erase what has been written about them — their histories — would require the obliteration of human civilization virtually everywhere on the planet.

I have no clear idea where or how far a name can carry us, but I suspect, like infinity, it exceeds even our capacity to wonder, and I believe a name bestowed well is another hedge against total annihilation and its realm of the utterly forgotten.

7

The Forgotten Expedition

T HE LIGHT BEGAN DROPPING, but it didn't vanish fast enough to hide the Tophet lying ahead along Arkansas 7, a stretch of road battered with illuminated billboards turning roadside litter into ghostly glowings: wraiths of shopping bags hung in bushes, and cups and bottles shone like burning brimstone. The Ouachitas come to their eastern decline not far beyond the highway, and there, a little north of Hot Springs, the agents of Mammon had marked the topographical terminus with a kind of aesthetic if not spiritual boundary and put the lie to the motto on Arkansas license plates: THE NATURAL STATE. Along Route 7, whatever the natural was, it served mostly to turn a buck.

A section of mountaintop had been cut open for "America's Largest Gated Community," an advertising slogan Q found poorly reasoned: wouldn't more people only increase chances of residents meeting up with those they're trying to escape? Expressing the reverse of what we saw, another slogan for the place — "Welcome to Heaven on Earth" — suggested a paradise residing in covenants about the color of a garage door and whether it could be left open on Sunday, as well as land prices assuring that thy neighbor shall not have a portfolio significantly smaller than thine because, as we all know, inadequate negotiables are a major cause of unmowed lawns and political preferences leaning toward populist positions. Q thought a pretty good alternative covenant could be hammered out of inclusion rather than exclusion, tolerance rather than suspicion, openness rather than fear. She said, "Why not call a state penitentiary a gated community?"

I mumbled how such a degraded stretch of mountain could drive a fellow to drink, and Q, who was at the wheel and has been known to rephrase my sentences into something I can only describe as more convivial, said, "Would a fellow settle for being driven to a drink?" He would, and she did, right after we took quarters in the historic Arlington Hotel a few miles south in old, ungated Hot Springs, in the heart of what was once called the Valley of Vapors. And vaporish it was on that cool evening as we walked along Central Avenue, wedged into the hills, to follow the stream that once carried off about half-a-hundred thermal springs formerly pouring forth openly from the eastern ridge — nearly a million gallons every twenty-four hours. No longer does much of the water rise to see the light of day, piped as most of it is to somewhere else. For Indians and French trappers and hunters, and, in the last century or so, for thousands of Americans who used to arrive by train, Hot Springs has long been a place to seek the loosening of a stiff joint or cleansing of a gland or purging of a tract.

On that Monday night I needed my memory of Heaven on Earth purged or at least loosened, so we went strolling on Central, a pleasant avenue, nicely influenced by the Bathhouse Row restorations of the National Park Service. Things were quiet to the point of being shut down, and cleansing a memory took some walking past gimcrackeries: a wax museum; catchpenny shops selling photos of monkeys in sombreros, cheap incense penetrating even closed doors, primitive wall masks plasticated in Bali, stick-on tattoos, peacock feathers, mood rings, **ELVIS LIVES!** bumper stickers. There were emporia offering T-shirts imprinted, in the manner of our time, with various notices to answer our pressing questions: I'M WITH STUPID. Or: DO I LOOK LIKE I CARE? And one for the motorcyclist: IF YOU CAN READ THIS, THE BITCH FELL OFF.

At last we came upon the healing potation we wanted, not an analeptic of sulfur or magnesium but one of spirituous heat rising from a distiller's craft: a jigger of hooch.

Maxine's Coffeehouse and Puzzle Bar, we were told, was once a place where ardor got engendered not so much by spirits or thermal waters but by human flesh. Maxine, now a citizen in the City Celestial, was the author of *Call Me Madam* and the operator of an upstairs bordello. To suggest that history, hanging from the walls were various ladies' intimates, unmentionables, and underlinens in various sizes, but every one of them crimson. Tacked to the high ceiling were smoke-stained dollar bills signed by customers as a kind of calling card. Q, expecting to be given a riddle, asked what made the place a puzzle bar, and Stevie, the bartender, set before us several little perplexities made from nails, or horseshoes, or twisted rods of steel and nickel. She said, "I've got more when you figure those out."

Quicker than was good for any man's mechanical self-esteem, Q succeeded in stacking up a half-dozen fourpenny nails in a way I'd thought impossible ten minutes earlier. This is one of the very things marriage counselors caution against, but men who wed a woman born a tomboy need either to sharpen their mechanical arts or to modify any notion of manly prowess based on contraptions. It may have been the first puzzle that gave our conversation a certain turn before she dismantled the nails to pass them to me and said, "I was taught calculus is a study of approaching limits, and this arrangement of nails is at its limit." As I failed several times to stack the nails, I was muttering about puzzles and the approaching limits of exasperation. "By the way," she said, "when we came out of the mountains and right into billboards and litter and sprawl-velopment, I think it was exceeded limits that got to you."

The evening was taking an untoward lurch into topics — like calculaic theory — that could only increase exasperation. For years, I knew calculus only as what a dentist removes from teeth. The conversation called for something desperate — like politics.

I began talking about the Presidential election coming up that autumn. I said we were going to get an update on how well the nation might be coming along in recognizing approaching limits and comprehending a new calculus both social and environmental. (Knowing my general innumeracy in mathematics, I put myself at risk in using Q's metaphor.) Across the country there seemed to be confusions,

fears of new vulnerabilities, a growing nihilism leaving people neither engaged nor enraged but just paralyzed in the face of corporate
mendacity and greed abetted by actions of a reactionary Administration and its Congress. Would the President's Orwellian politics
of manipulated fears continue to encourage a future of mountains
bulldozed into gated communities where residents see the demos as
demons? Q, the lawyer in her speaking, paraphrased William Sloane
Coffin: "People who fear disorder more than injustice will only produce more of both."

This conversation, which I give only the gist of, was broken
several times by the guitarist who'd been playing to an empty tavern until we came in. His gigs were short so he could sit next to Q
who is something of a magician in being able to make me disappear
right before the very eyes of certain males. I can be having a deep
conversation with some guy about his universal joint, and in walks
Q: Abracadabra! I'm no longer there. This is not a complaint. For a
writer, it can be most useful to become an invisible set of eyes and
ears. Technically, it's known as fly-on-the-wall reporting.

When the musician returned for another song, I told Q that the
last time I was on Central Avenue in Hot Springs, the words *gated
community* were more likely applied to a stockyard than to a housing
development. That visit, years gone, now seemed to exist in a simpler
time, but that perception was an illusion created by memory wearing thin — her quilt metaphor — for times are never simpler and the
complexities of existence don't increase; they just change, although
perhaps today they arrive faster and give us less time to duck. As
an example, I said the complexity of learning how to bring down a
bison with a stick and a sharpened stone is no greater than learning
how to buy a stuffed bison online. Q said, "So if I have a spear, and a
Quapaw woman of 1804 has a laptop with Internet access, she'll get
her buffalo about the same time I'll get mine?" That was the theory.

Her reference to 1804 was an allusion to our reason for being
in the narrow, thermal valley where precisely two centuries before
William Dunbar and George Hunter had reconnoitered for a month.

Above all else, the explorers were looking for potential resources there and along the Ouachita farther downstream that would produce commodities to yield fungibles. Unlike Lewis and Clark, the two Scottish immigrants showed scarce interest in anything beyond material resources, and it seemed to me that, could the men join us in a wee dram, their view of a gated community and its implications might not accord with mine. After all, the Hot Springs of our time produces fungibles that surely surpass their imaginings. Further, Dunbar was a wealthy owner of slaves (fungible) and a large plantation raising cotton (fungible); Hunter was a frequent speculator in realty (fungible) who also dabbled in distilling whiskey (fungible) and engaged from time to time in quests for valuable ores (fungible). In fact, Thomas Jefferson's instructions to Dunbar for the exploration up the Ouachita cautioned him to discourage Hunter from turning the voyage into a hunt for gold and silver.

Remarkable it would be if Dunbar envisioned what now lay outside the tavern door, and that implied incapacity in me to envision what, two centuries distant, would lie out there along Central Avenue (other than surely Elvis will yet live). One day, readers of this sentence will know the answer, and so to them, I pass along that question with the hope the refusal of my generation to imagine consequences has not got them into a real pickle.

I had to wonder: What would William and George say about the Valley of Vapors which they knew as a place empty of people and containing only a couple of derelict log-huts used seasonally by trappers seeking the healing waters? Would the fungibles brought in by gates and T-shirts, mineral waters, and visitors sipping in a tavern bestrung with crimson lingerie fulfill their hopes for what their explorations would open? Men of the old mechanical arts as they both were, would they see the arrival of a technological nation as inevitable, one that would necessarily doom ways of living the territory had sustained for ten-thousand years? And would they believe technology and its concomitant abuses of lands and human spirits were also inevitable? Was Hot Springs, Arkansas, two centuries after their visit, anything like what they had in mind? Did they consider anything beyond the extractive phase? Did they ever try to reckon consequences?

At that point in our conversation, the television replayed a spring-training home run by one of those jocks who points heavenward when he crosses the plate. I was paying no attention to the game until the admiring guitarist offered up to Q another aperçu intended to manifest his masculinely profound mind, this one on the role of possible celestial interest in the outcome of a small, horsehide sphere meeting an ash shaft. He said, "If God is spending time getting fly balls over a fence, no wonder this world is so screwed up."

Almost a hundred miles from Maxine's Coffeehouse and Puzzle Bar rise the headwaters of the Ouachita — although in 1804, before engineers tinkered with the river, the distance was greater — but Dunbar and Hunter went no farther upstream than Hot Springs. President Jefferson's original plan called for Dunbar to lead an expedition up to the source of the Arkansas, where the contingent would portage to the presumed nearby location of the wellspring of the Red River and descend it to its juncture with the Mississippi not far downstream from "The Forest," Dunbar's plantation a little south of Natchez. As an idea, it was fully Jeffersonian in its logical neatness. But the American West eats up logic and neatness, as it does those whose ignorance of the region causes them to misjudge and fail to live within its limits.

The headwaters of the Arkansas and Red rivers are not a portage away from each other unless you call four-hundred miles a portage, but it would be some years until any white man of influence would learn that detail. Not long before the Grand Excursion, as Jefferson called this southern counterpart to the expedition of Lewis and Clark, was to set forth, another detail of the American West arose. The Osage — people who usually got along better with whites than with any of their native brethren, even those of close consanguinity such as the Quapaw of Arkansas — gave indications that while Jefferson may have purchased from France a huge territory, it wasn't wise to assume he'd thereby also bought Indian lands.

Pawhuska, a leader of another group of Osage, alerted the President to a rogue band roaming around the western end of the Ouachita Mountains, and exerting its presence and demonstrating slight interest in a parley with a couple of Scottish immigrants carrying more astronomical instruments than firearms. Jefferson postponed the excursion until the following spring, and so began a run of poor fortune that dogged the endeavor even right to its conclusion. The remarkable good luck of Lewis and Clark wouldn't be repeated for the great rivers of the southern part of the Louisiana Purchase.

After Dunbar received Jefferson's letter deferring the Grand Excursion, he proposed to the President a far smaller reconnoitering, one able to serve as a shakedown cruise and hold the assembled outfit together until spring. Using boats Hunter had brought from the East, Dunbar recommended a retinue of the two scientists and thirteen soldiers put forth from a creek near his plantation, cross the Mississippi, and ascend a few leagues of the Red River to the Black River (as the lower forty-some miles of the Ouachita are called), and proceed to the "hot springs of the Washita," a place Americans then knew mostly by rumor, although Indians and French trappers and traders had long used the water route leading toward the springs.

Unlike Lewis and Clark, Dunbar and Hunter were not military men but entrepreneurial gentlemen of science: the former an astronomer and mathematician skilled in surveying; the latter a chemist-apothecary and mineralogist. Indeed, of the four Jeffersonian explorations of the Louisiana Purchase, only the Ouachita expedition was led by scientists, a model of leadership that proved unsuited to the adversities and mishaps of exploration, as you can see in these words from George Hunter:

The greater part of this day [we] were embarrassed by rapids & shoals, very often getting aground, & then delayed till a person would wade forward & cross the river, ahead of the boat in all probable directions in order to find the deepest water, before we could venture to proceed again. The men, or rather some of them, often grumbling & uttering execrations against me in particular for urging them on, in which they had the example of the sergeant who on many occasions of trifling difficulties frequently gave me very rude answers, & in several instances both now & formerly seemed to forget that it was his duty in such cases to urge on the men under his command to surmount them rather than to show a spirit of contradiction & backwardness.

For such insolence, William Clark would have pulled out the lash.

Gathering natural history, the two Scot scientists performed well enough, given limitations the season imposed on fieldwork. But their Ouachita journals, unlike those of Lewis and Clark, are almost barren of what we'd now call ethnology, partly because over their three-and-a-half-month trip, they encountered few people except whites attached to the fort near present-day Monroe, Louisiana. Further, humanity seemed to interest those two men of technical mind less than an unknown algae or a bit of odd rock (particularly novaculite, so-called Arkansas stone Indians used for tools of many kinds). Even the ancient aboriginal mounds along the lower Ouachita, of which I'll say more later, failed to rouse them beyond idle curiosity. Their exploration had the usual excitements, that is, difficulties of ascending a river — rocks, rapids, mud, opposing currents, cold water — but progress proceeded almost as planned, if we discount, as they never would, numerous intestinal infelicities and Dr. Hunter shooting himself in the hand.

Except for the excellent map drawn up from their survey notations about the large and navigable but uncharted Ouachita, the expedition results were small compared to other Jeffersonian explorations, and both men realized their accomplishment was limited, although they — especially the younger Hunter, who outlived Dunbar — became nationally known as a result of the excursion. Upon his return in 1805, Dunbar wrote Jefferson: "The objects which have presented themselves to us are not of very high importance; it must however be acknowledged that the hot springs are indeed a great natural curiosity." And Hunter told the Secretary of War of his regret the "course was not through a mineral country" and of a wish his "profession might have been more usefully employed." When the Grand Excursion, in something close to its original conception, set off at last in 1806, both Dunbar and Hunter declined to join it. Thirty years later George Featherstonhaugh, an English immigrant and a federally dispatched geologist, arrived in the Ouachita country to examine the hot springs; without mentioning names, he wrote in his report, "Certainly no man should be presumed a geologist merely because he is a learned chemist or a profound mathematician."

The reconstituted expedition, led by Thomas Freeman in 1806, got turned back by the Spanish along the Red River near what is now Texarkana, Arkansas, and was unable to fulfill Jefferson's plan of fully exploring the Red and Arkansas rivers. So, even including Dunbar and Hunter's Ouachita voyage, these southern excursions all add up to something useful to territorial expansion but scarcely to anything "grand."

That particular historic outcome in no way discouraged Q and me from our objective in following the Ouachita Valley; in fact, Dunbar's limited success, which helped it become the "Forgotten Expedition," added an element of intrigue to our path. Not far from Maxine's Puzzle Bar lay the only diamond mine in the world open to the public. It's not a shaft but a plowed field where one can lay down a few bucks and take a shovel out into the scrapings and likely turn up, if anything, a yellow or brown diamond in the rough the size of that filling in Uncle Ted's molar. Such diamond-hunting was an exercise reflective of the excursion we were on: scratching about among tailings of those before us in hopes of coming upon a gem of a quoz to adorn a chamber of memory, a quilt of remembrance.

Poor Q: I was on the other side of her, saying that if Dunbar and Hunter, penetrating the heavy forests of Arkansas, could choose a license-plate slogan intended to drum up fungible-producing activity in the heavily wooded territory, theirs might be COME SEE, COME SAW. Jefferson himself — and certainly the highly entrepreneurial George Washington — would approve, for they both wanted the land surveyed and opened to the ends of an agrarian society, the far-reaching results of which would prove the undoing of Jefferson's social and economic model.

To read the expedition journals of Dunbar and Hunter is to realize the last thing the men wanted was a "natural state" — that is, nature in its own state. Rather, they came to open the great wilderness cache of more than eight-hundred-thousand square miles Jefferson had just bought from the king of France for three cents an acre (four cents after finance charges), and they were there to gather knowledge and specimens to assist even greater extractions. They returned with latitudes and longitudes, with wild cabbages and oilstones and swanskins, all things leading, in their own ways, to a pair of red panties above my head and a baseball player pointing heavenward. Not to mention a guy saying to my wife, "If a jock can pray for a home run, I can pray to know your name," and she answering, "Blondie Bumstead."

8

High-Backed Booths

THAT MOONING — the public presentation of an uncloaked human rump — was practiced by American Indians in the eighteenth century, I think is not commonly known in this country. At least I was unaware of the long history of the fundamental moon until our morning in Hot Springs when I happened upon a passage in George Hunter's journal of his 1796 voyage down the Ohio River to Kentucky, a trip he would repeat eight years later on his way south to join Dunbar for their Ouachita excursion.

I came upon that bookish quoz while Q and I were in an old commercial springhouse, where we were drinking four-thousand-year-old water coming from eight-thousand feet down. It had fallen as rain when humankind, using reeds and damp clay, was teaching itself to write. Drinking the water was like quaffing cool drafts of time. (In that ancient purity from the Valley of Vapors, lunar scientists once protected pieces of the Moon until they could be studied for the presence of alien organisms. But it's of moons of another sort I speak now.)

Between quaffs, I read Q this passage from Hunter:

Yesterday we were met with a large, long keelboat manned with Indians and one white man from the Illinois country laden with skins. They set it up against the stream along the shore with great rapidity and kept time with their setting poles dextrously; I examined them with my spy glass and found them all quite naked except an handkerchief tied round their heads and a breechclout round their middles; as we approached their boat they perceived my Glass and immediately two of them lifted up their breech-clout and stuck out their bare Posteriors.

If you recall his earlier words about soldiers giving him back-sass on the Ouachita, you may conclude the good Scottish apothecary drew scant respect while on American rivers.

In rambling through the South, I've found displays of affability toward a traveler — even a Yankee — to be remarkably widespread. A couple of years ago, I encountered one source for it. I was in a Tennessee café, an old place with high-backed wooden booths — you hardly see them any longer — that gave visual privacy fore and aft. While I waited for a slice of chess pie, a pale, round head slowly appeared above the top of the adjoining booth, rising like a full moon coming up over the horizon. Once fully risen, the face, not yet of school age, examined me closely until I winked. It vanished quickly, only moments later to rise gradually again for further examination, once more ducking down when I crossed my eyes. Again, after a proper pause, it rose above the booth, this time to find a monster expression known to have sent mothers' boys running to aprons. The face disappeared in a flash. Moments later, another steadily deliberate rising. The boy took stock of me who had now tired of the game. Plotting a new tack, the little guy announced — with pride and as point of information — "I got a humdinger of a penis and two balls."

Before I could respond, the small moon of a head got pulled back down, and I heard a woman say, "Thank you for sharing that, Clevenger."

The woman, Clevenger's mother I soon learned, had not scolded the child either for his directness or for addressing a stranger. "His dad and I try to teach our kids to interpret instead of to judge," she said. They guided Clevenger in learning to evaluate rather than ignore or avoid someone unknown to him, certain he would learn on his own to smooth his conversational gambits. She had not encouraged reticence or excessive caution before a new face in town. He, so

I thought, was coming to understand something about words and community that people of the South can manifest so well. Travelers who cannot find impromptu conversations with almost anyone living south of the thirty-eighth parallel would do well to give up the road at once and get themselves to a qualified counselor.

I should add here that initial conversations in the South are rarely insipidly polite pleasantries to cover over otherwise awkward silences as they can be in, to pick a place, Hennepin County, Minnesota. Talk in Dixie is built on personal details, not usually egocentric bloviations but rather narrative particulars: the cottonmouth story, Cousin Otho's DWI arrest, reasons for the divorce, exactly why Flobelle's corn bread is good. A rural Southern waitress is, by assumption if not definition, a conversationalist. Within moments, the sojourner is likely to learn her marital status, her children's names, the mood of the cook, the quality of the preacher's last sermon. When I'm in a Southern eatery, if I learn any less than all that before the hoppin John arrives, I assume I've been scowling about corporate malfeasance, or maybe it was just that turnip pie or the peanuts in the RC Cola not sitting quite right.

During those hours I find myself alone on a long and numbing interstate highway, to speed the miles, I may retell the best story I heard that morning as a way of remembering it; or, when I've failed to find one, in desperation I might take up some question that could be seen as a precursor to mental unhinging. On a road across North Dakota a few years ago — do not judge me on this unless you've driven through North Dakota a half-dozen times — I began wondering how many people I'd meet if I lived to be fourscore and ten. I defined a "meeting" in the simplest terms: a face-to-face exchange containing a clear, if momentary, recognition between me and another. It could range from a hello, a wave, even a drive-by mooning, to a lifelong friendship (which counts as only a single meeting). Because the chance for error was so great and I wanted a high number, I tried to err on the side of a generous total. My high school had about eighteen-hundred students, so I tallied each one. You get the idea. I enumerated through my years, summing as I went, and what I came up with surprised me: only about a hundred-thousand people over ninety years. Then I reckoned — this was just guessing — that of those encounters, more than ninety-nine thousand were pleasant or at least neutral.

While it's true a crossing of the Great Plains can do things like this to a human mind, my reason for it was to learn how many stories or pieces of them I've missed over the years. It was clear: too often I've failed to rise above the high-backed booths of my life, show myself, and make an acquaintance. So many quoz awaiting, so many stories overlooked, even avoided. As Thomas Jefferson wrote his daughter Maria when he was concerned about her mental health:

> I am convinced our own happiness requires that we should continue to mix with the world, and to keep pace with it as it goes; and that every person who retires from free communication with [the world] is severely punished afterward by the state of mind into which he gets, and which can only be prevented by feeding our sociable principles.
>
> From 1793 to 1797 I remained closely at home, saw none but those who came there, and at length became very sensible of the ill effect it had upon my own mind, and of its direct and irresistible tendency to render me unfit for society and uneasy when necessarily engaged in it. I felt enough of the effect of withdrawing from the world then, to see that it led to an anti-social and misanthropic state of mind, which severely punishes him who gives in to it: and it will be a lesson I never shall forget as to myself.

Samuel Johnson said it in five words: "Solitude is dangerous to reason." Jefferson might have added that a democracy dependent upon mutual tolerance and shared concerns cannot long survive without open communication. I can think of no greater reason for taking to the American road.

. . .

The Ouachita River, following its mountains, makes an overall run due eastward until it nears Hot Springs where it jogs itself into three abrupt turns as if lost and uncertain which way to head next. The fall of the land decides things for it and sends the river off generally southeasterly, a course it holds until it gives itself (with a change of name near its mouth) over to the Red River a few miles above its juncture with the Mississippi. By the time it makes its last sharp bend below Hot Springs, the Ouachita has left the mountains and, soon enough, even any hills of consequence. In effect, the river, at this point, flows off what was, five-hundred-million years ago, the ancient continental edge of an emergent North America into the great Ouachita Embayment (today called by geologists the Mississippi Embayment of the Gulf Coastal Plain), a massive levelish landscape covering much of the lower South. I have no idea how many local residents realize they're living on a former sea bottom, although I do know I've not yet come upon anyone there who knew, despite that detail being fundamental in shaping their lives.

Beyond the sprawled, multilane strip of franchise businesses at Malvern, the land was rolling pastures broken by pockets of woods; those pastures — having replaced mountain forest — meant the means of earning a living also changed with the landscape, a crucial factor in determining the origin of early settlers, since migrants like to settle in territory reminding them of home. The Ouachita Valley was no longer Ozarkian-Appalachian Arkansas but now rather more expressive of a deeper South where sin lurked in the pasturage and perdition loomed above a fallen land heavy with impending Apocalypse. The Baptists were almost unchallenged, and their church signs carried bold ipse dixits: REPENT, or WHEREVER DEATH FINDS YOU — ETERNITY KEEPS YOU, or one interrogative, R U REDDY?

I confessed to Q what I was *reddy* for was a "meat and three," my preference being fried chicken, green beans, black-eyed peas, and greens, with a side of mashed potatoes and cream gravy. A bottle of pepper sauce at hand.

When we crossed to the west bank of the Ouachita, we entered a realm of convivially named communities forming on the map a truncated triangle anchored on the east by the river and centrally linked, perhaps to temper any excessive sociability, by a tributary called the Terre Noire. Within that trapezoid of congeniality were Friendship, Amity, Pleasant Hill, Delight, and Harmony Grove, but lying outside, as if excluded, were Ogemaw and Bodcaw, two pretty good names to keep in mind the next time you entertain a child with a tale of ogres and bogles from a dark land.

I discovered the trapezoid that night in Arkadelphia, a name coined to play not just upon the state but also upon a bit of Greek: an ark of brothers, an arc of friends. We felt the South full upon us.

Dunbar's Spectacles

I F I TELL YOU OUR QUARTERS THAT NIGHT — the best we could come up with — were not far from where the Caddo River disembogues into the wooded Ouachita, and if I say on the next morning we walked across a two-lane road to a little cookhouse of evident longevity serving up a good and freshly prepared meal right down to the yams, you may have an image of rural quaintness to make you regret being, at the moment, an armchair traveler.

Well, those descriptions are true, as is this: the motel was near an exit on Interstate 30 and right next door to the drive-up window of a burger chain boasting its quality with the slogan "Billions and Billions Served." (In American corporate logic, quantity *is* quality.) So: river juncture / interstate exit; historic café / franchise drive-up.

My thought that morning just north of Arkadelphia was, any eatery holding out against the omnipotence of the world's largest burger chain across the road might be doing so because of quality based on taste rather than on billions of anything. Perhaps the owner of Bowen's Restaurant had not yet become a purveyor of box food: grub, amalgamated in Hoboken or Fresno, some kitchen guy dumps from a carton, adds a little water to, gives it a couple of minutes of electronic zapping, and presto!, an entrée typically possessed of a single culinary characteristic — heat. Across a nation of speed-eaters, cooking has often come to mean heating. Even worse than the stuff being not very good is, you're likely to get a lot of it (quantity *is* quality). Gus Kubitzki, whom you're getting to know, threatened to open his own cookshack, the Munch & Crunch Lunch, and guarantee his quality with a mea culpa: "If our grub leaves you dissatisfied and yelping, please accept on the house a second helping."

A traveler in America today must look longer and with less success than a generation ago to find genuine regional food, and its discovery requires cagier research, such as questioning the town pharmacist or librarian, or reading hand-lettered signs advertising church suppers that might get you nothing more than chicken potpie and green Jell-O, but at other times might furnish you with a plate of panfried chicken delivered up by the county's last living-resident who still knows how to do it, a Presbyterian lady who measures out cream with half an eggshell and in all things culinarily Southern believes the lard will provide.

With such commentary in mind, I'll now offer not an alternative but an expanded view, drawn from road miles enough to give Q the idea of painting a yellow-striped centerline down the middle of my tombstone. We all know franchising has reduced many a Bert and Betty from owners to employees by sundering their little eggs-over-easy café or their chalkboard-special luncheries, but we can forget that a few good chains (not *always* an oxymoron) have also helped purge the land of many — to use a term no longer common — greasy spoons. It's easy to romanticize the food of yesteryear while forgetting Ptomaine Ptom's Ptamale Wagon.

You see, though, this is faint praise. Your own experience may have revealed the *even more* insidious intrusion of box food into places that look for all the world like a genuine local lunchroom; and, indeed, you might observe Bert and Betty in the kitchen. But she is now skilled in the art of microwavery and he's a peerless pourer who never saw a carton he couldn't open. At the time I write this, the apotheosis of this trend is the prefried hamburger, but it's only a question of time before you'll sit down, if we don't watch out, to a frozen-and-nuked BLT. I'm working to discover clues to identify such places failing to match up even to chain food, but I've come up with only obvious alerts like a door sign warning MICROWAVE IN USE. If the barbecue pit isn't smoking or the grill sizzling, you might as well kiss the ring of the King of Burgers, kneel to the Queen of Dairies, or salute the Colonel of the Fried-Leghorn Regiment.

The Arkadelphia downtown near the courthouse was groomed almost to the point of sterility, as if the churchly folk wanted to cleanse its historic soul of all those trespasses they so often seek forgiveness for in themselves, but in the library of Ouachita Baptist University, Q spotted some escaped remnants from earlier days. There, before our eyes, were several things not just of William Dunbar's time but once belonging to the man himself, including a few items from his excursion up the Ouachita, all of them unexpected: his compass, thick-lensed spectacles, ink-stained pen with metal nib, and, most remarkably, his logbook of the excursion, a journal that had come to light only months before. A video crew, under the direction of the leading historian of the Forgotten Expedition, Trey Berry, was making a documentary at the site of Dunbar's Mississippi plantation when, without warning, a man whizzed up on an ATV while the cameras rolled; he dismounted and pulled from a knapsack a worn logbook which, until that moment, historians had thought perished years ago in the fire that destroyed Dunbar's home. Cameras still running, Berry, then editing a new scholarly edition of the Ouachita journal, opened the book and laid eyes for the first time on William's original on-the-river text. A weaker scholar might have succumbed right there before the camera.

In the library, as I looked at some of the very words that had drawn Q and me into the valley, I felt I was seeing the tracks the man had left behind for us to follow, and his reality expanded from ghostly to an actual historic presence, physically perceivable: there were his neatly inked sentences set down perhaps by the pen now lying next to the logbook, words brought into focus by the spectacles. I could almost hear Dunbar's nib scratching across a page:

At 10 h. a.m. our people returned from the hot springs, each giving his own account of the wonderful things he had seen: they were unable to keep the finger a moment in the Water as it issued from the rock; they drank of it after cooling a little and found it very agreeable; some of them thinking that it tasted like Spice-wood tea.

Where is the American who has not had the urge to touch the sandal of the Statue of Liberty or buy a wooden seat when the old ballpark got torn down? Isn't there within us a basic urge to verify the past by tactilely connecting with it?

Q and I went again to the valley road and followed Arkansas 7 through tilled bottomlands that soon disappeared into pinelands, but the Ouachita was visible only from graveled side roads crossing it. Nondescript little houses of the '60s and '70s interrupted the forest, and in the opolis of Sparkman, oblivion was being held off for the moment by a new bank and its electronic-sign scrolling out mortgage rates and biblical citations. No moneylender there was going to be driven from the temple.

The road twisted its way on southward to another salvation-and-shekel sign, this one with rhyme seeming to trump reason: SAVE THE LOST AT ANY COST. Q eyed me, and I said, although I couldn't prove it, I had never intended to bankrupt anybody.

Beyond the few houses and trailers clinging to a couple of well-built churches that were Ouachita, Arkansas, the highway entered a broad clear-cut of broken snags and bent saplings. Come see, come saw. The detimbered place was so disabled and wasted it looked like a Mathew Brady photograph of the aftermath of Pickett's Charge. But, where the forest still remained, small lots opened for homes looked vacuumed rather than mowed, although the tidiness did not get neighborly and extend past one's own turf to the littered way-sides farther along. It was as if the sawed-down forest had taken the hearts out of the residents and turned them inward.

Camden, Arkansas, has that rare topographical feature along the river, a natural landing. Sitting at the head of navigation, it calls itself "The Queen City of the Ouachita," but it was another sign at the edge of town that brought us to a halt: *HOT BOILED CRAWFISH.* I tried the door. The place was shut up tight, I told a disappointed Q, and probably it was just as well because we were still too far north for good mudbugs. It was too soon.

The best arrivals in a region are those a traveler accomplishes gradually enough to see hints of change — topographic, cultural, culinary — slowly grow from promise to fulfillment, because nothing prepares you for a regional meal any better than a leisurely earned progress, where there's time for anticipation to whet imagination and appetite. Airplanes allow us to arrive before we're ready. Do you prefer quick bread or a leavened loaf? Bashed expectations, however small, require distance to play their part in the crescendo leading to a memorable repast: a crawdad shack with a locked door; a barbecue pit with dead embers; a whiff of roasting chiles and a sign: *WON'T BE READY TILL TOMORROW.* Still, the steadfast traveler abides, continues along, and then one evening the door's not locked, the crab pot's at boil, and the table's set. The most grateful eaters, like the most appreciative lovers, have known a heartbreak or two.

We walked the town center near the courthouse. The usual architectural uglifications following World War II had swept in and pillaged the historic facades of almost every building older than a seventeen-year cicada, and that left the place looking neither soundly established nor progressively prosperous; instead, the heart of Camden, as with so many other towns across America, looked exhausted here and mummified there.

But on a corner of the central intersection — instead of a parking lot — was a small park built atop the sepulcher of a former nineteenth-century bank, and on the east, like a giant garden wall, the two-storey side of a commercial building was covered with a large mural. Painted by an artist unafraid of colors mixed into hues just short of shocking, it was an impudence among moribund facades, and, although a somewhat standard compendium of local history from a Ouachita steamboat to a 1957 Dodge, it had excellent proportions and depth. Pictured at its heart, seemingly life-size, was the towered Ouachita Valley Bank once standing on the site, and around it were some forty human figures integrated spatially and racially, many sartorially snazzy. Better than any aluminized facade, the muraled brick wall suggested Camden was open for commerce. The intersection had changed from eyesore to eye-stopper.

A few blocks away, on Jefferson Street, we came upon a second mural, this one with another Ouachita stern-wheeler but dominated by a gowned vamp, the work clearly from the same hand. In fact, in one corner, the artist had effectively signed the mural by painting in himself painting the mural. Clever, we said. Then the artist's hand moved, sweeping a brush of red acrylic across the bricks. The painter was not painted in — he was still painting, pausing long between strokes to evaluate his work. If the man wasn't painted on the wall, that doesn't mean the wall hadn't painted him, for he wore evidence of his vivid palette from head bandanna to boots. I'm always reluctant to interrupt an artist working alfresco, but I was a moth drawn to his highlights. He, a wizard of quoz, was about to change the next twenty-four hours and the way I saw the Ouachita Valley.

❧ 10 ❧

A Fifty-Foot Femme Fatale

THE NUMBER OF AMERICANS who profess to have been taken aboard craft from beyond this planet is not innumerable but neither is it inconsiderable. Although I lack the figures, my guess is those who have merely dreamed of being taken aboard are far fewer. That very rarity could account for the transformative power in such dreams. In fact, had it not been for his doze on a Ouachita River sandbar in 1954, Indigo Rocket would have a life — right down to his name — surely different from the one he was about to show us in and around Camden, Arkansas. Oh, the painting of murals would still be there, but his cabin out at Mustin Lake, an ancient oxbow of the Ouachita, that would be something else.

As Q and I stood a discreet distance to watch the muralist's careful brushings, I eventually called up to him my admiration. To step inside a plein air painter's circle of awareness and observe the work for a spell and then slip away without a brief word strikes me as either rude or ungrateful for demonstrated artistry. If it's worth watching, it's worth commendation. A simple "well done" is enough.

To those words the painter descended the scaffold and began cleaning a brush rather than brushing us off. "I'm always glad to get down from up there," he said. In the unsequestered creation of exterior murals, an artist becomes used to everyone-a-commentator, especially so when a large portion of his painting is occupied by a languorous fifty-foot seductress. Other than her, the subjects in the mural were more traditional ones of local topography and history. Many citizens — of both genders — had not yet noticed a twenty-foot stern-wheeler steaming directly toward the vamp's (to keep the nauticals) well-trimmed stern.

The artist, Indigo Rocket, didn't really much like heights, in part because he'd recently fallen out of a tree. As he wiped the brush, he said, "For meeting people, I've never had a medium like street murals. But you can't talk from a scaffold."

He spoke of Camden seeing a small renaissance after some years of hard times brought on by changes in agriculture and the closures of the Camark Pottery factory and the kraft-paper mill, and there was even talk about remaking the town as a kind of creative colony where an artist could live cheaply. "Lots of new blood here," he said. "Artists and young people who want to approach things in new ways. That's how this mural happened." He was to do one a year until he covered all unseemly exposed exterior walls. "It's a way to paint the town and earn a little money from the fun." He mentioned how communities across the country were answering the megalomaniacal supercenters rising on their fringes by giving new reasons to come downtown, and murals were part of the rebirth, a change assisted by the development of inexpensive acrylic paint. A few years ago, who'd have thought an emulsion of thermoplastic globules could be a weapon to use against behemoth sprawl⁎marts?

"I grew up here," he said, "but I'd been gone for fifty years until I came back not long ago to be with my parents in their last days. Once I started that first mural, I was so exposed up on the scaffold, old friends began finding me. Now the murals help keep me here."

He was born Terrell Mashaw, but at the turn of the millennium he decided his art required a name more fitted to its new directions. Trim and angular but not tall, with strong hands, he was youthful despite a certain facial erosion reminiscent of a carved limestone visage long exposed to weather; his profile — a nose with an almost imperceptible arc like a slightly drawn bow — might have been taken from a courthouse-lawn statue. His hair was dark and straight. He had tried engineering at Louisiana Polytechnic Institute in Ruston before changing to art and design, studies he continued at the old

Art Center School in Los Angeles. Like most American males of that generation, he'd served the required military stint, his with the Army. He was sixty-six years old.

Rocket's education — both engineering and art — led him to Detroit where he designed tire treads, unfulfilling work leading him to take up a sequence of jobs and a life as peripatetic as that of a nineteenth-century itinerant sign-painter, work he'd also done. In Dallas he illustrated annual reports but soon burned out on advertising, so he sold most of his belongings to continue hithering and yonning: San Diego, Port Townsend, Sonoma, Boston, Providence, Woods Hole, San Antonio.

He had a knack for finding distinctive habitations: the Nobska lighthouse in Massachusetts, a tent in Massasoit State Park, a winery cottage in California, and now the cabin on the Ouachita oxbow. For a while he and his girlfriend, Blue, painted trucks and carousel horses and kiddie rides for a carnival, and sea creatures on walls for a couple of marine wonderlands. He spoke in an unassuming manner, his gaze often directed toward his bespattered boots. I asked what it was like to walk past and look up at one of his own murals, and he said, "I'm glad I'm still alive."

When Indigo learned we were following the valley of the Ouachita, he began a story about a dream he'd had on a river sandbar years ago, but decided the telling was too involved for a sidewalk conversation. I asked him to join us for supper, and he nodded and started back up the scaffold, pausing to call down, "Have you got a place to stay?" Not yet. "Come out to the cabin. There's a four-poster for you."

At seven, we met him at a little restaurant not far from the elegant slippers of the fifty-foot femme fatale, and it was she who led us into talk about the difficulties in painting large murals: heights, weather, public constraints, distortions caused by viewers looking from thirty feet below the painting.

"On that first mural," he said, "I struggled longest with how I should represent the black community here and its history. Do I put them in overalls and field dresses? Kerchiefs and shoeless? Are they picking cotton and walking behind mules? Does the mural end up with blacks in torn dungarees and whites in suits and dresses? What part of the past do I put up on a wall forty-six feet wide and three storeys high? I couldn't figure it out until one Sunday. That's the day people dress up down here — everybody, black or white. That was my answer — put some of every group in their Sunday best. I mean, who wouldn't get into their best bib and tucker for their portrait?"

Q said, "That made people happy?"

"Not everyone. Some guy drove past in an old truck one day when I was on the scaffold and yelled out, 'Hey! Why don't you paint another nigger up there!'" Indigo paused. "That's going to happen when a street is the gallery."

We talked about public murals in a democracy as being an art of inclusion, how art in a forum *demands* inclusion. I paraphrased José Orozco, the great muralist of Mexico, who said of all the arts, mural painting is (I quote him now) "the most disinterested, as it cannot be converted into an object of personal gain nor can it be concealed for the benefit of a few privileged people. It is for the people. It is for everybody." Great mural artists understand the power of the forum and use their work to instruct, inspire, remind, maybe amuse, and sometimes provoke. I could see Indigo's murals doing all those things.

"I've never had this much fun with art," he said. "I've earned more money but never so much pleasure. It's almost performance art. Rednecks in pickups, church ladies in Buicks, guys on Harleys — everybody wants to join in some way. One woman stopped to tell me I was using too much pink and purple. I told her enough murals in Arkansas are green and brown. Besides, bright colors fade."

I said, speaking of purple, the only thing on the first mural that wasn't generalized was the Grapette delivery truck. (I noticed it because I might have won a footrace in 1949 had I not drunk that second bottle of Grapette soda pop just before the competition.)

"It was invented here in Camden right about the time we were born," Indigo said. "Benjamin Fooks. He started out by selling brooms, among other things. You'll be sleeping in his former cabin tonight. He was my uncle."

That detail seemed rationale enough for me to boast I'd once taken the company slogan, "Thirsty or not," to heart and drunk six bottles in a day, and Indigo said, "I did thirteen one time between breakfast and going to bed." Q asked what the slogan meant, and he said, "You don't have a glass of wine because you're thirsty. You don't drink coffee for thirst." We both, I assume, were looking proud because she said, "Are you boys bonding over guzzling purple sodas?"

After we ordered sandwiches, he said, "Above the Grapette truck I painted a bright-yellow Stearman biplane, but there was something about it that bothered me. But I couldn't see what it was. I kept looking, and it still escaped me. One evening when I was up working on it, the bucket slipped out of my hand and fell thirty feet — yellow paint went everywhere. Something didn't want the plane up there. Right after the accident I finally saw how the Stearman was flying directly at the bank tower in the mural. Shades of Nine-Eleven in the brightest yellow. The next day I went up and painted clouds over it. In five months, that yellow plane was the only real accident."

Our waitress came to the table, cast a sweet eye on Indigo, a man now of local renown, asked whether his (full) glass needed refilling, and sashayed herself off again. Q asked, "Are you married?" Not now. "Do you have children?" No children. "How about when *you* were one? Were you a little artist?"

"I liked toys that *worked*," he said. "That *operated*. Things I could assemble and disassemble and reassemble in different ways — Lincoln Logs, Erector Sets. But those toys were all based on angles, and I wanted curves and circles. When I got older I built little flying things, but I always dreamed of machines that could be totally versatile to move in all the elements — land, water, and air. I guess I was more mechanical than artistic. A screwdriver instead of a crayon. Later, when I worked for the company that makes Transformers,

I had to design instruction books, but I wanted to do the figures. I didn't stay there long."

The waitress brought our supper, simple fare, nothing to distract the conversation. Indigo said, "When I was about sixteen, I saw in a *Popular Mechanics* plans for a small boat. Eight-feet long with a nineteen thirties–style racing hull. I made it out of spruce and marine plywood. At my mother's suggestion, I covered the bottom with fiberglass cloth, a new material then. I got an old Mercury outboard racing motor and rebuilt it. It'd do about forty miles an hour on the water, which is a little fast for the Ouachita. You know, bends and barges, snags. But I was a kid. One evening I was going full-bore up the river and hit an out-of-control ski boat which didn't survive. But the fiberglass hull saved me. My mother's idea. What did she know about boat construction?" We toasted his survival, and he said, "Maybe I should never have named that little racer *Miss Fit*. But I heard it's still out there somewhere, running the river."

Q said, "This afternoon you mentioned a dream you had about the Ouachita."

"Not *about* the river — *on* the river," he said. "It happened in August. I'd gone up the Ouachita alone. Stopped on a sandbar to get a little sun. I was a teenager. Nineteen fifty-four, a time of lots of talk and books about UFOs. I fell asleep, I guess. For how long, I don't know, but I dreamed a spacecraft came in above the water and hovered over me and blocked the sun. I can't remember it all now, but I do remember the ship spotted me, and three beings — willowy females — came down and took me aboard. I was helpless. All I could do was look back and see my body sleeping on the sand. The airship was like a chameleon — it kept changing colors, according to mood, it seemed. Inside, a huge vertical-axis gyro was turning. I don't remember what happened on the ship, except I can see now certain ideas got planted in me that began sprouting years after. The three females might have been expressions of yin principles — art, grace, and beauty. Who knows? Then I got returned to the sandbar. When I woke up in the hot sun, I had no sunburn, and my skin was aromatic. It was like I'd been under a big shadow the whole time."

Did he ever dream of the ship again? "Once, about a year later, in a fever. That time the thing — or the dream — was scary, but I don't know why. Something had changed." He shook his head. "Now I don't know whether the dreams were a blessing or curse."

Q asked whether he dreamed much about flying — body flying without mechanical support, that wonderful free-floating stuff. Indigo said, "Not enough."

❥ 11 ❦

Architect of Phantasmagoria

Soon after dusk, we followed Indigo Rocket across the river and into the low backcountry to the Fooks cabin where he lived on the woods-fringed oxbow fed by cold springs he could feel rising when at night he swam the dark water. His uncle built the retreat in 1946 on proceeds from Grapette and its sister drinks: Orangette, Lemonette, Limette. I felt a kind of proprietary interest in the place: my boyhood nickels must have bought a shingle here and a nail there.

Benjamin Tyndle Fooks (rhymes illogically with Cokes), after many months of experimentation, created his signature drink with real grape juice and cane sugar, and the resulting excellence of his beverage caused it, over the following decade, to reach from little Camden across the nation. (An early slogan: "Particular Folks Drink Fooks Drinks.") After the family sold the company, Grapette eventually ended up in the hands of a rival that let it decline until yet another group brought it back and returned it in a small way to certain areas, one of them its natal town where once again you can find it in the little clear bottles.

"Let me go in first," Indigo said as if he needed to open a safe passage for us through a lair, and he disappeared inside the cabin. Suddenly the dark windows took on an unearthly glow, and we heard him call out for us to enter, and in we went, Q keeping so close behind me I heard her mutter her grandfather's strongest oath, "Cheese and crackers!" As I looked about, mine came out stronger.

Our eyes had to adjust to the dimness and shadows, but before that could happen fully, Indigo, nowhere to be seen, must have hit another switch because the room seemed to change. Cheese and crackers indeed! It was a phantasmagorium!

Entering Indigo's parlor was like stepping into the back of a vacuum-tube radio of the same vintage as the first Grapette: the space was full of inexplicable objects, some glowing and others only seeming to glow from reflections; shapes curvilinear and right-angled, bulbous and boxy, yet all in a complex order it would take a schematic drawing to explain; the lower objects were ostensibly attached or anchored or plugged in, while the upper things appeared airborne. A chamber aloft, a room in hover.

I'd never seen so much light — *particles of light* — in a dim room; it was as though they were little bungs and stoppers to keep the cool darkness from leaking in and extinguishing everything. Clobbered by surprise, I saw two or three sparklings where perhaps there was only one. Yet the effect wasn't a banishment of darkness but a shivering of it with fractured radiance: glistenings, glisterings, gleamings, glintings, glimmerings, glowings, refractions and refulgences, candescence and luminescence, little shining beacons, small shimmering bulbs, twinklings and blinkings, lamplets and lanternlets bespangling the walls in a carny of luminations. It was as if a cut-glass prism full of entrapped sunbeams had fallen and shattered, each brokenness still shedding its wavelength of spectral light. A color wheel spun so fast the pigments had flown off to bespatter whatever they hit: ceiling, floor, Q's head. Her flaxen hair now magenta, now vermilion, and, with another step forward, orchid, heliotrope, cobalt blue. A student of chromatics could go mad. "Your face!" she said. "You're a chameleon. A redskin. No, now you're a green man from planet Quoz."

I said, Let it be like this when I cross over, and she said, "Maybe you just crossed. Maybe you're there."

Where was Indigo? Not the color, the man, because the color — and a hundred others — fluoresced everywhere.

Did I hear music? Was sight turning to sound? A little night music? Light music? A true chromatic scale sung sotto voce? A chorale of colors? Was I seeing radiance or hearing ragtime? The disassociation of synesthesia. Where the devil was Indigo?

Ah! Of course we couldn't see him, because we were inside his kaleidoscope skull where he'd transformed his imagination into light and color splattered all over constructions made from hundreds upon hundreds of found objects: buttons, beads, baskets, bottles, Christmas ornaments, saucers, seashells, vases, candlesticks, small brass horns, stalks of river cane, gelatin molds, twigs, a flyswatter. Look long enough, and somewhere there'd be green cheese and crackers, shellacked and polished and reflecting light like the evening star. He'd turned the place into a loom where he could weave a two-dimensional world of murals into a three-dimensional warped and wefted tapestry seeming to have movement, and that meant he'd embraced the fourth dimension.

The chamber, although large, seemed full, almost claustrophobic, as though it could hold nothing more, not so much as an exhalation, yet I could walk through it, along narrow aisles and alleys and avenues leading into little piazzas with chairs under long, thin, cut trees, decurved into leaning bows hung with bright picked-up objects, small arbors decorated by a magpie, all of it under a beamed sky of a ceiling — the only thing keeping me from floating off into some fifth dimension.

The nature of quoz is synergistic. Like stardust lying over the planet, quoz is potential recombinant energy seeking union with an open mind. A crevice is all it needs. Ready your emotional membranes, and it enters, passes through. To the implicit force in quoz, any idea that's ever crossed your brain is a latent zygote. This wasn't psychosis — it was zygosis.

And then Q came from someplace, her hair chrome yellow, her face puce, and she said, "Where've you been, Little Boy Blue?" Under the haycock, fast asleep.

But where the hell is Indigo? And then he was there too, coming into the room on a boy's bicycle painted in carny colors, nodding hello, and again out of the room, and soon again back into it, slowing to say, "Want a ride?" And my wambled brain thinking, *Just had one, thanks.* And here he came around again. "Thirsty or not?" And that time I got out a real answer: Thirsty!

I sat down in a chair under one of the tree limbs in front of a large fireplace, the chimney sided by a mural of half-mad Edward Lear's "The Owl and the Pussycat." I was fit to dance by the light of the moon. Q asked if I was all right, and later she alleged I said a candle has no opposite because if it did, you could take a couple of sticks of darkness into a lighted room and extinguish it.

Sans wheels, Indigo reappeared carrying a tray of three ice-cubed glasses and three bottles of Grapette, the old-style little fellows, and he poured us a round of Uncle Benjamin's secret formula in the very room where inventor Fooks used to take his, and Q asked again, "Are you okay?" and I said, For a minute or two, I think I transitioned.

Indigo may have smiled. His art had succeeded.

Sitting, sipping, collecting myself, I could see the room now more clearly. It wasn't airborne, but I still felt it could be if my attention wandered, because it was deliberately fitted out to permit the ordinary to transmogrify into the alien in an auxiliary cosmos where the immutable laws were those of fancy, and the goal was to unhitch a visitor from the mundane and the presumed in order that he might flitter like a bat through the darks of imagination. An emporium to disorient one's sensorium.

At the center of the Great Parlor, for that's what it was in its lodgelike setting, were large wooden tables topped with spired towers made entirely from found objects gathered by an artist on jolly terms with that elusive chimera of the late last century, one's inner child. But the craftsmanship was from experienced hands. If you know Erastus Salisbury Field's huge painting *Historical Monument of the American Republic,* you'll have an idea not of the architecture but of the folk vision inherent in Indigo's world of spires. Or perhaps closer is the fabled Watts Towers in Los Angeles, structures

Indigo loved. Nothing was pointless or daffy, although everything was whimsical.

On the far side of the room was a four-by-eight-foot spacecraft, airborne except for a small, hidden pedestal. A compact person could board it. Oh, to be again nine years old! Cross a hydroplane with a jet fighter, add in a few details from a Formula 1 race car, paint it in harmonious metallic pastels, tip the nose with small nodules of stained glass, and you'd have Indigo Rocket's rocket-ship, a piece of sculpture waiting for its gallery. He said cryptically, "A transition between air and water and land requires certain metamorphoses in design — for efficiency." I interpreted that to mean rotors for flight could metamorphose into propellers for water, sails could change to wings, wheels to pontoons, and maybe even the machine into man — or woman.

He called it *The Mother Ship* — driven by imaginative fire through dreams of earth, air, and water — the ur-craft spawning three much smaller but more intricate dream ships he brought out and held aloft one at a time to demonstrate their capacities to "transition" from element to element, from physical substance to the ether of one's dreams.

The vehicles functioned according to four guidelines: they were *stressed* like a bow, *pressurized* like a pneumatic tire, *charged* like a storage battery, and *articulated* like a skeleton. "I call them creature ships because they have a certain life force." Rotors on one craft had the shape of a well-turned feminine leg, and a fuselage on another had the body of a porpoise. They were devilishly clever, like da Vinci's drawings of machines. But if Leonardo conceived contraptions that one day would indeed exist, Indigo built deliberate impossibilities.

The ships belonged to his world of spires atop the tables. "It's all related," he said. "It's a family." Within each object was a consistent and continuing unity of vision, something often visible in the best folk art, and sometimes on beyond. "When I start building a tower, all I know is that it's headed for the sky." Q, who had been looking at a sketchbook of his spires, said, "That could be your epitaph."

Indigo constructed his towers from what he happened upon and could bring home: a rattan cornucopia for the body of a building, a belt buckle for a door, a woody vine became a spiral ramp, a goblet a tabernacle dome, a piece of costume jewelry for a cathedral window, a gourd turned into a house; all the constructions bright and airy and transformable into other shapes. He said, "I like to dream of building one I could live in."

He had created a narrative bringing the objects together: "A catastrophe wipes out all people over the age of three, and that calls forth the arrival of the Noggins, creatures of compassion and interchangeable intelligence whose lives depend on cooperation. Without harmony, they're dysfunctional." He was looking at a Noggin in his hand as he spoke, as if teaching it. "They raise the human children and teach them kindly wisdom."

Noggins? I said, and he, "If you have transport and towers, then you have to have creature life, creatures who use their noggins." From one of the skinny, ice-bent trees, he took down a plastic Easter egg that, as if painted by Picasso, had a face which changed with the angle of the beholder. Such an Egg Noggin — capable of interchange, transformation, and cooperation — was embryonic life to create a realm of benevolence.

"The Noggins," Indigo said, "have mastered the four elements and have acquired high, humane intelligence as they learned their mastery, but they're still a fusion of intelligence and machine even though they have emotions. Their highest transition is to blend with their operators — like a horse with its rider. This fusion comes from fantasy physics that works interchanges among matter and energy and being." So, a kind of *meta*physics.

He demonstrated certain physical transitions with the Noggins as he talked, at one point saying, "When I was doing the instruction books for Transformers — you know, those interlocking toy creature-machines — the company encouraged attacks and violence as a way to involve a kid's imagination. I used to wonder, *What if there were loving warriors? What if there were art attacks?* An alien ship arrives and dissimulates into multiple Noggins. Each one is skilled in an art technique unleashed by musically enhanced lasers that change surfaces into images like murals and patterns. They turn a gray world into colors. But the powers of blackness can fight back. They can shock the pastels and render them colorless for a while. It's an art attack! Pearl Harbor meets the Museum of Modern Art."

While he was saying this, he was disassembling one Noggin to build it into a second one. "What if violence got turned into art — dynamic art, performance art — and the child was the artist *and* performer? Don't children love performance where things are moving? They can visualize things in motion all at once like in real life — everything moving and transforming at every moment."

The Noggin in his hands now had feet instead of wheels, and its furry head had become feathery. "What if the idea wasn't to obliterate and vaporize but to create and actualize? What if the idea wasn't to actuate a preset program designed by an engineer but to help kids imagine something new for themselves, something the child hasn't imagined yet? Not destruction but construction where little kids are the creators and get to see their ideas hatch out of their own noggins." Now the second creature in his hands was ready to sprout what I took for rotors, but they could have been wings or fins or flippers or a clown's feet.

"It's a lot easier to knock down a sand castle than to build one," he said. "Destruction can even be fun for a minute or two, but wreckage doesn't leave behind any sense of achievement. It's empty, and kids soon feel that. They're left with nothing. We've got a world now where simulated attacks and virtual violence are probably more marketable than some toy or game that tries to create a vision and a physical expression of it. Kids are going to imitate us. We've taught them weapons are solutions. But there may be a time coming when search-and-destroy could change to search-and-design."

Q, who had been jotting down pieces of the conversation, asked if he thought any of these ideas had to do with his dream on the Ouachita sandbar. He said, "That dream opened a door to an idea. A theme. It was an inspiration that arose when the time was right. You know, a kind of dream ship that transported me to a mother ship for transference." He raised an arm to indicate the entire room, filled with his daedal inventions. "All this is the result of transitions."

Indigo pulled out a notebook of verse he'd written to illustrate his realm of Noggindom:

One by one the faces come
Out of the mist to be kissed;
Two by two enjoined as one,
Three or more joined in fun,
Ten or more become a sum
All together numbering many
Spinning together on the run.

At midnight he showed us to a room softened and charmed with arches and odd pieces of sculptured wood; the floor was steel blue, as if part of a ship built to travel between elements; a ladder, like one in a submarine, led to a small loft above a drawing table; a red velveteen settee, paintings of icebergs, and one of a cat done by his friend Blue. A four-poster bed. Everything was, to use Q's phrase, "in quiet resplendence."

I stood at the window for some time, looking out toward the old oxbow. I felt I'd dozed off on some river sandbar of the mind and been taken aboard an indigo rocket ship, and, if affirmation can be transition, I think I transitioned. I hope so. After all, transit without transition doesn't take a traveler very far.

The next morning when we went outside to say good-bye to Indigo and head on down the river valley, I looked back at the cabin. In the sunlight, I was surprised to see how small it was and how it was painted in a motley and unfinished way. He said, "I started painting it and realized I didn't know how to do the outside of a house, so I stopped. Maybe I'll figure it out one of these days."

❯12❮

The Goat Woman
of Smackover Creek

NOT EVERYONE A TRAVELER MEETS along the road is actually there. Unless we compress and distort it, existence just isn't that simple. Day in and day out, whether we perceive them or not, we continually pass through human shadows, ghostly presences that depend not at all on the supernatural but rather upon our openness to move in the deeps of time. Our predecessors often leave behind a quoz or two as a posthumous gift to direct us as we seek means to make of them what we will, perhaps using them to expand our own limited days or to remind ourselves of distant threads and successions, sometimes only pentimenti binding us even when we don't see the linkings.

In that manner, a traveler sometimes can know a person dead and gone better than one he just met at the next table: that lady who talked about too little rain, too much rain, rain just right for a good onion crop, the best onion for gumbo, her mother's onion-pie recipe, the time she got mad at her husband and baked him a possum stuffed with green onion and kudzu, that same lady who otherwise kept herself hidden.

The Goat Woman of Smackover Creek, I never met. She died sixteen years before Q and I crossed the stream twelve miles south of Camden and about the same to its junction with the Ouachita. Dunbar knew the creek, or perhaps one nearby, as Chemin Couvert, a "tree-covered way." The French description, corrupted by Americans, is probably the source of the name Smackover, although locals will offer several other interpretations ranging from the possible to the implausible.

The quoz that led me to the Goat Woman sits in the Arkansas Museum of Natural Resources, a colorless name, as if atonement for its proximity to a place called Smackover, or perhaps an overcorrection for its earlier name — the Arkansas Oil and Brine Museum — which could have led you to conclude it displayed historic machinery for pickling cucumbers. (Bromine, or brine, is extracted from underground saline water there.)

The quoz itself was a 1926 Model T truck that probably began as a factory "kit" — an engine mounted to a frame with wheels that became a rolling platform for crude and clumsy, though solidly built, living quarters within corrugated-metal sides and mullioned windows, everything but the glass creosoted black. The thing had more the look of a cage than a wheeled home. At its rear was a minuscule "porch" once serving as what must have been the tiniest performance stage in America. The museum staff called the rig a "circus wagon" and a "circus carriage," both terms misleading; more recent and accurate was "medicine-show truck." It was, the staff believed, "probably the rarest artifact that will ever be collected by the museum."

Between the large headlamps and the tiny taillights sat the six-by-twenty-foot box of wood and metal serving as home to the Goat Woman for more than half a century, virtually all of those years after the truck left the road. A man told me, "She got drove into the county but she never got drove back out again." He was speaking of the vehicle, but he might as well have been referring to its longtime resident.

How the medicine-show truck came to be hauled out of the mud along Smackover Creek after years of abandonment and vandalism is the story of Rhene Salome Miller Meyer. Her middle name seems peculiar unless you consider that her mother studied opera, and Rhene (pronounced RAY-nah) was born in 1905, the year Richard Strauss's opera *Salome* was first performed. Still, I wonder, did

Mother Miller choose to ignore the pathology of Salome's urge for the head of John the Baptist, or did she have in mind the other Salome, the one in the New Testament?

If you'll allow a few sentences of Rhene's biography, I'll get us to the part of her story I think carries well beyond the limits of one woman's life. Much of what I know came from Don Lambert who wrote a weekly column for the *Smackover Journal* and later was elected mayor, a man whose modesty led him to disprize his role in preserving the carnival wagon. A generation younger than Rhene, he met her as a boy when he went to burn trash on the back lot of his mother's department store on Broadway, where Lambert could talk with Rhene through a fence. Some years afterward, when she moved up to the creek, he delivered Lions Club Christmas boxes to her. He once wrote that "her story will forever be locked in an impenetrable and arcane maze." I would add, however, no matter the possible answers to her puzzle of a life, the very questions it raises reveal a way into the Goat Woman's maze. While everything that exists is a potential quoz for somebody, one must embrace the mystery for it to open itself.

One of six children, Rhene was born on a farm in Pennsylvania Dutch Country where her father staged occasional medicine shows to peddle a nostrum called the Miraculous Seven Sisters Hair Tonic that would "make your hair grow to touch the floor!" (Just who might want hair dragging the floor, I haven't learned.) Onstage, Father Miller would trot out three-year-old Rhene and point to her long and thick tresses as proof of the efficacy of the tonic. From the time she could strut a few steps, she grew accustomed to public exhibition and came to see the world as her stage. When Rhene was not displaying her locks, her chore, one she enjoyed as much, was milking the family goats. That pair of tasks set the fundamentals of her entire life.

In her midteens she went to Philadelphia to study art; then it was off to New York City for music at the Juilliard School and possibly a performance in Carnegie Hall, all of which led to training with a diva. But those impressive educations earned Rhene nothing more than a job with the Barnum & Bailey Circus as a "one-girl band," performing on seven instruments simultaneously (accordion, harmonica, drums, cymbals, traps, tambourine, castanets), or six if she pulled away from the rigged-up harmonica and sang. She also could play the piano, violin, harp, and bass drum.

During the '20s, Rhene traveled to Europe with another circus until it failed, forcing her return to New York to model shampoos and cosmetics. Don Lambert said, "Mrs. Meyer's hair was her glory." Indeed, in the two photos I've seen of her, her wiry mane didn't grow so much as explode into a dark nimbus above a face of high, rounded cheeks and seductively narrow eyes. Those photographs and her stage name and her European travel lead me to hypothesize that Rhene's art study exposed her to the famous Aubrey Beardsley illustrations for Oscar Wilde's *Salome* as well as to Gustav Klimt's well-known paintings of the two headhuntresses Salome and Judith, each portrait based on the same model whose hair and coloring Rhene could have seen in herself.

About 1927 or the year following, she joined a small, nearly insolvent carnival traveling to one-night stands in remote Midwestern and Southern villages, places that would turn out for anything if it promised even the slightest diversion from the quietude of local life: a tent revival would do as well as a medicine show (both having about the same results). For a troupe struggling on the fringe of the Depression, a one-girl band was both economical and a good come-on. In 1929 the faltering carny arrived in Camden, never to leave again except in pieces, broken up by economics. When the show folded its tents for the last time, Rhene may have been on the edge of destitution.

She was twenty-four years old, educated, broadly talented, attractive, the world before her, yet for reasons unknown, she decided to marry Charley Meyer, a quarter century older; he was presumably the business manager and a man with little education or talent, facially unblessed, and eccentric. The merest speculation suggests a marriage of convenience in such a May-December union, but that one lasted till Charley died a wizened octogenarian thirty-two years later. Perhaps because the old man may have physically and mentally battered her, Rhene did not remarry, nor apparently did she have any subsequent attachments.

As newlyweds, they drove the medicine-show truck from Camden down to Smackover where Charley found a rent-free "slap-up remnant" of the oil-boomtown days and opened a used-tire business providing a limited income. Abruptly, her life went from the most public of social intercourse to an inexplicable insulation, a segregation through a concealment.

At the back of the tire shop was the show wagon, and around it Charley built a board fence that Don Lambert said "presented a stockade appearance," much of it covered by an arbor to create a compound. Within it Rhene virtually disappeared for the next two decades, her society a tribe of goats she cherished and scarcely seemed to distinguish from people. The situation was made for a modern Chaucerian tale: a jealous aging husband fearing cuckoldry cloisters his bewitching bride while he buys and sells junked tires and vulcanizes flats. It's the classic motif of the maiden in the tower, Rhene's tower a wooden palisade: *Rapunzel, Rapunzel, let down your hair* (grown to touch the floor by the Miraculous Seven Sisters Hair Tonic).

Rhene's withdrawal into a Model T truck enclosed by a goat pen was so sudden and complete, villagers began to question whether her reclusion was that of a captive. Twice, the marshal came by Charley's little compound to ask questions and look inside, once asking to see a marriage certificate. No, the marshal told the people, the Goat Woman was not being constrained; as best he could determine, her isolation was of her own volition. Although no one used these terms, the childless woman appeared to be an anchoress whose sanctum was a cramped goat yard and her deities cloven-hoofed beasts.

Columnist Lambert, speaking of Smackover in the 1940s, wrote:

Most people would see her on those rare evenings late when she would walk down a darkened and deserted Broadway street in a brisk barefooted pace, her long hair in a wildly disorganized muss, with only a light-weight cotton dress covering her modesty. There was talk she was a deaf mute while others contended that she was crazed. We boys believed [the couple] to be German spies, with little consideration given to the fact that there was really nothing in Smackover to spy on. One fact was evident. She was different and to me resembled what I perceived to be a wild beauty right out of a Stone Age cave.

In a hamlet, anonymity doesn't exist because proximity won't allow it; there's no place to hide, no vanishing into a madding crowd available to the city dweller. A village resident is inescapably, ineradicably present in one way or another, and, since nothing is more conspicuous than attempted disappearance, imperceptibility is impossible; the best an eccentric can hope for is merely solitude.

Withdrawal affords an easy path to nonconformity, but to venture it in a village will only provide fodder to cramped lives where mockery is the usual first step to reducing an independent mind in order to pigeonhole it. Human enigma must be, if not explained, then at least accounted for, and those who set themselves apart through solitariness will be thought aloof, one of the world's oldest insults, and the common communal response will be a diagnosis of dementia. Society works to change self-imposed seclusion into banishment.

Contributing to Rhene's discrediting were her talents and good looks: she could do what other women couldn't, and simply by appearing, she showed men what they couldn't have. Such capacities must be brought within limits of ordinary tolerance, and the village accomplished that by reduction, by changing Salome into the "Goat Woman," the milker of bearded ruminants, the captured maiden of a (what else?) lecherous old goat. And she? The goat of jest and suspicions. It all fit together on so many levels. To a woman who loved goats and who prided herself on the milk they produced, the lone grace must have been the deprecating appellation carried no insult or hurt.

For villagers, the mocking cognomen helped answer her threat to their ordinariness and allowed the emotionally hobbled to fetter an exotic stray. Her perceived challenge to the complacency of their constringed lives of ingrained patterns was blunted, and their restricted existence could continue undisturbed as long as she provided entertainment. She was still onstage, even if the boards were no longer those of a theater or carny wagon but ones intended to hide her behind a palisade. Whether the hamlet knew it or not, Salome was invisibly dancing down Broadway. Don Lambert said, "Hair down to her waist, she was really something to see." If she did not hold any severed heads of the baptized, she held their minds.

That's my notion of how Rhene went from a life on the public stages of two continents to a durance behind a high plank wall where the audience was a few devil-eyed goats, the males now and then coming into odoriferous rut. But I wonder, was she ever aware of any passersby pausing outside the stockade to listen to her soft soprano accompanied by her violin, perhaps sending forth strains from *Salome* or *Pelléas et Mélisande*? In the songs from behind the wall, did anyone hear Salome singing:

> *Why does my king look at me*
> *all the time with his mole eyes*
> *under those twitching eyelids?*

Or did someone hear from her Mélisande's desire:

> *My long hair is descending*
> *to the threshold of the tower,*
> *my hair is waiting for you,*
> *all down the tower,*
> *all the long day,*
> *all the long day.*

Did anyone hear Rhene's songs as cryptograms of confinement with a jealous old eccentric?

If the Goat Woman's story ended there, it would be a sorrowful one indeed, but her life, still free of segues and legatos, again leaped over passages into unexpected movements.

About 1952, the couple fired up the old sideshow truck and sputtered four miles north into the woods where the wagon would "endure yearly baptisms from Smackover Creek" for the next half century. Charley, ill, his wick burning short, became more approachable and less intent on his wife's quarantine. Perhaps he, well into his eighties, was seeing the end, or maybe his jealousy just plain wore out with his body. A few volunteers, Don Lambert among them, built onto the Model T a small side room made from the old fence planks. It was little more than a hovel. Apparently, Charley lived in it while Rhene continued to reside in the show wagon. Lambert wrote that the couple, once away from Poplar Street, "seemed happy with their circumstances. They entertained whenever anyone cared to visit by showing silent movies followed by Rhene's musical presentations." She and her herd, visible to travelers on Route 7, became an inadvertent wayside attraction, and the medicine-show truck, a landmark; even yet in Camden, citizens speak of how they would put on the brakes to gape at the one they still call the "Goat Woman."

Not long after the move to the boggy, frog-riddled creek bank, Charley died, and Rhene's story shifted unpredictably once more. Now into her fifties, she forsook hermitry and stepped out of her unexplained shackles and commenced reclaiming the life she'd been educated for. She began performing on a local television morning show that aired her singing, accompanied by her own hand and sometimes by one of her goats which would, said Lambert, "join in songs with distinctive bleats at all the appropriate intervals." The village seemed to accept the lady who could so single-handedly divert them through one means or another, even if she remained the Goat Woman and they appeared to countenance her amusements much as a street-side audience does an organ-grinder's monkey: "Why, look at that little thing bang those cymbals!"

Although no longer sequestered, Rhene continued to live apart, and I don't believe she entirely slipped the village tether; rather, she found ways to express herself within its constriction, not letting it choke off her song. She continued lifting her seven instruments until her final few years when true dementia dropped a slow curtain down over her bright performances, and she went into a nursing home, and there she died at eighty-three.

Should you visit Smackover someday, you can see the little medicine-show wagon and you'll hear about the Goat Woman, but ask after Salome, and you're likely to get only a "Who?" Don Lambert finds apropos a poem from Emily Dickinson:

> I'm Nobody! Who are you?
> Are you — Nobody — Too?
> Then there's a pair of us!
> Don't tell! they'd advertise — you know!
>
> How dreary — to be — Somebody!
> How public — like a Frog —
> To tell one's name — the livelong June —
> To an admiring Bog!

❧ 13 ❧

The Ghost Bird

W HAT HAPPENED THE NEXT MORNING was either an author
sighting or a case of mistaken identity; but whichever, Q believed
I was happy the Louisiana state line was not far distant.

From Smackover we joggled onto a county road as near the Ouachita as we could get — although the river was out of view — to follow
Route 68 southeasterly until it cut away toward the oil-and-gas town
of El Dorado (a more accurate name would be El Dorado Negro).
Like so many other settlements west of the Appalachians, it was
named purely out of optimistic expectations. Untypically though,
three quarters of a century after its founding, El Dorado managed
to consummate its name when oil was discovered near the town in
1920. (Speaking of oil, we were now far enough south to hear the
word pronounced to rhyme with *bowl;* and some people had added
an *r* and dropped the *i* in the name of the river: the Warsh-taw.)

El Dorado (Elda Rayda) is also the county seat, and its flourishing
courthouse-quadrangle gave some historic polish to the usual crudi-
ties oil produces at the fringes of a town. On the square, we went into
a bookshop I hoped would have something about the Ouachita, but I
came up with, as I recall, only a natural history of polecats and, from
an accommodating clerk, detailed descriptions of various routes to
Louisiana, none of which would get us to a shore of the river. We
were inside long enough for a sunny day to turn stormy; as the rain
fell, the clerk, a smiling sexagenarian, said, "The Devil's beating his
wife." I took it for the title of a new book. "No," the man said. "I
mean the rain. My mother used to tell me it rained when the Devil

beat his wife." I hadn't known Old Harry had a wife. "Mildred," Q said. "A shapely number, although that long tail was a drag."

As we were going to the door, the shop phone rang, and I heard the clerk, in almost a whisper, say, "No, still here, but you better hurry if you're going to catch him." I presumed he was talking to the mother of the teenager standing at the science-fiction shelf. When I opened the door for Q, the clerk called out, "I know who you are!" I looked around to see whom he was talking to, and 'twas I. He gave a confiding wink and said, "Coming soon to a town near you." I returned one of those smiling nods we use when we fail to comprehend and don't really want clarification. That was a mistake.

Once outside, Q asked what I made of it. It's possible, I said, that he took me for an itinerant vinyl-awning salesman. "No," she said. "It sounded more accusatory. Like you're on the loose. An escapee from an institution." We all, I answered with manifest profundity, are on the lam from one institution or another. With that, we took up the road again.

While it's true on the way out of town I checked the rearview mirror once or twice — only in accordance with safe driving — and drove a mere one mile per hour below the speed limit — as was prudent — and signaled well before a lane change — courtesy my only thought — Q asked, "Are you keeping an eye out for cops?" Of course not, I said. No more than the next guy on the loose. And to prove I was in no hurry to cross the state line, I took a digression eastward to the Felsenthal Lock and Dam in the Ouachita swamp-lands. I rest my case.

She asked whether I'd ever paid the parking-meter violation I'd been tagged with in that beach-town tourist trap. Attorney that she is, her next questions, I thought, employed the words *warrant* and *arrest* rather more freely than clarity required. At the lock, to prove my conscience nearly clean (who would pay a fifty-dollar fine for failing to put a quarter in a meter at midnight?), I said I was going into the headquarters to get information from a uniformed Army Corps of Engineers ranger — one, for all I knew, authorized to wear a large-caliber sidearm. "That," my attorney advised, "is just how guys on the lam get apprehended."

Although marital counselors are divided on the issue, I stand with those — mostly male — who believe a husband appearing timid in front of uxorial authority cannot later expect a wife's acceptance of his reasons why, say, roundabout Route 58 is a better choice than direct Route 52. Gentlemen readers, you catch my drift.

Inside, I demonstrated a professional interest in the lock and dam, evidenced by informed questions (so I thought), but the result was a rebuff: "Can't allow you out there — not since Nine-Eleven." At that moment in our national history, a citizen who questioned anything linked, however far-fetched, to the airliner-as-weapon events of three years earlier could seem unpatriotic, even unfeeling, never mind that the strategic value to a terrorist of a little-used lock in a remote swamp was only somewhat greater than that of the nearest Arkansas chicken coop.

Not long before the rebuff, I heard this story from a man whom I will introduce you to later. He, a highway historian specializing in resurvey photography, told me: "I stopped in western Kansas along a stretch of old U.S. Route Forty in the middle of nowhere so I could photograph the road. Almost immediately a deputy sheriff pulled up and began questioning me. He refused to believe I was writing a book about an old highway, even after I pointed out my license plate: ROUTE 40. He went over to feel the plate for embossed letters to see if it was the real thing. After running the usual radio checks, he told me to move on. I asked what possible target was anywhere within view of my camera. He said, 'Have you ever heard of Nine-Eleven?' That was supposed to explain everything."

Well, I've heard of it too, and I've also heard of bored officials wanting to throw some weight around. To many travelers in America these days, it's clear those paired, historically horrendous digits are more effective in rationalizing unnecessary denials of public access to public places than the earlier "Insurance regulations won't allow it." No one today wants to put national security at risk by taking a snapshot of sweet Granny Davis as she toddles through the airport metal-detector.

Q and I left the office. A man I'd spoken to earlier, on seeing our license plate, asked how turkey hunting was in Missouri, a topic I'm versed in about to the same degree I am in oxidative phosphorylation. But this was the South, only six miles from Louisiana, where technical knowledge is less important at such a time than one's willingness to call up some little ol piece of relevant lore. I said I had early acquaintance with turkey tracks but I didn't hunt the birds, although I sometimes fed them. He saw we were willing to listen, a simple act that will earn as many friends in the South as buying the next round. So he talked turkey, and that led, unexpectedly, to his saying, "If you want to see the dam, I'll take you." He was a lock operator and, out of season though it was, dressed ready for a turkey hunt — should one present itself. To keep his invitation from coming back to vex his employment, since I'm not sure we were within the new (alleged) regulations, I'll leave him anonymous.

He led us into the lock house and across the dam, much of our conversation going on while we watched a beaver swim up and perch itself on a washed-out tree trapped below the tainter gates where the animal began a nonchalant grooming. Given that the beaver is an unofficial mascot of the Corps of Engineers — America's dam builders — I asked whether the critter was trained or an animatronic thing. "He just started showing up," the operator said. "I wish he'd tug that log out of there."

Formal engineering of the lower half of the Ouachita began in the 1870s with the removal of snags and proceeded to deepening the channel and the eventual construction of six locks and dams between Camden and the mouth at Jonesville, Louisiana, near where the river enters the broad floodplain of the Mississippi. That work created 337 miles navigable not just during seasonal rises but throughout the year, a modification that required turning the free flow of more than half the river into a stair of slack-water pools. Felsenthal, elevation fifty-four feet, gives the Ouachita the distinction of dropping from near the highest point in Arkansas to its lowest. Over its last half, no other navigable river in America is so removed, so hidden away from the common haunts of humanity. The Ouachita is a long meandering off by itself.

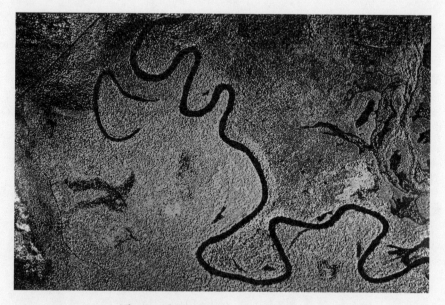

The Ouachita River in southern Arkansas.

After the calamitous Mississippi River Flood of 1927, engineers of the Ouachita began adding levees, dikes, "drainage structures," and pumping plants. There's even a flood wall in Monroe, Louisiana, that can fold down to serve as a walkway and observation platform. Because the terrain of the Ouachita, all the way from a little north of the Arkansas-Louisiana line on southward to its mouth, is dissected by natural wetlands fed by creeks and bayous, it was sensible during the engineering of it to create several wildlife areas, large and small, which now sprout from it like leaves on a stem. Those places have become havens for aquatic life and birds both resident and migratory.

This region, formed by the sea and shaped by flowing freshwater, by rainfall and humidity, is sodden and soggy here, saturated and soaked there, a land where periodic inundation is the heartbeat of its natural body and the determiner and enforcer of its ways of life, whether fish or fowl, moss or mosquito, mollusk or man. Even the hopefully named town of Waterproof, in its first location, got washed away by the Mississippi.

The terrain isn't easily adaptable to human ends, and that has made it a sanctuary, an adytum in the temple of nature for the so-called Lord God Bird (people seeing the large ivory-billed woodpecker for the first time supposedly uttered, "Lord God!"). It is the most famous American ghost bird, which is to say, it may or may not still be with us beyond those in specimen drawers. The last unquestioned sighting of an ivory-billed woodpecker occurred in 1944, less than forty miles east of the Ouachita, along one of its tributaries, the Tensas (pronounced and sometimes spelled "Tensaw"). In his 1842 *The Birds of America,* John James Audubon says of the crow-sized woodpecker:

> It is a beautiful bird, and its rich scalp attached to the upper mandible forms an ornament for the war-dress of most of our Indians, or for the shot-pouch of our squatters and hunters, by all of whom the bird is shot merely for that purpose. Travelers of all nations are also fond of possessing the upper part of the head and the bill of the male, and I have frequently remarked that on a steamboat's reaching what we call a wooding-place, the strangers were very apt to pay a quarter of a dollar for two or three heads of this woodpecker.

The remarkable power of the bird appears in an incident related by an earlier ornithologist, Alexander Wilson. One evening, after he returned to his North Carolina hotel room with a wounded ivory-bill he'd collected, he stepped out for forty-five minutes. When he returned, Wilson found "the bed covered with large pieces of plaster, the lath was exposed for at least fifteen inches square, and a hole large enough to admit the fist, opened to the weatherboards, so that in less than an hour he would certainly have succeeded in making his way through."

On a hunting trip in 1907, President Theodore Roosevelt, keenest of Presidential birders, came to the widely spread bottomland-forests of northeastern Louisiana. He wrote of the trees: "In stature, in towering majesty, they are unsurpassed by any trees of our eastern forests; lordlier kings of the green-leaved world are not to be found until we reach the sequoias and red-woods of the Sierras." Although he wasn't after ivory-bills — birds on the wing a hunter could mistake for ducks — Roosevelt said, "They seemed to me to set off the wildness of the swamp as much as any of the beasts of the chase."

Over the next quarter of a century, the ivory-bill range — once covering portions of a dozen southern and midsouthern states — contracted ever more, largely the result of loosened timber laws allowing unconstrained logging. Ornithologists began to suspect the bird was nearing extinction, with only a few still remaining somewhere on the continent, perhaps in the wetland forests between the Ouachita and the Mississippi in the northeast corner of Louisiana. In 1932, a lawyer–cum–state legislator from Tallulah set out into the deep woods of Madison Parish to prove to state wildlife officials that at least one ivory-bill was still living in the bottomlands of the Tensas River. He spotted it, shot it, and brought in the dead bird. That was an attorney who understood a writ of habeas corpus.

Nine years later, a national campaign to create a refuge for a creature on the edge of extinction began. By that time, though, one ornithologist estimated only a couple of dozen ivory-bills survived, perhaps all of them near the upper Tensas in the most extensive primeval forest then remaining in the South. The best habitat was on land owned by the Singer Sewing Machine Company. A paper published by Cornell University, the acknowledged authority in ivory-bill research, says:

The logging rights to the Singer Tract had been sold to the Chicago Mill and Lumber Company. The National Audubon

Society mounted a campaign to save the Singer Tract, but it only accelerated the rate of cutting. [The lumber company] had no interest in saving the forest or compromising with John Baker, the president of the . . . Society. Baker wanted to buy the rights to the trees and obtained a pledge of $200,000 from the governor of Louisiana for that purpose. The lumber company refused the offer, and the Singer Sewing Machine Company, which still owned the land, refused to intercede.

The Society sent a researcher into the tract two years later to look for any surviving ivory-bills, those vigorous eaters of injurious beetles. In a small and isolated stand of unlogged trees, he found a single bird. Until recent reports of sightings in east-central Arkansas can be generally confirmed, that lone female will remain the last proven ivory-bill in the United States. The Tensas River National Wildlife Refuge finally opened in the 1980s — forty years too late. As for the Chicago Mill and Lumber Company directors who collected the profit from deforestation, they are also extinct, but we must give them their due: they did their dead-level best to take with them a creature whose residence thereabouts was at least a hundred-thousand years longer than theirs.

In the 1970s, the original six navigational locks and dams on the Ouachita were replaced by four larger ones, each backing up about a hundred miles of river. That's a lot of water, but on the spring afternoon we watched the beaver, the difference in water level from one side of the dam to the other was only six inches, although in summer it can be fifteen feet. Fluctuation that great explains how early steamboats, unaided by locks and slack-water pools, sometimes could ascend the river into Arkansas to almost within view of the Ouachita Mountains. Even today, in a wet season, by taking a high-water passage, towboats move past Felsenthal Dam without using the locks.

Over the miles, engineers have widened the channel to a hundred feet and deepened it to nine, and they have cut through numerous tight bends that would otherwise challenge a string of barges; but the convoluted Ouachita still forces tows to be much shorter and narrower than those just a few miles east on the Mississippi.

During the time we talked with the lock operator — and long after the beaver had paddled off — not a single tow or even a bass boat approached. The timber mill just yonder of the dam didn't use barge transport, nor did many other industries near the Ouachita. The operator said, "Up here at this season we'll get only three or four tows a week, almost all of them carrying petroleum from the Gulf on toward Smackover for refining." I said to rebuild more than three hundred miles of a natural river for three or four tows a week seemed like a boondoggle in the boondocks. "Things change in the summer," he said. "Then, every month we'll lock through almost four-hundred wreck boats." Wreck boats? "You know — recreation boats."

Because taxpayer subsidies to get crude oil from the Gulf to Smackover — or a bass boat to a fishing hole — are not insignificant, I asked why the oil wasn't refined closer to the wellheads and sent north by pipelines. "Hey!" he said. "You're talking about my job!" And Q, in all civility, said, "I'd think we're talking economic common sense."

❥ 14 ❦

When Eyeballs Develop Taste Buds

T HREE THINGS REVEALED we'd left Arkansas and crossed into Louisiana: a small signboard of welcome, a few trees strung with Spanish moss, and an observably less-littered roadside. But Union Parish was cutover country, so thoroughly cut down that a *REPENT* painted on the lid of an old fifty-gallon oil drum and hung from a scraggly surviving pine may have had environmental import. Gus Kubitzki, remembering former years when such arboreal urgings were more numerous along Southern and Midwestern roads in scripturally overdosed counties, called them Jesus Trees. In this era of slick electronic-lures to redemption, I confess to missing those earlier notifications of the necessity for immediate contrition (*THE END IS NIGH*) and improved conduct (*DONT NEVER DO NOTHING GOD DONT WANT YOU TO*). I realize my attitude is a simple nostalgia in the same category as a preference for little Burma-Shave signs instead of monstrously massive and wattaged monopole-billboards. But what the hell? Once upon a time, even a shaving cream could wax eschatological with happy doggerel that for miles could stick in your head — or, worse, a ceaselessly chanting child's:

THE MIDNIGHT RIDE

OF PAUL

FOR BEER

LED TO A

WARMER HEMISPHERE.

BURMA-SHAVE

The old Jesus Tree tidings, homemade as they were, invited participation, although some responses edged toward blasphemous sarcasm. In Alabama in the '50s I was on a piece of scraggled, scrambled blacktop through exhausted and eroded fields, a place relieved only by a series of spiritual dispatches hanging from or leaning against Jesus Trees. Here was postwar recycling, for that painter of penitence had used household appliances otherwise headed for the nearest gully: a refrigerator door, the side of an oven, the lid of a washing machine. When he'd exhausted those, he turned to dismembered pieces of automobiles: doors, hoods, trunk lids, tires, and twice an entire vehicle.

Painted across two wringer washers and a barrel was *ARE YOU ON THE PATH TO HELL?* to which a second hand had added *WHERE ELSE COULD THIS ROAD GO?* To *WHERE WILL YOU SPEND ETURNITY?* the same second brush had appended *PLEASE NOT IN THIS COUNTY.* On the side of a defunct Hudson, a single word had been painted over to read: *PREPARE TO MEET THY MECHANIC.* The last sign, on a vintage school bus carcass, was *VENGENCE IS MINE SAYETH THE LORD* with a phone number added by the telltale, ministering, editorial hand; when I called it, a woman answered, "County Road Department." A traveler in that day found more community along the highways because there was something personal in those expressions; as an Alabamian told me then, "You know, don't you, neighbor, every dang one of them little peckerwood signs was all hand-did?"

The highway turned east to cross the river for the first time in a hundred miles, and it entered Ouachita Parish, dropped south again, and led us to a stretch of multilane in sore need of either repentance or vengeance. It wasn't so much the local *P* industries (paper, plastics, phones) escaping control as it was a congested franchiseland shot through with billboards: here was the veritable face of Anywherica, a hub of Nightmarerica under the control of the Lord of Misrule, this one subclassified as the Outskirts of Monroe, Louisiana. We were complicit with the Abbot of Unreason in taking a room along the Strip (our only choice, as far as we then could determine), but we sought atonement by heading to the river flowing past the old heart of the city. I had found in the phone directory a listing for a restaurant with three qualities to commend it: its name (Mohawk Tavern), its longevity (since 1952), and its downtown address.

The Mohawk existed somewhere between historic and weary-worn, neither fully one nor the other, a place Q described as history-worn. You probably know the Mohawks are as Southern as any Upstate New York native can be; my guess is the number of full-blood Mohawks who have ever set foot within a mile of Louisville Avenue in Monroe, Louisiana, is about proportionate to Apaches on the observation deck of the Empire State Building on Tuesday last. For that reason I liked the name as much as the wall-mounted turkey-on-the-wing and the cast-concrete pelican perched on the bar, a bird big enough to serve as a bollard to tie one's dinghy to. If you'll discount dust on a stuffed sailfish and on the racks of antlers and Jack Dempsey's sparring gloves hanging from on high, the tavern was like a well-groomed dowager who manifests her age not by trying to hide it but rather by keeping herself brushed and sponged and knowing the secret of flattering lighting: turn the lamps down, boys. The dark wood-paneled walls absorbed so much of what the fluorescents cast from the high ceiling, the light seemed to wear out before reaching us, bathing Q in a foggy dusk.

It wasn't until we took a seat at the long bar where a man was shucking oysters that I noticed what would prove to be the best feature of the Mohawk beyond honest food: the waiters wore dark trousers and pressed white-linen jackets giving off more brightness than the overheads. All the waiters were men, each was Negro, and every one of an age to have just missed service in World War II. They were, perhaps, selected for their distinctive physiognomies. Should I ever actually pursue my long-dreamed book of photographic portraits, titled something like *Faces in America,* I think I'll begin with the staff of the Mohawk.

I'll mention here that African-American settlement along the length of the Ouachita, for a Southern river, is far less than you might imagine, especially compared with the Mississippi or even with the rich flatlands immediately east of the lower Ouachita. It was to this latter country that a free-Negro New Yorker, Solomon Northrup, was taken in 1841 after being abducted and sold into slavery to work the cotton fields. A dozen years later, having regained his freedom, he wrote in his poignant *Twelve Years a Slave* about his labor near Bayou Boeuf, a tributary to the Ouachita:

> When a new hand, one unaccustomed to the business, is sent for the first time into the field, he is whipped up smartly, and made for that day to pick as fast as he can possibly. At night it is weighed, so that his capability in cotton picking is known. He must bring in the same weight each night following. If it falls short, it is considered evidence that he has been laggard, and a greater or less number of lashes is the penalty.

These days in America, when a black and a white unknown to each other meet, they both do well to consider — even yet — where such history lies, and if the two are to become friends or colleagues, sooner or later that question must be acknowledged and answered. When the meeting is brief and purely transactional, it can be glossed over, although I assume everyone longs for the day when such history, while not forgotten, won't impinge on the potential for humane relations.

The white-jacketed men enhanced their distinction of countenance by a comportment rarely seen these days outside of a restaurant in Italy. They neither introduced themselves nor stated the obvious ("I'll be your server tonight," as if to clarify they were not standing beside your table to repair a transmission); nor did they violate privacy ("How's that plate of jambalaya taste?" Didn't know a plate could taste); and certainly they didn't refer to eating as labor ("Are you still working on that rice?" Are we seated in a construction zone?). *And* they were content to allow the artifacts of a good meal — bowls, cutlery, crumbs — a long-enough presence to justify the preparation: there was no untimely sweeping the table clear in hopes we'd pay up and get out.

Like experienced court reporters, the waiters took down our words precisely and remained virtually invisible until called upon, at which sign they came forward with a deliberateness not to be altered by a choleric chef or a cranky customer. Movement so lentissimo, a perfection of age, is a lovely thing (if it's not in the left lane, in front of you). The men, attired and choreographed so smartly, made fine theater. Q said, "I think the decline of service demeanor in restaurants coincides with the demise of waiters in white jackets." I said, Isn't that about the same time restaurant patrons — including church ladies in Sunday bonnets — became "guys," as in, "You guys want nonsmoking?" (I should acknowledge here the South is still largely and blessedly free of that gender-corrupted phrase, the ubiquitous "you all" continuing to hold at bay the loathsome "you guys.")

My tip, the *pour boire* (this *was* La Louisiane), amounted to a quarter of the bill, which the waiter accepted with a simple nod as if expecting no less for capital service he knew to be more lost than practiced in America.

"The food!" you cry. "What about the food?"

Very well, anticipant reader, food at Mohawk Tavern: the menu made it clear we were in the northeastern corner of bayou country and not all that far from the Gulf. We each took a bowl of gumbo with rice to lead us to a plate of boiled Gulf shrimp atop a bed of chopped iceberg lettuce encircled by slices of hard-boiled eggs. It was simply served. There were no dishes overwrought with froufrou flourishes worked by a graduate of a culinary institute. The emphasis was on palate, not presentation. While I understand what I'm about to quote edges toward boorishness, I believe it has merit: Gus Kubitzki once said when faced with an overpriced, pretentious restaurant entrée (his description I can scarcely believe, but he claimed the dish was "Abyssinian nicket-goat" stuffed with curried truffles simmered in ewe's milk), "If the evolutionary process wanted me to like this, my eyeballs would have taste buds."

❯15❮

To Photograph Every Mile

A COUPLE OF MONTHS BEFORE setting out to travel the Ouachita Valley, I had an electrician rewire a storage space I was converting into a small exercise room. I explained to the man, only a few years younger than I, old folks don't need storage — they need muscle. The remark found resonance in him and considerably slowed the job, since he apparently wasn't able to talk while simultaneously holding a tool or length of conduit. He put down his screwdriver to exposit more clearly his means of teaching his grandson rudiments of basketball to help the boy make his school team.

"I never played down to him. He had to match me, but it didn't take long before he could outrun me, outjump me. That young body! Hell, he could get it to piss over the hood of a pickup." He stopped. "Excuse my phraseology, but you know what I'm saying."

He took a length of conduit, measured it, and put it down once more. "Oh, man! To be seventeen again!" (Conduit up, conduit down.) "He could outdo me in every way but one, and I had that advantage only because he couldn't see it, no matter how I tried to explain it." (Screwdriver in hand, screwdriver back into tool belt.) "Time!" he said, referring to what he was using too much of for my project. "The boy doesn't know what to do with time except to burn it. That's my one advantage. If he isn't fiddling with an electronic game, he spends his time dreaming impossible things — climbing Mount Everest or dating some starlet of the hour."

Having forgotten the conduit measurement, he remeasured. "I tell him, 'Okay, you can outrun me, but what good is it if you're not running to some productive place?'" (Here, a piece of conduit actually got attached to the wall.) "I tell him he's like a trash collector, except he goes around just collecting days so he can haul them off to dump them." (Junction box screwed to the wall.) "Time's his enemy because he's got too much of it, and it's my enemy because I'm running out of it." I could see why. (Next length of conduit measured and set down.) "Old Mother Nature's a smart-ass, you know. When you finally learn how to use time, you can't even piss over a hubcap." (Conduit remeasured.) "Excuse my phraseology, but you know what I'm saying."

The electrician's ramble was to come back to me across the Ouachita in West Monroe at Gabbeaux's Bayles Landing Restaurant, a riverside place, once a small fish market where *warp* and *lean* would be among the accurate words to describe it. Q and I were there to have lunch with a man, Glenn Gore, whose work she had learned of a month before I met the electrician. At Gabbeaux's, beyond its interior of angles skewed enough to serve as a film set for a surrealist dream sequence, we took a table on a patio of generally true plumb lines.

Across the Ouachita rose several multistorey buildings in downtown Monroe where stood the large courthouse at the site of the 1790 Fort Miro, the Spanish outpost that received Dunbar and Hunter and rented them a boat better suited to the ascent of the river than the clumsy vessel they'd struggled to drag that far upstream. Fifteen years after the Forgotten Expedition passed through, the steamboat *James Monroe* reached the garrison. The settlers, hoping to encourage further custom, toyed with the name of Fort Miro as if playing with alphabet blocks and managed to erase the Hispanic lineage by commemorating both the economic promise of the first steamboat bravely ascending the Ouachita *and* the current President who, as a plenipotentiary, was a signer of the documents conveying title to the Louisiana Territory to the United States. Miro became Monroe, and with the change, the citizens turned on its head the more common practice of naming ships after cities. Later residents have fuzzed over the Spanish founding even further by pronouncing the name of the old fort to rhyme with *high flow,* a parallel not frivolous given the rise the river can effect there.

Few courthouses so boldly face a watercourse as does that of Ouachita Parish, the third building on the location, a neoclassic edifice of white stone and Ionic columns, one that might have been lifted from Pennsylvania Avenue in Washington. The federal government, in a sense, helped clear the grounds of an earlier and lesser building by authorizing Admiral David Porter's ironclad gunboats to cannonade the town in 1863. Nothing of Fort Miro or of a couple of previous courthouses still stands, and vanished too are the early-twentieth-century houseboats where lived mussel-shell gatherers who once supplied button makers. And also gone with the winds of changing technology is the carbon-black industry that manufactured, among other things, pigment for ink out of natural gas from nearby wells. Now the gas is sent elsewhere for heat and power generation. Some street names in the old African-American section of shotgun houses proved equally evanescent: Adam and Eve Alley, Concrete Quarters, Owl Lane (all changed to honor civil rights workers), but Congo Street remained, as did, in a white section, Polly Anna.

Still in existence too, although no longer on the banks of the Ouachita, were creations of the first inhabitants, ceramics of wondrous beauty found in an oat field on the former Glendora Plantation, later demolished for an industrial site. Thirteen miles north of what would become the Mohawk Tavern, archaeologist Clarence Moore in 1909 turned up pots, bowls, jugs, bottles, and receptacles with sculpted figures, all made from local clay incised and painted with remarkable scroll patterns. One cannot really apprehend the Ouachita Valley without laying eyes on the ceramic art of those people. Here is a pre-Columbian vessel, its hues buff and brick red, that in itself may convey a deeper sense of the river valley.

On the morning we sat beside the Ouachita, it was making an easy descent, its passage as insouciant and heedless as an adolescent's hours. Had the old river a mind, it would surely see us all — William Dunbar, the mussel-shell collectors, even the Glendora potters — not so much as sharing a continuum as belonging to the same moment. Could I only develop a like notion of time, maybe a few more things would make some sense.

We read the menu: five-pound bucket of boiled crawfish, price on request (Q: "You aren't, are you?"); spicy boudin balls (waitresses tired of that old wisecrack); fried crawfish tails (and that one too); catfish chips (not to be confused with those of the buffalo); an assortment of gumbos, étoufées, bisques, jambalayas; and, of course, red beans and rice. The menu in mind, Q said, "Does this mean we'll be staying an extra week?"

Glenn Gore was a man of modest height, sixty-four years old, dark hair with a little seepage of gray at the temples. He carried some Choctaw blood, signs of which showed if one knew what to look for (not coloring or cheekbones of popular perception; earlobes are a far better indicator). He was born about thirty miles downriver, near Columbia, but he had been in Monroe since his second year. For almost a third of a century, he'd been living on the banks of the Ouachita where he started fishing and hunting at an age when he was too small to see over the steering wheel and too big to stay inside the fence. Around 1910, his grandfather sold vegetables to the steamboat crews when they stopped to lock through the old dam below Monroe. Because the city takes its municipal water from the Ouachita basin, you could say that the river flowed through his heart as well as his brain. Take away the Ouachita, and you'd not have Glenn Gore, at least not one anybody thereabouts would recognize. I should mention here that he preferred listening and modest statement of fact to the free-flowing palaveration so happily abundant in the South.

An engineer trained not formally but in industry, he identified himself as a photographer, although his initial work as an artist was with scratchboard, a nineteenth-century technique of engraving a reversed and negative image on a coated surface. It was a scratchboard scene that led him to discover a link between his art and the river, which is also the link between his being alive and the reason *for* his being alive. In 1989, needing backgrounds to use in his wild-life engravings, he took a camera and went down to the Ouachita to shoot not rabbits but scenery. Then he began trying to find published images of and information about the river but came up with only bits and pieces so limited and scattered that, even if assembled into one volume, the book would still be woefully incomplete.

Gore began working to photograph *every mile* of the Ouachita from head to foot, Rich Mountain to Jonesville, most of the lower miles accessible only by traveling the river itself in a sixteen-foot johnboat; but in the Ouachita foothills and up into the mountains, it was largely legwork. His first search was fifteen years ago, some six-thousand photographs of the Ouachita ago, 120 hours of video of the river ago, dozens of concerned messages to legislators ago. His unpresumption led him to say only, "Maybe I got carried away." I said, Rivers could do that.

The sense of riverness he had discovered within himself seemed to exist in few others, so he decided to try to change the disregard, neglect, and abuse of the major natural reason his neighbors lived where they lived, the very source of almost two-thirds of their bodies.

Of the six-hundred miles of river, he had, after fifteen years, multiple photographs of something less than half the Ouachita. It was a project other people could have undertaken, but no one had, and it seemed unlikely anybody would, at least not before accelerating changes — *deteriorations,* to use his word — obliterated much beauty and history along the river. Already it was too late to bring back things like the stunning aboriginal pyramid — and the knowledge its artifacts could have led to — bulldozed in 1932 for road fill at the mouth of the Ouachita. Too late to save the Glendora site, once yielding several hundred peerless ceramic vessels. No longer was there opportunity to capture images of the river before virtually all of it beyond the mountains was forced into pools and reservoirs. Yet he believed much still remained that William Dunbar and

George Hunter would recognize, views the Ouachita people themselves would know.

Seven years after his discovery of the skimpiness of documentation of the river, he organized the Ouachita River Foundation, essentially a one-man venture assisted only by his wife, son, and a board of directors. He feared open membership and acceptance of grants might impair advocacy. Nevertheless, his work garnered enough respect to draw a few small contributions from businesses and individuals. He had made five videos for showing to all who asked, and every year he published a full-color calendar, each month illustrated by a photograph of the Ouachita. To many of the dates, he added relevant river history (*March 3: During the Civil War five gunboats shelled the town of Jonesville, La., from the Ouachita River, 1863*), national history (*June 2: American Indians became U.S. citizens by Act of Congress, 1924*), or American lore (*March 18: Electric razor first marketed, 1931*). Sale of the calendars underwrote his documentation of the river.

His efforts to awaken and inform have inspired others. Reca (pronounced "Reesa") Bamburg Jones, a woman standing only three inches above five feet, once sat down and, so to speak, dug in her heels in front of a bulldozer sent by a timber company to clear out a hunk of riverine woods protecting a five-thousand-year-old archaeological site. Mrs. Jones managed to redirect the machine and prevent a total deforestation. She was later able to enlist archaeologist Joe Saunders to establish the remarkable age of the mound complex, today completely hidden in the woods. Because of their efforts, the State of Louisiana purchased half the Watson Brake tract so that it might one day become an archaeological park. The heel of a hundred-pound woman exerts more pressure per square centimeter than an equivalent area under the steel track of a bulldozer: a law of mechanics — and sometimes of society.

I suggested to Glenn a historic soft-drink bottling plant, now shut down and yielding nothing to the community, could make a good Ouachita River Center. Precedent was there for the change: a World

War II B-24 bomber training field near town had been turned into a museum. Gore thought it unlikely the city council would see a living river as worthy of commemoration and interpretation as is aerial warfare. That same bureaucracy paid scarce attention to the other side of the Ouachita and the success West Monroe had achieved in transforming itself and its little Main Street into a reawakened town of history and new businesses serving a new century. Leaders on the east side seemed to have no interest in creating a downtown where Auntie's Antiques could coexist next to Titanic Telephone, each contributing something productively different.

What, I asked, was the attitude of the city newspaper toward the motto of the Ouachita River Foundation, "Preservation of Beauty and History"? Gore said, "The *News-Star* isn't locally owned anymore, but in the past, it showed interest mostly when the river was rising." (Q: "I think you might be causing a rise.") "Maybe," he said. "Sometimes I think I see good changes."

What about the black community for whom, historically, the river was so important? "Getting them involved is a struggle too," Gore said. "I know they have other issues of real importance, so how much can a man ask?" He was watching the water slip by as he spoke, and then, without taking his eyes off the Ouachita, he said, "It's a struggle all the way, all the time, but I believe what we do matters. If we do it in the right spirit, we can shape the future for the good of the river and ourselves. They aren't separate."

It was apparent: long after his shutter stopped clicking, Glenn Gore would continue to work on behalf of the ancient Ouachita — efforts of which, like some of those who draw life from it, the river was oblivious. What he didn't say because he didn't need to was that the struggle also yielded many fine sunrises and sunsets to a man in a johnboat on the river, fishing rod and camera at hand. Being a guardian and advocate and documenter does not exclude joys.

When Q and I left Monroe to continue down the valley, I told her of another lunch I'd had a few years previous, one near Dayton, Ohio.

I was eating a sandwich on an overlook above the seventh tee of a golf course. Perhaps because it was about noon on a weekday, all the players were in their retirement years. (What I'm about to say should not be seen as an extension of a possibly distorted view of mine that any game capable of being played while smoking a cigar might belong in a category other than "sport.") As I watched the balls rise and bounce, I wondered for how many of the players those were golden years of tee shots and tee-vees and little else. Were some of them looking for purpose beyond birdies and *Wheel of Fortune*? Were they citizens whose potential the rest of us were ignoring?

To be of use and thereby earn remembrance — what person of good heart would say no? How many of those men had told a pal, in effect, "Now that I can't piss over a hubcap anymore, I don't know what I'm good for"? (Excuse my phraseology, but you know what I'm saying.) How many women (in different phraseology) had wondered something similar? Let me play with the words: isn't it a given that giving gives the greatest reason to be alive?

Q said, "Do you remember the Smith sisters up on the Blue Ridge in Virginia?" She referred to a pair of spinsters who spent half their lives documenting every wildflower they could near one stretch of the Parkway. Helen and Julia Smith left behind a catalog of data that botanists, ecologists, and who knows who else may one day find to be of crucial significance. And the sisters *by themselves* persuaded the National Park Service to change its mowing practices along the route for the benefit of botanical diversity.

There can never be enough scientists or humanists to gather the simple, quotidian facts of every existing thing, even though accurately understanding the world demands no less. To hell with the height of hubcaps and the reach of one's stream — it's the reach of one's curiosity and civic dedication we need. The power of a single self lies in its capacity to escape and go beyond itself to leave a gift behind. How can any achievement be lastingly significant if it lies outside a community of others? To live more otherly is to live more lastingly. It's a fundamental law of biology.

❧ 16 ❧

The Buzz Under the Hornet Nest

THE HIGHWAY OUT OF MONROE, U. S. 165, ran due south and stayed on the east side of the Ouachita, paralleling it more closely than we'd found since leaving the streamlet below the headwaters in the mountains, although a levee still kept the river from view most of the way. Despite dropping two-thousand feet and gathering tributary waters for five-hundred miles, the Ouachita appeared not to have enlarged appreciably below the uplands, nor had it become more occluded with sediment, unnatural uniformities I attributed mostly to the dam-and-pool engineering of it. From about Monroe on southward nearly to its terminus, the channel ran against the eastern edge of the low hills of pastures reaching all the way to the Red River; but eastward to the Mississippi lay cotton fields and wetlands, so that for some miles the Ouachita was a kind of zipper between the old steamboating South and the cattleman's West. In fact, that afternoon we met a Stetson-topped octogenarian whose talk was like a B Western sidekick from the 1940s, by crackee, a feller who complained about rambling into one too many dadblamed DUI convictions and having his daughter take away both his car *and* his horse.

The route: fields of bright-green seedling corn and tractors tilling under cotton stubble; other plots left fallow; cotton wagons neatly lined up until autumn; a dilapidated cotton gin; and, isolated in a plowed field, an abandoned shotgun house from sharecropping days. Every view was of only three colors — spring green, earthen brown, sky blue — until in one landscape stood a single, bright-white cattle egret that drew the eye as does a cut diamond.

Then the highway turned west and crossed the Ouachita over a 1935 hoist bridge seeing its last days; next to it stood unfinished piers for a new, characterless concrete span. The old steel-truss bridge that had lifted and lowered for nearly seventy years and had been whistled and smoked by the last stern-wheelers was raised to let a diesel-electric towboat and its barges pass, the first we'd seen moving on the river.

To the west, below rolling pastures and woody hills, lay Columbia, Louisiana. Visible from the road just beyond the bridge was a sign painted on the brick wall of a worn two-floored building with one side against the levee: WATERMARK SALOON: OLDEST BAR ON THE OUACHITA.

From the western edge of the Mississippi floodplain, more than fifty miles wide there, the hamlet sat on a snaky river bend, a sharply turned S, one of a series of even more S's than you need to spell *Mississippi*. In its low country, the Ouachita is such a sinuous thing, its convolutions have proven too numerous for the engineers to cut through, and in that way the niggardliness of Congress has helped keep the Ouachita from having the appearance of a drainage canal.

We walked the heart of the village — the two blocks of Main Street — from the live oaks on the courthouse square to the Ouachita levee that hides passing barges but not the high superstructures of the towboats, so that a stroller on Main sees pilothouses seeming to glide effortlessly along the top of the earthen embankment like so many donkey carts. At the base of that dike was the Watermark Saloon.

The term *saloon,* thanks in part to old Westerns — both movies and novels — has lost its more elegant connotation of a large social lounge, a *salon,* as the word changed from referring to a drawing room to referring to a barroom. To speak of the earlier meaning, the first saloons reaching Columbia were those built into the heart of passenger steamboats, a detail suggesting to me the Watermark Saloon might carry something of the older concept, since it stood as close to the Ouachita as a large building could without standing in the river. Better yet was evidence in the front window where four players sat at a domino table. Although I needed no further proof, near the entrance was a small sign suggesting a social stratigraphy not uncommon to the life of a salon: HIPPIES ENTER BY SIDE DOOR. Of side doors, there were none, not even so much as a coal chute.

Because I've never found spirituous beverage and sunlight a salubrious combination, I ordered us a couple of "cola drinks." The barkeep, Maggie, set them out, and with them a question that blesses a traveler's quest and promises initiation into local rites. She asked, "What brings you to our town?" I pointed north, toward the river, and said, That. Maggie turned to see what might be behind her she'd never noticed before, something to lure in outsiders. She said, "A brick wall?"

The Ouachita, I said, and in two sentences laid out our descent from the mountains to the river flowing behind the levee behind the brick wall. Maggie, with only a raised eyebrow, stepped away as if suddenly remembering the jiggers needed polishing; her towel went to work while she looked out onto Main Street. Bartenders, along with psychiatrists and barbers, hear many a thing they could term, if they're indulgent, eccentric. I should think, after forty years, I'd be able to foresee a woman's retreat in the face of an oddball; but then, eccentricity exists only in the eyes of a beholder. I have yet to meet a true eccentric who knows he is one; in fact, to be aware of it is evidence it's phony.

Maggie returned and placed her hands flat on the bar in a manner often preliminary to an invitation to leave. It was clear she had considered what she was about to say, and it was this: "You need to talk to Tom, the owner, upstairs." She returned to her towel, but before I could figure her import, she came back to name half a dozen other people with a link to the Ouachita, all residents we should meet. Her invitation wasn't to leave the place but to enter it — and not by the side door or even a coal chute.

A broad-shouldered, former construction-worker, Maggie was natally a Minnesotan, one of those Northerners who decide (at least in November through March) precipitation in the form of rain measured in feet, and humidity measured in muttering, is preferable to its more solid boreal expressions. Although she spoke in different terms, she was of the school believing that if warm weather — and what it has created — got removed from the South, then Virginia could as well be Vermont; or Alabama, Alberta. This school holds that had air-conditioning preceded William Faulkner, he'd have become not a book writer (to use Southern lingo) but more likely a bookkeeper. This line of latitude-based thought avers that the mint julep — if invented in a colder climate — would be made not with Bourbon but with schnapps, and it would be sipped not on a leafy front porch but in a pine-paneled rumpus room. Some Northerners with those notions even outrageously maintain nippier Southern weather would result in faster speech which might have helped Dixie turn that war Southerners know by a dozen names.*

I asked Maggie where we would find all the people she named, the list now nearly a dozen strong. "Sit tight," she said. "They'll find you." And, indeed, for the rest of our time in the river village, Columbians singly and in twos or threes found us, whether at the Watermark, or out on Main Street, or fifteen miles downstream when we went looking for fried catfish. In a room that let us sleep beside the levee, in a century-old house once the home of a riverman who engraved on the window of his front door not a steamboat but the 1906 battleship *Louisiana* of Roosevelt's Great White Fleet, even there the next morning someone came by with stories, each proffered in welcome as if a bouquet.

On the north wall of the saloon, once a general merchandise, a painted line marked the water level inside the building during the Great Flood of 1927 when the Mississippi backed up the Ouachita all the way into Arkansas; the muddy pool in the store had been deep

---

* Anyone thinking Southern speech is slow has not traveled enough among the magnolias, for a true Southerner can roll out the words as fast as any Brooklynite about to miss the F train; in truth, below Mason and Dixon's Line, most verbal slowing down is for narrative punctuation, an art the youth of Yankeedom could well stand to learn.

enough to force a long-legged dog wanting out to swim for it. Also on the wall were boat propellers, a pilot wheel, and photographs of Ouachita paddle wheelers.

But, most important for a salon-saloon, hanging from the high, tin ceiling was a pinecone-shaped, papery nest of bald-faced hornets, the insects, of course, having long ago evacuated themselves as they do each autumn. Somewhere in one of my other books, I've suggested a correlation between the dispensation of local tales and a tavern exhibiting taxidermic specimens. Let me here refine that affinity by saying a stuffed moose-head on the wall is most likely to elicit the richest conversations and should be considered the equivalent to a four-star rating; a bison or elk or pronghorn sconce is a degree down, but, in the matter of storytelling, each is superior to the ubiquitous buck deer.

In this system you see a bias toward size — both of the animal and the taxidermist's bill — and there's only one exception I know of, and that's the little jackalope. If that name is new to you, jolly reader, you won't find it in many dictionaries (lexicographers, please note), for it exists almost exclusively in saloons of the western Great Plains. Fake as it is, an antlered hare proves an ideal indicator of oral fabrications made, like the jackalope itself, from mostly genuine elements recombined into something of another order. In your own travels, you have perhaps encountered a cursing man who comes before an image of the Cross or Holy Virgin and is temporarily dispossessed of oaths stronger than *Dash!* or *Golly gee!* In an opposite yet analogous way, a man beneath a jackalope will discover his treasury of improvisations and concoctions, figments and fables, easily unlatched.

Of late, I've noticed that conversations under a hornet nest, one affixed to its natural branch hanging from a saloon ceiling, seem to draw forth a similar flow. A few miles upstream from the mouth of the Missouri River is a convivial taproom with a dozen nests (more in the basement), so many, in fact, when they get mingled in December with other decorations, you may fairly ask whether it's Christmas or

Halloween being celebrated. While the Watermark had only a single nest, you must remember, down South it takes far fewer hornets to put a buzz in the yakkety-yak, whether the talk is verifiable facts or blatant bosh or even inebriated rodomontade.

During our calls on the salon (daylight) and saloon (after sundown), Ouachitalogies buzzed through the Watermark like, well, you know what. There was one about the farmer who planted "Spanish daggers" — yuccas — under the bedroom window of his comely daughter to discourage Peeping Toms. That item led to somebody pointing across the taproom to the peephole in the covered stairway to the second floor, which, allegedly, allowed an earlier owner's wife to keep tabs on a husband possessed of less than churchly penchants. Then followed an intimation he might have been one of the Toms under the window of the farmer's daughter.

Somebody said anybody who pronounces the state name *LOO-zee-anna* is a hick, but his proposition didn't find consensus. A story drifted up about Miss X who learned of her fiancé's infidelity after she discovered tampons in his medicine cabinet and rejected his defense they were for cleaning nooks and crevices of his motorcycle. A man told another unhappy tale, this one about his "daddy" who used to whip him with a broken fan belt. Then came relief in some jawing about a pair of opposing politicians whose views were "as different as a dozen-and-a-half is from twelve-point-five," followed by a further mathematically fouled debate about whether those terms had the same meaning since one had a decimal in it, which surely carried greater exactness. And finally, bobbing up was a piece of flotsam from river history about old whiskey boats ascending the Ouachita into dry counties in Arkansas to sell quite legally all the booze a man could carry ashore — either on his shoulder or in his belly.

Lest I mislead you, I should say other buzz was higher on the brow, such as the one about the woman who kept urging somebody at the Schepis Museum, which happened to be right next to the Watermark, to come out to see Uncle Jack's paintings. But because every town, especially in Louisiana, seemed to have an Uncle Jack —

an Oncle Jacques — who paints or whittles, nobody listened until a few months previous to our arrival, when a museum associate finally went to look at the paintings. Uncle Jack proved to be Andrew Jackson Grayson, the "Audubon of the West," who created a corpus of ornithological illustrations that expands to the Pacific slope and northern Mexico Audubon's brilliant but topographically limited, grand catalog of birds. Grayson, a native of the lower Ouachita country, started his career as a shopkeeper in Columbia, Louisiana, before moving to St. Louis and then on again across Missouri where in 1846 he joined a wagon train that for some distance included the Donner party.

Soon after our departure for the end of the valley, an exhibition of Grayson's bird prints went up at the museum, once a two-floor mercantile built in 1916 by an Italian-immigrant couple trained in the arts — he in architecture and she in music, her pianoforte once sending down to the street the only classical notes Columbians could then hear this side of Natchez or New Orleans. When Giovanni Schepis finished his building, still the most impressive along Main, he wanted to honor both his native land and his new one. The way to do it, he thought, was to make molds of river sand for casting in concrete a matching pair of life-size statues portraying two entrepreneurs. He hoisted atop his store Christopher Columbus and George Washington who for years beyond Giovanni's have continued to look down the Ouachita.

A woman in the Watermark commented how odd it was their village history seemed to come out of four general merchandise stores: the very first structure in the hamlet, Grayson's shop, the Schepis Museum, and the initial use of the oldest saloon on the Ouachita. She said, "But back then, more things happened in a store than in a church." For a hamlet once on the fringe of forest and swamp, a community even today of only five-hundred souls, Columbia was made singular more by its arts than by its commerce. Where another town might have a feed supply, Columbia had a gallery displaying nineteenth-century treasures of American wildlife.

The local history gave perspective on words from the Reverend Timothy Flint, a New Englander who came into the lower Ouachita country in 1835; in his trip journal he wrote:

> How rapidly the remotest frontier forests of our country are filling up with the current of the westward tide of emigration. Whenever after ploughing through the waters, we approached a high and arable spot — an island in the swamp — we found it already occupied with the cabin and the field of a squatter. It strikes one with surprise to see these deserts, so remote that one would almost imagine he could claim them by right of discovery, actually peopled. The western states are already comparatively populous. The tide having there found its level, continues to roll on, eddying, disparting, and forcing its secret currents into every nook and valley of the wilderness. The smoke of hearths arises, and man with his axe, gun, and human incitements to action is there. It is much to be regretted that so great a proportion of the emigrants are of the class of poor, vagrant, and worthless foreigners, the scum of despotic governments, unacquainted with our institutions, and unfit for them.

Looking for supper, Q and I moseyed down the valley several miles and crossed the Ouachita on the ferry at Duty (no charge to travel west, but to go east costs a dollar). Along the river we found Jim Bowie's Relay Station, the name of more genuine history than the building. It sat with its back to the wooded hills overlooking the damp bottomland exuding water transfused into soil and vernal shrub, new leafage and boscage, sweetly rank, lush and teeming. After all the miles, at last we could breathe in, if not the Ouachita itself, then at least its expression.

A retired school principal, John Ed Bartmess, had built the place in the spirit of an earlier time, and he was methodically surrounding it with historic structures he hauled in or new ones built according to nineteenth-century lines. Inside he had covered the high ceiling with political yard signs that, while more colorful than a hornet nest, didn't much seem to evoke tales and fabrications — a peculiarity, since American politics is mostly just that.

But, with John Ed's fried catfish before us, who cared? And his hushpuppies. Across the country, what has happened in cafés to genuine french fries has happened in the South to café hushpuppies which, once frozen, also fit too readily into a box. But at the Relay Station, the freshly made fritters were cooked in a chile-laced corn-meal batter and served alongside a juglet of light Louisiana cane syrup. I mentioned to Bartmess something about his meals being food from another time; later, as Q and I reached the door to leave, he gave her a tin of his private-label syrup along with a pail full of stories that spilled out the front door onto the porch and on into the dark land of dewberries and possum hunts where, just beyond his words, flowed the Ouachita.

17

Connections and Continuums

CERTAINTY ON THIS MUTABLE PLANET belongs to the doctrinaire in whose ranks I try to keep out of step, probabilist that I am, a lowly foot soldier following probabilities. It is probability that leads me to believe American Indians of sixteen-hundred years ago did not intend to assist materially the construction in A.D. 1935 of the Huey Long Bridge at Jonesville, Louisiana. Yet they did, and the story of how that happened, with its deplorable consequences for the current residents living at the mouth of the Ouachita, became apparent as we neared its terminus.

But those last miles began less ominously.

The east-side river road out of Columbia was a pleasant run allowing an occasional glimpse of the Ouachita where once the cotton boats headed south with a thousand or more ginned bales and returned northward with sugar and coffee and durable goods for the isolated hamlets. Even beyond mischief in the river, it was a trickish business, causing one captain to say in 1929, "A steamboat man always has two worries: One is, will I get all the freight I can handle this trip? The other is, will I get more freight than I can handle this trip?"

The Reverend Flint, on his tour a century earlier, wrote:

On the long bayous of our river, on each side of which the great cotton plantations spread like prairies, you may travel thirty miles amid continuous lines of plantations, and nowhere see what may fairly be called a single fruit garden. To make money through cotton is visibly the first and the absorbing idea. The maxim of life seems adopted from the epicurean motto quoted by St. Paul, though otherwise not severe students of the scriptures — *let us make cotton and money, for to-morrow we die.*

When Q and I had again crossed on the Duty ferry and were on the western shore, we found the way south bestrung with the opened, blanched-lavender blossoms of wisteria as if hung out for a parade to welcome somebody home. Although the drier piney upland was never far away, the pavement, keeping to the floodplain and the old territory of cane brakes, rode atop a berm raised from the marshy flats so level that even the back of a box turtle would have a discernible elevation.

At Harrisonburg, the highway again brushed the escarpment before leaving it behind once and for all. It was there Confederates built Fort Beauregard in a short-lived resistance designed to halt the advance of Union gunboats up-country. I'd like to give you a nugget or two about that campaign on the Ouachita, but the topic, as far as I know, like the river itself, has yet to find its historian.

Failing that, I do have for you, if you like tales of nineteenth-century crime and detection and are accepting of digression, another few sentences from the Reverend Flint, who (I say belatedly) gave in his journal one of the few, therefore important, early pictures of the lower Ouachita country:

A man with a considerable sum of money was known to have crossed the Ouachita. He mysteriously disappeared. Suspicions were excited. His horse's footsteps were traced to the bank of the river. They were discovered on the opposite shore. Search was made for the horse, and at no great distance in the woods the animal was found saddled and feeding. Search was then made for the body of the rider below the point of crossing. It was soon discovered. The people of the vicinity, as usual, collected to the inquest. Said a knowing one, "Let each one of us in succession walk over the body, and when the murderer passes, he will stumble." The trial was immediately adopted, and the people, with a good deal of solemnity, walked, one after one, over the body. One person was observed in making the transit to walk uncommonly erect and firm and when going over the body, to raise his feet higher than the rest. "There," said the wizard inquisitor, "is the murderer." He went further. "Let his feet be examined," he added. He wore moccasins, and one of them was tied at the heel with a knot. At the point where the deceased had come to the river, it was a damp, soft clay. The footprint of a man was discovered there, who had worn a moccasin, that had impressed in the clay the visible indent of this knot. The suspected person was called upon to compare his footprint with those before him. Astounded, stupefied by such unlooked for evidence, he complied, and his foot exactly filled the impress, convincing everyone that he was the identical person who had followed the person whose body was before them to the point of the river where he had disappeared and below which his body was found. The man was arrested, tried, and, having confessed the murder, was executed.

On the south edge of Harrisonburg, in the shadow of the courthouse, the road entered a welter of waters, a wedding of them in many permutations that, in their natural state before hydroengineering, must once have looked from above like a prodigious entangling of giant serpents, a native symbol of rivers. In a way similar to the Mississippi twenty miles east, the Ouachita has been lopped and chopped as if it were in fact a snake daring to startle the gardener. The land there, if you can call it such, is rife with oxbows, bayous, bogues, diversion canals, drainage ditches, relict swamps and marshes, cypress bogs, moss-hung fens, lakes, catfish ponds, pools and puddles, a place squelchy and spongy, muddy and miry, and the home of a quadrillion creatures finding haven in the riverine-lacustrine realm lying under four and a half feet of yearly rainfall.

This is the country where the Ouachita ends, or perhaps I should say vanishes.

For a couple of sentences, tolerant reader, allow me to anthropomorphize the river that had for so many days carried us not on its current but in its wide presence.

Unhappy the Ouachita must be to see its lengthy and serpentine descent — a drop, were it accomplished all at once, that would surpass a dozen stacked-up Niagara Falls — usurped by a pair of comparatively lengthless, conniving pretenders at the very place it should be crowned queen (to travel *atop* a river is to witness woman in all her moods and phases). Imagine you've been creeping forward in a royal queue six-hundred miles long; then, as you are at last within sight of the throne, your promised destination, an officially sanctioned interloper pushes in ahead of you and snatches the crown to pass it off to an infant without experience of statesmanship. That's what happens to the Ouachita at Jonesville where the Tensas River (250 miles long) and the Little River (twenty miles), within a couple of hundred yards of each other, flow into the big river more than twice their combined length. The reconstituted waterway — its dismal name reflecting the injustice — is the Black River. (Whenever you read here "Black River," translate in your mind that inaccurate tenebrousness to one of euphony and history: Ouachita. As for the Little River, I'll call it by its older and more evocative Indian name, Catahoula, which one historian translated as "River of the Great Spirit.")

To modify my anthropomorphic metaphor, the Ouachita is the lead runner in a marathon where a faker slips in a hundred yards from the line and sprints freshly to the finish. Is there no official to cry foul?

Someone will say, and correctly so, that for two-hundred-million years the river has been a mindless thing propelled by only the laws of gravity to reach its progenitor sea, so a two-hundred-year-old name tacked onto its tail matters not a whit.

It is the issue of mattering a whit that returns me to the topic I began with: Indians of A.D. 400 and the Huey Long Bridge of A.D. 1935.

All the way from the domino table in the Rich Mountain general store at the headwaters of the Ouachita, I'd been looking forward to having my curiosity rewarded by the discovery of whatever quoz lay at the end of the river. While it's true I'd passed through Jonesville years earlier, I was then too callow and uninformed to recognize the outward facts of what was there, let alone any ramifications in them, so I did nothing but slow to the posted limit with not so much as a pause for a MoonPie.

Years later, but still before I knew of the Ouachita debouchment at Trinity — a cluster of houses across the Catahoula from Jonesville — I learned of the Troyville Mounds. And sometime afterward, I discovered Troyville was now Jonesville, the first of several poor decisions here, especially considering the new name appeared only in 1870 following a feud that, wrote a local historian, "ultimately cost the lives of at least five prominent citizens of the parish, and in a measure, put an end to two of the most cultured and outstanding families of that part of the state." (Other voices speak of the woman who insisted on the change to Jonesville as being widely known for her cruelty to slaves.)

Were I granted a week vacation anywhere in the American past, it would be to one of the great, aboriginal earthworks at the zenith of its existence: Cahokia, Poverty Point, Etowah, Spiro, Serpent Mound, the Newark Octagon in Ohio; maybe even one of the effigy mounds of the Upper Mississippi Valley. Earthworks at the tail end of the Mississippi Valley go back at least seven-thousand years, a span conceived of by some Americans no more accurately than the duration of the Upper Carboniferous. But to consider *our place in our place* — even a perception of the shallowness of human history — can wonderfully improve one's planetary comportment. If a visitor could return with a digital slide show from one of those grand earthwork civilizations in full native use, our comprehension of America would be enriched beyond imagining, and history textbooks could begin with more than the misleadingly cursory nod to any past before the European incursion.

Q and I live less than a mile from the valley of the lower Missouri River where high bluffs of limestone are sprinkled with small mounds fifteen-hundred years old — that's to say, structures from the time of Visigoths sacking Rome and Saxons doing similarly in Celtic Britain. In one place, before it got overtaken for a hunting tract owned by an outsider, was a mound I would visit to sit nearby and look across the two-mile floodplain toward the Missouri. When the mound was built, probably for a burial, the river flowed at the foot of the bluff.

Those mounds are where they are — I'm again speaking as a probabilist — because the people who made them believed a river could carry the great mystery within a human to another place on a presumed journey reflecting the provable one. Specific places lie at the heart of every Indian cosmology I know because human genesis arises from the land — *from a place.* To the indigenous people who lie within those mounds of earth and stone along the Missouri, a sense of the sacred began and ended with an earthen quoz pushing reverence into recognition of mystery.

While probabilists can do little more than postulate the possibility of a post-corporeal journey along a river, they can unquestionably make a verifiably veritable one (in what some "believers" consider our *pre*-afterlife). Over the years, from that mound above the river, I've imagined voyages departing there for distant shores, and I've even actually taken a few. From it, I could set my canoe upon the Missouri and — until the last few miles — using no power but what resides in rivers themselves, reach the Ouachita, a voyage of eleven-hundred miles. Wherever you are reading these words — Sydney, Nebraska, or Sydney, Australia; Florence, Oregon, or Firenze, Italy — the nearest floatable stream could start you too on a voyage to the Ouachita.

Once again, nimble reader (you who are so often ahead of me), you catch the drift. We belong to the land; the territories are one because the waters are one, and nothing so reveals that oneness as the courses of rivers. You know the old analogy: arteries and veins in a single body. I believe the ancient minds of America also understood this, and that's the reason sources and junctures of waters were important to them, for it is, perhaps above all else, sources and junctures that create not just quoz but the sacred in any cosmology. I believe those intellects, like ours, comprehended existence, if a human is to comprehend it at all, through the discovery and honoring of connections and continuums.

These notions came into play soon after Q and I arrived in Catahoula Parish on a late-March Saturday afternoon in quest of, if you will, the "bottom" of the Ouachita at Jonesville, Troyville, Trinity — the last league of the river. The Louisiana state road dumped us onto U.S. 84 at the edge of town and its spread of outskirt businesses, perhaps only one older than Daffy Duck. It was the kind of place I call a ZONE: Zoning Ordinances Non-Existent. But the homely strip was somewhat ameliorated by Sonny's, Home of the Italian Burrito, a rolled tortilla plump with fourteen ingredients more appropriate to a pizza than anything Mexican. For a five-spot, on two occasions, Q and I made a shared meal of one of them.

As we tried to reach the heart of Jonesville, population 2,700, my usually reliable seat-of-the-pants compass somehow went awry and caused me to misguess enough directions to create a tour of the village and its de facto, semisegregation. In the Negro section (we were soon to hear it called "Over the Tracks"), the citizens were outside in the mild air, gadding about, jollifying, getting ready for Saturday night; barbecue smokers scented the afternoon, voices called from porch to porch, coolers got stocked with ice and beverages. But in the white section, the doors were closed, shades drawn, stoops empty, and gadding about was nil; it could have been a January afternoon in northern Michigan.

By eliminating one direction after another, a brief task in such a small place, I eventually fumbled us into the historic center of Jonesville, the spot where it began. I am obligated to report what we saw, and that was considerable evidence of one of the poorest parishes in one of the poorest states. It reminded me of Gus Kubitzki's description of another town to be unnamed here, "an agreeable place once it's well behind you."

The impoverished commercial buildings had a lone saving grace: there weren't many of them. But those yet standing ranged from the crumbling, collapsing, and crippled to the decaying, deteriorated, and derelict. Remodeling meant boarding up a window and painting *KEEP OUT* across it. Here was another wreckage of that ship of state, the *U.S. American Dream,* that merchantman which founders and comes to grief whenever the winds in its sails — voracity without limits, profit without responsibility — inevitably slacken. Of the endeavors an impartial observer might honestly term "prosperous," I saw only two: Catahoula Bank and, behind it, the Addictive Disorder Clinic, a proximity a novelist of Main Street America would have to avoid to keep from being accused of clangingly obvious symbolism.

As we walked, neither Q nor I said anything for some time. At last she broke the numbed silence. "It looks like a place that lost its soul." Catahoula perish.

[**READER ALERT:** Although there is no bloodshed or vileness in it, this Huey Long Bridge story is only going to get darker, so I pause here for readers with heartstrings easily tightened to seek the refuge of chapter 20.]

❧18❧

A Grave History

THE DILAPIDATIONS in the old mercantile heart of Jonesville could not entirely overcome — I don't know how else to term it — an aura. Over several hours of trying to define it, I finally realized it arose from *what had been* — I don't mean crumbling bricks and decaying wood; rather it came from something much older, something not yet fully eradicated. A long and deep human past will stain the land in ways beyond discolorations of soil and will leave a scent perceptible not to the nose but to the imagination.

My interest in Jonesville may have been similar to John Milton's indubitable absorption with powers of destruction and evil in the face of salvation, an interest fully evident in his great, paired epic poems: not only is *Paradise Lost* a greater work, it's five times longer than *Paradise Regained*. Or consider Dante's unmistakable captivation not with the beatific souls in his *Paradiso* but with the tormented dead whirling in the *Inferno*.

I hope you will tolerate — those of you who have not gone on to chapter 20 — my use here of the word *evil*, because what happened in Jonesville was wrong, although it was a wickedness having nothing to do with the more usual — to judge from our popular entertainments — murder and mayhem, knives and napalm. It was not an evil of weapons but of tools: spades, scoops, scrapers, steam shovels. It's a tale of a past and a future that got, you could say, abridged.

On its ascent of the Ouachita in 1804, the Forgotten Expedition passed by what is today the historic center of Jonesville, and William Dunbar wrote in his log about a lone resident, a Frenchman whose "house is placed upon an Indian mount with several others in view: There is also a species of rampart surrounding this place and one very elevated mount, all of which I propose to view and describe on my return, our situation not now admitting delay." In late January 1805, Dunbar did return to make the first record of one of the most spectacular constructions in the entire region of Mississippi Valley aboriginal earthworks. Even Hunter, usually attracted more to resources of future profit, said, "If one may judge from the immense labor necessary to erect those Indian monuments to be seen here, this place must have once been very populous."

A couple of hundred yards below the crotch of the big Y that is the juncture of the Tensas with the Ouachita, at about the place where the little Catahoula River joins, once stood more than a half-dozen (observers gave varying numbers) prehistoric mounds protected on two sides by a large, defensive, L-shaped earthen embankment about a mile long running from the Black River to the Catahoula, with a pair of water gaps allowing dugouts to enter the enclosure. The right-angled rampart inversely reflected the juncture of those two rivers and protected the center. Rising near the middle was, to use a later name, the Great Mound, its height and structural design then unmatched among the large earthworks of the United States.

When the expedition came through, the Indians — both builders and later denizens — were long gone, and the only resident was the Frenchman who operated a ferry across the Black River. At the time, although Dunbar wouldn't have known, the Great Mound was more than a thousand years old, an age commensurate with the First Crusade. It was also the second-highest native mound in America; only the huge Monk's Mound at Cahokia, Illinois, across the Mississippi from St. Louis, stood taller, but just by a few feet. Because the Great Mound rose from a far smaller base, its steeply angled upper portion, Dunbar's "cone," created steep and high architectural lines probably found nowhere else in the United States. Despite being heavily overgrown with cane, the thing was unique — the Empire State Building of prehistoric America. (Its complex of stacked, geometric shapes makes a single term for it difficult, but the structure was clearly much more than a "mound"; recognizing the simplification, I'll refer to it now and then as a pyramid.) It was a giant earthen exclamation point, a grand monument fitting to a grand river at its terminus.

I fear my words will fail to show the pyramid precisely, so I'll resort to a diagram I've taken from a theoretical one that Winslow Walker, the archaeologist who conducted the fullest investigation of the Great Mound, made in the early 1930s. The apex of what you see in the figure, all of it made of clay, rose to the height of an eight-storey building; when Dunbar visited, the pyramid was the tallest native structure in the South.

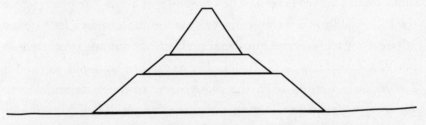

Diagrammatic reconstruction after Winslow Walker of the Great Mound as William Dunbar would have seen it in 1804.

Walker established the footprint of the structure, and then, combining Dunbar's 1805 vertical measurements with his own horizontal ones, he was able to reveal through geometry the upper portion, the truncated cone, had to rise at a fifty-degree angle from its base atop the double terraces, or tiers, below. The angle of repose (angle of slide) for dry earth is thirty-nine degrees, but for damp clay, of which the mound was made, the angle can decrease to seventeen degrees; with that in mind, you might consider the engineering of the Great Mound in a rockless, fluent land as at least the equal to the stone pyramids in Egypt, Mexico, or Central America.

Referring to the edifice as a "mound" denigrates and did not help its survival. The tenacious soils of what the usually unimpassioned Hunter called a "stupendous turret" were packed down hard and perhaps locked in by buried cane mats. That peerless work stood for more than a thousand years in a climate notorious for hurricanes and for saturating downpours lasting all day. The pyramid would be there now for you to witness had a couple of decisions, otherwise of little significance, turned out differently. Although many archaeologically rich native mounds and middens around the country have been destroyed for simple road fill, nothing as splendid as the Great Mound has fallen for that mundane purpose.

Dunbar wrote that because the "ascent is extremely steep, it is necessary to support one'self by the canes which cover this mount, to be able to get to the top." (The Indians may have used a narrow spiral ramp, perhaps one of timbers, but the answer to that mystery is now also lost.) Assuming hundreds of years of erosion must have reduced it, Dunbar thought the tower was originally even higher, although with the diameter of the crest only eight feet, the pyramid could not have held much more packed soil or had space at the top for a large structure.

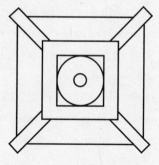

Simplified overhead diagram of the Great Mound as configured by Winslow Walker.

So what was the purpose of that extraordinary quoz at the heart of what may have been the "capital" of a region blessed with the conjoining of three rivers? Dunbar guessed a watchtower, but that function could have been more easily accomplished in a tall cypress. A signal station? A monument to a deity or person? A ceremonial pyramid? A giant gnomon for astronomical observations? Apparently, like most of the truly large Mississippian earthworks, it was not a mortuary, at least not initially. Then what was it?

Jon Gibson, an archaeologist who has studied the ancient earth-works at Poverty Point eighty miles north, speaks of such constructs as metaphors of creation and the cosmos once helping to link a people — and not just the elite — to their land. He writes:

> Mounds . . . manifested one of the strongest emotions shared by individuals and small communities — the sense of place, or home. Mounds turned meadows and woods, lakes and bay-ous, houses and hunting grounds into centers of the cosmos. . . . Mounds metaphorically expressed the southern native world view in which secular and sacred, home and chapel, corporeal and spiritual, and reality and magic were inseparable. [The prin-ciple behind the mounds] gave people common knowledge and feelings of a shared past.

We shall never be able to confirm such ideas, argues the probabi-list in me, because what a millennium of fifty-inch-per-annum rain-fall (the record there is three feet in a single month) had not wreaked on the Great Mound, Southerners accomplished in seventy years. In America, we like to get things done.

Heavy destruction began during the Civil War when soldiers dug away the top and shoveled it down the slopes to make a rifle pit for shooting at anyone ascending the Black River or perhaps coming along the road out of Natchez, twenty-five direct miles eastward. The ineffectiveness of minié balls or light artillery (who was going to drag a mortar up even that reduced slope?) in stopping iron-clad gunboats suggests the military destruction of the upper por-tion was senseless — sheer and utter waste of a singular American wonderment.

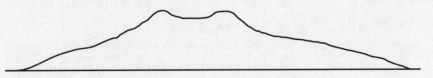

The Great Mound as a Civil War soldier would have seen it in 1864.

Six years after the end of the war, the new village of Jonesville was laid out *exactly* within the hundred acres enclosed by the prehistoric embankments and the two rivers. In spite of open ground running southward for some distance along the west bank of the Black River, a few Louisianians nevertheless chose to set a sixteen-block village squarely atop the ancient site, and that made certain the eventual destruction of several smaller mounds in front of the big one. Yet even then, enough of the Great Mound remained to provide significant knowledge of the ancient place and its peoples *if* an archaeologist had arrived anytime in the subsequent sixty-four years. To the loss of America, one did not.

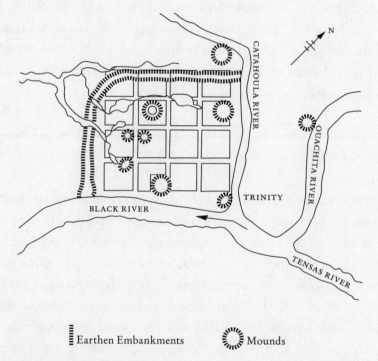

Troyville, now Jonesville, as laid out in 1871. The Great Mound (circle within a circle) is at upper left.

In 1931, as part of Governor Huey P. Long's get-people-back-to-work programs, the Louisiana Highway Department began building a bridge to replace the ferry that was a descendant of the first one of 1796. An approach ramp was necessary to get the span above a potential flood, and what more convenient source for the dirt fill than the Great Mound? One generation's expedience is the grand-children's expense. On came the steam shovels.

By the time archaeologist Walker learned of the devastation — publicly sanctioned vandalism that plundered the future at a time when any notion of stewardship thereabouts was more remote than flights to Pluto — and got to the site that summer, the pyramid and its trove of revealing artifacts had been dug and hauled a few hundred feet south and compacted into the bridge approach. He wrote, "A contract was made with the owners to permit the removal of 21,000 cubic yards of dirt, which resulted in reducing the mound nearly to street level." If you've ever driven U.S. 84 in eastern Louisiana and crossed the Huey Long Bridge, your wheels have rolled directly over the soil of what once was one of the great monuments of ancient America.

Remains of the Great Mound as Winslow Walker first saw them in 1931.

Walker thought the shovels might not have gone below the current surface far enough to reach the original base of the mound, and, surely enough, six feet down he exposed its footprint still intact. He immediately began investigating what little remained, but four days later heavy rains stopped him. Returning in early September 1932, he and his father and a few "Negro laborers" for the next two weeks conducted archaeological excavations of the residuum. Even on such unpromising ground, even in that time, a good scientist could turn up information to assist a hypothetical reconstruction of what once had been.

A citizen to whom historic preservation and its links to economic vitality mean anything at all has to think, *After a thousand years, if only Walker had arrived a few months earlier!* Archaeology could have revealed so much more about the ancient residents and their lives.

Ah, archaeology! There's the glitch. Walker reported:

Unfortunately, the people on whose land the great mound had stood were at first suspicious of the intentions of the excavators, and knowing little of scientific aims or procedure, believed instead that the real purpose was to search for the "Natchez treasure," which, according to popular tradition, was buried in this or some other large Indian mound. It was, therefore, with reluctance that they at last consented to any excavation of the site at all, and then only on the stipulation that any such "money" found would belong by right to them. But as the work progressed and this form of remuneration did not materialize, their cupidity led them to formulate other demands, which finally became so unreasonable and so impossible to grant that the excavation of the great mound site had to be summarily stopped.

Walker's barely checked vexation, unusual in a scientific report, indicates his disappointment and frustrated hopes. A few other townspeople, however, with greater intelligence and foresight, did help by lending him tools.

One of the many unexplained facts of the Troyville Mounds has to do not with residents or even the structures themselves but with an earlier archaeologist, Philadelphian Clarence Moore, who, over thirty years, discovered and excavated mounds across the South as if they were as common as clods of dirt. (You'll recall the decorated Glendora pot shown in chapter 15.) From 1891 to 1918, he steamed up rivers and bayous and coastlines in his own small shallow-draft stern-wheeler, *Gopher,* to dig indigenous earthworks and amass a collection of prehistoric, Southern artifacts paramount in number, quality, and range.

The *Gopher* and its crew came to Jonesville in November 1908, and Moore disembarked. A mere two hours later, he headed on up the Ouachita, recording in his log no reason for shrugging off the Great Mound; reduced though it was, it was still bigger than all but a few he'd excavated elsewhere. His overlooking the smaller mounds at Jonesville may reflect their degradation by the current inhabitants as well as his awareness of hundreds of other sites lying less molested elsewhere.

But how, of all people, could Clarence Moore steam away from something like the Great Mound, even then the tallest structure for many miles? My guess is that he met with venality, as would Walker twenty-four years later; perhaps the demands asked of Moore were even larger, since he was known to pay landowners for digging rights. I think his unnatural silence about neglecting the Troyville site indicates his disgust with a property owner he encountered there, perhaps the same family Walker later dealt with. Although the speed of Moore's excavations in other locations has raised questions about his scientific procedure, even a hurried dig at Troyville would have yielded knowledge we lack today: better Moore's quick spade and trowel than highway department steam shovels. And what if he had found a vessel or two even half the significance of those in the splendid cache of ceramics he came up with only sixty-five miles north at Glendora? The number of pottery sherds that Walker and others have excavated since the leveling prove the soil in and around Jonesville was far from culturally sterile.

Winslow Walker's highly limited, salvage archaeology in 1932 is the fullest we will ever likely have of the grand pyramid. Most artifacts and skeletal remains he excavated were crushed almost beyond recognition, and many other finds were too fragile under the difficult conditions to be preserved. Still, his work would have revealed even more had not — once again — some residents, unwilling to recognize the difference between a souvenir and a scientifically interpretable artifact, interfered. Walker said about his excavation of a mound at the mouth of the Catahoula River where he unearthed a few human burials:

Unfortunately it was not possible to remove any of the bones for study, owing to the intense and insatiable curiosity aroused in the local populace by the discovery. Not content with flocking around the site in such numbers during the day that they seriously interfered with the work of the excavators, they returned to the scene under cover of nightfall, tore off the coverings placed to protect the skeletons, and committed such acts of vandalism that the owners of the ground felt obliged to put a stop to the nuisance by requiring all work to be stopped immediately and the bones to be covered over as before. Time was allowed only to take a few photographs of the burials.

Henceforth, artifacts reburied or not, plunderers knew where to dig for a piece of broken pottery or a crumbling tibia to set up on a windowsill or to keep in a bean sack under the bed. Today, the situation has changed little: current reports of one recent scientific dig are classified to keep looters from using them.

When Q and I began walking Jonesville, all we could see of the vanished prehistoric settlement lay at the foot of Front Street above the Black River; there, a grassy mound with a height on its western edge that failed to rise above my eyebrows had been shaved and half-squared by two streets. The evening view eastward over the slope and across the flood wall, and on to the river, and on beyond the flatlands, was pleasing, but from eighty feet higher, what must it have been like to see first light of day? Archaeologist Gibson believes the early inhabitants considered "unblocked vistas provided an entry portal for good spirits, which originated in the beneficent east, and an exit portal for disharmonious spirits which built up inside enclosed spaces."

Atop the remaining, mutilated mound was an Anglo cemetery of about forty broken tombstones and two big, concrete vaults like septic tanks, half-sunken boxes built to slow some future power shovel from dislodging their contents. Standing in the middle of the cemetery, Q said, "The message here is that it's okay to desecrate the grave of a heathen savage, but curst be he that moves my sacred white bones." Indeed, Cyrus Thomas, another of the great names in American earthworks archaeology, wrote that in the digging of modern graves at Jonesville, "skeletons and pottery are frequently thrown out." But then, those Anglo bones kept that small mound from being entirely obliterated.

Under the lowering sky in an eerie dusk, I walked the grassy hump to read the markers — one name was Hobgood — and Q stared for some time at crypts under a big dead tree well on its way toward stumpdom. She said, "This place is out of Edgar Allan Poe." Looking at the disgraced ancient mound, I said I wished I could quote the raven.

We walked on two blocks west to where the Great Mound had stood for a millennium. I imagined the view without the five houses and a Catholic chapel sitting on a corner of the site. At the same scale as the other drawings and with modern structures removed, here's what I saw:

The site of the Great Mound (without current structures) as it was in 2004.

The sequence of these mound diagrams reminds me of the image on a cardiac monitor progressing from the electronic pyramids of a healthy heartbeat to that direful flattened line of the dead.

❥ 19 ❦

Extracting Sunbeams
from Cucumbers

JONESVILLE SITS on the low second terrace of the Black River, only about twenty feet above it, and not always elevated enough to keep the rivers away, although high waters never topped the Great Mound, even in its reduced state. During the Flood of 1882, a New Orleans newspaper, which Mark Twain quotes in *Life on the Mississippi,* reported on the area: "On the inside of the houses the inmates had built on boxes a scaffold on which they placed the furniture. The bedposts were sawed off on top, as the ceiling was not more than four feet from the improvised floor. The building looked very insecure, and threatened every moment to float off."

The earliest image of Troyville — by the African-American illustrator Henry Jackson Lewis whose work preserves so many nineteenth-century scenes in the Mississippi Valley — is a picture of that flood made only a decade after the founding of the settlement; Lewis shows a couple of dozen inundated buildings in front of several mounds raising their tops above the water.

[**DIGRESSION ALERT:** Not only here but across the South and Middle West, aboriginal mounds became prime homesites, perhaps an admission of which people truly understood how to live in concert with the land. I leave it to you, percipient reader, to decide whether this final extract from Reverend Flint's 1835 journal of the Ouachita territory draws a merited contrast:

Our ferryman, living on a high Indian mound, had a small field above the overflow. We found him and his habitation among the real curiosities of the country. He was a little old Hollander, dressed about half in Robinson Crusoe costume, with his house and garden on the summit of a mound, rearing its solitary elevation above the vast swamp, and at some miles' distance from any other dwelling. Flourishing peach and plum trees and a little garden covered this summit. The cabin had two stories, the under one a sort of lumber room, dug in the side of the mound. We ascended the upper one by a ladder, to his parlour and dormitory. Himself, a dog and cat, were the sole tenants. The man, the habitation, everything in and around it, were such as Walter Scott would have assigned to a wizard. His family utensils were horns of strange forms and dimensions; his vessels cypress knees; his bellows a long reed with which he blew up the fire, blowpipe fashion. His dog and cat, his barn and buildings, were all in perfect keeping. The strange looking old being was himself, I judged, a fancied adept in astrology; for he showed me a Dutch book, which as well as I could make out his explanation of it, taught the occult science of the stars. . . . This lone old man, a century ago, would have been in danger from superstition. At present he will occupy his solitary swamp unmolested, and some morning of no distant day, will be found stiff in his dormitory, resting just above the bones of the unknown dwellers of the former generations; as he seemed feeble and suffering, and complained of having experienced a fit during the thunderstorm of the preceding night.

Of other past events at the mouth of the Ouachita, I should mention the possibility that Hernando de Soto passed through the Indian settlement at the foot of the Great Mound. If that village was Anilco, as some historians believe, then those people saw the fatally ill conquistador in his last days before being sent by his men on a final voyage to the bottom of the Mississippi River.]

. . .

Searching for a view of the terminus of the Ouachita, the place where it loses its name, Q and I walked down one afternoon through a gate in the flood-wall linked with a low levee, so we could reach the sandy edge of the Black River to behold the juncture of waters, but it wasn't visible from there either. I asked a young fisherman in hunter's-orange camouflage (Q: "Is he hiding from catfish?") where we could find a viewpoint. We needed to cross the Catahoula to Trinity, he said, only a couple of hundred yards distant, but getting there required directions and a vehicle.

To the south we could see the 1935 bridge and its mundane ramp built from a priceless past. On beyond it, standing in the middle of the river, were three concrete columns connected on top by lateral beams. The assemblage looked like a temple gateway, a Japanese sacred torii with an extra leg: TTT. Could it possibly be once-blasé Jonesvillians (I came within an ace of writing *Jonesvillains*) were trying to atone for the (okay, I'll use it) villainy here a generation ago? Such a junction of waters was undoubtedly a sacred place to the indigenous peoples, and that means destruction of the pyramid and its collateral mounds was desecration. But was there now hope that a wise and generous enlightenment, however belated, had come to the hamlet? I asked the fisherman what the thing was. "Piers for the new bridge," he said. "The old one's coming down — at least it's supposed to when the politicians quit arguing over who gets paid what for the right-of-way, so we can finish the bridge."

"You mean," asked Q, "a thousand-year-old marvel got turned into road fill that lasted all of sixty-some years?" He was taken aback. Thinking her words sounded harsh, she added, "Maybe in nineteen thirty-one they didn't know what they were doing."

"You've heard about the mound?" he said in surprise, and then, cautious with his words, "Oh, they knew what they were doing all right." While he helped his five-year-old son rebait a hook, he said, "You can't tell it by these clothes, but I work in a bank, and I see every day how economically depressed Catahoula Parish is. People here don't like to admit it, but it's obvious to outsiders. The local catfish farms are about gone because of Asian imports, and cotton is way down. Okay, soybeans are up this year, and a few people make money raising pet turtles, those little green ones. Cooters. Most of them go to Asia. But trading cooters for catfish doesn't make a real broad economic base. All you have to do is look at the town up there. Those buildings show how hard-hit we are."

His line jerked around, then went taut, and he wrestled in a fourteen-inch blue catfish he would grill that night. When he had reset his line, he said, "They knew back then what they were doing to the big mound, but I doubt they figured they were shoveling our economic future into road fill. For a town this size, a good tourist attraction could be the base of a nice economy." I mentioned Poverty Point, eighty miles north, a sprawling archaeological site almost four-thousand years old, which had not long ago become a National Historic Landmark even though nothing there was quite so dramatic as the Troyville pyramid had been. "No question," he said. "If the big mound was still here, we'd have some tourist business."

I asked whether he knew about Cahokia, how the State of Illinois, over the years and without the use of eminent domain, bought up a '50s and '60s housing development — including a drive-in theater — at the foot of the giant mound and gradually removed structures and streets to re-create in increments a landscape fitting to a prehistoric cultural center without equal in the United States. A balloon-frame house can be moved anywhere if need be, but an earthen structure like Monk's Mound, a thousand feet long and covering sixteen acres (a base larger than that of the Cheops pyramid), is going nowhere except where unchecked erosion might take it. The changes at Cahokia, including a new museum, materially assisted its designation as a World Heritage Site, and the last I'd heard, two-hundred-thousand people a year came to see it.

He was still listening, so I went on. Why not create for depressed Jonesville an economic-assistance plan, one to be developed over time through fund-raising and finding willing sellers? Buy the half-dozen intrusive houses (as they come up for sale) and the chapel on the block where the Great Mound once stood, remove them, conduct full archaeological research. Restore the embankment and small mounds, then culminate the project with a reconstruction of the Great Mound by delineating it with so-called ghost architecture, perhaps an open steel frame bearing the outline. Maybe include metal ramps — similar in design to the conjectured originals — that visitors could take to the top. There would be nothing else in America quite like it.

"That's pretty radical for us," he said. Radical? Hell, people here — like everywhere else — are heading for the outskirts anyway. Why not let the American urge to sprawl away from town central work economically for Jonesville?

Either out of interest or in disbelief at such notions, he seemed still open, so I kept going although I knew my words sounded like, as Lemuel Gulliver has it, "a project for extracting sunbeams out of cucumbers." How about, in one of the derelict buildings on Mound Street, a visitor center to display the discoveries and interpretations of the archaeologists? A museum that, among other things, might explore the mystery of who the aboriginal people were and why they settled there and why they later deserted the place, an inquiry that could shed light on how a later people are using it.

And I would have added to my blatant quodlibetic — had I then thought of it — any eradication of knowledge of a place is as deleterious to a community as the destruction of the place itself. Such a new undertaking might help citizens see some connections between their Addictive Disorder Clinic and their disassociation from their past and the economic consequences. It was too late for true preservation and restoration of the earthworks but not for further investigation and interpretation and some edifying reconstructions. To rebuild a place wisely is to rebuild lives. An attuned economic engine can also be a spiritual engine.

"Like a theme park?" he said. Not at all. It wouldn't be drive-by history but a center with national ramifications to educate and — given the losses — help a town do what it could to reclaim a great inheritance a previous generation had squandered. A way to undo the rapacity of an economy based upon principles that ultimately impoverish a community. (This last sentence I didn't say, but only because the words then failed me.)

But I did say, since I was talking to a bank employee, too often we all live in ways guaranteed to divest our inheritance. We've become, at least nationally, great violators of the old Quaker apothegm *Thee shall never touch the principal.* Weren't reactionary politicians in Washington wanting to sell off Department of the Interior lands to pay for a deficit brought on by corporate handouts and a disastrous Mesopotamian war?

He'd stopped looking at me, and I realized I might have gone too far for him. He was watching his little boy, whose interest in fishing was exhausted, pile up small mounds of river sand as if he'd been illustrating the conversation; after he had six or seven piles, he swept his hand across them, leveling them as though they never were.

❧20❦

A Cannonball Clean
Through the Parlor

GUIDED BY THE FISHERMAN'S DIRECTIONS, Q and I drove back through Jonesville and on around to the north side of the Catahoula River, following it a short way to its terminus at Trinity, across the water and less than a quarter mile from where the great pyramid once had been. We stopped and walked a lightly wooded area to the edge of a thirty-foot bluff overlooking a wide expanse of water, and Q asked, "Is that the mouth of the Ouachita?" Without a more detailed map, I couldn't be certain. She said, "I wish somebody would come along." The words were still in the air when I saw a squarely built man coming toward us, probably to run us off. Hoping I was wrong, I met him to give our reason for trespassing. Before I could say anything, he introduced himself: Tuffy Parish. I said we were hunting the end of the Ouachita River, and he said, "You're looking at it."

Q came up to explain our descent from the headwaters, which she now could relate with polish, and he motioned to follow him back to the edge of the bluff, several yards beyond where we'd been. He nodded to a small sign, blue letters on white, each side painted so both river and road travelers could read it: OUACHITA RIVER. Tuffy, whose given name was James, pointed northeast. "That's the Tensaw." Then pointing northwest, "That's the Ouachita." Motioning south, he said, "On down's the Black." He started walking again. "This way," he said. "The view you're looking for is best over here."

Over here was a platform on long and slender steel piers allowing the high deck a gentle sway above the last mile of the Ouachita. "We call it Parish's Peaceful Point."

He kept a barbecue grill there and had made benches on top of watertight boxes holding picnic supplies and a few books. "It's a good place to read and watch," he said.

Q looked at me. "I never thought we'd find treasure boxes of books at the end of the river." That pleased him.

The woodland beauty of the last lap of the Ouachita was fittingly modest but not inconsequential, especially if one imagined afloat on the wide waters some dugouts of the builders of the Great Mound, pirogues of French trappers, Dunbar and Hunter's clumsy barge, Union ironclads, Clarence Moore's *Gopher;* perhaps even Hernando de Soto, about to give up his ghost, his bodily voyage almost done, and he so far from home, his conquest incomplete but nevertheless deadly, and maybe one way or another the cause of the abandonment of the settlement around the grand pyramid.

We watched the Ouachita until it began to disappear in the dusk, then Parish said, "Let me show you something else," and led us off the deck and into a wooden cabin he'd saved from destruction and rebuilt as a guest cottage, turning the interior into a little gallery for his inventive opuscules: curtain rods made from tree branches, an American flag with stripes fashioned from old fence pickets and the union from a four-paned window with a half-dozen Gulf Coast starfish glued to the glass. He said, "Come back sometime and stay here."

Parish was sixty-seven and retired from a local company that manufactured twine and rope products. He was smiling. "I used to have good connections." He believed living along a river entailed responsibility, but his words for it were "Whatever we do here can keep on going downstream." Seeing me pull out my little notebook to write that down, he added, "You put in how we take care of the end of the river." Here was a man, were he a generation older and owner of the Great Mound, who might have made the history — the well-being — of Jonesville sweepingly different.

He went to the door. "Come on over to the house. I want you to see something in the garage, and you tell me if it's not the only thing like it along the river." Tuffy built his house in 1973 by incorporating where he could portions of an 1830s home originally on the site. Although the place was more than thirty feet above the usual river level, a couple of forty-foot rises had twice put water up to the windowsills. His wife, Ginger, a retired teacher of third graders, joined us in the garage while he went to a cooler to find four bottles of beer. I stood looking around for the curiosity he wanted us to spot.

When I was nine or ten and traveling the highways as my father's navigator, I would imagine going up to selected front doors across the country and knocking and introducing myself and my assignment: a researcher with the Committee for American Curiosities whose task it was to discover all the peculiarly worthy things people squirrel away in their homes. I would show my credentials signed by Harry Truman and the Secretary of the Interior (interiors were our special domain), papers that would make a person eager to share treasures pulled from attic trunks, cartons at the backs of closets, even from a secret compartment in the chiffonier: the Mister's cloth napkin Jackson Pollock spilled spaghetti red on, the Missus's diary of Great-Grandmother Lavinia's trip across the plains in 1848, Sister's collection of roller-skate keys, Junior's cigar box of subway tokens, Granny's shelf of player-piano rolls. After full examination, I'd give the family a booklet of instructions on the best ways to pass along one day their troves to posterity. We would then all sit down at the kitchen table for a slice of apricot upside-down cake and a glass of apple cider. (You, astute reader, now see how so long ago this business of quests for quoz got started.)

While Tuffy opened the bottles and tried to match varieties to each of us, I looked around the garage for the something: surely it wasn't the vehicles or basketballs or mower or the three pairs of rubber boots or the — *hold it.* What's that thing on the wall above the Wellingtons? Something related to his picket-fence flag? Of similar size and shape, this one made of two planks, riddled with blackened nail punctures, two vertical smears of yellowed white paint, the right side with a jagged hole:

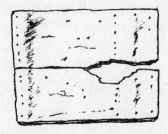

The Parishes watched me stare at it, and when I turned to them, their faces revealed I'd found the something. I said I knew I was seeing an oddity but I didn't know what the oddity was. Tuffy said, "You mentioned an interest in river history, and that's a piece of Ouachita history made out of cypress."

I said I was going to need some help. He explained how in using components of the 1830s home to build his new one, he'd uncovered original planked walls, two exterior ones and two inside, all with a similar hole broken through them. The peculiarity was that the puncture in the front wall, the one facing the river, was much lower than the hole at the back; then he noticed all four breachings were in parallel walls and aligned at an ascending angle, with a base that had to be down on the water. Then he understood: the perforations marked the trajectory of a cannonball fired from river level, one likely from a Union gunboat during the Ouachita campaign. He found no other damage, so he cut out the planks around the four holes and turned them into hanging sculpture.

But why only one shot? "I think it was a warning, because a battery here did fire on the fleet," he said. "Maybe somebody up here at the house took a potshot at them." The cannonball reportedly ended up in a field a half mile away.

Parish passed a beer to each of us, a good thing since I've long believed calling-card cannonballs shot clean through a parlor a signal invitation to — if not a prayer — then at least a toast celebrating everyone who's still alive to raise a glass. I said something along the lines of On behalf of Admiral Porter, may I tardily apologize for such an uncivil action against a domicile. And we drank to that. Then Q raised a second toast: "To that grand old Ouachita and all the wandering feet that reach her shores, long may she wave up!" And we drank to that too.

II.
Into the Southeast

Florida

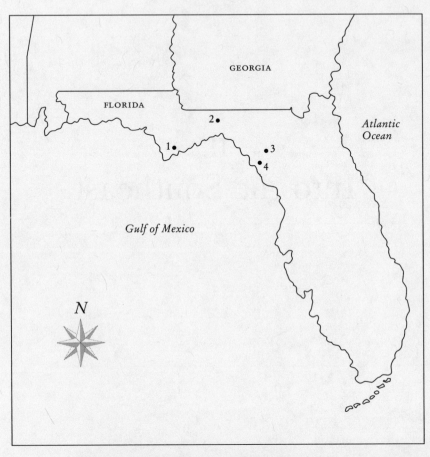

1 Apalachicola, Florida   3 Perry, Florida
2 Tallahassee, Florida   4 Steinhatchee, Florida

Into the Southeast

Doing What They Hadn't Ort to Do

Steinhatchee has always been a close-knit community and isolated in as much as it is off the beaten path. The people are independent, resourceful, and filled with pride. All of this is a definite asset if one lives in an isolated, rough territory. But many others have taken advantage of this isolation to use it for hiding from the law or doing something they hadn't ort to do.

Many old timers wish for better times and hope someday to be rid of the reputation that had spread far and wide. As the nation becomes over-populated, we need these off-the-beaten-path places to renew our lives and spirit from the rat race of daily living.

> — Elsie Lee Adams,
> *Steinhatchee River Falls,*
> 1991

❧ 1 ❧

A Quoz of Conviviums

THE NEXT LEG OF THE JOURNEY began in 1969 in Columbia, Missouri, and the source of it was an utter concoction created by my close friend Motier DuQuince Davis. We were then undergoing the academic abuse attendant with getting a doctoral degree in English literature. As PhD candidates, we called ourselves Phuds. Mo and I were pushing thirty, married, and had served our required stints in the military — he in the Army (where he learned to do a parachute-landing fall, and with enough malted relaxant would demonstrate) and I on an aircraft carrier.

All that is to say we had experience enough to recognize professional hazing, even when disguised by tradition and open acceptance. Although the college was rich with teachers who gave meaning to the term *human studies,* we happened to fall into a cadre of inflated, neurotic, pluckless, costive-spirited literature professors who possessed a single skill: they could read artfully assembled words and spin out interpretations. If any youthful moisture of soul remained in them, it had turned to mildew. The range of their dry-hearted, withered passions ran only from annoyance to worry, with every petty stage between and nothing beyond. Genuine emotions were only topics in their lecture notes, where they could discourse safely on the rage of King Lear, the suicidal despair of Ophelia, the jollity of Falstaff. Yet it was those sciolists, those hollow Prufrocks never daring to wear their trousers rolled, who dictated our lives, and we dispiritedly acquiesced by assuming our eventual end at some quiet liberal-arts college would justify our acceptance of their means. We fools, as my friend called us, managed such delusion through spine-less mutterings over mugs of cheap draft-beer.

Early one evening, several of us sat in a bar on Broadway in Columbia. Among us was an angular, sinewy student, younger than either Mo or I and innocent of military experience, full of repressed resentment and given to sudden and sometimes violent expressions of it, all of them prudently beyond the oversight of the professors. As the beer began to rile him, he said, "Tonight I'm going to find a fight or a fuck." Mo, always of calm facade even if turbulent beneath, said, "Sonny, you got yourself there a pretty fair country-western song." The kid shrugged. "Why not?" he said. "What are we but graduate-school rednecks? Who are we kidding?" He was working himself toward the fighting rather than the other. "What motivates us isn't a professor. It isn't even literature. It's the *fantasy* of a future professorship. So here we sit in a college-boy bar when we ought to be swinging a pool cue at somebody in a Cracker tavern."

Mo, who grew up in Macon, Georgia, said, "Bobbie Cheryl's Anchor Inn. Outside Davidson, North Carolina. It's an old road-house, falling down the hill into the creek. Men's toilet's got no door." What was he talking about? "Above the bar there's a ratty stuffed boar's head wearing a Tar Heel necktie. The floor sags from two generations of dancing feet. There's a fist hole in the wall above the urinal, but swinging a pool cue will get you tossed out. But you're not going to find any doctoral candidates in there and no associate professors trying to snuggle up in a rickety hideaway with a coed their daughter's age."

How many words do we hear in our lifetime that are inconse-quential flotsam immediately washed out of our lives to leave behind nothing, not even a residue? On the other hand, how many ordinary utterances — lacking apparent significance and free of indications they will survive beyond a moment or two — are there that seem to vanish, yet in some way resurface later, ready at last to shift a life? Bobbie Cheryl's Anchor Inn — four words — did just that to me, but I had no awareness of its implications for a third of a century. I was blind, in nautical lingo, to Mo's hook well-set in a hard bottom. I could recognize a metaphor on a printed page but not one in my life.

His précis of the Anchor Inn put me in it: I could see the red-neon anchor flickering in the window, and on a wall the name spelled out in a script of old ropes, and the back door held closed with barbed wire. I could hear pieces of conversations about deer hunting, women, government regulations, tractors, women, crank-shafts, women, football, wives, death. I could imagine us there in front of Bobbie Cheryl herself: she in midlife, married three times and not again, missing a couple of incisors, chain-smoking, tattooed in a time when women had no tattoos, tolerating neither loud cuss-ing nor putting your head down on the bar.

The Anchor Inn was, surely, a rendezvous of men — and a few women — wearing fertilizer and implement-company billed caps, who let fly with whatever might be going on beneath those hats, their sentences pungent and without pretense and rarely free of egre-gious solecisms. In the Anchor, a fellow like me would be tolerated and allowed to listen in as long as he kept his education to himself. A fair exchange.

Such a place had to be empty of vicarious life; it was an out-county dive, a crossroads tavern both in its topographical location and in its people gathered for conviviality. Despite the literariness of the High Professorhood running our lives, those men, several of them failed seminarians, would not deign to recognize the etymological relation between tavern and tabernacle. In their recently resecularized view, a trivial beer-joint could never be a house of Communion.

The ancient Romans, heathens to the new Christians, had a word for the Anchor Inn: *convivium,* a place of wine and song and con-versations on matters requiring no decisions of consequence. Bob-bie Cheryl's, I was sure, was full of what our lives lacked because it wasn't found on a written page; rather it was a place where we might find firsthand stories to put on a written page. It was the difference between secondary and primary sources.

That night, so long ago, my friend's talk of the Anchor Inn started a voyage for all of us, although several soon gave it up along the way. We talked how sometime we'd go together to Bobbie Cheryl's to celebrate our graduation from Phuddom and our release into a world not drawn from fiction but from actuality. After that night, for me at least, the Anchor Inn became archetypal and legendary, and — *I see now* — it helped carry me on through and smack out of academia. I think these very sentences — and likely most of the others I've written over the last quarter century — wouldn't exist without that anchor of a roadhouse and its promise of convivium. Bobbie Cheryl sang a siren song that for years I could only hum because I didn't understand the words.

But I'm getting ahead here.

Mo and I both eventually emerged with our Phudentials which in the end proved useless in those years when teaching jobs in our field all but evaporated. He joined the advertising department of a large Southern insurance company and earned a good salary, more than he ever would have from any imagined life dispensing nimble conspectuses to enraptured undergraduates. I continued to spiral down for some time, even after I hit the road to pursue stories of a kind the Anchor Inn surely was full of. Mo earned enough among the underwriters and adjusters to buy a thirty-seven-foot sloop and become a blue-water sailor whenever he could escape the office; he no longer needed an Anchor Inn, to confuse my metaphor, to buoy him. As for me, I underwrote my writing with a job clerking in the county courthouse and, later, one hoisting things on a loading dock, and yet another delivering bundles of newspapers in the wee hours. But always, I knew, out there somewhere in America were the Anchor Inns, the Dew Drop Inns, and all those taps owned by all those Shortys and Luckys.

Not long ago, when the Ouachita was still flowing fresh through my life, I received a letter from Mo saying he'd left the insurance office with enough in a retirement account to free him at last to write, and he was eager to pursue a book about the vanishing watermen's taverns along the Florida Gulf Coast. He'd met an artist who was ready to paint watercolors of what he hoped to find. His letter suggested a quest was key to his idea. The taverns, lying at the end of roads stopping at a waterfront, avoided advertising, and in effect put themselves in secret locations, allowing patrons the joy of discovery. He was anxious to start right away, before the dwindling places vanished entirely. In his letter I saw the promise of a quoz of conviviums. At his side, I'd follow his tracks.

2

The Black Lagoon

Q AND I STARTED for the Florida Panhandle south of Tallahassee. There we were to meet Davis. At sunset on a Sunday we came into a landscape of subterranean percolations of water rising through limestone to form rivers and creeks and lakes, only to, as if having seen enough of the new Florida, disappear again into the pervious rock, sometimes reemerging as a spring or resuming as a stream willing to try the territory again. While not hollow, Florida a few inches down is as porous as a weathered thighbone you might find in a High Plains pasture. Lake Iamonia, near the Georgia line, has come and gone more than once during my years of traveling the state. In this view, water surrounds Florida on four sides: east, west, south, and underneath. It's a piece of loosely stuck geology not so much affixed to the continent as merely anchored for the night.

That invisible hydrological nether-realm creates almost all the allure I'm able to find in a place afflicted for some years by nearly a thousand new residents a day. Even though it was the first "state" successfully settled by Europeans, as late as 1900 the greater part of Florida was still wilderness, a situation the people ever since have been working to eradicate. (Given the flooding population, Floridians ought to cotton to a visitor like me who comes in, spends a few bucks, fails to see what they see, and soon gets out, leaving folks a dollar or two ahead.) If you have neighbors thinking of moving to Florida, recommend they first drive multilane U.S. 19 from Crystal River to Clearwater; if they can view that stretch as the happy fulfilling of their dream and of the American way, then the state may indeed be for them. If, on the other hand, they find it a harbinger of the end of sensible life, then they may be better off redirecting their exodus. That's why, after all, North Dakota exists — for those who want, for the price of only five or six months of winter, to kiss good-bye life-absorbing congestion in search of a mall.

But synthetic Floridorable was elsewhere on the Sunday evening Q and I arrived in the Apalachicola National Forest in Wakulla County in the eastern end of the Panhandle. Although just fifteen miles south of Tallahassee, we were surrounded by an ostensible wilderness. In the falling darkness, the narrow road through the thick hummock-land rose only slightly above the swampy terrain and appeared to be floating on pontoons. The air was thick with the scent of woods and water, and when we stopped once to take the place in, from the thicket came squeaks and rasps and murmurs, stridulations, tremolos and low caterwauls bemingling into a polyphonic, boggy concert of contrapuntal voices. It was an ancient kingdom, not a "magic" one but real, safe for a little while longer in a piece of vanishing Florida. A half century earlier, Edwin Way Teale, the American naturalist, wrote of that very place in his *North with the Spring,* a narrative about one leg of his seventy-five-thousand miles of road trips around the continent:

It was the voice of the dark, the swamp, the vast wilderness of ancient times. It links us — as it will link men and women of an even more urbanized, regimented, crowded tomorrow — with days of a lost wildness.

When Teale reached the banks of the Wakulla River in 1953, he wanted to photograph the snail-eating limpkin, a bird once "highly esteemed as food," he said, and so intrepid or unsuspecting it was easily slaughtered until nearing the edge of extinction by the 1920s. Unlike the passenger pigeon, the limpkin shed its fearlessness, became more suspicious of humanity, less tolerant, and retired to newly created sanctuaries where, after several of its generations, it again had become bolder and more visible by the time Teale arrived. Yet, at Wakulla today, the limpkin is still listed as rare.

We stopped at the Wakulla Springs Lodge, a Spanish Colonial–style building — white stucco walls, Moorish arches, red roof tiles, marble floors, grand fireplace — that seemed to fit the lowland, if any human structure can fit a swamp. Old Joe, the eleven-foot stuffed alligator whose age allegedly was two centuries, lent his presence to the mood. After hours of long miles, to stumble into a corporate motel is merely to end the day, but to reach a place imbued with its own native territory is to *arrive* (the word comes from the Latin, *toward shore*), to fetch up on a distant strand.

The lobby had a high ceiling of exposed cypress beams painted with what were, perhaps, Aztec-inspired designs; the guest rooms — furnishings, bathroom fixtures, and possibly the lightbulbs — were from the 1930s when the lodge was built. In its aura of forgotten Florida, the place was ideal for a search into its disappearing remnants. As we went outside to survey the terrain in the moonlight, the clerk warned, "Keep your eyes open for gators, because they're out there."

The freshwater spring, with the largest volume issuing from a single fissure on the planet, is the source of the Wakulla River and the reason the lodge exists. It was into that fountain, which Indians considered the home of four-inch-tall homunculi who danced in its depths on moonlit nights, that Tarzan (in the person of Johnny Weissmuller) made several high dives. And from it some years later emerged a creature to disturb the sleep of many a child in the 1950s. Soon after Teale's visit, a movie crew came along to gape 185 feet straight down into the clarity of the pool to determine whether filming in its depths was feasible. They asked a young Tallahassee man, Rico Browning, to swim it for some test footage to see if native aquatic plants looked exotic enough to stand in for a lost Amazonian river.

The director watched Browning's powerful and rhythmic underwater stroke, a strangely beautiful quarter-rotating crawl. It was perfect for the antediluvian creature in the 3-D fright film he was about to make. He had Browning fitted out in a sponge-rubber suit that turned him into the amphibious subhuman Gill Man who performed marvelous aquatic maneuvers. It helped that Browning, so I heard, could swim underwater while holding his breath for four minutes.

Over the past fifty years, I had believed *The Creature from the Black Lagoon* (a movie that inexplicably keeps appearing in my books, although I've seen it only a couple of times) was filmed on a Southern California back-lot pool. I'd never thought it possible to look into the real "lagoon." The spring and its surround, while neither a back-lot set nor a piece of Disney World plasticity, nevertheless were once in the sights of those very theme-park developers.

There are thousands of springs in Florida, several of them famous attractions, including one with mermaids performing underwater modern dance with the help of air hoses. But Wakulla is a quieter place, and that quiet allows its distinctions — geological, ornithological, mythological — to arise quietly and naturally like its translucent water. There is even the legend, claim a few local historians, it was on the Wakulla River where an Indian shot an arrow into the neck of Ponce de León to end his quest for a Fountain of Youth Eternal.

As I was wondering aloud what it would be like to descend into water so deep it holds ice-age mastodon bones, Q asked if I'd actually do it. Maybe tomorrow if we have time, I said. (All marriage counselors agree that tarradiddle to a spouse is acceptable — *if* it's patently obvious bunk.)

Mo had left a hand-drawn map directing our way southward a few miles along a road paralleling the Wakulla to its junction with the St. Marks River about six miles above its mouth in Apalachee Bay where, five more miles from the open water of the Gulf of Mexico, one entity after another contested the area since at least 1677: Indians, pirates, England, Spain, France, America, Confederates and Federals. That long and curving shore of upper Florida, fretted with stream outlets and heavy marsh grasses and impenetrable thickets, had until recently proved too topographically uncertain to lure big-dollar development. Yet, with the rest of the coast at last largely built-upon or being readied for draglines and dozers, the northern section had become highly vulnerable.

Some years ago, Floridians started naming their coasts: the stretch around Miami became the Gold Coast, the reach above St. Petersburg was the Nature Coast, Pensacola lay on the Emerald Coast, and — although its limits varied — the curve of the Gulf from about Cedar Key to Panama City belatedly turned into the Forgotten Coast. Just who it was who forgot it, I never learned, but it certainly wasn't developers and speculating buyers of land. Throughout that area, realty signs sprouted in the underbrush like palmettos, and a billboard summed things up: IT'S ALL ABOUT REAL ESTATE.

At the little counter in Posey's Oyster Bar on the St. Marks River sat my friend whom I'd not seen for so long; on one side was his wife, Celia, and on the other, Rosalie Shepherd, the watercolorist for his book. Also waiting were two bottles of beer at two empty seats for Q and me. Arriving soon after us was a bowl of fish dip, a name sounding like some piscatorial prophylaxis, a parallel to what farmers use to disinfect sheep.

I now believe mullet fish dip, a delicacy tricky to find, is deliberately unappetizingly named to conserve a limited resource. Recipes for it vary, but most begin with smoked fish pulled from the bone and then minced before adding differing ingredients: crumbled crackers, cream cheese, pickle relish, celery, mayonnaise, but always with spices remaining secret from maker to maker. Q, as she quite possibly took more than her share from the bowl, asked why I'd never told her about smoked-mullet spread. I said the classic fish dips of Old Florida, like state-champion trees, must be kept secret to protect them from excessive appreciation. (My second falsehood of the evening; in truth, Mo had just introduced me to them also, a detail raising the question why *he* had never before mentioned them to me.) To avoid missing out on such discoveries is another reason for traveling often to see friends, even when they live halfway across the continent. For the next several days, he and I would be looking for smoked-fish dips along the coast, comparing recipes and executions. As he talked about second-to-none amberjack spread, the rest of us were piling soda crackers with Posey's mullet dip; I could have made a fine meal of it on saltines had not baskets of fried-snapper sandwiches and coleslaw come to the table. At moments like those, all the yellow highway stripes between Missouri and Florida seemed as nothing.

The old café, its floors showing more relief than the surrounding land, had commensurately undulating wooden walls and ceiling, the latter mostly concealed by a gray cloud of signed dollar-bills that, like an approaching storm, had begun descending earthward along support posts. At Posey's, the custom got started years ago, explained the bartender, when a commercial fisherman flush from a sale of mullet put his name on a few bills and tacked them overhead so he'd have money for beer the next time his nets came up empty. On the night we were there, his original four dollars had multiplied into about fifteen hundred. Mo said, "The authenticity disappears once tourists start adding their autographed bills," to which Q responded, "Maybe it's a new authenticity beginning."

After supper, he and I walked out back to the porch at the edge of the St. Marks River, once a haven for pirates. Buccaneers long dead, my flashlight beam revealed only dark water alive with slow gliding red dots — eyes of alligators. Did Posey's qualify for his book? "It's authentic and unpretentious," he said. "And it's aged to the point of being beat-up. The food's local and good. The building's right on the water, and it's out of the way — a place you have to search for. But, like so many other places today, it's missing a key element." Which is? "Where are the commercial fishermen? Here instead you've got college students." I said Posey's, then, must not be a kind of Bobbie Cheryl's Anchor Inn. He looked blank for a moment before the memory returned. "No," he said with a smile more enigmatic than joyful. "The Anchor's something else."

On our return to the black lagoon, I mentioned moviemakers using the great Wakulla Spring as a stand-in for the Gill Man's Amazon and Tarzan's Africa. How is it visitors by the millions seek a passive voyeurism of the fake rather than an examination of the genuine? Perhaps a corner of Nebraska or Kansas could use the plasticated boost of a Magic Kingdom, but why would anyone willing to enter the once-abundant native landscape of Florida need any such falsity? Tell me, O Swami.

Swami didn't really answer. Rather, he said, "Maybe because most of the authentic is gone. What's left for them?" Well, I said, but he went on: "You can see how a place like Posey's, with a water view, sits in the eye of a hurricane — one that may never hit. And now, all those places are in a more deadly eye of some developer or speculator in California or Chicago who wants to turn them into a Magic Kingdom of commercial fishermen's taverns. Or worse, knock them down for waterside condos."

We rode quietly through the dark and wet land. Almost inaudibly, he said, "Maybe my guidebook will help preserve, and maybe it'll only speed up change. Maybe identifying the few places left will push them right into a developer's portfolio." For a mile or so he was quiet again, then, "Maybe instead of a guide I should write something that'll leave them anonymous. Maybe I shouldn't write it up at all." If anonymity is necessary for survival, I said, then they're probably doomed with or without your words.

His search, I'll mention here, was inspired and informed by Ray Oldenburg's 1989 book, *The Great Good Place,* which analyzes "happy gathering places where unrelated people relate." Among such "third places" (after those of home and work), Panhandle Floridian Oldenburg writes about Viennese coffeehouses, German beer gardens, French cafés, Greek tavernas, English pubs, and the American country-store. Mo believed commercial fishermen's taverns of recent years served a similar purpose in bringing watermen together as well as linking them with their community. Given a certain closeting of American life of late, abetted in no small way by electronic communications and entertainments, he feared the demise of third places, and it bothered him. He was a son of old Middle Georgia where civilization — and that includes civility — requires a proper forum. A convivium.

❥ 3 ❧

Arrows That Flieth by Day

THE NEXT MORNING Q and Celia headed south on a trip of their own, and Mo and I struck out on old U.S. 98, but we got no farther than a dozen miles before pulling into the woods to follow a sign nailed to a tree: *TUPELO HONEY & MAYHAW JELLY*. The makers, a couple in their late seventies, were just departing on an errand, but they paused to sell us honey. I asked what put the tupelo in it. "Our bees," the woman said in a Panhandle lilt ever harder to hear even in Wakulla County. "In spring they visit tupelo blossoms down in here all along the river. Your mouth will tell you it's not like other honeys." That evening after I dribbled it over a couple of crackers, I said, echoing a phrase I'd heard two days earlier, "I knowed we shoulda boughten more."

Motier Davis saw his thick black hair change early to titanium white, a topping that distinguishes him and befits his courtly manners, they in turn enhanced by his distinctive speech known among linguists as Plantation dialect. As if his regular features were not enough, his pronunciations — at least when he was at the University of Missouri — were a veritable magnet even to the most bronze-clad feminine hearts. (The virtual voice on his dashboard GPS hears his "I-95" as "Mighty fine.") With his intelligence, that Plantation locution has stood him in good stead wherever he's been. Even in Florida, people will talk to him just to hear *him* talk, and that he does well. Getting to know this gentle man, a Georgian Don Quixote forever tilting at the windmills of his dreams, did much to set straight my youthful misconceptions about the South. Without his friendship and counsel, although he's a year younger, my travels in Dixie would have had a different cast.

Sagging down like a line of wet laundry, old U.S. 98 followed the curve of the Gulf about as closely as a road could, the sound of the waves sometimes overcoming the hum and thrum of auto tires. We rolled through little Panacea, its name likely coming from waters once alleged to heal ailments beyond counting; the promotion by Bostonians of that spring is a story of nineteenth-century speculators — a history begun by Ponce de León's legendary and unfulfilled quest for his Fountain — that continues even as new remunerative "springs" of a manufactured sort come forth.

Carrabelle, a town I remembered from a couple of decades earlier, now looked more prosperous, less down-at-the-edges, less frayed, less of a commercial fishermen's town. We saw more deck shoes than Wellingtons, more spinning reels than nets, more cruisers than shrimp trawlers. The new prosperity was much the result of Forgotten Coast marketeers realizing how marketable forgottenness can be in a state gaining forty new residents every hour. Crowding apparently improves human memory.

All of that had translated into a northern Gulf coastline of ever more housing built atop twelve-foot pilings designed, in theory, to let saltwater storm surges wash in and wash back out, leaving behind not even so much as a soggy doormat. Those places looked like spindle-shanked fat men waiting to tiptoe into the Gulf. The dwellings weren't exactly flimsy unless you consider the meteorological forces they challenge, but aesthetically, they had the lines of matchboxes atop chopsticks. A day earlier, a man had described them to me as "unneedless hurricane bait." The Calusa people here, prior to the arrival of the Ponce de Leóns, lived with the wind and not against it. But the Western hubris is to try to invent ways to withstand hurricanes and storm surges, the residents acting like a boxer who believes he's too good ever to have to dodge a solid punch.

I asked Mo if he thought for most people vacationing there,

whether cognizant of it or not, the best part of a day at the beach was the *idea* of a day at the beach. Concept over actuality.

I spoke of a friend who thinks he likes to travel, yet whenever asked whether he enjoyed his last trip to wherever, he answers unfailingly, "Not really," and he begins to enumerate the reasons. What he enjoys isn't travel but rather the logistics of travel, the contemplation of discoveries, the premeditation of trains leaving on time and carrying no crying babies, hotels with windows that open, restaurants free of sour waiters, roads dry and straight and uncongested, and above all a digestive tract never challenged by unaccustomed fare. He loves the architectural drawing of a journey and not the actual structure where the bubble of true plumb is always a couple of degrees askew, where two-by-sixes warp and hinges loosen, where a carpenter needs a sledgehammer as much as a tape measure. And indeed, to love the reality of the road, a traveler does well to pack a small, emotional sledge ready for frequent application.

Along old 98, I was having to beat down memories that not so much made me long for what once was there but simply left me almost sadhearted over what likely will be. As dyspepsia is to a diner, so personal nostalgia is to the traveler.

The challenge in Mo's project was not only finding a few surviving watermen's taverns but presenting them historically rather than nostalgically — and that's always miry ground for a writer depicting places of what used to be. After a couple of hours on the road, he grew disappointed we'd not turned up anything remotely authentic. "Maybe I'm too late," he said. And then, perhaps to urge his search on, "I guess every historian of any topic is always too late."

Let me here, in my words, suggest what he was looking for: a cast of ordinary people who establish the character of a place and set a tone free of pretense and class distinctions, everything carried on in an atmosphere offering escape from the demands of jobs and family, while opening into a congeniality that sloughs off any decision beyond naming one's potion. About the physical structure itself, I'll say more later.

A big fist of a thundercloud rose in the southeast, the sky occluded, and at Eastpoint, a settlement as smack on the Gulf as one can get, we stopped to walk around. Propped in the window of a shut-down tavern was a card with these words: *FOR IVAN — PSALMS 91.* It was a reference to the last hurricane to lay low that piece of the coast. Mo said, "Between hurricanes and developers, my guidebook's getting thinner by the day." He nodded toward the sign. "Here's another page that won't be." Later we looked up the biblical citation:

> Thou shalt not be afraid for the terror by night, nor for the arrow that flieth by day; nor for the pestilence that walketh in darkness; nor for the destruction that wasteth at noonday. There shall no evil befall thee, neither shall any plague come nigh thy dwelling; for he shall give his angels charge over thee. They shall bear thee up in their hands lest thou dash thy foot against a stone.

The tavern owner, though, must have had in mind not that King James Version but some condensed and revised bible of the American developer: "Thou shalt buildeth directly in the path of the terror by night and putteth thy life investment into the hands of angels."

A few steps away was a place, built only an increment or two beyond sticks and straw, easily reconstructed should the next Ivan or Charley or Katrina send it flying across Franklin County. The Eastpoint Oysterhouse and Raw Bar, right beside a shucking house for Apalachicola Bay oysters, squatted under a corrugated metal roof mangled by some destruction that wasteth, the oystertorium in need of little repair beyond a tacking back down by a kid with a twelve-ounce hammer. American architecture should have a place for the deliberately, flimsily, permanently provisional.

Of several hand-lettered signs hanging on the front were two we wanted: *FRESH MULLET* and *SMOKED FISH.* On the back stoop at the edge of St. George Sound, a fellow was just about to pull amberjack from the smoker and mash it into a paste of cream cheese, mayonnaise, and freshly squeezed lemon juice. We sat at a table near him, the damp Gulf air getting damper as the rain moved in, a pelican on a piling continuing to hold out her wings, whether still trying to dry them or, having rethought the weather, trying to wash them, I couldn't determine. Perhaps she was readying herself to be borne up in angelic hands.

The smoker-man set before us two servings of fish dip. "Amber-jack," said Mo after the first taste, "the consummate spread." We ate, he took out his pad to make notes, and both of us felt we'd at last found a temporary survivor from the terrors by night and arrows that flieth by day, and I said so. He asked, "Are you talking about hurricanes or developers?"

The manager, Wally, a retired Ohioan, came out with two glasses of beer, and I asked him what changes he'd seen in his three decades there. "This is a last frontier that's about gone," he said. "They've found us out. Forgotten Coast? Baloney. Today, nothing in Florida with land under it is forgotten." Pointing eastward across the sound, he said, "Out on Dog Island a few weeks back, five acres went for almost a million-and-a-quarter, and that's for a piece of scrub-covered sandbar with no access except a landing strip or whatever shallow-draft boat you've got." He sat down and said, "What do you call a piece of open land in Florida?" A memory? "No." An over-sight? "A future condo hole," he said.

As he talked, a hard rain rattled on the metal roof and the cor-rugations poured off hundreds of rivulets to draw down a watery curtain. The difference between the water on the roof and the humid air under it was distinguishable largely by the noise. I asked Wally whether he still noticed the humidity, and he shrugged. "You know why little old ladies come here?" To find little old men? "They come here to rehydrate their skins. Get one of them good and damp, and she can shuffle off ten years. Who wants to feel a dry sponge when he can have a damp one?" He noticed me scribbling. "You've heard of the Southern beauty? The Miss Americas? That's all about humid air and eating Southern vegetables and wearing sunbonnets — or it used to be, anyway. Ever been to Arizona? Have you seen those old gals out there? The short ones turn into raisins and the big ones look like prunes. No Georgia Peaches in that desert." To slow him down, I stopped writing.

Mo and I went back onto the road to wander into what had turned to drizzle, but he found no further places for his guide. Finally, in Apalachicola, an agreeable town letting its history show to advantage, at the Seafood Grill of 1903, we hung up the day with a glass of rum and a grouper sandwich. My friend, knowing recent hurricane devastation had been worse westward, figured any promise of a watermen's place would be greater farther south, down along the Big Bend, the heart of the Forgotten Coast.

A woman just shy of her middle years, whose eyeliner the rain had redrawn into something like black teardrops, was talking to the bartender. She spoke of a dead-end job, about domestic infelicities, about fading dreams. Without anger, she said, "I got a livin room, but in my life I got no room to live in, and that means I'm doin some wrong livin." Mo, who's written a couple of good country songs, perked up. I was scribbling when he whispered, "Did you get it?" I said maybe she'd been reading too much Gertrude Stein.

We took a third-floor chamber in the old Gibson Inn, a wooden-veranda place immaculately kept, a genuine and pretty piece of an earlier Florida, and I think the quarters lifted his hopes that his quest wasn't too late. The next morning I found him in the dining room, already fed, working in his notebook, a good sign. He was again anticipating his search.

A few miles westward, we checked his assumption about damage beyond Port St. Joe, and indeed found nothing useful to him, so we turned back east, dropping south to pick up Florida 30-A which led us to Indian Pass on St. Vincent Sound, the southernmost point of the Panhandle. And there, in faded clapboard, was another qualifying place, and Mo was smiling.

≫ 4 ≪

Dead Man Stream

THE TRADING POST, a 1929 country store, sat at a T intersection between the Gulf and a large spread of pine forest, and inside the building at the oyster raw-bar lay the center of Indian Pass — not the opening to the sound but a settlement too small to be even an opolis. Among just enough canned goods and bags of pretzels and billed caps to keep the term *general merchandise* more or less accurate were University of Florida football mementos: helmets, pennants, and posters. Also on display was a superannuated, stuffed squirrel we were able to identify by a few bits of fur still clinging to its desiccated skin. Next to it was a little pinnace, aluminum sails full, ingeniously made of cut-up beer cans.

We sat at the short counter, within talking distance of a man shucking oysters. Mo ordered a tray of raw ones, and I asked for a dozen roasted. The shucker, watching me watch him, pulled an oyster from a bucket and said, "You want to open your own?" He tapped the shell with his oyster knife. "All you got to do is make yourself a hole between the shells, then wallow her out." I took the thick blade and began wallowing. I stopped at a dozen, handed them to a broken-toothed man wearing a GATORS cap pulled down far enough to bend over his ears. He slid the oysters into a little oven. I asked if he was the chef. "Chef! Hell, I'm just the oyster guy." Mo opened his dozen as he listened to the shucker who was also the manager, a youngish fellow smart enough, since he wouldn't have time for supper, to put an occasional fresh oyster onto a cracker, sauce it, and eat it.

Intently serious, he talked of the effects of two hurricanes a couple of decades earlier. "Those storms wiped out the oystering and shrimping beds along in here for a while," he said. "That's when the place started turning to tourism. This building where we're at had four feet of water in it. After that, some of those other buildings outside just got ate up by termites." He took another oyster, aligned it on a cracker, doused it, and swallowed it down. "The oystering beds are now about ninety-five percent state owned and about five percent leased out private. It's a different business these days, and people argue about whether state management is better or worse. But for sure, we're now into more and more tourism, but this used to be turpentine country. From the pines. That's all gone."

The oysters came to us on metal beer trays, the established way to serve any Southern mollusk or crustacean, although I'm not yet entirely convinced it's truly the tray that imparts the last bit of flavor. We seasoned them with pepper sauce and went at them slowly, but my friend, observing they were a snack and not a meal, advised against ordering another round. I countered that, while he, now a Gulf Coast Floridian, could get to a raw-bar almost anytime, I could not. What's more, any author of a guide to watermen's hangouts should double-test the offerings of the house; otherwise, there could be judgmental errors impairing future sale of a future book just then on his mind. Alas, my failed logic suggests that even a good and companionable friend — or an honored spouse — may prove to be something less than a foreseeing comrade of the road. As Gus Kubitzki once counseled, "A fried chicken-leg on your plate is worth two plump hens in the coop."

We turned back eastward through the pine-and-palmetto woods punctuated by signs, not clumsy ones like we'd seen yesterday — *WORMS AND BEER* or *YARD SALE IN BASEMENT* — but elegantly painted expressions of another sort: HORSEBACK RIDES ON THE BEACH and DENTISTRY BY THE SEA and VOTE YES ON TOURIST TAX and HALF ACRE FOR SALE WILL SUBDIVIDE. It was my third trip — the first in the '50s — over that section of U.S. 98, and I knew, should there be a fourth, my memory then would no longer recognize the route.

When we came again to Posey's in St. Marks, we stopped — professedly to stretch our legs, and it was only chance that a cup of mullet dip happened to be in the cooler, and when the bartender insisted it had our name on it, we had little choice but to let her set it before us. Rudeness does not benefit a traveler. I asked her, a lively woman from Pennsylvania, why there was ice in the long trough serving as the men's urinal. She said, "That's how we make our light beer." On that score, our beverages were safe.

It may have been the dip that turned Mo contemplative as he began talking about the watermen's taverns he was in search of. Were I to set down all he said, I'd infringe on his book, so I'll only suggest a few of his notions. Such places, once commonly beginning as commercial fishermen's depots and chandleries, are of necessity on the water, at the very source rather than removed to a shopping-center parking lot; that crucial seaside-proximity allows a patron to become, however briefly, a part of the source and to connect to something genuine and historic. The sine qua non of the taverns is that they were initially workplaces where function dominated all else. Often built quickly, cheaply, and solely with an eye on practicality, they are of wood, tar paper, sheet metal, and in their age they manifest a temporariness to remind a patron of a good reason to hoist a glass to a friend (while we can) or as thanks for a good catch. In fact, they even seem to celebrate the ephemeral by turning a derelict dinghy into shelves for bottles and glasses, or by hanging walls with tools of the trade: a harpoon warped by age, a broken oyster-rake. Dangling from the ceiling might be a chicken-wire crab trap rusted to inutility, and on a windowsill, colored-glass net floats. The critic who sees here a quest for such places only as useless nostalgia quite misses the urge in humanity to connect, to find links — in short, to belong to one more of the possible continuums that help us accept our brevity.

We drove on east, that is, inland, leaving the coast only because no continuous stretches of highway exist along it for some 160 miles southward. I'd been told the swampy terrain there had helped keep away highway engineers, but I still imagined I could hear a digital pencil scribing across a sheet of electronic drafting paper up in Tallahassee.

Beyond U.S. 98, Taylor County is mostly Southern forest, the parts of it near the Gulf a ferociously tangled undergrowth affording haven to creatures great and much less so: alligators to no-see-ums (the latter sometimes called "nature's little-bitty bastards," a not inelegant description to those who have encountered them). Taylor and Dixie counties, lying low between the Aucilla and Suwannee rivers, are the two least-trampled areas remaining in Florida. Even Floridians from other parts of the state find those counties to belong to, if not another place, then at least another time, so much so that recent reports of the presence there of ivory-billed woodpeckers cannot be discounted out of hand. In fact, about half of the old specimens now in museums came from the watershed of the Suwannee. Were a developer today to spot one, he'd need to shoot it on sight to keep an endangered species from putting a halt to his machinery.

Some years earlier, I'd stopped at an oyster house on the highway just outside Perry, the Taylor County seat. I had to ring a bell for someone inside to push a button to unlock the front door, as if the place were a high-rise apartment in Manhattan. When I stepped in, an old shucker cried out in a near falsetto voice, "The finest people in the world walk through our door." I thought it a damn jolly welcome. When the next customer came in, the same greeting. And the next, and the next. By the time I left, half-crazed from the greetings, I'd noticed that all the finest people were of the same race despite the large percentage of blacks living nearby. No one would confess it, but the buzzer was a Negro filter. I'd never encountered such before, and that one had survived long past the time of overt jim crow practices.

To my surprise, Deal's Famous Oyster House was still there. We pulled in to see whether the buzzer also remained. It did not, although a little sign inside yet welcomed the finest people in the world. So early in the afternoon, the Famous Oyster House was empty of other customers, but we got assurance some of the finest people in the world were now also black. I should say here, on certain issues of sensitivity, Mo often asked the questions because his Plantation dialect didn't immediately call forth the word *Yankee*.

The mullet dip wasn't ready, the hour was too late for an oyster sandwich with a side of Deal's swamp cabbage, those two details suggesting a lack of foresight in a particular decision about a second tray of roasted oysters at Indian Pass. We settled for colas and a little conversation. Mo talked of his quest: "This place is almost remote enough to qualify, but it's too clean. Almost sterile. Look at this bar — it doesn't look like any toasts have ever been spilled on it." He ran his hand across the top as if to feel for stains. Perhaps, I suggested, his requirements were becoming a little overrefined.

In Taylor County there is only a single looping highway — although under differing numbers — that swings down into the low forest and marshes to reach the Gulf, and that's what we followed a few miles out of Perry after a dish of ice cream to lock down any loose oysters or migrating fish-dip. Good digestion demanded it. A sense of remoteness came over us, and it increased when we came upon a large red-haired thing lying dead beside the road: a wild boar with long, bloodied tusks still in a snarl. The destruction feral hogs wreak on forest life across the country makes such a death almost cause for celebration, in spite of the animal being a more beautiful, powerful-looking creature than its domesticated forebears. What their hooves don't crush, their snouts root out.

Several miles beyond, condo Florida reappeared at Keaton Beach, an upthrust of new, multi-storey buildings, most of them unoccupied until the snowbirds began appearing. I asked Mo how many days a year Keaton Beach had more than a busload of residents. "Maybe half the year," he said. "Maybe less. But that's likely to change. No — it's certain to change."

The road returned to the interior at the Blue Creek inlet and followed a ridge just high enough to lift us a couple of feet above

the coastal swamp where again something like ancient Florida surrounded us, although the grand longleaf pines had been logged out
and replaced with fast-growing slash pines of the timber plantations.
As a Black Angus is to a bison, so slash pine is to longleaf, as utility
is to nobility.

Just before sundown we left the forest that was destined to become
sacks for toting home frozen chicken potpies and kitty litter. We
came into Steinhatchee, an erstwhile commercial fishing port nes-
tled along the river of the same name, recently spanned by a new
and cleanly designed concrete-bridge arching high enough to give
an excellent view extending two miles westward to Deadman Bay
and the Gulf beyond. Despite the Germanic-looking first syllable
(rhymes with *seen*), the name Steinhatchee comes from Creek Indian
words loosely translated as "dead man stream."

The village, once a turpentine camp, gains its pleasant appearance from an especial authenticity and the modest way it lies in a
crook of the narrow river dividing it from Jena (usually, JEEN-ah)
which was a string of waterfront and roadside buildings and several
small homes along streets with names like Mullet and Shark. A few
dilapidated fish-houses, where the catch used to arrive for shipment
elsewhere, lined the north side of the river and gave it regional character sufficient to distinguish it from, say, a town in Iowa. But the
last Steinhatchee fish-house had just gone out of business.

The place was neither quaint nor notably historic, its architecture
humdrum, post–World War II stuff. Entwined higgledy-piggledy in
its dozen or so streets, not all of them paved, were some diminutive
seasonal bungalows admixed with house trailers, most in deplorable
condition. The quirky layout of streets was a grid of short lanes often
interrupted by lots overgrown or stacked with unneedless stuff, or
by marsh greenage trying to return. The intersection of Center and
Fourteenth streets, to name one, were it there, would sit in the middle of a pond. Beyond the riverfront, small commercial buildings —
four cafés, gas station, bar, motel, boat shop — were sprinkled about
so that the place with its live oaks appeared to merge seamlessly

into the piney woods. Steinhatchee was unincorporated, unplanned, unpretentious, and for years unwanted by anybody other than its native residents, although two new buildings and a resort, each on the river, were evidence that the unwanting was a thing of the past.

To listen to the inhabitants, as we began doing that evening, was to learn that a few years ago — some said three years, others said four, but nobody went further back than half a generation — it was not the bay that deserved the name Deadman but Steinhatchee itself. "It was a near ghost town," a woman in Perry had told us. "And that was just dandy with people there. Around here, all this is old-time Cracker country, especially down there, and lots of those folks wanted nothing more than to be left alone. The last thing they wanted was for condo builders to find them out." She paused. "You've heard about the illegal stuff?" I must have looked blank. "No? Hang around, and sooner or later you will."

Those words were to change the nature of our quest.

⅀ 5 ⅀

Road to Nowhere

THE FIRST APPEARANCE in Steinhatchee of a new economy arrived benignly enough. Just above the right angle the river makes on its last miles was Steinhatchee Landing, an upscale if small resort built in among the native trees, the houses clustered, the architecture derived from classic Cracker and Victorian styles, albeit air-conditioned and hot-tubbed. The Landing set a standard for intelligent and unobtrusive innovation. Looking like a cross between a Southern neighborhood in the era of hitching posts and a piney-woods encampment, the place fit in, even if some of its visitors perhaps did not.

In small-town America anywhere, change will draw out a few loud, wrathfully frightened voices, usually those who prefer to see a place die rather than transform, but the Landing apparently entered loosely organized Steinhatchee with at least some grudging local appreciation for its contributions to a restructured economy. And, as the woman in Perry had mysteriously added, "The money for *that* enterprise was legal, as far as I know."

On our second evening in Steinhatchee, at Fiddler's Restaurant by the river, Mo and I made a supper of oyster stew and black-beans-and-rice, and finished with a glass of rum that drew us into a reminiscence overheard by a fellow in search of conversation. Our rambling took a useful turn when he couldn't answer a question I asked. By way of apology, he said, "I could write a book about all I don't know. What about yourself?" I said that was how I made my living. He didn't take me literally and began talking, talking to the point of letting a feline or two out of the bag — just what a reporter needs.

Although not a native, the fellow often came into the county to tend "accounts" of a kind he was vague about. He said, "The main use of land here is to treat it like a commodity. You know, like stock you hope to buy low and sell high. Then you take your profit and go get a yacht or you invest in building a new condo somewhere else. I'm not talking about the locals. This is about outsiders from across state or across the country. Half the property here that's selling is going to speculators — mom-and-dad speculators mostly. They don't want to move here. I mean, look at this place. Hey, if you don't fish or hunt, what do you do? Read a book?" He spoke the last sentence as he might ask, "Commit suicide?"

Mo said we'd heard about differences in zoning between Steinhatchee and Jena. "I don't know anything reliable about that, except anything goes in Jena." He wet his whistle and ignored a question from me. "Today you can call this place Little America. They're doing the American Agenda — profit at any price. They ought to change the name Jena to Grabola or this place to Hatchascheme. But at least it's not on the Road to Nowhere anymore."

For the third time that day, mention of the "Road to Nowhere" came up. I was beginning to suspect the phrase might not be a metaphor of an old, doomed economy. Mo asked what it was. "Cross the bridge," the man said as he headed for the door, "and take the road south. See if you can figure out why it's there and why it's paved."

There being no true watermen's taverns in Steinhatchee or Jena, my congenial way-fellow was willing, perhaps because of his abiding interest in writing a mystery, to pursue for a couple of days a different topic, one promising intrigue.

The next morning at breakfast in the Bridge End Café, I asked for his help in marking the Black-Eyed Pea Line, the northernmost extent of cafés serving as a matter of course those esteemed members of what Gus Kubitzki termed the Fraternal and Protective Order of Nature's Little Guys: raisins, capers, olives, peppercorns. Today, it's more useful to any traveler wanting to honor the Southern regional menu to know the demarcation of the B-EPL than the Mason-Dixon Line. I told him the Pea Line didn't reach as far north as the Grits Line, and that was a shame, given the greater nutrient value of a legume over hominy. After requesting the waitress add black-eyed peas to my eggs and grits, I heard loudly from the kitchen, "He wants *what* with his eggs?" evidence the cook might be from Kankakee or Lompoc and really should not yet be entrusted with the preparation of anything Southern beyond warming a MoonPie.

Across the river, we went south until we were encompassed by alterations of marsh with low, almost impenetrable undergrowth of cord and salt-joint grasses. Yet, running through it all were twelve miles of good, wide pavement, straight as a drag strip and showing black streaks of spinning tires. The asphalt, County Route 361, paralleled the coast a bit over a mile distant, but Deadman Bay wasn't visible until the road turned into a sand lane for a few hundred yards, then ceased altogether; from there we could see a far shoreline perforated by thousands of inlets and baffled by hundreds of islets and keys. Okay, I said, if this road isn't for dragsters, who's it for? What's it for? Mo shook his head and drew his words out. "Something's going on down in here."

References to the "Road to Nowhere" were as numerous as ones to the "No-Name Storm," so we tried to hook the two together. The big blow of 1993 wasn't a hurricane, not technically anyway, but it was, a carpenter told us, "one mother of a tropical storm and tidal surge that plastered all of the Big Bend of the Gulf." In Steinhatchee, it hammered many of the older buildings and sent them downriver or flying off into the woods and quite literally became the high-water mark in current Steinhatchee history and a central reference point in most citizens' memories. Stories were set BS or AS — Before Storm or After. To eliminate it from their past would produce a different Steinhatchee, perhaps one less able to face the flux of new people arriving, because in a way, the storm prepared the village for change as a bulldozer does a construction site.

But what did violent weather have to do with a road wandering off into the middle of a sea marsh?

Up on the main highway through Dixie County, we went into Cross City, the courthouse town on the edge of the coastal swamp. There, in the library, a former store in a homely shopping center, Mo sat down at a computer to search while I talked to a librarian, a sad-faced woman four or five steps away from the back-half of a hearse. Where, I asked, could we find material of any sort on the Road to Nowhere or on Steinhatchee or Jena? Although the hamlets were only fourteen direct miles west, their isolation made them appear, even to up-county natives, somehow remote, and the mere mention of the names seemed to make people edgy. The librarian said in surprise as if I'd asked about Yachats, Oregon, or Slapout, Oklahoma, "Why, I lived in Steinhatchee for a while!" Then she seemed to catch herself. "But I never learned much about it. My memory wouldn't be trustworthy anymore." She did a charade of trying to recollect some innocent tidbit to toss to me so I'd go away. "I do remember we were so poor then. Everyone was so poor. I just don't know what to suggest to you."

Mo also found nothing. I told him the librarian knew more than she was willing to share. We were beginning to notice how a conversation would tumble merrily along until we'd bring up the Road to Nowhere. Abruptly, it would be time to get back to work, to pick up the kid, to open the mail. I mentioned to Mo three movies where a stranger rides into town, asks a couple of wrong questions, and never rides out again. He said, "That puts me right at ease here on the edge of Deadman Bay."

At the Dixie County Courthouse, we again came up empty. Then we drove on to the Taylor County Courthouse in Perry where, at last, somebody admitted knowing something about the Road to Nowhere. A clerk took us into a side room and pulled down two large criminal dockets. In them we found just enough clues to improve our questions and to lead us to the right places to ask them: a used bookstore, a certain bar, a particular café. Out came an item here, a document there, a recollection, a dodged question, a paragraph in a newspaper, a magazine article. Slowly, ever so slowly, the story of the Road to Nowhere began to emerge. It was a tale of two counties.

6

Bales of Square Mullet

S OMETIME IN THE EARLY 1970s, memories varied on the year, Steinhatchee became an entry point and entrepôt for large bales of Colombian marijuana smuggled in from the Gulf to be trucked to cities all over the East. The residents called it "pot hauling" or simply "hauling." Although Steinhatchee wasn't the only coastal community thereabouts so engaged, its isolation, river access, myriad coastal inlets, and position between two county jurisdictions gave it advantages.

Because the "trade" was spread throughout a community of linked families, it became difficult for anyone in Steinhatchee not to know about it and dangerous to talk about it. The safest course was to pretend it wasn't happening, and in that way smuggling bore resemblance to moonshining in the southern Appalachians during Prohibition, where snitching could be more dangerous than involvement. In a nutshell, the setup was this: so-called bird-dog boats motored out to a mother ship offshore to pick up bales of marijuana and haul them up the Steinhatchee River to a waiting truck.

Many residents figured the dope was going to city people who deserved what their excessive incomes could buy, those urbanites who were responsible for the quaaludes reaching Steinhatchee teenagers. (Parents considered ludes the real evil.) What's more, native inhabitants saw the trade as giving them at last their fair measure of American prosperity which for so long had eluded the two remote villages. In the late '60s, a fisherman might earn ten-thousand dollars a year for the laborious and often dangerous work of pulling in nets of mullet and other fish, an income he (males worked virtually all the boats) could match or exceed with a single good night of moving dope in the '70s. Truckers could collect twice that with a load, and men at the next level made even more.

Instead of a load of wet, slimy, cold fish pulled up into a skiff, now the catch was dry bales known as "square mullet" that could be stacked and transported as easily as packets of twenty-dollar bills. After all, this was an economically depressed area open to desperate measures. In the late '60s, the Cross City school-board was suspected of burning down its high school to collect the insurance and selling the salvage for its own personal compensation. And there was a billing of insurance companies for rebuilding after a hurricane, reconstruction never undertaken; when a grand jury was impaneled to investigate, it sought instead to disband itself. And what about the brother of a county commissioner who shot down a deputy sheriff to keep from being arrested for drunkenness, only to be acquitted? These were crimes by white men, but a black man found guilty of selling ten grams of marijuana for twenty-five dollars drew a sentence of five years in prison. One of the stories Mo and I turned up, this one in a 1983 *Harper's* article by John Rothchild, said, "The judge . . . remarked that a person who peddles small amounts is, in a way, worse than someone who hauls it by the ton." It was such logic, in an isolated terrain ideal for clandestine undertakings, that allowed the trade to flourish. But increasing brazenness eventually drew the attention of state and federal agents, and pressure on local lawmen intensified enough for them at last to arrest a hauler. He was from Kansas.

Before long, the smugglers found it more efficient to bring the cannabis to shore not by little bird-dog boats but by airplane. The Dixie County Commission at first leased the airport to known smugglers and then built a wide and straight highway through a marshy remoteness toward a coastline (the Road to Nowhere) it never reached. It was a landing strip for light planes bearing loads of square mullet, a name no longer particularly accurate, unless somewhere there were winged mullet.

With the addition of cocaine to shipments, the packages began to change. But, over time, it was another innovation that became fractious, and it led to trouble: Cubans and other Hispanics became increasingly involved and created rifts among Floridians living in an area never known for ethnic tolerance. When the haulers began hiding bales of dope in the swamp as insurance they would be paid, the Cubans responded by cutting off the cash altogether and making the stashed bales the entire payment, and the former fishermen countered by setting aside yet more bales.

As wealth grew, so with it did envy. Boats, for whatever purpose, got bigger and fancier, ratty house-trailers turned into new double-wides or real houses, and money filled some pockets fuller than others. One defendant later explained in court the source of his $125,000 in cash by saying, "Like, when I go home at night, I throw my change into a glass-jar-type thing, and it accumulates over the years."

A man, who as a boy had cleaned real mullet on the docks of a group later deeply involved in the smuggling, finally agreed to put on a drug agent's wire to gain for himself and his brother immunity from prosecution. Soon after informing, he moved — escaped — to Texas and opened a restaurant. Apparently no one knows exactly how many tons of marijuana came into the United States through Taylor and Dixie counties in those years, but it's certain there will be readers of this sentence, living far distant from Deadman Bay, who have toked Steinhatchee stash. (One may ask how such blatant activity could operate so long beyond the scope of the law.)

In the Taylor County Courthouse, Mo and I read in only two of the criminal-court ledgers more than a hundred names of men charged with some phase of smuggling or trafficking. About half the names were Hispanic; many of the rest were local people, including one county commissioner who was convicted and served forty-two months in prison only to be released, whereupon, shortly before we arrived, he had run again for office but was defeated.

Eventually, the trials became so numerous they had to be held in a half-dozen out-county towns, and the convictions for a spell put a noticeable drain on Steinhatchee males. A clerk in Perry said, "I don't think much of the drug money did any lasting good down there, but it sure helped some lawyers up in this end of Taylor."

❧ 7 ❧

A Taste of Manatee

O NE MORNING, Mo and I followed our usual practice of going to a café for breakfast and letting a chance conversation with whoever turned up to direct our day. In a village, things can assemble rather quickly like that.

On my travels, especially ones I write about, I'm forever aware of the difficulty of learning enough to report accurately in a limited time. Being an outsider keeps me away from some stories but also lets me in on others when a native sees his anecdote will soon leave town with the stranger. For this reason, I ask people appearing in my books to check the accuracy of what I've written about them before it goes into print. (Once in a while, though, that isn't feasible; in those instances, I may change a name but only with full admission to you, the vigilant reader.) That morning, we heard a story from a man unafraid to tell it and willing later to stand by it.

At the Lynn-Rich Restaurant on the east side of Steinhatchee, we watched a large man eating a slice of pie and speaking earnestly to another fellow who seemed uneasy about whatever the topic was. Between them lay a thick binder of blueprints. Although they sat several tables away from us, it wasn't difficult to hear sentences the big man emphasized, ones he clearly considered especially pithy: "Five percent of five million is a nice piece of chump change." And later, "Look, at any point I'll sell out." Later still, "Share the pie, and you eventually get more pie." Since he'd already eaten his pie, I assumed he wasn't speaking literally. And then the words that drew us to him: "If you want to develop land anywhere, you'd better know how to do an end run around a city council or a county commission." It seemed evident that a piece of the future of Steinhatchee was getting laid out between a slice of pie and two cups of thin coffee.

After an hour, the quiet man left and the other gathered up his documents. We walked over, and Mo asked if he knew whether the village had a sewage system. It was a leading question, a test question. I expected the man to rebuff us and make a hurried exit, but he opened his binder and explained a little about the problems of sewage in an area of porous limestone and abundant springs, where streams, including the Steinhatchee River, can have miles of subterranean flow. One current sewage method there — septic fields of mounded earth — was barely adequate for only a few scattered homes.

The man, Charlie Kinnard, was in his late sixties, about six feet tall, his balding head cropped close as was his white beard. He was articulate, capable of turning a phrase in the Southern manner, possessed of an affability that appeared to match a capacity to intimidate should he need to. He'd been in Florida for seven years and lived now across the state. "I'm a Tennessee hillbilly," he said, but later clarified that he grew up in Nashville and had attended a prestigious prep school. He'd married more than once and divorced more than once.

To my surprise, Kinnard began explaining amiably his proposed development for the area, being quite specific about where it was to be. As he laid out blueprints, maps, aerial photos, and photographs, he said, "Two and a half years ago I'd never heard of Steinhatchee, but right now I've got approval for four twenty-five-storey condos. That's four-hundred units." I said he could house more people than now lived in Steinhatchee and Jena combined. "After those units, I want to do even more. You know the Road to Nowhere? That's a paved road waiting for somebody to use it, make it go somewhere. How about two ten-storey condos — two-hundred-fifty units — out there?"

Mo said we'd heard there was a thirty-two-foot height limit on new construction. "That's Steinhatchee. Across the river in Dixie County, they've got no limit. There's already a six-storey building going up now. And I've got questions about how well it's being done." As he talked, he pointed out each location on a map and held up sketches of his proposed buildings. "If all my units get built, they'll be fifty percent of the tax base in Dixie County. That's pretty persuasive."

Kinnard closed the binder and lowered his voice and said ominously, "Step outside." As we followed him to his car — a sunbleached top-of-the-line Central European model, one of two he had there — Mo whispered to me, "Is this the part where the Yankee asking too many questions takes a little ol ride back into the swamp?"

Tapping the hood ornament, Kinnard said, "She's got a lot of miles on her. I want a Bentley." He shook his head at his remark and added, "I've got as much junk as a white man ought to have. These plans of mine, when you get down to it, they're plans to build a fund for more toys."

He looked around, measured our interest in his pursuits, and said just above a whisper, "The difficulty here is with local contractors. Their attitudes — it's all small-town stuff. I'm not in the family, and I don't want to be. I just want reliability and quality and no messing behind my back." Moments later, as if to illustrate, a local builder pulled his pickup in next to Kinnard's automobile and blocked an exit. To the bulky, tough-faced man, Charlie said, "You're in a driveway." The other said, "Is it your business?" and went into the café. Soon he was back out to move his truck; after he'd done so, he said menacingly to Kinnard, "Does that satisfy you?" and he stepped close for a further exchange of theories about the duties incumbent with tidy parking. Neither man, each big enough to hold his ground easily, gave an inch. The contractor headed toward his coffee but paused to call over his shoulder, "You're an idiot."

Kinnard, who still had not altered his casual lean against his car, smiled at us and said calmly, "You see what I mean? You can't work with stupidity. One time it's a fool, and somewhere else it's a fricking environmentalist crying about a frog — or a manatee." Still smiling, he said, "Have you ever eaten manatee?" Good god, I said, everybody loves a manatee! I said Christopher Columbus, after seeing his first manatees, wrote in his log he'd seen mermaids (they weren't so beautiful as painted). With a nod, Kinnard said, "Sure, we love them because their taste is between a bald eagle and a spotted owl." Trying to realign the conversation, I made a display of writing in my notebook. Kinnard watched for a moment, then looked at Mo and said, "Why save something that's too dumb to get out of the way?" I wrote that down too.

As he left, he invited us to come by his condo site to see what he had going. The next morning, Mo had to return home, and not long after, Q rejoined me. The two of us drove out to view the location where the high-rise condos were to go. We found Kinnard inside a semitrailer he'd set up as an office in a bulldozed area of low-lying land I'd have thought too soggy to set a fishing shack on, let alone a high-rise. Among the few jaggedly broken trees still standing, palmettos and scrub growth were trying to return as if to heal the stripped earth. He greeted us warmly, surprised I'd followed through with a visit. I asked what would happen when potential investors or residents learned they couldn't see the Gulf three miles distant from the site. "That's one reason we're going up," he said. "The footprint will be small, but the view big. I brought a seventy-foot crane out here and took pictures from the top of it to give people an idea of the view they'll have from upper floors."

We talked about construction, problems of sewage created by several hundred new residents, "skyprints" that block views from the ground, the low and porous land, the effect of a changed tax base, hurricane bait. He planned to hire outside builders whenever he could. "You saw the problem yesterday in the parking lot," he said, paused, then added, "I'll tell you something." Lowering his voice, he stepped close, although no one else was within a half mile of us. "That contractor yesterday — I could have shot him. Legally. Maybe you don't know it, but Florida's got new handgun legislation."

He was speaking of the so-called "stand your ground" law, propagated by the National Rifle Association in Florida with the idea of spreading it across the rest of the nation, as the organization had a couple of decades earlier with the "right-to-carry" gun laws. I was confused about the reasoning of Florida voters: many were recently enraged by a judge who granted a natural death to a brain-dead woman, yet now they were content to permit the living to shoot it out over a parking space. None of this, of course, came into our conversation. Q was becoming apprehensive and was secretly pulling on the back of my shirt to get it to leave.

In words of utter calmness, Kinnard explained how a few months earlier he had dealt with a neighboring tenant, widely known as a scofflaw who kept trespassing on commercial property the developer owned on the Atlantic coast. One night, he and a friend (a potential witness) got the trespasser — a big, meaty guy holding title to adjacent commercial land — and *his* backup to make threats as the four men argued over boundaries. Demonstrating for us, Kinnard became dramatically deliberate as he acted out the incident, using the bulldozed scrub as his stage. Q was as uneasy as I've ever seen her.

After listening to threats from the trespasser, Kinnard alerted his own witness to observe closely. Then, for us, just as he did that night, he took two slow steps backward and reached inside his shirt to demonstrate how he'd drawn his .22-caliber pistol and shot the man in the shoulder. Kinnard said, "The fool yelled out to his goon, 'Goddamnit! He shot me!' He couldn't believe it."

The police showed up, filled out some reports, and that was about it, except for one officer saying, "We ought to arrest you for poor marksmanship." No further investigation, no prosecution. The trespasser's body-mass took the bullet and saved him, but — even had the man died — Kinnard knew his own safety was secure within his new legal right. (Ah, the American pistol! That old righter-of-wrongs now become a wronger-of-rights, such as the right to judicial process.)

Looking at Q, Kinnard added, "I'd rather be judged by twelve than carried by six. Wouldn't you now?" While still pulling at the back of my shirt, she said it was time for supper.

≫ 8 ≪

Playground for the Rich and Famous

O N MY LAST DAY IN STEINHATCHEE, I wanted to ask somebody with expertise whether the new money from realty transactions, much of it coming from outside speculators, was likely to imperil the long-established ways of life there. With no shortage of real-estate offices in the hamlet, I picked one at random and walked in. I'll not describe the people of this encounter for a reason that will be obvious; perhaps their words will let you see them.

A woman, a former Californian, greeted me warmly and lessened her warmth only slightly when I said I wasn't looking for property, but I did have a few questions. "Okay," she said. I asked when the realty boom around Steinhatchee began, and she considered: "No more than about five years ago, I think." Not wishing to spend time with a man who wasn't going to be a customer, her responses became shorter, so I tried priming the pump with a debatable observation. I said it seemed to me that recent history along the river had been shaped, for better or worse, by the No-Name Storm and — avoiding the word *smuggling* — illicit importations, and lately, overwhelmingly, by rapid real-estate development. The woman shook her head. "I haven't been here that long." It was one more dodge.

Another agent, a native, a woman with a pleasant face but a fully charged load of suppressed anger behind it, interrupted forcefully from across the small office. "Look," she said, "Steinhatchee's going to become the playground for the rich and famous. Clearwater, Miami — they're used up. Where are they going to go now?" She stopped abruptly. "I can't talk about it. I've got work to do."

Trying a more oblique approach, I turned again to the first woman to ask whether there were density regulations in Taylor County. Her answers were perfunctory but polite. "Yes." Were there city limits? "No." Was there a formal town council? "There's a project board with regular meetings." What about incorporation? "It's inevitable."

The other agent, perhaps further inflamed by my honoring her wish not to talk about it, cried out, "Hey!" as she rose from her chair. "Somebody's going to make the money! Somebody's got to sell it! I grew up here! Who's got a better right?" She sat down again. "I don't have time for this."

There I was, angering people in "stand your ground" gun-law territory. Were such questions provocation enough to plug me? In a somewhat theatrical way, I picked up my things to leave and said I was just trying to understand a place I found quite interesting, especially its history. The agent who had no time launched into a topic that had not come up. She said, again with more volume than required for a small room, "We can make an X, you know! We can sign our names! We're not hicks! You know, we're proud! People from outside —" She caught herself and stopped. She looked directly at me. Her interior serpent was coiled and ready to strike. "You go talking about changes," she said. "I can tell you what changed things here." She waited for me to ask, and I did. "The net ban," she seethed. "The net ban is what changed everything! Those people will be the end of us! *The end!*"

"Those people" were not smugglers, realty speculators, or develop-at-any-cost builders. They were not snowbirds or the guy who bulldozes a lot into the forest for a rental house-trailer having a septic system made from a fifty-gallon oil barrel with holes punched in it. "Those people" were the National Marine Fisheries Service and the Florida Fish and Wildlife Conservation Commission.

A decade earlier, a constitutional amendment to modify certain outdated fishing practices — ones clearly shown to be destructive to the sustainability of the resource and, eventually, to people whose livelihoods depended on fishing — was put to a statewide vote.

Although the measure didn't win in Steinhatchee, nearly seventy percent of the rest of Florida approved it.

The agent rolled on so furiously I couldn't take down her words fast enough, but the argument was this: the net ban had made earning a living from fishing impossible, and that was forcing natives to sell their land to outsiders. The whole thing was a scheme by various government entities that didn't care a hoot about protecting fish or fishermen. No, their secret plan was to take away private property. But she didn't want to talk about it.

9

In There Own Sweat

THE REAL-ESTATE AGENT'S ALLEGATIONS sent me to a telephone to call a field office of the Florida Fish and Wildlife Conservation Commission up in Perry to ask for an interview with an agent or two. The next day Q and I drove to the edge of Perry where the Commission had quarters in a trailer and a couple of outbuildings. We talked first with Karen Parker, retired from the Army and now the Public Information Coordinator, before she introduced us to Lieutenant Bruce Cooper, the patrol supervisor, a graduate of Auburn University and a former outfielder on its baseball team. Both of the agents, in their early middle-years, were personable, calm, and open to any questions I had.

Among Parker's duties was assisting people affected by the modified fishing regulations (widely but inaccurately called the "net ban"), then more than a decade old. She listened closely before responding to my questions, weighed her replies, and was unafraid to admit when she didn't have an answer but always added she would try to find it. The changes in regulations not only had been voted in by a significant margin but had been upheld later by the Florida Supreme Court. Parker, speaking of the earlier, looser regulation of nets, said, "A lot of Floridians thought outdated fishing-regulations were killing Florida. This is the fishing capital of the world. Most people could see what was happening to a key resource."

The new measures prohibited only *certain kinds* of nets, mainly ones that entangle fish. Such nets, some of them the length of six football fields, are quite effective at ensnaring not just mullet — the

203

targeted fish — but also a couple of dozen other species, even game fish like grouper, pompano, or sea trout. Mullet, sleek-bodied vegetarians, migrate in enormous schools and thereby become highly vulnerable to massive commercial nets — that is to say, vulnerable to harvesting in numbers beyond their rate of reproduction. With the earlier gill and trammel nets, sustainability was rapidly declining, as became evident from what already had happened on up the Atlantic coast at least as far as North Carolina: over the last several decades, the number of mullet and species preying upon them had so decreased that commercial fisheries dependent on mullet were collapsing.

Texas was the first Gulf Coast state to outlaw old-style entangling nets, then Florida. At the time of our conversation, Alabama, not often known for its environmental foresight, was about to make a similar change because of the demonstrable evidence that modified nets help increase the number of mullet — once the staple fish of Florida — and species dependent on them.

Cooper said, "This spring I saw the largest school of mullet I've ever seen, and it's due to the new nets. And that increase has happened even with some illegal fishing still going on." He nodded toward a fenced area. "Right now, over there, we've got two illegal nets we picked up just recently. The technology we have today to apprehend outlaw fishing has surpassed the capacity to harvest illegally. Without governmental enforcement, certain fish would be seriously reduced and others of them would be gone."

He took us inside the fenced area and showed us two big rolls of entangling nets. I asked who still used such things. "Mostly older men going out at night," Cooper said. "When we come up to their boats, they tell us the fish jumped into the boat because those guys know courts require evidence of an illegal net *being used.* Just having possession of the fish isn't illegal."

Despite the misleading name, the new regulation did not ban nets, but it did require reduced size of both the total area of a net and the openings in the mesh, and it limited the use of nets to only two at a time. Those changes necessitated more hand casts, a bodily demanding task that made some fishermen no longer want to expend the effort, while others simply resented having to change their old ways.

An opinion I'd heard the day before now made sense: a man who once used the old netting method told me he thought the young were too soft to go after mullet and the old were now too down in the back for it. His words seemed to reflect what I'd encountered that morning at Pouncey's Restaurant in Perry where a woman supervising several teenagers on an outing wore a T-shirt embossed with:

WORK HARD!
NO ONE EVER DROWN
IN THERE OWN SWEAT

Karen Parker said of the coastal town forty miles south of Steinhatchee, "People in Cedar Key have switched to clamming with some success. And the University of Florida offers a course in developing commercial clamming-beds that can produce a harvest in eighteen months. It's a renewable resource. They call it Clamalot. But I haven't heard yet of anyone in Steinhatchee taking part."

Cedar Key — once a port on an early cross-Florida railroad and a center for the manufacture of wooden pencils — has an economic and cultural history quite different from the more isolated and insulated Steinhatchee from whence much of the timber for pencils came. (Many an American learned to write with a stick of Steinhatchee forest in hand.)

"The talk today in Cedar Key isn't about a net ban," Parker said. "People there are more concerned about preventing pollutants from wiping out the economic advances they've made with clamming. They see their situation much differently today." She paused to phrase her words. "When people have to start changing established ways, it's difficult anywhere, and some communities resist it — maybe I should say *feel* it — more than others. But when it comes to the new fishing regulations, there's help all around to make the transition easier."

Resistance to transition in Steinhatchee cropped up one night a couple of years earlier when a conservation agent, out of uniform, went into the local lounge, a place where, during the day, I'd seen elderly women playing Scrabble. Recognized, the agent caught a barrage of hostility and was soon dragged into the parking lot and beaten before he could break free and cross the road to the river. He leaped in and swam to the other side. There, a young woman saw the battered man and, in apparent sympathy, offered him a lift. She promptly returned him to the parking lot where he was battered again. He recovered, and the new regulations remained unchanged, but he'd provided an evening's diversion for men who preferred altercation to alteration.

Various agencies created several programs to assist commercial fishermen affected by the new provisions, including a standing offer to buy their old, illegal nets, as well as unemployment benefits and job retraining in both aquaculture and agriculture. People elsewhere around the Gulf who shifted to clamming or crabbing could bring in good pay, and so could those fishing for mullet with redesigned nets, but they were people who believed "no one ever drown in there own sweat."

Still, at night in Deadman Bay, violators were going out in their bird-dog boats, a number of them motivated as much by the thrill of risk as by a quest for money. After all, when darkness comes down in the Steinhatchee country, some people can't come up with much to amuse themselves, and a game of cat-and-mouse on the water or a fox-and-hound high-speed chase over dirt roads through the timber plantations can provide stories for several evenings at the lounge. It was almost as good as beating up a conservation agent. And, in a fashion similar to Appalachian moonshiners of another era, law versus outlaw was a contest where a hot-blooded fellow could try to make himself into a local legend.

The Steinhatchee story, as I came to see it, was of a village being changed not by a misnamed "net ban" but by a juggernaut of increasing human population and the refusal of people both there and elsewhere to set and follow reasonable guidelines for realty development. The true enemy of Steinhatchee was not some governmental agency imagined to be after private land; it was blind stubbornness and — even more — greed. In those ways, many of the residents themselves were active participants in a full-momentum — if doomed — pursuit of the quick-and-easy.

My guess is that Steinhatchee and Jena were headed toward a new order — one initially more prosperous, at least for outside investors — but one that would soon enough further impoverish their lives emotionally and spiritually, because the forces they were embracing rarely accommodate native traditions and values like those developed locally over generations. But if anger, hopeless resignation, anomie, and unconsidered acceptance of the steamrollers of contemporary Florida could be replaced by common sense, imagination, and wise leadership, a seemingly implacable new American economy might be turned to serve the people.

But first they would have to show a resilience capable of forming a future rather than being flattened by one. Instead of simply reviling aquaculture, how about trying it? Instead of living beyond the law, how about finding the benefits of living within it? And what about considering the implications of Steinhatchee Landing where native traditions of northern Florida Cracker architecture had been reinterpreted sympathetically along the river to create new jobs and a sound pillar in the local economy?

The right choice in Steinhatchee, I concluded, was not to continue fighting to resurrect doomed ways but to shape a future to honor and enhance the most salubrious aspects of their past where lay innovative avenues rather than roads to nowhere. The choice at Deadman Bay, as across the nation, was whether to comprehend and reshape history or to continue the current course and become history.

Maybe it was even beginning to happen. In Perry, I picked up a leaflet with the headline

JUST SAY NO!
NO BOMBING RANGE
NO MISSILES ON OUR NATURE COAST

Below was this: "Save our health, the environment, our homes, and our property values!" The sheet was a response to a plan to move the bombing range at Eglin Air Force Base east of Pensacola (one of the largest forested military bases in the world) a couple of hundred miles southeast to the timberlands north of Steinhatchee. The leaflet said, "We have a new developer in Taylor County who stands to get rich quick if he can pull off a land-swap deal with the military. We get the bombs and he gets the beach."

❧ 10 ❧

The Truth About Bobbie Cheryl

A COUPLE OF DAYS EARLIER, on our last evening together in Steinhatchee, I asked Mo before he headed home whether his quest for watermen's taverns was succeeding. I said we hadn't come upon any in Steinhatchee, and the most likely spot for one there was a lounge where ladies played Scrabble in the afternoon and conservation agents got thrashed at night. "I think we hit Steinhatchee too late," he said. "We missed out on the fish-houses and the whole culture connected to them. Maybe I'll just write a book called *Too Late*. That should about cover it all."

I suggested his revised title was a reminder we'd better get ourselves up to North Carolina before we'd be saying the same about Bobbie Cheryl's Anchor Inn. Hadn't the dream of that Great Good Place helped us through those sorry days of Phuddom? We owed it an honorary visit. After all, Miss Bobbie Cheryl wasn't going to live forever.

"Miss?" he said, surprised. "Bobby Sherrill's no miss. He's a guy." Mo looked at me as if I'd just popped out with something about Shakespeare's latest novel. He spoke kindly, taking his time to let me down gently. "Didn't you ever catch on? We needed a dream, an escape. Bobby Sherrill's Anchor Inn was my invention. I concocted it to save us. It was an anchor for a couple of guys adrift on a sea of near insanity." He put his hand on my shoulder, as he does from time to time. "And it worked, at least for you," he said, "because it was mythical." He paused again. "Even if it really did exist, would you want to find it?"

209

III.
Into the Southwest

The Near Southwest

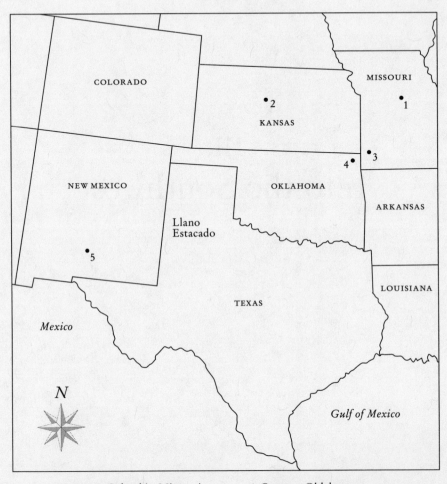

Colorado, Kansas, Missouri, New Mexico, Oklahoma, Arkansas, Louisiana, Texas, Mexico, Gulf of Mexico, Llano Estacado

1 Columbia, Missouri
2 Galatia, Kansas
3 Joplin, Missouri
4 Quapaw, Oklahoma
5 Alamogordo, New Mexico

Into the Southwest

On a Ring of Light

The next day the Indian told me their name for this light —
Artoosoqu' — and on my inquiring concerning the will-o'-the-wisp,
and the like phenomena, he said that his "folks" sometimes saw fires
passing along at various heights, even as high as the trees, and making a noise. I was prepared after this to hear of the most startling and
unimagined phenomena witnessed by "his folks"; they are abroad
at all hours and seasons in scenes so unfrequented by white men.
Nature must have made a thousand revelations to them which are
still secrets to us.

I did not regret my not having seen this before, since I now saw
it under circumstances so favorable. I was in just the frame of mind
to see something wonderful [that night], and this was a phenomenon
adequate to my circumstances and expectation, and it put me on the
alert to see more like it. I let science slide, and rejoiced in that light
as if it had been a fellow-creature. I saw that it was excellent, and
was very glad to know that it was so cheap. A scientific *explanation*,
as it is called, would have been altogether out of place there. That is
for pale daylight. Science with its *retorts* would have put me to sleep;
it was the opportunity to be ignorant that I improved. It suggested
to me that there was something to be seen if one had eyes. It made
a believer of me more than before. I believed that the woods were
not tenantless, but choke-full of honest spirits as good as myself any
day — not an empty chamber in which chemistry was left to work
alone, but an inhabited house — and for a few moments I enjoyed
fellowship with them. Your so-called wise man goes trying to persuade himself that there is no entity there but himself and his traps,
but it is a great deal easier to believe the truth. It suggested, too, that
the same experience always gives birth to the same sort of belief or

religion. One revelation has been made to the Indian, another to the white man. I have much to learn of the Indian, nothing of the missionary. I am not sure but all that would tempt me to teach the Indian my religion would be his promise to teach me *his*. Long enough I had heard of irrelevant things; now at length I was glad to make acquaintance with the light that dwells in rotten wood. Where is all your knowledge gone to? It evaporates completely, for it has no depth.

— Henry David Thoreau,
The Maine Woods,
1864

➤ 1 ◄

Apologia to Camerado Reader

Never, young authors, open your story with another writer's words. I, being young only in comparison to mud or a Galápagos tortoise, have earned — at least in my own mind — the liberty of violating the axiom. Exceptions prove rules, so it's said. Here's my contravention, this from the eighteenth century, from Laurence Sterne's *The Life and Opinions of Tristram Shandy, Gentleman:*

> Of all the several ways of beginning a book which are now in practice throughout the known world, I am confident my own way of doing it is the best — I'm sure it is the most religious — for I begin with writing the first sentence — and trusting to Almighty God for the second.

And so can it be also with journeys where a traveler makes a first step, goes the first mile, takes up the first day, and thereafter more or less follows along as the Almighty Way-gods ordain.

The initial sentence of the next leg of the quest for quoz with Q — one expressing our first step, as you'll soon see — is "Q knew of the Quadruplets and planetary Parcheesi long before we set out, so they weren't in our road conversation as we headed for the Quapaw Ghost Light." But before we get to those words, I must say a few preparatory things. (If you've ever dreamed you disembarked from some vehicle in some distant city and found yourself without luggage and clad in only your pajamas, then you know what arrival without preparation is like.) We both had long wanted to verify or debunk the Quapaw Ghost Light, and, happily, it lay more or less along our route to southern New Mexico; of course, for a circuitous traveler, any place is along the way.

The Almighty Something — I won't lay it off on deity — did indeed give me the second sentence (the one actually opening this chapter), even though, as far as I could see initially, its connection to the original first words lacked reason and certainly didn't rhyme. Almighties often work like that: mysterious if not mystical ordinations reach us so full of gaps and blanks we have to stumble along on our own and in so doing find our way and thereby reveal ourselves, expressing our lives for better or worse. In this manner, we write our autobiographies with wandering feet and the tracks they leave behind — despite many of those traces being blown to the winds before anyone else can pick them up.

Gus Kubitzki held that life is a cosmic board-game played against an invisible, invincible opponent who spends most of his time saying, "Your move," then forcing your hand before you're ready. The game, patently, isn't to see whether you win or lose — loss is preordained — rather it's to see the pattern of the traces you leave behind and where they lead others.

The first time Gus spoke of this — although it's not original to him — he apologized for the apparent crypto-Christianity in his analogy before citing the Epistle of James: "Wilt thou know, O vain man, that faith without works is dead?" Gus then modulated the assertion of James: "By his tracks a man is justified." This view is considerably less deterministic than Master Tristram's and requires an effort greater than simply listening for cosmic directions. It is, Gus maintained, laying down tracks that puts the travail — the meaning — into travel. (An early American spelling of *traveler* was *travailleur*.) Indeed, tracks are one reason some people believe a pilgrimage — following in the steps of another — to be the highest expression of travel. We are all, Gus would say, whether we realize it or not, forever in the traces of others.

With pilgrimages and planetary Parcheesi in mind, able reader, here we go into the Southwest via the Quapaw Ghost Light, with an excursive run into Galatia, Kansas, circa 1920, and another into 1901 Joplin, Missouri, but only after I give you the third sentence some Almighty just gave me, apparently that Mightiness wanting you to have it at this point rather than at the top of this chapter:

The size of America challenges the plans of travelers as much as their comprehension, and for scribes of the road, it's useful to answer to an organizing principle before setting out in search of edification, although simply going forth blindly is in itself an organizing principle, a common one that often translates into a wide-ranging circulation or occasionally into only a small rotation through a region. I've used both in my days on the two-lanes, even writing about the results a few times, but for these roads to quoz now in your hands, I want something looser, more serendipitous, more open to vagaries, more embracing the vagrant because that's the way life works.

An ideal approach might be to go aloft in a balloon, a craft dependent on capricious winds for direction, and at some unappointed moment be pitched out of the basket to parachute into whatever territory lay below and, unbuckling, say, "Well, look where the hell I've landed this time." Could we as newborns speak, many of us just might utter that very sentence with our first breath.

Given the impracticalities of such a course, I've resorted to selecting some hithers and thithers and striking out for them, the connecting roads (since I've already traveled many of them) of only intermittent relevance, usually the relevance coming simply from happenstance. It is the customary lack of significant happenstance along the way in rail travel, it seems to me, that's the biggest drawback to it, especially with the limited coach trackage in America, where one knows exactly the route beforehand and even the posted hours of arrival and departure. (As for commercial airlines, I won't deign to speak of them as travel, since they provide nothing more than movement: the passenger-victim, like a bit of eaten potato, is hapless in being moved from the point of entry to the place of exit.)

I don't want percipient readers to feel the locales here are put before you willy-nilly, higgledy-piggledy, helter-skelter. I have no wish to set down a scrambled ramble, no matter that life on this planet often seems unarranged just so. I'm after an open structure rather than a metaphoric one. Why didn't I tell you this sooner? Because in open structures, as in open travels, logic is something we come to discover once we set forth and only thereafter gainfully lay upon them, form reflecting content. (Anyone who plans out his life day by day on January 1 and works diligently to follow it till New Year's Eve will not likely take to this approach. So, free-souled camerado, we'll leave those suffering chaps to board Flight Double-Aught-Naught to Humdrumania.)

With that, I've set myself up to have to answer for my table of contents, with its orderly compass bearings. Let them not mislead you because, other than serving as simple directions to head off in, they've been added only after accomplishing the experiences behind them. Keep in mind a publishing writer must face an editor who exists to administer to your comprehension.

When I'm writing about America, I often summon up a mental map of the forty-eight states to help me shape my thinking. The map has many variations; one of them, the simplest, is the Quadruplets (there's that seventeenth letter again) which rather neatly comprise the contiguous United States and the four central sections of this book. Four great rivers — the Potomac, the Ohio, and a short stretch each of the Mississippi and Missouri — laterally divide the eastern half of the country; if you attach that natural division to the more arbitrarily determined one of the northern borders of Kansas, Colorado, Utah, Nevada, and California, you then have a three-thousand-mile, coast-to-coast dividing latitude. (If you prefer, shift that line a few miles southward to the thirty-eighth parallel, roughly marked out by U.S. Highway 50, and you have an even simpler division.) Now, take the western boundaries of five states — Minnesota, Iowa, Missouri, Arkansas, Louisiana — virtually the ninety-seventh meridian, and you have another useful line, this one border-to-border, clearly indicated on almost every map of the country. You can see the pattern in your head and always have it handy, even in your dreams.

Cross those two lines and — Shazam! — you have quadruplets of roughly similar area, provided we treat Texas and California as the lone stars they often wish to be. As I write these sentences, the center of American population is remarkably close to that intersection, lying this particular afternoon somewhere (depending on how many people moved into Phoenix yesterday morning) in the weeds along U.S. 50 in Missouri. When I was born, the center of population — that migratory mathematical spot recapitulating Euro-American historical movements as if it were itself a westering pioneer — was off in an Indiana cornfield. (As for Indians, depending on how rigidly you define them, their population center too has westered since the coming of whites, but their shift, of course, is one not of territorial expansion but of contraction.)

Also near that intersection are the places where I was born and where I grew up and from whence all these journeys for quoz have begun. My view now of my life as a board game played on this grand, quadrated map is that some Almighty Something placed me virtually at that crux of the Quadruplets to make sure I belonged no more to one region than to all of them; I see that placement as perhaps a celestial — or certainly a terrestrial — utterance: "Your move, sonny."

Of my many answering moves over the years in this planetary Parcheesi, the earliest was my youthful goal to spend a month in each of the forty-eight states — four years of days and nights spread around each state. From it I hoped to come away with an idea of America and a knowledge of the best places for return visits. It's taken longer to achieve than I imagined at age ten, and some states have gotten considerably more than their original share of tomcat prowlings and sleeps. A few years ago I raised the goal, despite lacking a month of nighttimes in Delaware. (An errant traveler has to work to keep from slipping out of the little First State; getting careless and driving on to the next town will readily put you somewhere else.)

Let me emphasize that this particular quadrate-topographic organization that you see in the table of contents has no more value to a journey than a file folder to its papers, a tin to its crackers. It's a mere receptacle for stories — *after* serving as scarcely other than a gossamer suggestion of where a few might be found.

Now, at last, here comes that promised first sentence, ordinary though it is, in its proper location (as it turns out) in chapter 2.

❧ 2 ❧

That Batch from Down Behind Otis

Q KNEW OF THE QUADRUPLETS and planetary Parcheesi long
before we set out, so they weren't in our road conversation
as we headed for the Quapaw Ghost Light. What *was* there was an
old, decaying, overturned outhouse — a donnicker, a privy, a classic wooden Chic Sale, as they were called in the 1930s — along Missouri Route 123 just south of Humansville (which Q thought a more
accurate name than, say, most of the Springfields, virtually all of
them no longer evincing a spring in a field; on learning the town was
not named for the resident species but for its founder, James Human,
she said, "Happy for those folks his surname wasn't Mudd").

Missouri has eight-thousand miles of federal and state highways,
and I have been over all of them — most several times, several many
times, and a few more than a thousand times (the reaper's going to
catch up with me before I can travel all the paved county-roads whose
distance equals the planetary circumference). Across the years, that
familiarity has turned certain objects along the routes into waymarks to direct my course or my attention. Like snapshots in an
album, they visually bespeak moments in my life. To lose a photo
is to lose a material connection, a mnemonic of what's gone before.
It's hard to resist humanizing such waymarks into an old friend who
says, "You remember me?"

On several recent trips, I'd watched that particular outhouse lean
ever farther to the south until, when Q and I passed, it had gone to
ground; it was end-of-an-era prostrate, at last ready to feed worms
and centipedes. After a certain age, a fellow can find it difficult to

keep from seeing in such change a forecast of his own days. When I said something along those lines to Q, she, comparable youth she is, said, "You see your life as an outhouse?" Well, not until now.

And that's when I remembered Galatia, Kansas, circa 1920. (They pronounce it Gah-LAY-shah.) An uncle by marriage told me this story once so I could record it, and again later on the road to New Orleans where I took him at age seventy-six to fulfill his long wish of seeing Mardi Gras. For three days we walked the French Quarter, he holding to my arm nearly the entire time. The version I gave Q along Route 123 on the way to the Ghost Light, unlike the one coming up, was necessarily less detailed and more in my voice than in my uncle's, he whom I'll call Julian to save the living possible embarrassment and me from charges of invasion of privacy.

Galatia sits astride the ninety-ninth meridian, the one next to the longitude where any westbound traveler, no matter how numb or purblind, sees the American West unequivocally begin. From corner to corner, if you draw a big *X* across a map of the great rectangle of Kansas, then hop in an auto and, at the posted speed, drive westward from the center of that *X* for thirty minutes, you'll be in Galatia, only eighty miles south of the geographic center of the forty-eight. For people who aren't Kansans, and even for many who are, Galatia lies squarely in the heart of the Kansas of popular imagination: a landscape somewhat flat, rather arid, naturally treeless except along creek bottoms. In truth, it's not entirely devoid of a rise or two (which out there can pass for hills), nor is it without moisture or trees. You can see all of those elements in Barton County — but not necessarily at the same time.

Because there was, to use the terminology of the era in question, a picture-show of sorts in Galatia, Saturday night-double-features could lure off the farms residents from miles around, sometimes almost as many as lived in the opolis itself. Julian's parents were immigrants from the Volga Republic, Lutherans who probably carried some long-ago suppressed Jewish ancestry. They were a clan of braininess surpassing brawniness, not always an asset among boys,

224

especially boys on the Great Plains where a perceived excess of intelligence (reading something other than Bible verses or letters on a can of beans) could turn daily life — like making it home from school without getting thumped — into a challenge. It mattered little that Julian's speech was perfect Ike-Eisenhower Kansas: still, he understood the German spoken at the kitchen table, carried a German surname, and had to answer for World War I of which he knew almost nothing.

Within a few years, the family moved to Kansas City to run a theater on the Kansas side of town, and there they prospered. (Incidentally, it was through my uncle I met Gus Kubitzki, also a theater man.) Julian was a smallish, dark-eyed boy, one who would rather, said my father, make you chuckle with him than cuss at him and, failing that, negotiate differences with his feet. (Here's another story trying to overleap itself.)

At certain seasons of the year, when the almost unrelenting labor on a wheat farm could be briefly ignored, the beefy sons of those wheatmen liked to come rolling into town about sunset, ostensibly for a movie but in truth coming not for Tom Mix but to mix it up with the Galatia boys of commensurate age. Their unespoused goal — beyond the testosteronically driven gratification of fisticuffs — was to give to girls of both town and country evidence of the physical superiority of the back-of-beyond boys, commonly referred to as — no matter where they lived — "that batch from down behind Otis." It's unusual in America to find triple-linked prepositions carrying such social stigma, but the Teutonic community had learned its English pretty well by then.

Although this was the Kansas of Carry Nation Country and also the years of the Eighteenth Amendment, cheap malt beverage was often an ingredient raising and changing things as yeast does dough. Those encounters usually became unsanctioned athletic events offering track or pugilistics: in the words of Uncle Julian, "Run for your fuckin life, hurdle a fence, and jump for cover." *Or,* make a stand with your fists up.

Such embarrassments, while never lethal, could prove to have regrettable longevity. Take Otto "Mudhead" Maschmeyer who lost his race to cover and got put to use as a human mop to swab up a miry spot in the middle of unpaved Steinert Street. Even after he became a locally successful something or the other, he was still Mudhead. The name stuck, and even his later move all the way down to Wichita couldn't entirely wash it away. Those renamings were a kind of prevenient vengeance the slower-witted worked on males who one day might hold their mortgages or judge them in court or assess the value of their tractors.

Enough. Here's the story from my uncle:

"About sundown, especially after harvest, we'd have to start watching for long, dust trails heading for Galatia. They were like skinny tornadoes, but these weren't going to veer off. They were going to arrive on Main Street, sure as hell, and touch down like a thrown punch. And they were coming for the likes of us. We townies — except maybe sometimes for the biggest of us — we'd scatter like mice running for holes in the wall. If you were young enough, though, you didn't have to worry. You could stand back and watch and learn that your time was coming some year. It was kind of an initiation rite, but we never saw it that way. We wanted to avoid it, not pass it.

"Even though I was kind of a squirt, one Halloween I made a miscalculation and learned I'd come of age. I stood watching the batch from down behind Otis come riding in on their dust clouds that curled back behind them like the tail of a giant bull. I wasn't worried, because I thought I was too young, and besides, for the last couple of years I'd been picking out hidey-holes all around town. No place, of course, was very far from any other place in little Galatia. I knew about an empty cistern, two storm cellars, an old shack — I can't remember all of them, but I remember all of them were dead ends, you might say. The way out was the way in, so you better not be seen going in. We were like prairie dogs — get too far from one of your holes, and you've had it.

"That Halloween the dust clouds started rising from the east, then from the south, then another from the west. Those things were scary. You see, Galatia was at a kind of crossroads, and the damn Otis batch had us in a pincer movement. They didn't know the term, but they knew how to hunt. Karl Klinghammer and I stayed around to watch the streets empty till it was just us two shrimps. When the farm boys unpiled from their jalopies and rattletrap trucks, they got mad they couldn't find anybody. They'd come for bear, and the bears were in hibernation. So they milled around and decided to go for mice.

"One of them said for us to hear it, 'Let's get them two little turds.' They were hoping somebody bigger would come out to rescue us. Karl took off one way, and I went the other. He told me later, when they caught him hiding down behind the gas station, they stripped him to his drawers, took a bucket of used crankcase oil and daubed him top to bottom with thick, black oil and grease, and sent him home which was back across town. Half Galatia staring out their windows at the poor kid. From then on, I'm sorry to say, little blue-eyed Karl was Sambo. The name even came up in his obituary.

"I was short, but I was fast, but their longer legs covered more ground. I saw I wasn't going to make it to any of my hidey-holes, so I dodged behind old-man Schenk's place because he had a dilapidated Chic Sale he'd stopped using when he plumbed out his house. We didn't call it a Chic Sale then. It was just a privy or some other terms that are on the coarse side. The thing was nothing more than worn-out boards full of knotholes and wide cracks between the planks. You could say it was well-ventilated. Half the boys were right on my heels, and I barely managed to make it inside and throw down the latch just in the nick. They really had their piss and vinegar up by then. Piss and beer's what I should say. They were a pack of dogs smelling the kill. They pounded on the door and shook the Chic Sale and shouted in at me, 'Come out of there, you little fart, and face the music!'

"I didn't think they'd tip the thing over because old Schenk was known to enjoy slapping around troublesome boys, especially when he was drunk. Besides, he had folks down by Otis and up by

Milberger. Those country boys were yelling, but there wasn't any cussing except to call me names of a certain sort. One of them said, 'Who's in there?'

"That was good news. If they didn't know who it was, I might survive without any long-term damage. They were looking in, but it was too dark inside for them to tell, even though there was moonlight on the grass, and I could recognize some of them. And I kept my cap pulled down low. They started arguing about lifting the privy up to pull me out like a nut out of his shell. My only hope was old Schenk would hear the ruckus and come out and start laying hands on them, but there wasn't any light on in his house. He probably was in there with his bottle all right, three sheets to the wind. Couldn't hear, and if he could hear, couldn't move.

"One of the bunch said he had a better idea and pulled them off a ways to huddle. Then they came back and surrounded the privy. I just knew I was going to get stuffed down that hole and end up with a name worse than Mudhead.

"They all sort of turned away from me, then, one at a time, turned around again. They had a plan. They were saying, 'Where is he?' 'Over in the corner.' 'Okay, he's yours, Richter.'

"Then this skinny thing comes through a knothole. You know I don't like snakes, so I whacked at it with my cap, and Richter Diebenkorn let out a yell. It wasn't a snake. It was Diebenkorn's dipsey-noodle. Then it popped in through another hole, and he let loose with it and hosed down my shoes before I could jump away. Then another stream came in through a crack in the door, then one from the other side. I got up on the seat. It was a one-holer, so that was good. The streams were arcing before they could get higher than my pant legs. I was mostly out of the line of fire — you know, out of the trajectories. But then somebody got boosted up to the little vent-window under the eaves, and there wasn't any escape, except maybe down the hole.

"Oh, they got me. Did they get me! *Head to toe.* Didn't leave a dry inch. All I could do was put my hands over my face. Hell.

They'd been drinking beer, so their reservoirs were full, and they took turns. I mean, there were so many peckers coming through those planks, that privy looked like a horse chestnut turned inside out. They were saying things like 'Come on! Let me have a shot at him!' Or 'Aim for his eyes!' Or 'If that little pizzle of yours can't hit him, mine will!'

"The only justice was when somebody yelled at the fat boy, Albert Tesselhoff, 'Damnit, Tesselhoff, you just got me! Watch your goddamn aim!'

"But I refused to yell, so they still didn't know who I was, and there was no way on earth I was coming out. Then they started going dry, and finally one of them says, 'Man, he stinks!' And they all left.

"They were probably waiting for me around the corner. I knew they weren't going to touch a pee-soaked kid now, but they'd like to know who they got so they could pin a name on him. You know, something like 'Carry Nation's boy, Yuri.' The day would come when I might be over to Hoisington or down at Great Bend and somebody would walk up and say, 'How you doing, Pisspants?' And my future wife would ask me to explain it. Or maybe I wouldn't even have a wife. I mean, what girl would want to marry a boy who'd been hosed down like a scarecrow on fire? You see, right there along with me, my future was locked in that Chic Sale.

"I wasn't coming out until I was sure the coast was clear, so I sat there, first steaming, then shivering. Teeth chattering. Trying to huddle up in those stinking clothes. But it was better than getting recognized.

"About midnight, after when they usually left town, I dared a sneak for home. I crept through backyards, behind bushes, wherever there was shadow. Like an old alley cat. Which is also what I smelled like. Have you ever walked in soaking-wet corduroy pants? Shoes squeaking?

"It was so late I knew Ma would be worried and waiting up for me, but hell, I had no choice. I went down to a little dug-pond and slipped in real quiet. Cold? Man alive! Then I got out and went on home. She was always the kindest woman you could hope to meet, even when she had the paddle out. She looked at me and only said, '*Gott im Himmel!*'

"I told her I had to hide in a pond to escape that batch from down behind Otis. She was proud of me. She ran a hot bath with a bar of lye soap, and gave me hot tea, and let me have a jigger of schnapps, and put me to bed under the best quilt. The next morning Pop said, 'I hear you used your head, boy, but next time find yourself a *dry* hole.' But there wasn't any next time, and I never got a nickname, and I later got to marry your beautiful aunt. But I waited till we'd been together a few years before I ever told her about that Halloween."

❥ 3 ❦

In the Light of Ghosts

ALLOW ME, LUCID READER, to argue the existence of ghosts. Set
aside for the moment your suspicion this writer has at last gone
around that bend immemorial, a trip three or four of you may have
deemed already accomplished sometime back when he began prais-
ing a particular letter of the alphabet. I won't defend my position
on that bend, but I do hope to persuade you to an enlarged view of
ghostdom.

If a ghost is an immaterial immanence able to work changes in the
material world, such as scaring somebody, then its actuality seems to me
no more questionable than other immanences, such as love or morality,
mathematics or logic, or — the greatest of all — memory, that force
from which our humanity, our humanness, our civilization, our loves
and lives, proceed. We can survive without morality or arithmetic or
logic, but without memory, we haven't a chance. We are who we are
and where we are in no insignificant measure because of immaterial
memories. If you are not yet in accord, try this test: point to love —
not the object of love or its expression but *the "thing" itself.* Or wrap up
a carton of courage and send it prepaid to one fearful; give a birthday
box of belief to the skeptical; for the corrupt, pour them a healing draft
of invigorating ethics; go down a lane and seek the fountain of truth.
Take any concept we live by — fidelity or deity or gravity or any other
invisibility that keeps us from floating off into the ether of one realm
or another — and snap a photo of it and stick it to the refrigerator for
those moments when you need a reminder of its importance. Do we
not live according to immanences as much as substances?

You know all of this because you know that to speak the name of anything, real or imagined, is to give it existence in the actual world of sound. From nothing instantly rises something. I might say to you, before we start our stroll into a deep woods or down a dark alley, "Keep an eye out for the Nodgort. It can be dangerous here." With those words, at least for a moment, I've put the dreaded Nodgort into your life, and you must make a decision about the reality of its threat to you. (Lest I lose you in needless speculation, I confess I coined the word and, as far as I know, in setting down that sentence I'm likely the only person on Earth who has ever uttered or written *Nodgort*.)

In some ways, the following pages are about Nodgorts — quoz of a certain immaterial kind, and how they came to shape the route and events on the road Q and I were slowly finding into the Southwest. I hope now you'll sanction talk of ghosts of several orders and at least for the moment accept their theoretical existence.

On a rainy Tuesday we were in southwestern Missouri, six miles from Kansas, eight from Oklahoma, and a half hour from Arkansas; more specifically, we were at the intersection of Fourth Street and Main, the historical center of Joplin, where old Route 66 once passed through. I sat at a table in the southeast corner of the public library, and before me was a three-inch file of articles and clippings about the Quapaw Ghost Light, also called the Hornet or Seneca Spook Light, the Ozark Mystery Light, the Devil's Jack-o'-Lantern, or a couple of other combinations of those adjectives. I'd heard about it for half-a-century but had only then finally gotten around to looking into the truth — or untruth — of it. Q was in another place in the library where she was reading microfilmed newspaper accounts of a certain dire event in 1901 that I'd first learned of a decade before hearing about the strange light near Hornet, Missouri, ten miles distant, down along the Oklahoma border on the old Quapaw Reservation.

After a couple of hours, finding me halfway through the Ghost Light reports, she placed in front of me several photocopies from two Joplin newspapers of a little more than a century earlier. "You'd better set the Ghost Light aside," she said, and returned to the microfilm reader. I pushed back the file and began reading her gatherings from 1901 when the place where I sat had been a bank lobby in the corner of the Joplin Hotel, then the social and political locus of town. A long sequence of events had culminated only a hundred feet away, at the southwest corner of Fourth and Main. Instead of stories about a Ghost Light, I took up the shade of one William Grayston.

I want to tell you this calamitous tale not necessarily objectively (for human objectivity, like ghosts, is possible only in theory and has even less substance than a Nodgort) but at least accurately and even-handedly, although when I reach the conclusion, I'll have to interpret. The story, one I've long wanted to relate, was earlier impossible to me because I didn't have the details until Q, an investigator of no mean order, began dragging them into the light, a ghostly light. Or perhaps I mean the light of ghosts. I am, in a sense, a participant in this crime, and my life has been turned a certain way because of those occurrences in 1901. While you read the next some pages, your life too will be participant.

By the end of its first quarter century, Joplin, Missouri, was a mining community on a rapid clip toward high prosperity, a lead and zinc boomtown full of situations and characters commensurate with such development. Any place whose early history contains a Three-Finger Pete and a county coroner surnamed Coffin is bound to have a past as lively as it is deadly. What cattle were then doing to Dodge City (not far westward), metals were doing in Joplin. We all know, in America, ore cannot be taken from the ground below without the assists of saloons, games of chance, and houses of ill fame on top of it. When such gathered enterprises lie within a gallop of two "dry" states and an alcohol-prohibited Indian Territory, booze will determine things as rainfall does a forest. The usual lubricant of a spinning roulette wheel or a bordello is alcohol, and without it, mechanical rotations and purchased pleasures tend to come to a frictioned, squeaking halt.

One of Joplin's folk historians, Dolph Shaner, wrote in 1948 of that town named after a Methodist preacher:

Several decades ago, when a crusade was being organized, one of the speakers libeled the city as being as bad "as Babylon with its hanging gardens." But it wasn't that bad. There were saloons, gambling places, assignation houses, and bawdy houses. Time was when a circus parade brought faces of dozens of female denizens to upstairs windows along Main Street.

Those denizens, of course, were not one-flight-up dentists or lawyers or even typists; their profession was older, at least as old as hanging gardens. A man was to tell me, "Fourth and Main in nineteen hundred was a place a miner could come up above ground to wet his whistle *and* his weasel until his Saturday wages were gone."

At that intersection of Fourth and Main — the topographic, political, and social heart of town, the location where north-south electric trolleys crossed east-west lines — stood the two best hotels: the three-storey Joplin (the center of the "brick hotel ring") and the newer, eight-floor Keystone built by a Pennsylvanian and therefore not a component of an oligarchy I shall soon speak of. On opposite corners were the Worth Building and its aptly named House of Lords Restaurant and Bar at street side, with a gambling den on the second floor and a flesh parlor on the third. Catercorner stood a two-storey, ramshackle frame building that had been moved fifteen miles by mules across the Kansas border in 1873, the year of the official founding of Joplin. On its upper floor were blossoms in a hanging garden, and at sidewalk level was the Club Saloon where, a few years before our year in question, a fatal shooting happened.

(Here's a little incident from about 1900 to help set the tone for events to come: An attractive guest in one of the Main Street hotels arrived in Joplin by train. She was selling encyclopedias. Aware that a mining town is only slightly more literary than, say, a mine shaft, she had learned how to circumvent such unlettering. Counting on her shapeliness to gain entry to a businessman's office, she would pointedly mention her wish to see the beauty of the countryside: *If only she had a buggy — perhaps at eleven on Tuesday morning.*

At that hour on that day in front of her hotel, the number of shined buggies with men, mustaches waxed to perfection and hat brims dashingly rolled, was unusual. At half past eleven, one expectant blade went inside to inquire after the bookish miss. "What!" said the clerk. "Why, she caught the evening train for points west last night!" Evidence of this story may be the large number of unsoiled encyclopedias showing up at estate sales a few years later.)

In 1924 Joplin became so desirous of cleaning itself up it prohibited "cheek-to-cheek dancing, extreme side-stepping, whirling, dipping, dog walking, shuffling, toddling, Texas tommying, the Chicago walk, the cake-eater or Flapper hop, and stiff-arm dancing." Whether you might be cited in Joplin eighty years later for, say, an excessive side step or a bit of toddling, I don't know, but I do know the city is no longer much of a mining town or particularly "wide-open." Where once stood the House of Lords Restaurant and Bar and its upstairs sportations is a pocket park not of wetted whistles and weasels but of birdsong and squirrels. At the time Q and I were at the historic crux of Joplin — accurately depicted in Thomas Hart Benton's mural in city hall — words like *tavern* and *saloon* were in some circles almost as coarse as *whorehouse,* and it took me three inquiries in the library to learn the location of the nearest spirituous beverage, although it was only a block away in a restaurant I'll call the Blue Tomato.

It is not digressive, as you will see, to mention here a sign, partly overgrown and showing decay, I saw on the north end of Main Street. The hand-painted words came from Alexander Pope's "Essay on Man":

> *Vice Is A Monster Of So Frightful Mien,*
> *As, To Be Hated, Needs But To Be Seen,*
> *Yet Seen Too Oft, Familiar With Her Face,*
> *We First Endure, Then Pity, Then Embrace.*

For a pint and a quiet place to discuss ghostly histories emerging before us, Q and I walked a block east of Main to the Tomato, a pleasant establishment free of hard spirits, as one might guess from cash-register receipts imprinted with "SERVING JOPLIN IN JESUS NAME!" Ignoring the beloved American Aberrant Apostrophe (the one on the tab having wandered from the register and out the door to end up down the street on a *CLOSED MONDAY'S* sign), I asked our "server," Jessie, a bubblelating young blonde, about the slogan. She said, "What slogan?" After she poured our glasses of ale, I mentioned to Q the catchphrase had me hoping to have service from the Anointed Himself, and Q responded, "How do you know you didn't?" Alert the tabloids: JOPLIN JESUS, AKA JESSIE, SPOTTED SERVING SUDS.

Once again, humoring reader, my tale wanders from its path. But then, as Master Tristram Shandy says, "Digressions, incontestably, are the sunshine, they are the life, the soul of reading: — take them out of this book, for instance, you might as well take the book along with them." But that was long ago, and my editors believe contemporary readers to be less tolerant, so I'll return to the story fully mindful, nevertheless, that service to the House of Lords — and to the Anointed Lord Himself — lies quite within this dark matter. Perhaps I should begin there.

❥ 4 ❦

A Poetical History of Satan

WILLIAM GRAYSTON, born 1862, came with his family soon after the Civil War to near Sparta in Christian County, Missouri, on the edge of the northern Ozarks, about eighty miles east of Joplin. The county took its name not because it was rich with fact-free fundamentalism but rather from a district in Kentucky bearing the surname of a Revolutionary War soldier killed by Indians. That Missouri area, even with its ardent foot-washing Baptists, was a hotbed of vigilantes: at a public hanging, praying over one of them on the scaffold was William's father, David, an English immigrant stone-cutter who made his way west by finding work along the Erie Canal. Once in southern Missouri, David discovered he could outpreach, outwrite, and outdebate any ordinary Methodist, Presbyterian, or Freethinker daring to take him on.

He wrote "A Poetical History of Satan," "Poetic Rambles in Search of the Church," "Millennium," and *The Poetical Bible* wherein (if you can imagine it) he set the entire holy writs from Genesis to Revelation into couplets, that least tolerable of rhymes. He and his brother-in-law, B. J. Wrightsman, at someone's behest, composed "Missouri" and offered it as the official state-song; after a performance in the capitol concluded with an ovation, the tune vanished, except for my copy of the sheet music in Q's piano bench. From time to time she pulls it out to amuse me with its notably unanthemic melody, although it's something you could shake a jolly bustle to. As for David Grayston's *Poetical Bible* and his history of Old Clootie, I've never succeeded in finding those.

William grew up in a household thick with sermons from a brilliant if aloof father, a man who was (wrote the *Joplin Daily Globe* in 1901) "a power in shaping both the religious and political destiny of Southeast Missouri." Young Willie, a handsome boy of acute intellect, took in the religionizing designed more to prove fallacies in other sects than to set forth its own theosophical base interpreting existence. The earthly task of humankind, so he heard repeatedly, was to acquiesce and simply believe; after all, things would be explained later in the beyond. But the presumed superiority of willful incognizance over freedom of inquiry made no sense to him. If a Creator gave intelligence and the power to inquire and discover truths, why would It then insist on beliefs demanding blind faith?

The boy wondered whether life eternal could be bought with nothing more than a mindless, even uncomprehending, confession of sin preceding a profession of "I believe." Didn't such mindlessness make escape from one's own iniquities easy while minimizing — if not negating — the significance of good works? Could a mass murderer do a confess-and-profess and thereby earn eternal redemption while a freethinking physician who healed thousands would be forever damned? How could such a concept advance humanity? What kind of god would encourage blind faith to trump mercy and generosity? Wasn't a quest for "personal salvation" the ultimate expression of self-concern?

Moving gradually away from a religiosity emphasizing iniquity over inquiry, piety over percipience, William learned to orate rather than preach, and as he came into manhood, he found his principles of morality and ethics, of social justice and public duty, residing far more in humanity itself than in deity. If such a thing as heavenly redemption existed, it would not be through a declaration of belief that can evaporate in a moment — it would be through kindly works which can long remain markers of one's life. He began to comprehend the greater challenge — and risks — in bringing people to reason rather than merely to belief. For him, the way to a better life for all was to be discovered through the light of examination rather than through unquestioning faith. His means were inductive thought and scientific method. As his father would later sadly write of his son:

> *Darwin and Spencer his guide*
> *Instead of Jesus crucified.*

Young Grayston wasn't afraid of the demanding effort of seeking a spirituality based not on supposition, strictures, credulity, and dogmatized opinion but rather upon a close reasoning leading to consequent service to other people. His sacred texts became the writings of Thomas Huxley and Charles Darwin and especially Herbert Spencer ("struggle for existence," "survival of the fittest"). In 1901 the *Globe* was to write of William: "He knew as much about the contents of *On the Origin of Species* and *The Descent of Man* as anyone in the state of Missouri perhaps. . . . No phase of either physical science or speculative thought escaped his attention."

Grayston was a man in search of evidence wherever it lay, and that led him into law after finding a congenial example in attorney and orator Robert Ingersoll of New York, another preacher's son whose freethinking, rationalistic speeches — "Why I Am an Agnostic," "Some Mistakes of Moses," "Superstition" — may have kept him from running for the Presidency. (Or maybe it was quips like "With soap, baptism is a good thing.")

The relation between the son and his biblically doctrinaire father grew strained, especially so when Will went westward to the new colony of Freethinkers in Liberal, Missouri, thirty miles north of Joplin. For a short spell, at age twenty-three he became the principal of the school soon to grow into Free Thought University in (said opponents) "a godless town" having neither churches nor saloons, where the freethinking residents said they kept "one foot upon the neck of priestcraft and the other upon the rock of truth." In Universal Mental Liberty Hall, Will listened to or lectured or debated all who came: scientists, Baptists, atheists, Jews, deists, Catholics, or anyone else of capable mind willing to observe the lone rule of maintaining "respectable decorum."

Such a place, of course, drew the ire — if not fear — of certain intolerant Christians who could see it only as "a practical experiment in Infidelity" and who condemned and cursed anyone associated with it. (On the day Q and I visited Liberal — population seven hundred, about the same as it was in Grayston's day — the major change since then, as far as I could determine, was there were now only two "liberals" anywhere about and, according to certain laws of physics, the pair of them departed town at the same moment and in the same vehicle as did we.)

Soon after the founder of Liberal and Free Thought University abandoned inductive process and descended into spiritualism, Grayston returned to his home area near Springfield where he married and became the father of Gertrude who bore her sire's intellect but not his internal strength. (I name her because she will appear

William and Molly Grayston with daughter, Gertrude, Springfield, Missouri, 1889.
An observant reader may see in this and the following two photographs of calmly posed people, forever locked safely within the old frames, an appearance of orderly lives showing no hint of the unfathomable madness that can afflict a human existence in the click of a cosmic shutter.

again in this story.) After the birth of a second child, Herbert (for philosopher Spencer), the mother struggled with what appears to have been postpartum depression exacerbated by the death of little Herbert in infancy.

The marriage collapsed after four years, and Grayston was granted a divorce. His petition says:

> [Plaintiff] faithfully demeaned himself and discharged all his duties as the husband of defendant and at all times treated her with kindness and affection, but that defendant, wholly disregarding her duties as wife of the plaintiff, has during the greater part of said married life, abused, wronged, and mistreated the plaintiff in various ways by calling him vile names and applying to him opprobrious epithets.

The mother, as was then the nearly unbroken practice, retained custody of Gertrude.

Having prevailed in the divorce but lost his daughter, his wife, and his home, Grayston left Springfield and his law practice for two years of roaming the Ozark Mountains of northern Arkansas, supporting himself by writing newspaper dispatches about the metallurgical resources being discovered there.

When his mind cleared, William returned to law and moved to Joplin in 1892, just ahead of its second mineral boom. He was an outsider and a Freethinker in a religiously conservative region, yet he became a respected stump-speaker for selected Democratic candidates, and he spoke on behalf of both the Law and Order League and the Anti-Saloon League. He espoused certain early Spencerian notions of evolutionary social progress ("A people's condition may be judged by the treatment which women receive under it"). He supported the early positions of William Jennings Bryan, long before the Great Commoner's descent into simplistic antievolutionary views. (As geologists began reading the ancient fossil records, Bryan later said, "It's better to trust in the Rock of Ages than know the ages of rocks.")

Less admired by Grayston were Joplin men like Thomas Connor, an illiterate Irish-immigrant saloon keeper down at the state-line settlement of Seneca ("Hell on the Border") who purchased at a dime on the dollar six-hundred acres that proved to be rich mineral lands he quickly leased to eastern companies. Through a good investment and blind good luck, Connor became the first millionaire in Joplin and got the attendant title of "First Citizen." Shrewd enough thereafter not to rely on luck, he bought the local waterworks and the Joplin Hotel which he subsequently would raze to build on the same site a monument to his own name, the luxurious, eight-storey Connor Hotel. He died just before its completion. Years later, in 1978, on the very morning before it was to be imploded to make way for the public library where I sat reading about it, the hotel, as if anathematized, suddenly collapsed on its own accord, killing a worker at that accursed intersection of Fourth and Main.

Unlike old Tom Connor, Grayston had no spare dimes and his luck may have been blind but it wasn't good. Instead, he had only a remarkably relentless curiosity always in pursuit of reason, a mind driven by the conviction that evolution could be shaped to benefit humanity. (Spencer: "All is well since all grows better.") Grayston's capacity to be disturbed by public vice and corruption was unsurpassed in Joplin, and his stump speeches and lectures and his flow of words endeared him to some while making him a vexing pariah among the town fathers, those men of secret-handshake societies,

those eating aged porterhouse steaks while cutting deals with figures written on the white tablecloths of the House of Lords. Grayston's success in persuasion made him a man to be watched, because he could prove dangerous.

His looks, his impassioned speeches, even the sense of danger surrounding him, drew glances from a petite blonde, a seventeen-year-old "of remarkable beauty

William Grayston, 1896.

widely known as the Belle of Joplin." (Quotations, except where I note otherwise, come from 1901 and 1902 issues of Jasper County newspapers.) Although her family was of less than modest means, she was the niece of a recent Lieutenant Governor and the daughter of a former Joplin fire chief. Her name was Pearl Payton.

Almost exactly twice her age, William married Pearl five months after they were introduced, and ten months after the marriage, she gave birth to a daughter. Although Grayston was prominent for his public speaking, his law practice was not sufficient for the family to have its own home, so they moved into the cramped Payton boardinghouse run by Pearl's mother. There, after a year, marital deteriorations began between William and Pearl, each unfathomable to the other.

As Grayston's dashing mystery faded for his wife, she was left only with what was truly remarkable about him: an individualistic mind happy to explain the usefulness and implicit morality of truths discovered through scientific method. He spoke about the justness of pensions for miners' widows and about the ways universal suffrage was in accordance with social evolutions necessarily carrying requisite dissolutions; he showed her distinctions between credence and reason, superstition and demonstrable evidence. He pointed out how civic criminality aborts democracy, and he asked her ideas on why liberty and happiness did not always proceed from the pursuit of the public weal. He suggested, were a Heaven to exist, it likely would have to be of human creation. He, if selectively, quoted Spencer: "The ultimate result of shielding men from the effects of folly, is to fill the world with fools."

But to Pearl, William might as well have been speaking Bantu; she grasped his mind as a queen bee does the mind of the beekeeper. And he too was baffled. One night, after their third separation, he wrote his father:

> I lay in bed, . . . thinking as to how it was that my wife, who I
> knew and felt was one of the sweetest and best meaning little

girls in all this world; how it was that the things that made me shudder did not even interest her, but failing to impress her as they did me she seemed to think I was only irritable, and kindly asked me not to think ahead and borrow trouble, but just to go along and let the world run as it wants to run. Her words sounded as if flowing from an inexhaustible fountain of kindness and good will, and my heart ached from the depth of the same feelings for our daughter's welfare; but oh! how differently we looked at things! I wondered and wondered, "Why is it we look at things so differently?"

On his business trips, Grayston frequently carried along their little daughter, and he read to her and tried to explain the world by looking at facts and evidence; what he could not be to his first daughter, he tried to be to his second. During his absence, the young mother seemed satisfied to be unencumbered by the demands of a four-year-old and unaffected by gossip about how she longed to make up for a youth too soon given up.

After the first brief separation and reunion, William began to believe their life might be better in a city where he wouldn't be a notable nonconformist at odds with the temper of the town; where he wouldn't be a Freethinker in perpetual contest with the mining and commercial factions of the knights and fellows of loyal and ancient clandestine orders running Joplin. A man with such auspicious promise surely could make a more significant social contribution if the eternal struggle to create open minds and generous hearts could be taken beyond lesser issues of booze and keno and doxies. Wouldn't Kansas City or St. Louis be a better place for his family, his practice, and the quest for social justice? In the spring of 1900 he crossed the state, his little girl with him, to stay with his sister while he looked for ground for a new life in St. Louis. He was gone seven weeks.

Returning to Joplin and the pinched room in the Payton boardinghouse, William had scarcely set down his luggage and laid out gifts for Pearl before she told him about her divorce petition alleging an "impossibility of compatibility" and claiming his travels to find the family a new home constituted nonsupport.

He was thunderstruck. How could that happen? Where had such a decision come from? Yes, Herbert Spencer said evolution must be accompanied by dissolutions, but such a turn of events seemed beyond Spencerian reasoning. Once again, he had to leave the house. He rented a dollar-a-night room in the Forney Hotel downtown, not far from his Main Street law office now shared with his younger brother and new partner, George.

Attorney and believer in inductive method, seeker of evidence, William began investigating the source of Pearl's action. As he took down depositions, he narrowed the circle of influence on her, then reduced it again until at last it pointed to a single source: the roomer down the hall, the big and well-dressed man, he of dark hair and eyes, the black-mustached widower six years younger than William, a migratory man whom Grayston himself had brought into the boardinghouse after learning the fellow, president and superintendent of the Joplin Waterworks, was looking to move from his twenty-dollar-a-week lodging to something cheaper. Although a comparative newcomer from New York City, he wasn't needy by any means, yet for some reason he took Payton's eight-dollar-a-week room in East Joplin, across the tracks of the Kansas City Southern Railway.

That peculiarly minimal twelve-buck difference doesn't seem to have been William's first clue to Pearl's behavior, yet he couldn't have been unaware of rumors the widower was sweet on Mrs. Grayston. But the second clue was, you could say, conclusive: the man paying for Pearl's divorce petition was the lodger himself, Superintendent George Grant Bayne, and the attorney representing her was Bayne's lodge brother, Thomas Dolan, whom William had faced off against in court on several heated occasions, a man, like Bayne, with more influential connections than genuine friends.

Grayston told Bayne to get out of the Payton home, but the superintendent refused, as he also refused to address any questions about Pearl's petition. On several occasions, William told the foot-loose Bayne to move until eventually he was telling him not just to leave the house but to *leave town*. Each time, Bayne's answer was silence.

Gossip increased: how Bayne and the Belle of Joplin had been seen hugging and kissing near the window of his room in the Payton home; how they'd been spotted riding snuggled in a buggy over in Byersville. Hardly anyone questioned why a man of means and position would remain in the humble boardinghouse, because every gossip *knew* the reason was to stay close to Pearl.

The only change the superintendent made was to begin carry-ing a hammerless .38-caliber Smith & Wesson, a pocketable revolver made for the sole purpose of killing a man. Later, Bayne alleged he took up the pistol only after William told him to get out of Joplin or he'd "shoot him down like a yellow dog." Grayston, a member of the Law and Order League, owned no weapons.

Over the next many weeks, William's investigations convinced him that his wife was innocent of any intimacies, and he continued to work for their reconciliation until, growing desperate, he tried to force negotiations by writing up a "cross suit" asking for custody of their daughter. On someone's advice, Pearl refused, so William rewrote his suit to ask for only rights of visitation in the event of a divorce, but he didn't file that second one. Pearl remained intrac-table, refusing to proceed with her divorce petition beyond filing it, although she still allowed him to take their daughter on his business trips. Yet, on someone's counsel, Pearl kept the threat hanging above William. But why?

Grayston was determined he would not lose a third child, cer-tainly not to some rover whose business dealings, he had discovered, couldn't withstand even cursory scrutiny. Unearthing the truth, he believed, would surely lead to a way of protecting what he most loved, his little girl.

His investigations made it easy for him to dismiss the gossip, but his insistence on Pearl's innocence did not silence rumor, nor did it keep people from interpreting the bad blood between him and Bayne as nothing more than a love triangle. Wasn't adultery, said the tittle-tattle, the reason the interloper, too craven to answer Grayston, carried a pistol instead of simply moving out of a dismal room? What's more, in the face of Grayston's charges and threats, wasn't Bayne's long and perfect silence de facto proof of his dalliance? Wouldn't a younger, larger man, *if innocent*, take some action against his accuser?

For almost eighteen months, things dragged on without resolution. On the nineteenth of November, 1901, in that same letter to his father, William cryptically encouraged him to "read between the lines" and closed saying he would soon send more:

> A year ago last spring I was preparing for a business trip to St. Louis, and lay awake thinking of the awful corruption in Joplin and how terrible it would be for me to allow my little daughter to be educated in the schools of East Joplin unless the atmosphere of those schools should be radically changed. As I lay thinking most intently, and my little daughter huddled in my arms, waiting for her mamma to come to bed, I thought I would speak of this feature of the matter to my wife and listen to her views. . . .
>
> [My thoughts] seemed to open up an ocean of problems and to suggest a new standpoint from which to view almost every problem before me, and that minute I decided to revise every opinion held by me on every subject coming up before me and to see if it were possible to discover and weed out any serious errors in my views and plans and methods of business conduct. Well, I have kept the resolution steadily in mind to the present hour and am happier for having done so.

Such was his Spencerian interpretation of evolutionary change being accompanied by dissolution that he saw a single human life reflecting the course of its species in a kind of emotional ontogeny recapitulating phylogeny. Through reason, he was at last reaching a rational untangling of the situation, and a new and different life could emerge from the old.

The morning after sending his letter, Thursday, the twenty-first of November, Grayston went south of town to examine the Panther Mine and returned that afternoon with a sample of lead ore in his pocket. It was not the piece of lead about to change his life.

He stopped by the office, just a hundred yards beyond Fourth and Main, one flight up, to talk to his brother about some legal matters, he showed George the ore, and at about four thirty William left smiling in his new, raised spirits. He walked to Sixth Street with an acquaintance, then, his motive unknown, abruptly turned around and, striding swiftly, headed back to that hexed crux of all Joplin, where stood the two hotels, the House of Lords, and the Club Saloon.

Grayston was moving toward the very place where, a little more than a century later, I sat reading old newspaper accounts about his approach. His time was four thirty p.m. and mine was four fifty. His day was a pleasant Thursday afternoon a week before Thanksgiving, and mine was a drizzly Tuesday just past the vernal equinox.

What comes next is a conjunction of hour and place and three men's lives, a ghostly triangle redrawing itself into something different, as if it were evolving: William, George, William. Once the new figure was accurately drawn and understood, none of those men would emerge from it unchanged.

❯5❮

Gladiator Without a Sword

H E IS NOT HERE TO SPEAK, that peerless speaker, and he cannot tell his story, not a word of it, and what is about to happen comes from others, almost all of them adversaries. I will, for reasons to become clear, presume to speak for him, because without him, this sentence, this book, would not exist. I set down sentences with the hope they are inspirited and that the truth of what occurred near the end of the second year of a new millennium will at last come to light, however ghostly — ghastly — it may be.

21 November 1901, 4:30 p.m. The shops and offices are about to close, and workers begin to crowd the Joplin sidewalks, and the new electric trolleys fill with riders, the overhead wires sparking and popping at each juncture and the rails gleaming among the brick pavement. William Grayston is thirty-nine years old, of middle height, muscular, his hairline in retreat. He has a vigor unmatched in his family except by his father who, nearing seventy, can still stand forth to lay out the perils of Hell and bring strong men to their knees in hope of redemption, that word his son heard so often back in Christian County.

4:35. William is walking south on Main. He wears a dark, three-piece woolen suit, a tan chesterfield draped over his left arm, derby on his head. In his pockets are a few slips of notes, a key, a snapshot of the Panther Mine, and a sample of lead ore from it. Nothing else. For some reason, he turns around from his acquaintance at Sixth Street and heads north along the west side of Main, moving fast, as if in pursuit. Something apparently has been said to him to cause him to alter his course. No record of what those words were or of their import will remain, but from them there will be no turning back. His renewed good spirits seem to have vanished in an instant. Clearly, reaction has replaced reasoning.

4:37. He weaves his way among the crowd, the trolleys rumbling and clanging; out of a shop comes the scent of fresh cigars, from a tavern the odor of soured beer, and there's the smell of new shoes, ladies' cosmetics, the unmistakable emanations of a hardware store and a drug counter and a newsstand. The streets are rank with life.

4:42. As he nears the intersection of Fourth and Main, he calls out to a man walking ahead. No response. Grayston closes the distance and calls again, louder, "Say there! Bayne!" The big man hears the voice but only quickens his step until he reaches the corner, and there he stops as if according to plan, and strikes a nonchalant lean against the front of the Club Saloon where two bartenders stand talking about the funeral that has briefly (and conveniently) closed the tavern. They are Frank Geier and George Bayless, and they go silent when Bayne takes his incongruously casual stance, seemingly on a mark, against the worn building covered with old advertising signs, a place that should have been torn down years ago. Across the street is the new, round-towered Keystone Hotel with an elaborately executed facade of Carthage limestone accented by wrought iron around the entrance to the Joplin National Bank; next to it is another elaborate entryway recently changed into the compact Mirror News and Cigar Stand — Freeman and Lawrence, proprietors.

4:43. In the block north, a couple of hundred feet away: Are men standing at the windows above the House of Lords Restaurant and Bar? Are they looking to get a good view of something, as if the intersection is about to become an arena? William Grayston is familiar with arenas, but this one is not a speaker's stump or an orator's stage or a debater's platform. It is a marketplace Colosseum, and entering is the eminent attorney from Sparta, Missouri, a gladiator, albeit one lacking sword, shield, or helmet. *Ave! Moriturus te saluto!*

4:44. "Say there!" he calls out again. "Bayne, you son of a bitch!"

Now Bayne is waiting for him. Grayston shouts for all to hear: "You can't live in the same town I do! I've told you and I mean it!" Bayne straightens from his devil-may-care slouch but does not remove his right hand from his overcoat pocket, nor does he speak. Can nothing provoke this man to response, not even a theatric and public insult and challenge? Grayston whips back his right arm and hits Bayne on the left jaw hard enough to send the big man against the door of the saloon. There's only one punch. Hats go flying.

4:45. The superintendent recovers his balance, thrusts the right side of his overcoat forward and, from the hip, squeezes the trigger on the pistol in his outer pocket. The bullet strikes Frank Geier just above the heart. Even before the bartender hits the sidewalk, Bayne pulls out the pistol, and as William begins to rise from picking up his hat, the gun gets shoved right above his heart, only the chesterfield over his left arm to protect him, and point-blank, Bayne fires again. The bullet penetrates the coat, pierces William's weskit, perforates the left ventricle of his heart, punctures his liver, and passes on down to his pelvis where it ricochets off the bone and stops.

4:46. Grayston turns, lunges into the street, drops his smoldering, powder-burned coat, and takes another bullet, this one in the back, above the heart, shattering his left shoulder blade. Bayne fires two more shots. They go wild. The gun is empty, but he has hit two men with three shots, all of them into the upper left side of the body, either into the heart or just above. It is skillful, almost professional, shooting.

4:47. Frank Geier lies on the sidewalk by the saloon door. He will survive. Grayston, still holding his derby, unable to stand straight, reaches the east side of Main and staggers one step into the little news-depot, and there, between printed words, those pleasures so much a part of his life, he falls backward as proprietor Harvey Lawrence catches him by the collar and lowers him. His twitching legs lie in the ornate doorway and his head on the sidewalk. Under the amphitheater of the Roman Colosseum was a small exit for the slain: the Portal of Death.

4:48. A man claiming to be a doctor from Kansas City, not to be heard from again, comes forward as if a deus ex machina, feels for a pulse, and finds it: weak, weaker, gone. Except for the dark splotch on Grayston's vest above the heart, there is not much blood. At the bottom of the circle of silent, gaping faces, William stares blindly into the sinking light of the implacably godless sky of the Thursday before Thanksgiving, and a woman at the back of the crowd says, "What's the matter?" and a man answers, "Oh, nothing — only a man killed."

4:49. Someone else goes into the street where the trolleys have come to a halt, and he stomps out the burning chesterfield and hands it to a helmeted man — either a taxi driver or a constable (he will testify later), both of whom wear similar headgear.

4:50. Then a second deus ex machina: the acting county coroner comes from nowhere and rifles through Grayston's pockets. He finds no weapon. He appears disappointed.

In a struggle for existence, the fittest has survived.

The next day, the *Press* in Carthage, the county seat, wrote: "Joplin was the scene of another awful tragedy yesterday afternoon and another was added to the long list of crimes which has been growing there so rapidly during the present month." Reporters in Jasper County and across the state presented the deadly events as a classic love triangle, and that was what most of Joplin believed, and so did my father who first told me the story, and so I believed until a few weeks after that rainy day in the Joplin library when Q and I began trying to follow the tracks of the killer.

The moment Bayne emptied the revolver, he returned it to his overcoat pocket. With remarkable calmness and assurance for someone who had just shot down two people in public view, one of them a prominent lawyer, and thereby transformed a young woman into a widow and a little girl into a fatherless child, he walked away, accompanied by a man large enough to be a bodyguard. The pair was headed toward Bayne's Waterworks office a block distant and behind the Joplin Hotel owned by his boss, Tom Connor.

Before they could reach it, two police and an ex-constable stopped them and asked the killer why he shot Grayston, to which he, speaking at long last, said, "The son of a bitch hit me." The police took the pistol from him and checked the cylinder to find all five bullets spent. The assassin had fired until he could fire no more. Then a third deus ex machina in the form of two more people: Bayne's lawyers — one the author of Pearl's divorce petition, and both men Grayston's frequent adversaries in court. They somehow quickly got from their offices and made it through the big throng filling the streets to reach Bayne just in time to tell him to say nothing more. The killer went into his second public silence, that one lasting seven months.

William's attorney brother, in their office only a few hundred feet from the site of the shooting, for reasons unknown, took two hours to get a warrant sworn out for the arrest of Bayne. Even then the gunman was not formally arrested but simply turned over to Walter Fletcher, once a miner, an uneducated man who had been elected justice of the peace and who right then also happened to be the acting coroner, neither position requiring knowledge of law or medicine. While Fletcher, he who searched Grayston's pockets, wrangled and stormed over jurisdiction with a constable trying to serve the warrant for Bayne's arrest, the murderer sat watching, utterly silent, fully placid, as if guaranteed the outcome of it all. One reporter wrote the killer was "cool and unconcerned, [showing] no agitation."

Finally, Fletcher spoke of "an understanding" that Bayne was not to be placed in jail but merely taken into custody by a deputy constable, a secret-handshake brother of the slayer, and escorted to their lodge hall for supper before going on to Carthage and a room in the elegant Harrington Hotel, the social center of town. Later, when asked about such an unorthodox arrangement, Justice Fletcher told the deputy to say there was concern about mob action. That explanation might bear up for anyone who sees a dining table in a lodge hall and a room in a hotel as providing greater security than a cell in a police station.

During all of these shenanigans, Fletcher managed to retrieve the burned overcoat and the bloodied vest (*it* would never be seen again), and he even argued for the murder weapon to be given back to the assassin, but the city marshal refused to hand over the pistol. Justice Fletcher also contrived to take bartender George Bayless, the key witness, into Bayne's office for a private conference and then on to the *Globe* office for a chat with a reporter.

At the coroner's inquest that evening, five carefully selected jury men gave the only verdict possible to a murder executed in broad daylight before dozens of witnesses: "W. E. Grayston came to his death from a gunshot wound inflicted by one George G. Bayne." But two jurors, at the urging of Fletcher, tried to insert the interpretation that the homicide was done in self-defense. A coroner's jury, of course, does not exist to establish motive. But if Justice Fletcher's connivances were obvious, it wasn't then apparent why he would expose himself to charges of several manifest malfeasances.

The following morning, November 22, Bayne was returned to Joplin where he waived arraignment and was admitted to a bail set by Fletcher of only three-thousand dollars. The *Press* wrote, "There is general surprise in Carthage that the bail should be so low, even if Bayne should be admitted to bail at all." Also brought about that day was the first of three eventual changes of venue — not out of Joplin but out of the courtrooms of certain judges and into the purview of the uneducated justice of the peace, Fletcher.

Again at liberty, the murderer went immediately to the Payton boardinghouse, his access to Pearl at last unfettered, and he packed his bag — that simple act Grayston had demanded for eighteen months — and returned to his office where he stayed the night, using for a pillow his rolled overcoat, the one he wore while gunning down William. The next day Bayne boarded a Frisco coach for Illinois where he spent the succeeding several days with his mother.

As he, lips sealed, waited for the homicide trial, he never exhibited anything but quiet certainty about his case, despite shooting point-blank an unarmed man bending over to pick up his hat, and firing a second bullet into his back, both shots directed at the heart. Bayne did not once attempt to aim for a leg or arm; he fired no warning shot; he did not brandish the weapon; and he did not respond with his own large fists. Yet he seemed assured his argument of self-defense against a man who punched him once but clearly intended no further blows would prevail in the murder trial.

An undertaker's ambulance, a new horse-drawn vehicle, came to take Grayston to the morgue for an autopsy. The county physician removed the slug from William's broken shoulder blade but left in the other, deeply embedded mortal piece of lead, and today it lies with William's remains under a few feet of flinty soil on a hillside north of Sparta in Christian County, in a forgotten family cemetery big enough to hold only seven other related burials, one of them his infant son, Herbert.

Those eight Graystons rest beneath five old cedars, the graves marked for a century by only small, rough fieldstones that look more accidental than placed, meager memorials from the man who put them there, the paterfamilias, the old stonecutter from England, "the hermit poet-preacher" who apparently saw things of this realm as dross, distractions from the true life-eternal promised to the delivered.

The last words I've been able to find from him reveal *his hope* that his freethinking son — the one who believed any heaven would be of human making — had changed his mind and at last joined that blessed gathering of the redeemed waiting somewhere beyond this particular vale of tears.

And, of tears shed during the justments for the deceased, none exceeded those from William's first wife who, wrote the *Press,*

arose in the church and stated in the presence of the living and the dead in a voice broken with sobs, that the trouble which caused her separation from W. E. Grayston was her own fault, and that she felt it her duty at this time and upon this occasion to offer this restitution, this exoneration from blame to his memory; that had she been a little less impatient and had acted as she should have done, that they might have been living happily together today, because she had always loved him and him only.

People witnessing her shocking eruption in the crowded chapel feared the emotion-racked confession revealed temporary derangement. Among those gathered was William's first daughter, fifteen-year-old Gertrude. Twenty-three-year-old Mrs. Pearl Grayston chose to stay home in Joplin.

Gertrude Grayston, Springfield, Missouri, 1900.

❥ 6 ❦

God Help the Jury

Y OU'LL RECALL that Q brought reports of this homicide to me while I was reading about the Quapaw Ghost Light before we were to go in quest of it. But I want to keep William's story together, so I'm going to step ahead in sequence and travel only in time to get you to the outcome before I return to the road leading to the purported Light along the border of the old Indian Territory.

The murder of Grayston, as far as I could follow it, seemed to have more loose ends than a frayed hawser. Discovering a threadlet here and an inkle there still didn't allow me to bring them into coherence, and the unraveled strands lay parted and tangled, failing to tie together the century-old interpretation of a crime of passions. The record was replete with incompatible details and cryptic utterances even a master boatswain's mate couldn't braid into a plausible line. It wasn't that *something* was missing — it was that a full locker of lines looked to be missing.

For a time, the new information led only deeper into a dead end. Then, a small gleam, a kind of ghostly beacon, if you will, rose above that cul-de-sac to shine and beckon, and behind it were truths waiting for more than a century to come into light.

The skeleton of the story lay in several newspapers of 1901 and 1902, most of them from Jasper County. I continually had to evaluate political orientations that colored and, at times, distorted reporting: the *Joplin Daily Globe* was a Democratic organ and the *News-Herald* and *Carthage Press* were Republican. While what I'm about to tell you, as much as possible, is evidential fact or testimony corroborated by confirmed events, I've still had to referee variations and contradictory details, always trying to discount the overwhelming conjectures and speculations at the trial. I struggled against the loose standards of reportage in that era not far removed from the days of yellow journalism, and I had to weigh obviously biased assumptions and rumormongering presented as truth, especially when they contradicted established particulars. The amount of sheer reportorial incompetence — corrupted quotations, names spelled differently (not just from day to day but within the same sentence) or given entirely wrong (*Price* changed to *Pratt*), grammatical errors ("he had threw that away") — left me confused at one moment and amused the next. And then there were the typesetters' hooters. Here's a single line *quoting* the judge's instructions to the jury:

arguments, ou are yhereb nyotified not to.

Q discovered Grayston had once brought a libel suit against the Republican *News-Herald* (later dropped for reasons unknown) and also had political clashes with Democrats running the *Globe*. In a small town with fifty barrooms, William's Anti-Saloon League lectures put him at odds with influential men and their cohorts who owned and operated highly lucrative establishments, the House of Lords supreme among them (the editor of the *Globe* held title to the building). Working against relative newcomer Grayston was his belonging to neither lodge nor church as well as his support of issues such as women's suffrage and pensions to miners' widows in a town controlled by mining magnates and their associates and underlings.

One last detail: despite several searches across the state, attorney Q could find no transcript of the trial, *State of Missouri v. George G. Bayne.*

On June 30, 1902, from a jury pool of almost sixty men, the attorneys selected twelve, most of them farmers, ages twenty-five to sixty-five, only one from Joplin. In the middle of the growing season, the men were pulled out of their fields and away from their stock to be sequestered for an unspecified period but almost certainly including the Fourth of July, when there would be nothing for men of the open air to do but sit confined in a hot hotel.

The trial began on July 1 in a filled chamber where "standing room only" meant people at the rear stood on chairs to get a glimpse of the faces and demeanors of the killer and of the Belle of Joplin. A third of the audience was female, among them "two very pretty women, the sister of Grayston . . . attired in deep mourning." She was the only person present whose grief exceeded her curiosity. "The other of those more than ordinarily pretty women was Mrs. Grayston . . . attired in a soft white wool shirtwaist." William's father, the renowned man of the cloth, remained in Christian County. The question for the spectators was not who did it or why he did it — they already "knew" that; what they didn't know were the terms of his punishment. But, even more, their curiosity wanted to hear somebody break into a steamy confession.

The state opened with its plan to press for murder in the first degree, a verdict that would require proof of malice aforethought. (When Q read of the prosecutor's plan, she said, "I can't believe it! He's opened and lost.") Despite numerous denials from the victim himself based on his several investigations, the motive the prosecutor and his three assistants intended to prove was that George Bayne had been intimate with Pearl Grayston while William was traveling. (As Q read on, she said: "What've they found that William's investigation missed?")

The defense answered: Grayston was a volatile and "dangerous" person whose several public threats to Bayne virtually forced the defendant to protect himself with a concealed weapon for which he had a permit. Lawyers for the accused held that Grayston was a large, strong, unstable man, and they trotted several witnesses to the stand who alleged they had *heard of* his being "dangerous" or they had *surmised* as much, although not one of them himself (they were all males) had witnessed anything beyond a vocal threat to Bayne. Their ex parte testimony being expressed in such similar language suggests considerable pretrial coaching, virtually confirmed by subsequent leading of witnesses. The prosecution did not raise an objection to those tactics or to witnesses throwing out rampant speculations and judgments. In fact, on at least two occasions, the prosecutor's own witnesses spoke opinions that hardly assisted his argument. He seemed unable — or *unwilling* — to control their statements.

Again and again, the defense readily drew from witnesses variations of Grayston's "reputation was bad" and Bayne's "reputation was good," one man citing the time William told an opposing lawyer "to sit down or he'd pull his whiskers." Another testified he'd heard someone say Grayston "was the kind of man who'd come up behind you and blow your head off." (William had never owned a gun.) Yet another opined the slain man "was liable to kill anybody." Dolan, Grayston's perpetual courtroom foe, told the jury the victim "was one of the meanest men . . . or the craziest" he'd ever known. To all of that hearsay and supposition, the prosecution objected *not even once*. Judging by accounts in the Joplin newspapers, the first two days were trial by character assassination.

It was day three before the prosecuting attorney at last raised an objection, but only to Dolan's "bulldozing" a witness, which drew a rebuke from the judge for using such a coarse term in his courtroom; but he did sustain the objection.

Assisted by Grayston's brother, the prosecution team was not undistinguished; if anything, its credentials appear to have outshone those of Bayne's three lawyers. But even when the legally astute George Grayston took the stand, his testimony was listless and perfunctory, surely leading their sister to wonder, *If he won't speak forcefully for our brother, who will?*

The prosecutors based much of their argument on equivocal statements by three teenage girls who, during elocution practice in the Methodist church across the street from the Payton boardinghouse, alleged they saw from ninety feet away and through two windows a woman who was — or looked like — Pearl sitting on the lap of a man who was — or looked like — George Bayne, the pair "hugging and kissing" while he — or she — was inexplicably holding a newspaper. A woman testified she'd seen Pearl and Bayne riding in a buggy over in Byersville, to which the defense responded with a witness out of Oklahoma, one Mabel Price (a name to remember), who said it was she in the buggy and that she was sometimes mistaken for Mrs. Grayston; Mabel then stood before the jury in an attempt to show a professed resemblance. Throughout the trial, Pearl herself conferred frequently with the killer's lawyers.

At last, the petite beauty in her white shirtwaist took the stand as the crowded court murmured and then grew silent, not to miss a single of her words, every ear waiting for that titillating question. At last the prosecuting attorney asked it: "Have you ever had sexual intercourse with Mister Bayne?" Emphatically, Pearl Grayston said, "Certainly not!" The prosecution, as if rebuked, took that line no further and yielded to the defense which then established Pearl was at work on the afternoon the teenage girls claimed to have seen her smooching it up with Bayne.

The evening Q read the account of the trial, she said to me, "I keep waiting for the prosecution to argue that five shots from a thirty-eight — one while the victim was bending over and another into his back, both aimed at his heart — were hardly a *measured* self-defense against an unarmed man. Besides, William made no attempt to batter Bayne. It wasn't a fight." I suggested she keep reading, but she didn't, not just then. Instead she said, "If William was so strong and dangerous, the kind to come up behind you, why didn't he just beat up or shoot Bayne in a dark alley with no witnesses? I mean, he took action on the most public street in Joplin when it was most full of people." She was getting vexed. "And I've got another problem. Does a *dangerous* man make all his threats in public?"

She was shaking her head. "His open challenges had to be just a tactic to embarrass Bayne and get him to move away from Pearl." I recommended she read on, but she said, "Why hasn't the prosecution found and brought forth the bloody vest to show the jury? Juries don't easily forget blood. And why aren't those unethical procedures of that scalawag of a justice of the peace coming out? He had no legal training. He tampered with evidence. He tried to manipulate a key witness. He tried to influence the inquest verdict." Then she read on, but not before adding, "Where's any mention of William as an advocate of the Law and Order League? Come on now, this is an all-star prosecution team? A law student could show up such ineptness. It had to be deliberately executed incompetence."

Finally, Bayne came to the stand. For a couple of hours, he gave an account that hardly differed from what others had said except in two details: first, he saw Grayston put his *right* hand into his pocket before hitting him, and second, the blow landed on Bayne's *right* jaw. Grayston's right-handedness made both assertions highly dubious unless you accept that he struck a powerful blow with his left hand while his right was reaching into his pocket. An enraged righty leading with his left? Bayne clearly was trying to use the single testimony — denied by all others — that Grayston appeared to be going for a gun just before he swung his fist. The prosecution raised not one of those questions.

Of the defendant's assured testimony, the *Globe* wrote, "Bayne was decidedly the best witness on either side." Given the prosecution's insipid questioning of him, that's probably accurate.

After the Fourth of July recess, on the final day, the prosecutors at last seemed to take up genuine pursuit of justice, as each of them spoke in summary to ridicule the argument that unarmed Grayston was a "dangerous man." The concluding statement, given by the least-experienced prosecutor, nevertheless drew applause from spectators. On reading that, Q said, "I don't know how, but maybe the all-stars are going to pull it out." Then she read on to see that the closing arguments for the defense also had effect.

Just before midnight on Saturday, the fifth of July, the judge gave the unlettered jury his complex instructions: Although Bayne had been tried for murder in the first degree, the jury "could not find in the first degree . . . as the trouble resulting in the murder was not unprovoked." But, should they find the defendant not guilty as charged but rather guilty of premeditating a crime, they could find him guilty in the second degree. Or, further, if they "find the deed was committed in sudden heat of passion and done of malice," their verdict could be murder in the fourth degree. If that was their decision, the killer could be considered for the minimal penalty — a fine of a hundred dollars.

William's father in Sparta would write:

> God help the jury in this case
> To give our homes a sacred place;
> Without it, life is but a sham;
> To Thee we look, the great I Am.

And so, off into the night thick with July heat went twelve "thoroughly fatigued men," cooped up for a week like so many laying hens — farmers kept from the necessary care of stock and crops — to consider forty hours of testimony. On Sunday morning it took them a little more than a hundred minutes to reach a verdict, despite the first vote being ten to two. After brief further discussion, it was eleven to one. Then, although the last juror was still dubious, to keep deliberations from dragging on only to end up with a hung jury, he voted with the majority.

Monday morning the court reconvened, and the foreman stood to read the verdict in those first half-dozen words known so well: "We, the jury, find the defendant not guilty as charged." George G. Bayne, slayer of William E. Grayston, stood calmly, his assurance now confirmed, as he accepted the congratulations of his lawyers. Three days later the acquitted killer resigned from the Joplin Waterworks to take a similar job in Carthage, and nine months after that he married the petite blonde he'd taken for a buggy ride or two, the woman who testified in support of one of his alibis: Mabel Price.

The day following the trial, the *Carthage Press* reported: "One of the jurors remarked afterward that on general principles Bayne should have been given about two years for remaining and courting danger, but that under the law and evidence, the jury could do nothing but turn him loose."

And Grayston? Well, he was proven right: his wife was innocent of adultery.

Robert Ingersoll, the freethinking attorney who had inspired William years earlier, once wrote, "In Nature there are neither rewards nor punishments — there are consequences."

❧ 7 ❧

A Triangle Becomes a Polygon

THERE WAS SOMETHING WRONG with the entire story — not merely justice miscarried but something of even greater import; the evidence simply didn't fit what the public accepted: a mortal outcome of a marital triangle. A pair of facts kept trying to bend the human geometry into a different shape. *But what the devil was the true shape?* The first fact was Bayne's moving out of the Payton rooming house immediately after he was freed on bail the day following the murder, the very thing the victim for eighteen months had been demanding. Second, Bayne speedily married not Pearl but the woman he'd allegedly been glimpsed with during those months. If there was adultery in the Payton place, wouldn't his future bride also have demanded he move elsewhere? Were he truly innocent of adulterous dalliance, wouldn't she insist he clear his name?

Other nettlesome details arose: Why would a man who for months appeared craven and feckless even with a pistol in his pocket finally court a confrontation that would shame him at the most public place in Joplin? Why would a well-paid president and superintendent of a company insist on living a year and a half in an eight-dollar-a-week room in a small and crowded house not far from the honky-tonks of the Kansas City Southern bottoms? Why, three days after his acquittal, would he resign his job with Joplin Waterworks only to take a similar one just twelve miles away? Why would a man whose career was notable for its transience refuse to move even across the street to defuse a threat to his life? Why would a man fearing his survival be so dangerously stubborn?

I couldn't leave those questions alone. One night, when Q and I were home again from the Southwest, I began rehashing aloud all we'd learned about the events. Finally, hearing myself, I stopped and apologized for once again flooding her with what I called my obsession for the truth of the murder. "I don't think you're *obsessed*," she said. "I think you're *possessed*. William's ghost has you." I said she knew I believed in only ghosts of the Nodgort kind. She hesitated not a moment. "But you believe big-time in the persistence of memory."

Unbeknownst to me, Q soon went to the State Historical Society on the University of Missouri campus to begin cranking more reels of old microfilmed newspapers, trying to read the scratched and blemished and often barely legible words. When she returned, she handed me several sheets of gray photocopies. "You've been complaining of the blatant bias in the reporting in Joplin, so I went looking for stories from out of town."

As Carthage started planning a massively magnificent courthouse in 1891, Joplin demanded for itself a kind of "annex" almost as impressive, a place to handle criminal cases. Carthage, the "holy city" where mine owners went to live, could house the recorder of deeds as long as Joplin, the "sin city" where miners came out of deep holes to blow their wages, got the county prosecutor. After all, in the competition between the towns, what was litigable in one might not be so in the other. A jurisprudence of convenience — and control.

I sat down with the *Carthage Press* account of the murder but found nothing to alter or enlarge what I already knew. I must have read too fast, because a few days later when I went over it again, I noticed the final paragraph, a little piece seemingly tacked on as an afterthought, the kind of thing a compositor may cut off to fit a story onto a page, fourteen lines almost hidden in the shadow of smudged microfilm. If I did believe in ghosts, I'd have sworn they had just inserted the paragraph. Above it in tiny type was this subheadline — INVESTIGATING WATERWORKS — and following were three sentences, the last one a stroboscopic beam:

It is a fact that W. E. Grayston had been for some time conducting a searching inquiry into the Joplin Waterworks affairs. It is not known that this fact had anything to do with yesterday's trouble, but it certainly had no tendency to promote pleasant relations between the two men. Grayston charged that the city council had to an extent been bought up by the water company, and that he would shortly divulge some startling facts which would have important bearing on the spring elections.

So: the crime was not a triangle, and maybe it wasn't even a rectangle. Maybe it was a polygon of more angles than a spectacular billiard shot. The triangle, as presented by both the defense and the prosecution, was (to mix the image) a red herring, a lurid ruse readily comprehensible to a rough-edged populace wanting a smutty tale of criminal carnality rather than one of municipal turpitude. The papers in Joplin had not, in a suspicious silence over eight months, even once in several thousand words mentioned Grayston's investigations. What's more, neither did the prosecuting attorney (a Joplinite), although such evidence had motive for murder written all over it.

In search of items that before seemed contradictory, elliptic, unexplained, inconsonant, or downright nonsensical, I took up the murder again, rereading what I'd earlier gathered. No longer did I need a cudgel to beat loose details into a formation because at last they fell into place and marched along like a drill team.

After more than a century, not every piece was still existent, but plenty enough remained to build a ghost outline of the new figure — a polygon indeed. Q and I dug up long-buried news stories, most of them outwardly unconnected to the homicide; we got marriage certificates, divorce petitions, Last Wills and Testaments, obituaries, funeral records, civil suits in two states, minutes of city council meetings, lodge rosters, old maps, and photographs of faces and buildings in turn-of-the-century Joplin and Carthage; we did considerable footwork on the streets, even twice reenacting William's last steps, once with me playing the victim, and once the malefactor; we went off to find his unremembered and overgrown grave (a search leaving us crawling with ticks). We even later stopped in Illinois to see the mausoleum wherein since 1939 has lain the murderer in his marble sarcophagus.

Despite the sensational nature of the homicide, by the time of our visit more than a century later, Joplin had quite forgotten about it — acquittals reduce significance — but its drama readily drew in librarians and archivists who came up with documents we otherwise would never have found. Some of the records were in deplorable condition. One newspaper account of the murder, which might have shed even more detail, lay within a large, bound book, but the brittle paper was in more and tinier fragments than the Dead Sea Scrolls. And a possibly significant nineteenth-century legal document in Springfield had disappeared forever because it and hundreds of others had been stored in a shed alongside wet snowplows. Administrators in my own county courthouse some years previous had ordered a dump truck to back up under an attic window to catch old records pitched out for a trip to the landfill. (Beyond all that, how much American history everywhere has gone down the gullets of mice to end up as droppings, I can't guess.)

The *Joplin Daily Globe,* the organ that in its own way had once covered over the truth, published a story about my quest. For several weeks thereafter, the postman brought to me now and then an envelope of details. A perfect crime was, except in the escape of the perpetrators, no longer perfect.

I believe now, were those people involved in or witness to the homicide still living, Q could retry the case and convict George G. Bayne not of murder in the fourth degree, nor the third, nor even the second, but of murder one, and his directors as accessories to the crime. Yet, without those witnesses and their truthful testimony, my case must today remain circumstantial; but, as you will see, those circumstantials are so numerous and coherent, probability exceeds coincidence.

That little beacon of a paragraph out of Carthage provided new, more consonant interpretations to utterances like one from Pearl's father, which I'd previously taken as dissembling or as a simple-minded interpretation of a family tragedy: to a reporter's asking for "the occasion of this affair," George Payton answered, "If people would attend to their own business and let other people's business alone, there would not be so much trouble." He had to be speaking of gossips as well as Grayston's investigations into the waterworks. And when William, in the letter to his father, mentioned Pearl's asking him "not to think ahead and borrow trouble, but just to go along and let the world run as it wants to run," it was now clear she too was talking about his civic investigations.

Grayston's unwillingness to "go along" with public malfeasance appears also in that last letter to his father, as William asks him to "read between the lines," some of which address "the awful corruption in Joplin." He was, one way or another, a proponent for the "clean government" movement just then beginning to take shape in western Missouri, a cause that, a decade or so after his murder, would lead Joplin to experiment with a city-commission system.

He had once mentioned a "conspiracy" but later dropped the word, not because there wasn't a conspiracy, I think, but because the term, until proven in court, suggests paranoia. No matter who asked it of him, Grayston was a man incapable of letting "the world run as it wants to run" when that meant harm to the public weal and to his daughter. He was, wrote his father, "goaded by more than common strife," but I've found nothing to suggest he knew his challenge was putting the continuance of his days at risk.

❧ 8 ❧

Though Dead, He Speaks

O NCE I HAD ASSEMBLED ALL THE PERTINENT FACTS I was likely to turn up, here's what I believe happened in Joplin, starting in the spring of 1901 when the promise of the new millennium was only three months old.

Realizing Pearl's divorce petition prevented moving his family, Grayston decided to remain in town to investigate further the corruption of East Joplin and the related vice of West Joplin, baneful iniquities now reaching into his own home and threatening his daughter's future. For a man of an inherited, preternaturally crusading spirit, his decision to challenge those behind the jobbery was the only conscionable action. If not religious, he was indeed ethical and thoroughly philosophical, and possessed of an intellectual underpinning that gave reason and basis for trying to correct rottenness — Spencer's "dissolutions" — harming public welfare and his family.

But, astute as he was, apparently he did not at first recognize the role Bayne was playing in the corruption, for it was Grayston who suggested the superintendent take a room with his wife's family. Could William then only have read a quatrain from his father's funeral ode to him, "Though Dead, He Speaks," he might have lived longer. The lines confirm David's perception of the truth:

> *His home, selected for its lair,*
> *Foul serpent had been coiling there,*
> *Watching to make its deadly spring,*
> *A loathsome, filthy, deathly thing.*

Waterworks superintendent Bayne did not move into the Payton home to get cheaper quarters; he arrived as a lackey mole to look for means to force Grayston to shut down an investigation getting too close to him and his confraternity. Most of Joplin knew about the separations of the prominent couple, and every lawyer had heard of voluble William's hopes for reconciliation and his deep concerns for his daughter. The men who hired Bayne to run the water plant knew Grayston's vulnerability lay in his devotion to family, and they understood his heartstrings were attached to his Achilles' heel: his potential for intemperate response. Sooner or later, the oligarchs might be able to pull those strings in a way to rein him in.

Although the stooge Bayne was in the Payton house at first simply to gather information, as gossip developed, his confederates realized they might play rumor into a conclusive manipulation of Grayston. Their first tactic was to incite, pay for, and encourage the divorce petition, while at the same time discouraging Pearl from following through with it. To keep it hanging over Grayston could serve better to force him to desist in his inquiries.

The Lords of the White Tablecloth, shrewd as they could be nefarious, surely also saw they might be able to use against him his reputation for bold confrontation, widely recognized among Joplin lawyers; such volatility in the face of malfeasance could make him susceptible to a cunningly conceived provocation, a ploy to inflame him into irrationality. Here was a man who, said his own attorney, "fought his law cases with a good deal of heart," always refusing to back away from public misdeeds.

The protagonist in a blood tragedy must commit a deadly error of judgment, and even the names here seem suited to a drama: a house of lords sending a bane into the home of a man of will and his beautiful pearl. Had Grayston kept his plan silent until actually exposing the culpable, he would have had a protective shield of truth, and it would have been too late to silence him. But, as friends and foes alike testified, William was "quite a talker."

At last, the lords could not afford to wait longer; there was no more time for a subtle, restrained response. It had come down to Grayston or them, and they decided, if I may phrase it so, to pull the trigger. The hand to do that job was already perfectly placed and the true motive for the homicide conveniently concealed by rumors and Grayston's public statements of there not being room enough in Joplin for both himself and the superintendent. All the plot needed was something to force William to make the first move, a deed to be forced in broad daylight before dozens of witnesses who would, by their very presence, provide a cover of justifiable homicide. Grayston was too prominent — especially after his announcement — to be taken to a mine shaft and dropped in, a dark exit of some lesser Joplin men.

I believe Bayne's collaborators, neither thugs nor mobsters, and not at heart murderers, were (to use an old phrase) "just crooked enough to have to screw their hats on," mere businessmen with lucrative connections bringing in graft and bribes, people fearful of losing what they had connived diligently to get. Their motive, beyond continued greed and retention of their gains and power, was avoidance of prison. With the elimination of a single man, the lords and abettors and even the executioner could emerge innocent, with their ill-got gains intact. Aware that Grayston was a man of frontal assault and not one "to creep up from behind to blow a head off," they knew he had evidence to make a few heads roll.

The lords selected the hour and the arena and put all the actors in place, got every action ready to proceed as scripted: a gladiator with a derby for a helmet, an overcoat for a buckler, his sword a clenched fist. The crowd would be there when the emperor gave the thumbs-down, and as the man from Sparta fell, the rough-edged throng could almost hear a *Hoc Habet!* "Now he's had it!"

The immediate postmortem events and trial went as flawlessly as the perfectly placed bullets:

· The mysterious "doctor" who appeared from nowhere to take William's pulse and then vanish.

- The sudden arrival of the killer's lawyer through the milling crowd just as the police seized the murder weapon.
- The unqualified *acting* coroner getting to the body before it could be taken to the undertaker.
- His manipulation and destruction of evidence.
- His attempt to get motive inserted into the verdict.
- The killer not even for a moment being manacled or placed in a cell but instead taken by a fellow lodge-brother to their hall for supper and then to a comfortable hotel room.
- The absurdly minimal bail.
- Timing the trial for the heart of the growing season.
- Stacking the jury with farmers sure to be restive and eager to get back to their animals and crops, men with no inclination to argue their way into a hung jury that could lead to a retrial and a change of venue, ill-educated men struggling to interpret the judge's needlessly convoluted instructions precluding any verdict requiring serious punishment.

All of those measures were probably enough. But, given how much was riding on the outcome, the lords took no chances on anything they could control, including the prosecution:

- Its plan to pursue a verdict impossible to win.
- Insistence on trying to establish an adulterous relationship the victim himself had disproven.
- Reliance on insubstantial and refutable testimony from fourteen-year-old girls.
- Refusal to challenge repeated conjectures, speculations, and hearsay.
- Failure to point out that many of the witnesses for the defense belonged to the same secret orders as the killer.
- Failure to put forward that the victim was shot once while bending over to pick up his hat and a second time in the back.
- Failure to demonstrate that the defendant, allegedly intending only self-defense, did not attempt to aim for a leg or an arm or to

fire a warning shot or merely to brandish his weapon in the face of an unarmed man.

· Failure to discover what caused Grayston to turn around on Main Street — such as a threat to his daughter — and, after eighteen months of clandestine opportunities, to choose instead the most crowded of public arenas to confront his nemesis, a man who could have prevented the violence simply by boarding a streetcar for a home in lovely Carthage where, after all, he would go immediately following the murder.

But, the most convicting evidence of a corrupted trial is the refusal of the prosecution to introduce Grayston's sustained inquiry into municipal corruption involving the city council and the editor of the *Globe* (a man the *Carthage Press* called "Boss" Barbee when it printed a map showing his private, covered walkway into the House of Lords). William's investigation established a clear motive for his murder, considerably more convincing than the simple contrivance of a jealous husband who on his own public testimony had exonerated his wife of adultery.

This last failure of the prosecution virtually indicts Grayston's brother and partner: are we to believe William never discussed with him his extended probings so deeply connected to his life? Given William's years of studying scientific method and inductive procedures, given his professional awareness of the crucial importance of prima facie evidence, can anyone believe he kept no records to prove the dangerous charges he was about to announce? Who, we must ask, above all else would know about those records and their whereabouts? Who would have last access to them? Where did they go?

There is but a single plausible answer.

If that is not enough, then what are we to conclude from George Grayston's indifferent, listless, and occasionally slighting testimony supposedly in defense of his murdered brother? What about his comments immediately following the trial? "I desire to express my positive and complete satisfaction with the work of the attorneys for the state. . . . Their work was not only able but brilliant and showed the high order of legal forensic ability possessed by them." An able and brilliant prosecution with high forensic ability that could not even produce a hundred-dollar fine against the killer of his brother?

Consider a final pair of questions: What's the implication of the younger Grayston being appointed as city attorney only two years following the murder? And beginning soon after that, what are we to infer from his long professional association with the Joplin Waterworks?

Could I make my summary argument before a new jury, this would be it: William Grayston was descended on, laid into, sold out, and done in. He was set up to be shot down. He died in a political assassination executed so cleverly, the truth lay buried for more than a century, with only two innocent women and their daughters serving a lifelong sentence.

I, fair-minded reader, rest my case. You and all readers who come after you are now the jury.

The aftermath: Brother Grayston later served as counsel to corporations and wealthy Joplinites before succumbing at age fifty-nine — a life twenty years longer than William's — to appendicitis. The week he died, the circuit court closed for a day to honor him.

George Bayne, the man who refused to move out of a crowded boardinghouse, soon began moving from town to town, getting involved in a water department lawsuit in Tulsa, Oklahoma, and somehow slipping out of that one too, before returning to near his boyhood home in Illinois, accompanied by his new wife, the purported Pearl Grayston look-alike, who there bore him a son. The killer lived into his seventies, dying just three months after my birth (Q: "Did you pass word there wasn't room enough in 1939 for both of you?"). He died not on a public sidewalk but in his own bed, wife at his side, of a myocardial infarction. The undertaker's record gives his occupation as "mausoleum owner." George Grant Bayne, as if fulfilling his surname, at last found honest means to make money from what he was good at: as a minister of death. It is in that mausoleum where he lies today, shielded from the elements, his mummified cadaver safely locked in until the granite walls come down. To the very end, he proved adept at self-preservation.

Mrs. Anna Pearl Grayston worked as a bookkeeper in Joplin for several years before remarrying. Her daughter with William, the little girl whose education and future he was so worried about, a concern which fueled his investigation, became a schoolteacher.

William's other daughter, his first child, Gertrude, like her mother, was divorced not long after losing her second child at birth. She took her firstborn to Kansas City, San Diego, Los Angeles, St. Louis, and back to Kansas City where he, like his grandfather, became a lawyer, a man once described by another lawyer as "too honest to be a good attorney." Gertrude worked as a single mother for some years, usually as a manager of large, urban apartment-buildings, until she remarried well in her forties. But the lasting trauma of a father brazenly shot down on a street, a mother's hysterical coffin-side confession, a stillborn child, and her own growing mental frailty — those demons she fought but couldn't escape.

Thirty-six years after her father's assassination, Gertrude began writing more frequently to her mother (who had learned to gain strength from adversity), opening every letter with "Dearest Mother" and often closing them with "Heaps and heaps of love." But each month revealed increasing expressions of her failing will to live. In June 1937, in words strangely reflecting the last letter her father wrote, she said:

> [My illness] has been a so-called nervous collapse. Now you may think this all very silly, but it's been very serious. I am better today, but what I suffer I shall not tell you for you have your troubles too and [bear] them alone, but Mother, mine have been coming the past few years and possibly for years and years. Now I can look back and see how I should have handled some matters quite differently for my future's welfare. At any rate, I am sorry I didn't overcome worry in my younger days and take life and other's affairs

less seriously. I'm trying to now. So dearest, you do the same, for [doing otherwise] does not bring happiness or health.

Only two weeks later, on the third of July, almost exactly thirty-five years to the day of the acquittal of her father's murderer, at about three in the morning, she persuaded her nurse, Edna, to leave the bedroom so that Gertrude might rest quietly in the heat. Her husband, to give his ill wife greater repose, was asleep upstairs in the tall apartment-building a few blocks from Forest Park in St. Louis, a well-situated neighborhood.

Sometime in the predawn, Gertrude rose from the hot bed and stepped to the bathroom, to open a small window. At four a.m. and again at five, Edna looked in to see Gertrude apparently lying quietly under a sheet. An hour later, checking once more, the nurse noticed her patient still in the same position. Tiptoeing to the bed, Edna found under the sheet not Gertrude but two pillows neatly arranged like a resting body. She knocked on the bathroom door. No answer. Knocking again, opening the door, she found no Gertrude. Edna started to leave when she felt a morning breeze from behind the shower curtain. Her heart in her throat, she drew back the curtain slowly, and, *Oh, thank heavens!* No one was in the tub.

She leaned over to close the small window opening to the alley-side of the building. But, seeing the screen unlatched, she stepped up on the edge of the tub to peer out a window so narrow a child would struggle to squeeze through it. Looking straight across the alley, she saw only the city. Then, pulling herself up so she could look directly down ten floors to the concrete roof of the parking garage, Edna saw it: the thin housedress in disarray over the bloodied, broken body.

George Grant Bayne, slayer of William Edward Grayston, had managed to strike again, this time without ever lifting a hand, and once again his alibi was perfect, but this one was a fact — he was nowhere near the scene. Yet, across the miles and years, Bayne still managed to get my father's mother.

9

Dance of the Hobs

THE QUAPAW GHOST LIGHT began showing itself, so claim a few elders, just about the year William Grayston arrived in Joplin. I take the coincident timing as sheer chance, despite one corner of my imagination wanting to see something greater in the connection; it's that ancient urge in us to find indications of ethereal — cosmic — significance in our lives, a morsel of evidence to suggest our little twin-legged assemblage of atoms is more than a brief inconsequentiality.

The file of articles on the Ghost Light in the Joplin library seemed to establish that the apparition made regular appearances twelve miles southwest of the accursed crux of Fourth and Main. In the clippings were the usual hokum and humbuggery associated with unexplained luminous phenomena across the nation. I went quickly through yarns of a vicious, captured Civil War sergeant — vengefully decapitated by being stood in front of a cannon — who spends eternity hunting his head; of a lady walking moonless nights with a ball of fire where her noddle should be; of a miner following his shaking carbide lamp in quest of a lost you-name-it. My search was for plausible details from people who, unsatisfied with anecdotes about the Light, had gone out into the Spookville Triangle to witness it for themselves.

In a society deprived of the bewitchingly inexplicable, a floating, bobbing, weaving, dancing, hovering, flashing, fracturing light that turns red, yellow, blue, green, and purple, and purportedly has been doing so since the arrival into Indian Territory of the Quapaw dispossessed from the Arkansas Valley — *that* is a thing to be inspected and maybe even cherished. And so it is among the people of the Three Corners where Missouri, Kansas, and Oklahoma conjoin less than four miles from the hangout of the ocular confoundment. The hamlet of Hornet, Missouri, is about that same distance away. Spook Light Road, popularly called the Devil's Promenade and, officially, Ottawa County Route E-50, lies just within the quondam Quapaw Reservation.

I was reading the dubieties because, a half century earlier, a close friend who grew up nearby had told me of smooching with his girl on a dark out-county lane and being accosted by a scintillating ball of heatless fire hovering over the hood of his car. My pal, known to be truthful if gullible, spoke so assuredly and vibrantly of the orb that two years later we went in search of it. We found nothing, possibly not even the correct road.

Perhaps somewhere in Missouri or Oklahoma exists a local newspaper or magazine never to have carried an item about the Quapaw Light, more commonly known in the old mining area, as I've mentioned, as the Hornet Spook Light. Even Q, growing up across the state, had read about it, and she insisted on having a chance to see it after my research made one thing clear: down on the Devil's Promenade, people were truly encountering a most quozzical *something*. As a reporter along the American road, I am bound by duty to explore the veracity of such wayside incidents because, who knows, your very safety while passing through might depend on an alert about balls of fire accosting vehicles after sundown.

Reports, both in print and from people I spoke to, claimed the phantasm sometimes appeared briefly or not at all, and on other occasions would shine till dawn. Generally, it had a constancy rather alien in the realm of ghosts. "It's reliable enough, especially on cloudy nights," a librarian told me, "and I never heard of it harming anybody, unless scaring the dickens out of you is harmful — you know, out there in the dark, getting a whack put on your ticker."

In both Jasper and Ottawa counties, I came upon nobody

unaware of the thing, about half saying they'd seen it, and most of them believing it not yet properly explained by science. But one fellow, ignoring the many photographs of it, called it "the Hornet Spoof Light." I asked had he seen it, and he replied, "How does a sane person see what isn't there?"

Based upon no physical evidence except declarations written and spoken, and in spite of the sanity question, I still believed in the possibility of something spectral: not a specter perhaps but maybe a manifestation of a spectrum out on the wooded slope above the Spring River on the western edge of the Ozark Plateau. I further believed Q and I would encounter nothing, yet we nevertheless went forth, interested not so much in debunking as merely observing. I'm not a fellow whom ghosts — beyond the hypothetical — seem attracted to any more than a prom queen to the goofball next door. Apparitions snub me, won't dance with me (except possibly one night in West Virginia — but that's a story for another book). In their defense, I admit I've never been good at having to believe in something before being able to witness it (and that's a key reason my little tub of traditional theologies always sinks even before I can get it untied from the dock of factuality for a sail into the rising Mare Fundamentalensis).

So, on that rainy Tuesday after I'd begun pursuit of a murderer, Q and I headed south as the sky was clearing just enough to reveal a frail, crescent moon setting beyond the prairie of eastern Oklahoma. The Devil's Promenade, the name linking to Devil's Hollow, was a wooded vale dropping down to the Spring River to the west. The lane was less forested than formerly but yet woodsy and remote enough, despite a couple of tumbledown dwellings and a farm near the river, to create good darkness for a light show. Still, steady electrification had recently caused a few visitors — those managing to find the proper lane — to watch some electrical radiant and entirely miss the Ghost Light. Or so we were told.

The customary accounts concurred on the phenomenon earlier appearing in another location not far distant, but for the past half century it had taken its shine to E-50. "She jiggles around a little, but

she don't go straggling across the county," said an old fellow totter-
ing through the library. "She's a homebody. You just got to sit real
quiet like you was in Granny's parlor."

At Halloween, he'd often known the road to be lined with cars,
but on the March evening Q and I drove to the hollow, no one else
was around, and our expectation was tempered only by a sense we'd
not be lucky enough to glimpse the whatever. I rolled us along slowly
over the new asphalt running as straight west as a surveyor's transit
can lay a lane down, the engineered perfection having relief only
in its rise and fall over low hills of blackjack oaks. Melodious calls
of toads roused the darkness, and the damp air smelled of spring.
The isolation was less deep than in years past: Interstate 44, the Will
Rogers Turnpike, angled across the end of the Promenade where the
two-lane stopped abruptly as if afraid to enter the hollow, although a
little beyond the river the road picked up again to continue westward
into Quapaw, Oklahoma, about four miles from the vale. Except for
a couple of breaches in the woods, the trees and hills made the turnpike and Quapaw invisible.

Right after we crossed the Missouri line and entered the Promenade, a small light appeared in the distance on the left of the road.
My anticipation apparently got the better of me, and I blurted out
something to which Q said, "You're seeing some kind of vehicle way
ahead of us," and a pickup did pass by soon after. I pulled to the side,
shut off the engine, got out of the car. In a darkness so deep I could
see down only to my knees, I began walking as if I were wading
the night. When I returned, my sudden emergence from the thick
obscurity caused Q to jump.

In a whisper, as if the Powers of Spectral Illumination have ears,
she asked for explanations I'd read that afternoon: ball lightning,
will-o'-the-wisp, marsh gas, mine gas, fox fire, Saint Elmo's fire, sun-
spots, glowing minerals, static electricity, ionized plasma; headlights
from automobiles, billboards, a water tower, a landing field, a farm;
and, of course, those ectoplasmic souls in search of craniums —
theirs or yours.

"No Lucifer anywhere?" I forgot: a telepreacher claimed the glow was a sign from Satan that our souls would soon be his unless we renounced sin (and sent in a check). And another pulpiteer, thinking differently, contended the Light was notice of the Second Coming this time next Thursday, or maybe it was a Wednesday a year ago. More credible allegations mentioned pranksters sneaking from the woods to pop an electronic flash at a car or wave an illuminated plastic pumpkin over the windshield of entwined couples. And, to be expected, a small contingent claimed the phenomenon was entirely imagined and of even less substance than a virgo gloriosa appearing in a water stain on the wall of a chapel or bordello. A clerk had said, "Why do you think it's called the Spook Light? Maybe because it's as real as spooks?"

Thirty minutes passed, and no emanation of any sort appeared, so I drove back eastward to a higher spot with a longer view. A van had arrived, with four intent faces staring into the west. I stopped far enough away not to block their view, then walked to them. A woman of middle years and three teenage girls glanced at me only to ascertain I was possessed of a more or less standard head lacking any luminescence and in the accustomed location.

Had they seen it? Without looking my way, the woman murmured slowly, uneasily, "It's there right now."

I turned to the west. Blackness. Soot, pitch, ebony, the inside of a crow. Otherwise, zilch. She whispered, eyes still fixed forward, "In thirty years, this is the best I've ever seen it." I looked again. Nothing. Spoof Light.

Then, as if I'd suddenly regained lost vision, the dark got punctured — a white-hot poker thrust through a black tent. The whiteness rose above the distant road, waxed brighter, dimmed, then again brighter, its edge tinged bloodred. A not-of-this-Earth gleaming seemed to float a mile or two away, slightly shifting laterally, like an animal moving its head side to side as it fixes on its quarry. Great Caesar's Ghost!

After fifty years, I was at last seeing the Quapaw Light! I started off down the black road to tell Q, but I couldn't keep from turning around to assure that nothing was coming up from behind. Holy Willie! A Nodgort had found a crack in my rationality, and the pesky hob was dancing, mocking. I forced myself to stand still for a moment to prove reason yet prevailed, even if a bit equivocally. *There,* I thought, *that's a moment, that's enough.* But I had to restrain an impulse to quickstep back to the safety of the car. (Oh, reader, do you shake your head? Well, consider this: a jokester jumping out of the scrub at that moment could have put a whack on my ticker.)

"What's wrong?" Q asked, and I nodded westward, and she looked that way. "What am I supposed to be seeing?" The road was black again. "I don't see any — oh! Is that it?" It was it: waxing, pendulating, waning, throwing out a bubble of redness, sucking it back in, vanishing only to show itself again, making a tiny zig to set up a zag.

I watched Q's unblinking countenance. Though she rarely takes names in vain, her face was exclaiming in other ways, "Ye gods!" Nuns had taught her the only real ghost is the *Holy Ghost* — never mind the Witch of Endor summoning up the wraith of Samuel. But those earnest sisters never faced the Quapaw Ghost Light. Ha! Let Mother Mary Michael debunk this one. Jumpin Jehoshaphat!

The thing glimmered and shimmered, twinkled and blinked, flickered and fluttered, glistened and winked. We stared so long I began to believe our eyes were playing tricks, so we corroborated what the little dazzler was doing: Tell me what you're seeing, I said, and Q answered, "It just moved left." Yes. "Coming back the other way." Yes. "Getting reddish again." Yep. "Oops, just disappeared — no, it's back — and brighter." Exactly.

It was doing the pixy peekaboo. "The thing's playful," Q said. "No wonder people are fond of it — it's a Tinker Bell." In my satanic voice I rasped, No, my pretty — mistake not a tool of the Devil. Then, changing to a falsetto, I repeated the librarian's wisecrack: "Around here, we take it lightly."

Spooky, as it's sometimes called, resembled an evening star low in the sky on a clear night, but it upended astrophysics in its shifting from a red dwarf to a white giant, although it was never bigger than a bright planet seen with moderate-power binoculars.

A farm truck came from behind and passed, and we watched to see whether it would spook the Light, but the globe bravely continued its performance. I started the engine and went slowly forward to get closer; I was an infant reaching out to touch the first star he ever sees. At our approach, the gleaming kept its distance as does a rainbow or mirage, then it winked out. We turned around to go back to where we'd been, and again there it was, hanging above the lane. If we couldn't close the distance on it, then that eliminated explanations like will-o'-the-wisp or lights from a tower — anything with a fixed location. Q: "It's not a figment of the imagination. It's actually there — or somewhere. Something's somewhere. It's real as a rainbow. Maybe not as beautiful, but a lot more lively."

We gaped at it for nearly two hours because it was what we had wanted to find: an authentic optical phenomenon reportedly unexplained by science. A merry spectral puzzle. Observing it was like stepping back into the Dark Ages when nature was full of phantasmagoria, when mysteries overwhelmed explications and ignorance transcended illumination, a time when superstition could extinguish enlightenment, when priestly obfuscations manipulated folk into blind faiths where charms and potions, spells and incantations, holy relics and amulets, were defenses against hobgoblins going thumpity-bump in the night or rising in the woods to flicker their mischief. It was a time of ignis fatuus, fool's fire, burning in the forest; of corpus sanctum dancing across chimney tops; when fox fire was the Devil's footprint and spontaneous ignition of marsh gas the restless dead returned to exact vengeance. And even in Oklahoma, Ottawa County E-50 ran west only to the edge of Devil's Hollow before stopping until it could safely resume three miles west.

The Light was less spectacular than suggested by the most fanciful claims, so much so that had someone not initially observed it prior to the electrification of the county, the phenomenon might not be noticed today. In fact, when we arrived, I *had* seen it, only to be convinced by Q that it was a moving vehicle. As we were leaving, she said, "It's my first UFO," adding before I could cavil, "Unexplained Flickering Orb."

The Quapaw Ghost Light is remarkable but not incredible, modest but worth its myth, possessed of the power of the peculiar, and among the many phantasms of the Ozarks, Spooky is one of the few to come forth predictably and allow examination. You can't hear, touch, smell, or taste it, but you can't doubt seeing it if your patience allows. The Light's little, but it's old, now reliably older than nearly all who go out for a gander.

I might have been content to leave things at that, except for my curiosity about that last detail: just how old was the Quapaw Quoz?

[**READER ALERT:** Anyone wanting to encounter the Hornet eidolon wrapped in its mystery or those wishing to preserve its "inexplicability" should head for chapter 11 to join the mosey again a few miles west of the Devil's Promenade.]

❧ 10 ❧

How Tadpoles Become Serpents

A RETURN TO THE Joplin library and another look through the Ghost Light clippings clarified one aspect: most of the published stories about it came from writers who, not having witnessed it, relied instead on hoary hearsay or on witnesses of noticeably uncritical or biased mind (testimony from anybody who could turn a buck off Spooky was prone to distortions). In those worn-out accounts was a sameness with abundant repetitions of unsubstantiated and dubious allegations and considerable evidence of one memory enhancing, reinforcing, and doctoring another. Whenever a new claim got introduced, it would get repeated and adulterated as it evolved from fabrication to fable to virtual fact. Many of the scribes needed a close shave with Occam's razor. On the other hand, the few reports of empirical scrutiny (I exclude firing a rifle at the phantom) matched what Q and I saw, as did descriptions from the most informed residents we talked with.

We copied reports and returned in the light of day to the Promenade to walk part of it, take some measurements and photographs, set up binoculars to look west at noon. Watched by slot-eyed goats, I knocked at a dilapidated dwelling near where we'd first seen the apparition; the door stood open and within the dimness a single candle burned, but no one responded except an aged, barked-out cur either groggy or ready for the Other Side. We went west to Miami (in Oklahoma it's My-AM-ah) to the courthouse to examine early maps of Ottawa County. A clerk, averring she'd once jumped into her boyfriend's arms when the Spook came up to hover over the hood

286

of his parked car, rejected my suggestion he'd planted an accomplice in the bushes.

Later, I sorted the accounts into three stacks: one from writers who had not actually witnessed the Light (much the largest pile); another from those who casually saw the thing and wrote judiciously about it *soon* afterward; and the third and fewest from Occamists going forth with inductive razors.

Even though many post-1950 stories claimed the Light appeared in the late 1800s, to the last one they were anecdotal and unauthenticated, and only a couple acknowledged there might be, over more than a century, several causes of illuminations. The earliest published account I found (a few weeks later because it was oddly missing from the Joplin library) appeared in the *Kansas City Star* in 1936. Written by A. B. MacDonald (who had won a Pulitzer Prize for solving a murder in Texas five years earlier), the long piece was the first to cut through the manifest malarkey. Still, nearly all subsequent sketches either ignored MacDonald or tried to obviate his conclusion by asserting, in the disingenuous words of the current Joplin Convention and Visitors Bureau, "the source of the Light remains a mystery."

In late 1935 when MacDonald arrived at the Devil's Promenade, with him was Logan Smith who had lived along it for some years and had watched the occurrence hundreds of times. Its source was, Smith told the reporter, auto headlamps coming from the new federal highway east of Quapaw. On a map, he showed MacDonald the perfect alignment over several miles of Route 66 with the Ghost Light road, even though the Spring River Valley intervened. He pointed out the long view westward was essentially downhill: Quapaw, in spite of the interruption of rolling terrain, is almost two hundred feet lower than the east end of the Promenade. Convinced, MacDonald made no attempt to test the theory.

A decade later another *Star* reporter, Charles Graham, persuaded two men from the Army base at Camp Crowder, Missouri, twenty miles from the Promenade, to join him in an unofficial investigation of the Route 66 theory. Flashing automobile headlights from the west, they re-created at will the coming and going of Spooky: he danced at their command.

Over the following twenty years, new research confirmed those results, one of them noting local observations of the phenomenon increased after completion of 66, and someone else correlated appearances of the Light with traffic flow on the highway. An examiner noted that vehicles with different kinds of lights moving differently (passing, turning, speeding up or slowing down, heading east or west), as well as changing atmospheric conditions, would create variations in the display and activity of the phenomenon. Sometimes stars twinkle and sometimes they don't; sometimes they're visible, and sometimes not; the Moon has a halo one night and a cross the next; it may be yellow, orange, or white — maybe even blue. Graham attributed certain variations to afterimages that can occur in viewers staring at a brightness, and another researcher theorized refraction of light might also contribute. Of particular note, all of them said the luminosity could not be seen from any low point on the Promenade. Each one of the verifiable experiments on the headlamp theory coincided precisely with what Q and I witnessed.

I thought, *Well, that's that.* I realized I was almost — almost — disappointed at rational explanation. Some Nodgort, wanting mystery over factual revelation, worked to challenge what I'd found: What about all those claims the shining existed before automobiles? What about the discovery that Graham's and a later researcher's tests had been made not from the current Spook Light Road, E-50, but from a parallel one, E-40, the Hornet Road, a mile north and one that does not align with U.S. 66? Oberon and Titania danced and capered in the crannies of my skull. "Yes!" they sang out. "The mystery remains!" Q too, I have to disclose here, showed pleasure the solution was still, so to speak, up in the air.

Off we went into Oklahoma and on toward New Mexico, content in witnessing an event that trussed up science like a dead pig hung in a tree for country butchering. Some weeks later when we were home again and I was putting away maps of the journey, I looked once more at the forty-five-degree *angle* Route 66 makes between the Kansas state line and Quapaw, Oklahoma, a run of four miles. That's when I remembered: across the prairie country, the earliest federal highways did not usually make such an angle; instead, for economy, they followed the old section-line roads commonly running toward only cardinal compass-points. Ninety-degree turns were everywhere. Reason flashed on in my mind and sent dark-loving Robin Goodfellow back into his recess: the current route of U.S. 66 in northeastern Ottawa County is not the original used from 1926 to 1932. That first 66 ran the cardinal directions, as old road-maps and a close reading of Graham's *Star* story prove. On the north side of Quapaw, the first highway aligned perfectly with E-40, the initial Spook Light Road, the one from which the tests were made, thereby corroborating early claims the wonderment had moved south, as it indeed it had, south to E-50, the current Promenade which lines up with a later section of Route 66 now sharing traffic for two miles with U.S. 69. Commentators negating the early researches for being on "the wrong road" did not understand the reconfigured highway. Those unable to remember the past are condemned to botch the present. Or, to corrupt another Americanism, bungled history is bunk.

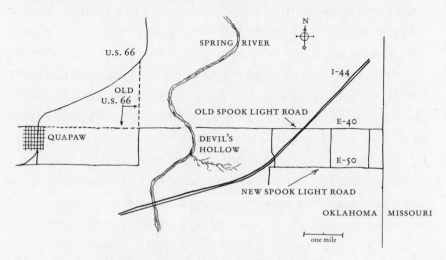

The Spook Light Roads in northeast Oklahoma.

I read again the investigations based on mensuration and found them making new sense. When reporter Graham asked an engineer, who claimed he solved the puzzle in 1930, why he'd not published his solution, the man said, "We thought it would be more fun just to let people go on believing the mystery."

That brought to mind an old psychological experiment examining the effects of suggestion and expectation: Volunteers in a room illuminated by only a pinpoint of light were asked to "draw on paper the path of a moving beam." Their pencils marked out arcs and angles and tangents and squiggles to create mazes of graphite. After the overhead lights came on again and the subjects learned the pinpoint had not moved even so much as a quintillionth of a millimeter, they expressed disbelief, disappointment, and more annoyance than surprise. Idols of the tribe are powerful.

Something else came to me: when I was in the Navy, at sea, smokers were prohibited from lighting up on deck because the flare of a match could be seen by enemy eyes a mile or more away.

And one final remembrance: that old story of the Episcopal pastor explaining sin by telling his congregation about drinking so thirstily at a spring he nearly swallowed a tadpole. A year later, a Methodist deacon in the next county over mentioned how Catholic Father So-and-So, getting senile, swallowed a tadpole that changed to a frog in his gut. And sometime thereafter, a fulminating Baptist told of a Pentecostal preacher going to a spring to get a salamander he could swallow and cough up before his stunned audience to prove the Devil lies within everybody. At the Episcopal pastor's death, several people two counties away knew for certain a Mormon in the grip of Satan had died from eating one too many serpents.

But, above all, what about the "fact" always trotted out to disprove the headlamps solution — those anecdotal reports allegedly as old as the first Quapaw into the territory — that the Ghost Light existed before the automobile? Even accepting such unsupported assertions, I suspect people in 1880 did not spend all their hours after sunset in darkness. A lantern, a bonfire, an eastbound locomotive, would offer illumination enough to create Spooky, especially if refraction proves to be involved. And, I should add, any piece of country over the years may well exhibit occasional luminescent appearances of several kinds from natural causes, particularly a place with wetlands and old mines. There likely has been more than one Ghost Light.

A few days ago I gave this explication to a friend who had long wanted to see the small marvel, and he said, "Now you've gone and ruined it for me!" I asked whether knowing a rainbow is a spectral display of refracted light kept him from enjoying one. I proposed that in the three million miles of American roadways, the physical factors necessary for the creation of the Quapaw Light are, if not unique, then at least rare and remarkable enough to make it worth encountering. In the long view, doesn't satisfaction from enlightenment surpass the tenebrifics of mystery? Isn't, in the end, a humble schoolmaster greater than the slickest magician?

And keep in mind (I should have added), the Quapaw Light exists on the fringe of the Ozarks where fable, fundamental faith, fabrication, and fallacy have long had their way with fact, where superstition suppresses science, where belief in evolution can defeat a politician or get a preacher drummed out of a church, where it will be a long time before a spectrometer can hold against a ghost-o-meter.

⊱ 11 ⊰

Last Train Out of Land's End

Y OU HAVE, PERHAPS, seen the old photographs or films of horse-drawn vehicles — wagons, buggies, traps — and men afoot lined up on a vast treeless stretch of the southeastern Great Plains, as white people ("boomers") took position to take possession: they were ready for one of the races ("runs") into native lands to grab a few acres of what was soon to be given away to anybody who could drive a stake into a piece of unclaimed soil. The Indian Territory was about to be remade into Oklahoma. In Choctaw, the name means "red people," but today, it's somewhat of an irony of American nomenclature.

Oh yes, tribal America is still there in numbers, but many a Pawnee or Ponca will give you a howdy and a blue-eyed wink. I don't know whether the Choctaw have a word for *amalgamated,* but as time steps along, a new name for the state could prove usefully accurate, if not popular. Across the country, when I meet a person with some Indian ancestry (even if in Vermont or California), the native strain is most often Cherokee; in fact, years ago, I was wed to one, and before that spent much time with two other women of that noble line. A Choctaw woman (she's another story) once said to me, "What is it with Anglos wanting to be part Cherokee? I think it must be the name — it sounds, well, cheery. Choctaw sounds serious. And Creek or Kaw? Forget it."

Those huge late-nineteenth-century land runs, repeated several times across the territory, might look benign compared to the immense giveaways of America to railroads, mining consortiums, and cattle barons. At least, as some Oklahomans point out, the people making the runs were predominantly landless and impoverished, although that meant once "landed," they still lacked resources to turn their newly got soil into successful farms. "The ground is free," somebody should have said, "but the plow will cost you sixty dollars. And then you gotta buy a mule. Don't forget seed." And so forth until you reach the tax man.

The aboriginal lands not "opened" by runs came onto the market in another, more furtive manner called *allotment*, whereby individual Indians were granted title to a parcel of their own tribal realty either to farm or dispose of as they wished. Growing up in a culture believing soil cannot rightly be owned by an individual, and having little knowledge of or interest in farming, many economically distressed Indians let go of their allotment, selling it to whites, so that four generations later a number of tribes began trying to reconstitute themselves by reassembling land once theirs by treaty.

A large segment of the people making the runs came out of the southern Appalachians and the Ozarks. Those citizens (Indians were not then citizens) brought along a fierce laissez-faire outlook that, to my eyes and ears, is still evident along the Oklahoma byways. There you can find both Mountain and Southern tinctures in the speech of residents who mix a penchant for the friendly conversation of Dixie with the openness of the West, their discourse touched by the relaxed attitude toward existence not uncommon among tribal Americans. A visitor who can smile, speak, and listen is not long a stranger in Oklahoma, a happy aspect of traveling the state.

But there's another aspect, one I believe also related to the early history of the runs and the people who made them; it's an attitude of disconnection, a notion that land is expendable, almost disposable, a thing you can use and walk away from. In such dislocation and displacement, I see ancient nomadic peoples intermixed with some make-a-quick-buck settlers. Washington Irving, in an unusual accommodation for an author, accompanied an 1832 military expedition sent into Indian Territory to cool a little native unrest. As he and the mounted rangers neared the end of their long journey,

Irving, in his *A Tour on the Prairies,* wrote about breaking an over-night bivouac west of Fort Gibson:

> I always felt disposed to linger until the last straggler disappeared among the trees and the distant note of the bugle died upon the ear, that I might behold the wilderness relapsing into silence and solitude. In the present instance, the deserted scene of our late bustling encampment had a forlorn and desolate appearance. The surrounding forest had been in many places trampled into a quagmire. Trees felled and partly hewn in pieces and scattered in huge fragments; tent-poles stripped of their covering; smolder-ing fires with great morsels of roasted venison and buffalo meat standing on wooden spits before them, hacked and slashed by the knives of hungry hunters; while around were strewed the hides, the horns, the antlers and bones of buffaloes and deer, with uncooked joints and unplucked turkeys left behind with that reckless improvidence and wastefulness which young hunters are apt to indulge when in a neighborhood where game abounds. In the meantime a score or two of turkey-buzzards, or vultures, were already on the wing, wheeling their magnificent flight high in the air, and preparing for a descent upon the camp as soon as it should be abandoned.

Lest an idealistic reader think the nomadic tribes conducted their stopovers with a greater prudence, here's an 1840 description by Vic-tor Tixier from *Travels on the Osage Prairies,* his superb account of Plains Indian life at the coming of the Euro-Americans. The hunting camp he describes was not far from the place Irving spoke of:

> Day by day our encampment became more disagreeable. A dead horse lay only a few steps beyond the camp, and not far distant another had perished after a rattlesnake bite. An insuf-ferable stink rose from the two carcasses and from the drying skin and the discarded meat. The Osages throw out meat the sec-

ond day after butchering an animal; in our plenteous living, you can reckon how much we wasted. The grass had become quite scant thereabouts, and the camp was full of manure the horses left around their pickets. Our long sojourn allowed a frightening number of dreadful insects to multiply, and several dogs became rabid. The great heat dried up many of the springs, and the horses and boys turned the few remaining into flowing mud. It became imperative to carry our lodgings to another place.

The itinerary Q and I took across Oklahoma was through a land of conspicuous improvidence, despite the many and various exhortations to residents to place their lives into the hands of a Providence upon whom no human eyes have yet been laid. Perhaps it's an imperfection in me that along the way I found it difficult to look beyond the roadsides to the far hills made lovely by distance because of what I kept seeing *between* the churches, with their warnings of eternal perdition: miles of abandoned buildings, of decaying house-trailers steadily vanishing under glomerations of cast-off appliances, toys, rusted vehicles (autos, busses, riding mowers, tractors, trucks, a bulldozer, a crane, a forklift), and a plethora of cheap things (shopping bags to wading pools) made from petroleum which the state pumped from beneath all that spent material. For a connoisseur of piles, stacks, and heaps, there were aggregations of broken-up asphalt pavement, chainsawed trees, used tires, raw red earth, oil-field pipes, galvanized ductwork, broken concrete blocks, aluminum siding, and one remarkable stack of refrigerators topped by a ragged American flag flapping a conqueror's tired glory over the rummage.

Some of the scrap mounds, as if emblems of the hills the ancestors hailed from, were festively entwined with poison ivy, the Western answer to kudzu that has served to cover over derelictions in the South. More than one enterprising person had set up a sign near an accumulation of things and called it a flea market. Above the door to one shack were scythe blades crossed in a heraldic manner as if sabers from Shiloh. Those folk knew the American method of getting rid of what a thrifty Scot might call clamjamfry was not to try to give it away but to attach a price of eye-catching cheapness. Anybody can pass up a rusted scythe or a chromed hubcap if it's free, but ask a dime for it, and it becomes irresistible.

One merchant had brought scatterings into an actual building called the Cheapo Depot, and indeed, the route looked like an open-air depot or an abandoned siding where the last train out of Land's End had passed through to empty hopper cars hauling the dregs and dross, the clinkers and sinters of our time. From the gigantic mounts of tailings dug out of the exhausted mines near Picher and for miles on beyond were long stretches where the roadsides seemed worn out, used up, and depleted beyond recovery. Any home or farm pleasantly in order only made the surround of rubble and decay stand forth as does a gold tooth next to a rotten one ready for extraction.

Amidst it all were New Hope or New Life or New Hereafter "worship centers" built with the architectural lines of an auto-body shop, many of them topped by undersized, tacked-on, cheapo-depot steeples far too small; they had the appearance of a father at his kid's fourth birthday party: befuddled dad under one of those little, shiny, conical hats with an elastic strap, he looking not so much a dunce in the corner as a fool on a stool.

Several metal-sided churches (once called by an uncharitable acquaintance "Tin-Can Temples of Ready Redemption," which was only marginally gentler than her "Tin Temples of Tax-Exempt Bias") announced the availability inside of *The* Truth, that very thing escaping all other temples. (Loathe thy neighbor — or at least his views.) Other New Hereafters recommended the desirability of life everlasting and noted its perquisite of salvation, although what the area needed was salvage.

The nation, the world, stands prepared with the Salvation Army, but where's a Salvage Army? A quest for life eternal, contended Gus Kubitzki, who freely admitted his limitations in speculative metaphysics, was spiritual avarice. "Fourscore and ten," claimed he, "ought to be enough for anybody." He himself, however, did fudge a bit, dying in his ninety-second year, but his daughter denied him at least one everlasting existence — a second life not postulated, but as real and certain as earth — when she refused to fulfill Gus's wish his ashes be added to the mulch of his rose garden.* Today I'd like to have a blossom resurrected from some of his oxidized dust so I could imagine a few recycled atoms of his right arm which helped me at age eleven break in my new catcher's mitt. There's a clear possibility (he himself might say), until evidence appears to controvert it, a human's best chance for something approximating life everlasting lies in the memory of others. There I go again, speaking of our tracks.

Q and I persevered on into a darkening morning until, not far from Sulphur, Oklahoma, I saw two signs of hope, one writ small and the other sculpted large. The first was *LAWN MORE BLADES SHARPEND*. Now there was a fellow aware of a time when a scythe didn't need throwing away, because it got steadily used and sharpened out of existence. The second, a tall sculpture perhaps made of recast mower and scythe blades, was a colossal human-hand rising from the earth to reach toward the heavens. On the uplifted index-finger pointing skyward rested a tremendous, steel butterfly.

Sulphur was Sulphur Springs until the citizens lowered the water-table enough to dry up nearly all the artesian sources that had refreshed and restored Indians for centuries and whites for a generation; gone were springs like Medicine and Bromide. When the mineral flowings ceased and the spas depending on them vanished, Muskogee Avenue began a slow slide from the prosperous to the desperate, although one source, a drilled one, yet remained to leak a lightly sulfurous vapor over downtown. We followed the odor to Vendome Well, formerly the fount of a large swimming pool (long gone), where we came upon a woman filling plastic jugs. I tried the water. It tasted like Hell — that is, brimstone — and I asked how

---

* In the year I write of Gus's dust, 827,000 gallons of embalming fluid and 100,000 tons of metals will be put into the soil to make newly deceased Americans comfortable. Kubitzki's cadaver remains even yet to turn in his coffin at the refusal to give him a green burial. He wanted nothing more than a cotton shroud.

she was able to get it down. "I don't drink it. My dogs drink it, and when they do they're not bothered by ticks. But I know a power-company lineman who's in the brush a lot, and he drinks it and says he's tick-free."

On the day we were in Sulphur, the Chickasaw tribe had recently finished clearing an entire town block, once the site of the old Arte-sian Hotel, to build a casino called Cash Springs. (A man said, "They want your brain to think *Cash-in-o,* but you know who does the cashing in.") Since it was Indians themselves who deeded to white men for safekeeping the vale where most of the artesian springs used to rise, the Chickasaws are smart to recognize a new way to cash in on the hope of a life restored and resurrected by another outpouring, this one from a jackpot, a dream only slightly more certain than life everlasting.

West of Sulphur (the town that traded in its national park for a national recreation area) and not far from an enterprise called Junk City, USA, was the Treasure Valley Casino, another of a baker's dozen owned by the Chickasaws who were happily fulfilling an Anglo urge to convert savings accounts into coins to drop into blink-ing, dinging machines that in return give a "player" a fleeting glance at little, electronic pictures. Indian slots are, possibly, a part of a Celestial Redemption Plan to take the territory back from usurp-ers for repatriation through realty purchases funded by small wheels going round and round as if they were land titles. Some Indians and whites alike believe the age-old mineral springs — briefly entrusted to no-deposit/no-return citizens who exhausted them in only a cen-tury — should now be given back to those who once knew how to keep them. Call it recycling.

❥ 12 ❧

A Quest for Querques

CROSSING THE RED RIVER into Texas from Oklahoma is like stepping out a back door onto an avenue instead of an alley, and the difference has little to do with prosperity but much to do with definitions of self and our place in the scheme of things. While I enjoy Oklahomans, I've never crossed the Red River southward without a bit of relief and a renewed respect for Lone-Star stewardship. The Texas waysides and the structures and landscape along them all looked flat-out better taken care of. If the alleged Texan braggadocio wants to proclaim its land ethic — at least in comparative terms — only the dim-sighted would try to gainsay it. Dizzy Dean once spouted something along the lines of "It ain't braggin if you done it."

Our route toward southern New Mexico was through the lower end of the Great Plains, formerly called by Anglo-Americans the Great American Desert, a land underlain by the Ogallala Aquifer which — were it on the surface and open water — would cover a larger area than the Great Lakes. (It could fill Lake Erie nine times.) The rolling and fertile savannah atop the Ogallala is the thorax and abdomen of America: we breathe it, we digest it. The Osage and Pawnee and dozens of other tribes were unaware of the immense reservoir held in erosional outwash from the Rocky Mountains, as was also Zebulon Pike who wrote in 1810, "These vast plains of the western hemisphere may become in time equally celebrated as the sandy desarts of Africa." For many years, his view appeared to be remarkably shortsighted, but with contemporary agriculture having so significantly lowered the Ogallala and turned loose a conjugation of problems reaching well beyond it, Pike's words now seem to be foresight.

From the Red River near Quanah, Texas, Q and I struck a staggered, forty-five-degree angle composed of numerous left turns followed twenty minutes later by a right turn and thirty minutes after that by another left turn, then a right again; in such a manner we "descended" southwesterly, always heading only due south or due west across the lower Panhandle of Texas. We were following back roads that rarely deviated from the Jeffersonian township-and-range system, staying within the grid as if it were a hog fence.

We entered the southern edge of the grand Llano Estacado, the Staked Plain, a description perhaps from Coronado's men in 1541, setting out sticks to mark a route they could retrace on their return across the naturally featureless and shockingly level and seemingly immeasurable grassland.

For an American traveler of stout heart, the Great Plains, and especially the Llano, are a good measure of one's capacity to enjoy a landscape apparently without limits, a topography to make patience struggle to remain sovereign over the anxiety of nonarrival. In a place where the dominating feature is an encircling horizon sometimes of nothing more than a thin, flat, unattainable line, where a thousand footsteps or even a sixty-mile-an-hour motoring from sunup till noon seems to have taken you no farther than a gerbil gets on its wheel, travelers can find admiration of the interminable uninterruptedness too much for their resolve to appreciate American spaciousness. The incessant miles challenge pleasure. That perceived vacancy, like the sea it once was, teaches, if not submission, then at least sufferance. You can accept its scope, but you can't master it. Crossing the Llano is a voyage into space — not the celestial kind, but one fully grounded and possessed of the requisite gravity: whether you're on wheels, on horseback, or afoot, there's no weightless floating. Instead, one hauls oneself across as if *towing* one's butt. At its perimeters, there should be stations offering to anesthetize the

unstringable, those susceptible to the heebie-jeebies, and any children scouring the backseat (although, now that I think about it, the
Llano itself soon enough can induce a beneficent stupor).

The Staked Plain, of course, is not vacant: it's covered with massive cultivations, although in the spring the tilled earth creates a
brown desolation that erases the awful magnificence of the native
grassland, and it's there human logic founders — the apparent emptiness can dislocate minds and displace reason with its ubiquitous
nowhere permeated by absence.

A traveler's brain will not for long abide infinity because sooner
or later we desperately want the other side of an itinerary. After all,
the goal of travel is to get somewhere, at least anywhere, because
going nowhere takes you into the realm of the insane. Trying to
avoid an unhinging, Q and I stopped at heres and theres: a local burp
and belch (enchilada), a dip and sip (ice-cream soda to lock it down),
a county courthouse (to stretch legs), and once by a fence post to
see what was nailed to it (a shot red-tailed hawk). But always reality
abides: *We're not there yet.* Where? *Anywhere, as long as it's somewhere other than this where.*

A tip for happy passage on the Plains is, as I reminded myself,
to see the grasslands as an expression of the great planetary respira-
tory system, and to hear the unslowed sweep of wind as the engine
powering that respiration. I recommended to Q she do as does the
seaman: lift eyes to the cloudscapes and view them as aerial hills and
dales, watch them change as if we were moving through them, as if
we were making actual progress. After all, the word *cloud,* related to
clod, means *hill* in Old English.

All well and good, but on the day we crossed, we were cursed
with a wonderfully clear sky untroubled by even a wisp of cirrostra-
tus, a sky vacuumed of everything but a diaphanous blue so merging
with the horizon as to erase it and make the roads seem to lead not
necessarily toward New Mexico but simply into a space as perceptible as the ether.

We fell into a steadfast silence rising from prolonged miles elastic enough I thought them incapable of ever stretching to a breaking point: Were they multiplying, self-generating? Did that last mile just hatch out two more? Like duckweed on a pond in spring, they appeared to propagate themselves with unnerving fecundity. My belief in finiteness taunted and made claustrophobia look like a small price to pay for boundaries, and I felt my mind being wiped clean of the petty detritus of daily life: "May I see your registration, sir?" It matters not, Officer. "You know what your speed was?" Speed? What is speed?

Q soon brought me back. She said (in Spanish either because her mind also was wandering from the chummy limits of accustomed routine or because of her conversation with the Hispanic waitress at lunch), *"Los conquistadores caminaban esta ruta. Que machos eran!"* Oh, they were men indeed to hoof across this plain. Coronado, Pike, a million natives — I admired them all as if they had walked to Neptune.

"Have you got a story of the Llano?" she said. "A *true* story?" There was this guy — "I've heard it." He was young and witty and friendly but not really a two-fisted chap. One evening he climbed into his car north of Abilene and went west, following county roads that took him into the Llano. He was headed to Albuquerque. Not long after sundown, not even halfway across, a rear tire blew out. He stopped and looked at the flattened rubber, stared uncomprehendingly at the "jack-assembly," realized he didn't know how to change a tire, and found himself unnerved and unmanned. He began to whimper, then cry. Then he threw up. He crawled into the backseat, wrapped his arms around his quaking body, rocked himself, summoned up a couple of his favorite show tunes (one of them "I Feel Pretty"), and sang himself to sleep. About dawn a woman rancher saw his car, roused him, showed him how to jack up the rear end, and left him. He turned his machine around and scurried toward home, promising himself he'd never again go alone into the Staked Plain. Moral: vastness teaches humility. Or maybe it's a modern jack-assembly that does it.

As we crossed into New Mexico, the horizon began to rupture into a marvelous irregularity, with undulations and touches of jaggedness, all of it now cast in a vague blueness that meant not more sky but the Rockies. Hello, the hills! Hello, the other side!

We were looking for a creature frequenting the east versant of the Guadalupe Mountains, a bird for years I'd wanted to see; by reading her a passage from the hand of American ornithologist William Beebe, I'd managed to spark Q's interest also.

The vermilion flycatcher, whose Latin generic name means *firehead*, belongs to a family of small and modest birds usually colored in every shade of gray between white and black, and it lives in arid lands where other animate life typically finds survival through a camouflage composed of the common dun hues of the desert, chocolate brown constituting gaudiness. Yet the male firehead flouts the logic of evolution by flaunting itself with a large scarlet cap with matching ascot and doublet. Were that not enough, he performs an aerial display a woodcock might envy. The degree of nonconformity evolution will tolerate can be limited, and to exceed it can be dangerous, can even lead to extinction. If not in numbers, then at least in its behavior, the firehead is a rara avis. It's a quoz of the desert everyone should witness while it — and we — last. Here's Beebe's passage about the vermilion flycatcher I read to Q:

> Up shoots one from a mesquite tree, with full, rounded crest, and breast puffed out until it seems a floating ball of vermilion — buoyed up on vibrating wings. Slowly, by successive upward throbs, the bird ascends, at each point of vibrating rest uttering his little love song — a cheerful *ching-tink-a-le-tink! ching-tink-a-le-tink!* which is the utmost he can do. When at the limit of his flight, fifty or seventy-five feet above our heads, he redoubles his efforts, and the *chings* and the *tinks* rapidly succeed each other. Suddenly, his little strength exhausted, the suitor drops to earth almost vertically in a series of downward swoops, and alights near the wee gray form for which he at pres-

ent exists. He watches eagerly for some sign of favor, but a rival is already climbing skyward, whose feathers seem no brighter than his, whose simple lay of love is no more eager, no more tender, yet some subtle fate, with workings too fine for our senses, decides against the first suitor, and, before the second bird has regained his perch, the female flies low over the cactus-pads, followed by the breathless performer.

Failing to see the flycatcher in one location, we went on to Rattlesnake Springs, south of Carlsbad. I'd no more than stepped from the car to take a position to allow sunlight to illuminate vermilion feathers, than a firehead flew up, cast my way a bold if not disdainful eye, and flew off, only to return to find its grounds again quiet except for a related bird so nondescript it has to carry a man's name for identification: a Say's phoebe flitted nervously while a pair of scaled quail scratched about, and a lesser nighthawk with eyelids half closed and body aligned with a fat cottonwood-branch ignored us all. As for the show the flycatcher put on, Professor Beebe might have furnished the script.

When the performance — actually two of them — ended, Q and I rolled on to Carlsbad for the night, arriving late, so we had to finish the long day by eating crackers and cheese in a motel room, the repast made tolerable by twin cups of an aged tequila. Crossing the Llano seemed like another existence, as I guess indeed it was.

The next morning we struck out for Alamogordo via a route of a couple of good Mexican cafés I knew, each serving its own interpretation of green chile. In New Mexico, if a place can't do a toothsome bowl of green-chile stew, nothing else is going to get done right either. The Cajuns have their roux, the French their white sauce, and the New Mexicans their peppers. Years ago in Socorro a man said to me, "Green chile makes a guy happy — and strong." As he spoke the last two words, he erected his index-finger.

Rolling on northward, Q told of when she was nine years old and beginning to learn Spanish, she heard about a desert city called

"Alba Querque" at the foot of mountains named after watermelons and near a mesa called Encantada. An enchanted place, to be sure! But a querque? Translating literally, she asked about a *dawn what-r-what*. Sister Maxima Gravitas (or some such) took the translation as impertinence and ignored it, so Q wrote a story about a querque, a quirky what-what that roamed about at dawn to hunt penguins. Sister Gravitas, in those days of black-and-white habits, passed over the penguin reference and corrected only the girl's misinterpreted etymology while quite failing to kill her mythology, the result being Q, once graduated, left eastern Missouri for a few years in southern Arizona where she began a life of hunting not penguins but querques, of whom, I believe, I am one.

That evening we reached Fat Cottonwood, that is, Alamogordo. We had come to visit another rara avis of the desert, a querque named Jean Ingold whom I'd wanted to see almost as long as I had a vermilion flycatcher. She, I suspected, was creating a quozzical life to give acquisitiveness a smart comeuppance.

❧13❧

One-Hundred-Seventeen Square Feet

WE TOOK QUARTERS that evening on the south edge of Alamo-gordo. Q had work to do, so I went up to the northwest corner of town near the School for the Blind and Visually Impaired, went on beyond the pale of urban lights, crossed the railroad tracks, found the irrigation canal — a weedy ditch of congealing pools — that served as my waymarker, and followed it past a small salvage yard (WE BUY JUNK CARS) toward the end of the road. In the distance on the highway was a lighted billboard showing a gigantic photograph of a tobacco-chewing young man having no mandible, with the caption something like LOOKING GOOD?

The western sky held only enough of sundown to furnish the San Andres Mountains a silhouette, but moonrise over the Sacramentos to the east lighted the Tularosa Basin, a place blanketed with gypsum sands of such brilliant whiteness they reflected moonlight and made the valley floor appear illuminated from its underside (in July they bounce off sufficient solar heat to allow a barefoot stroll at noon). The sands crawled with darkling beetles come up into the night from below where lay the saline residue of ancient Lake Otero. Dig down the length of a man's arm into the dry sand, and watch the hole magically fill with water, salty stuff that tempts and mocks a desert thirst. Some seasons, even yet, the deepest part of the basin farther south will briefly hold a shallow lake called Lucero: Lucifer, the Morning Star, the Prince of Darkness.

North of the white dunes and the Poison Hills and the alkali flats created by outwash from canyons with names like Lost Man and

Dead Man is the Malpais — the Valley of Fires — a vast upflow of black lava flung from the Abyss as Lucifer was thrown into it. It's a land of jagged, indurate rock where few people go and no one can easefully live. In another century, a fellow said of it, "Out there the only critters sleeping with both eyes closed are dead." Not a place for the visually impaired.

Out that way too are the Oscura Mountains standing above the northern limit of the Jornada del Muerto. And yet another terminus is there, this one the end of the preatomic age, an infernal locus of god-awful name, Trinity, where one early morning in July 1945, to use the phrase of the time, "the sun rose in the west" to start human-kind on its greatest journey of death when gentlemen scientists down from Los Alamos exploded the first-ever nuclear weapon. But Trinity? Trinity of what? Detonation, destruction, devastation? Degen-eration, decivilization, devolution? Depravity, deformity, destiny?

The names from that territory seemed in mortal combat at a kind of toponymic Armageddon: mountains of the Sacrament and of an apostle against mountains of gloom overlooking a dead man's jour-ney. And eastward lay a "bad country" leading to an unholy trinity of demonics of damnation and darkness, where to sleep deeply is to die.

The old residents, the Apaches, also had names for this desert, but I don't know what they were; in dust devils spinning downwind, the Mescalero listened for the twistings to speak, but I don't know what they said. I have heard an elder tell of the lake under the sands and how it waits for the time of man to pass so it can rise once again, emerge into the light, cleansed and pure and holding life, its waters beneath a sky looking down on a land devoid of two-leggeds who take all they don't desecrate. The promise of crystal water appears today in the rosemary mint (tastes like both) and in lemonade bush (from citruslike berries comes a beverage), each plant a result of nat-ural alchemies transmuting salt and alkali into sugar and spice.

The afternoon following my first evening (appropriate to an Armageddon, the date was 6-6-06, the Beast of Revelations), I was up in the hills north of Alamogordo, up at La Luz — another name of almost unbelievable irony and applicability, as if the Hispanic *viejos* were clairvoyant, people not of impaired vision but *prevision*. There a man told me as we looked across the long valley, "Ask in Alamogordo what goes on at the military base, and you'll hear about cutting-edge weapons of lasers and particle beams and neutrons and microwaves. Things to kill you or just give you a bad sunburn. Stealth technology. I don't know what the truth is, but I know I've seen a blinding beam of light fired the length of the valley right toward the Oscuras. And I believe this — we create monsters down there." Weaponry of luminescence in a land where residents say the sun shines three-hundred-twenty days a year (and on one of them, it rose in the west). La Luz.

The night was dark as all get-out when I stopped the car to stumble my way toward the pallid glow of a shabby house trailer, one of the stumbles noisy enough (or maybe it was my cussword) to bring out the hounds of Hell, a pair of charging mongrel pit bulls. I couldn't see the dust the dogs were raising, but I could smell it. A guttural voice cursed the curs into fanged growls, and it inquired about my approach with the indirection of "Are you one of them county morons?" I said I was the moron looking for Jean Ingold's trailer. "Next one north!" — the punctuation provided by an empty beer can pitched at the once-again-barking mutts that put one into a satisfying yelp.

I fumbled forward toward a strip of thin pines, shadows against the sky, dimly illuminated by the dimmest of light from a dim window in a dimmed house trailer. I called her name and went to the screen door, and there she stood, her hair freshly washed and in rollers, and she, slender, a small lark, the single bulb inside outlining her shape through a nightie worn down to sheerness, more a long veil than a gown, and her voice in surprise, "I thought you were arriving tomorrow. I go to bed at nine in the warm weather, but I'm glad you made it." Opening the door, holding it for me — "Maybe you can help me move my cot outside. I think it's too warm tonight to sleep in here." So we moved it. Later, she would lie down near the pines, covering herself with only a thin sheet, and she would watch the desert sky slip away over the mountains until she too slipped away into sleep.

With no place to sit under the trees and but a single chair in her single room, she offered it to me while she sat on the floor, her legs under her like a child at a storytelling. Jean Shirer Ingold was eighteen months shy of seventy, and she watched me with side-glances, speaking as her eyes searched the walls for what to talk about, and she gave frequent quick chuckles to things she said, although a few of her sentences had a somber cast to them. She was both sprightly and spritely.

For a decade, as she'd read through books I've written, she sent me letters — typewritten and single-spaced on both sides of the thin paper, key topics underlined for speedy comprehension, margins frequently annotated in pen with additional clarifying thoughts. Sometimes she wrote a short review of a book, usually one about human survival and what it will require, and sometimes she included relevant apothegms, often an adage, such as Gandhi's *We must be the change we wish to see in the world,* from a talk she'd given or heard at the Unitarian Fellowship.

Letters from her differed from many that I receive. Here's the first sentence from one of them: "Heat-Moon, Carrizozo's lava beds are one place I should have worn thicker-soled shoes." Another: "Heat-Moon, have I ever told you about Andre, who worked for a pesticide company?" For perspective, consider her opening sentences against these from other readers across the country: "Dear WLH-M, forgive this long letter for taking up your time, but I have the odd habit of reading your books." Or "Dear Author Least Heat-Moon: I'm eager for your next book, so please hurry up with it. I got your last book at a garage sale for a dime — and you know how long it takes before things get to a garage sale." While I'm sharing these, I'll not resist one more: "Dear Mr. Heat-Moon, I found your book about traveling around America to be most well-written, but what have you done since *Travels with Charley?*"

Ingold's sentences were precisely set down, each typographic misstroke from her portable Smith Corona neatly painted over and restruck. In ten years of her letters, I found but a single misspelled word; once she apologized for typing on only one side of excessively translucent paper, and another missive gave apology for a postal clerk who "tilted" the stamps on a large envelope containing a small packet of mesquite blossoms she had gathered and dried for use as a condiment. I should try them, perhaps on a salad.

Her arms were thin, composed of nothing but muscle and sinew, and her slender hands ended in digits thickened strong by years of manual labor in the desert soils of New Mexico. They were not the fingers of a bon-ton matron, although they once easily could have been. As time will do, especially under a desert sun, it had imprinted but had not stolen away her pretty face or taken her lively gait or made her uneasy in the night. Spiders, propane gas, and the tilt of the earth — those were something else.

The trailer — Ingold didn't own it any more than a car or even a bicycle — was only a couple of years away from qualifying as vintage, yet the relic was tidy, at least the twenty feet of it on the west end where she lived; if 117-square-feet of living area can appear spacious, hers did through an absence of material goods (Jean: "Who started calling *things* 'goods'?"). If significance in life lies in accumulation, Ingold was running on empty.

In her room was the chair, a table, cabinet, dresser, narrow metal-frame bed, a few hanging clothes, hot plate, toaster, and refrigerator (empty, it might hold a pair of gallon jugs of milk). There was also a propane furnace she refused to use, relying instead on an electric-coil heater to warm her fingers of a winter morning. I have not attached the adjective *small* in front of each of those objects because the repetition, while accurate, would be undeft, but small indeed everything was. The entirety of her belongings could fit into the back of a (small) pickup truck. When she changed location, her mover was the U.S. Postal Service, Parcel Post division. In a nation of bodily and materially increasing obesity, Ingold had mastered the challenge of living thin, or, in a self-effacing explanation, "I'm poor at owning."

On that southern desert, she conditioned the trailer air with a six-inch electric fan and an automobile sun-shield (found in an alley) set across the west window; in the afternoon, during a short lie-down on the floor, she might add a basin of cool water and a washcloth to wipe over her bare body. It made for a fair nap. That water usually came from rain barrels under the downspouts on the landlord's out-buildings or what could be collected off the trailer. When rain wasn't there (annual precipitation was nine inches), she resorted to the cold-water tap in the bathtub, but that stuff was hard and unpleasant.

Ingold owned two lightbulbs: a hundred watt and a sixty. She ground by hand dried beans "to hasten the cooking time and save electricity." The month before I visited, her electric bill, at three dollars and fifty cents, failed to meet the minimum payment (the cost of an ice-cream cone, which she declined the warm evening I offered to bring one). She had no phone, no television, no radio, no music player, no checkbook, no credit cards, no insurance, no debt. She did have a savings account. Her carbon footprint was that of a house cat. She quoted Thoreau: *It is impossible for me to be interested in what interests men generally.*

Paying no rent for her 117-square-feet, she instead mowed, trimmed, weeded, and watered the landlord's scraggly trees and his perpetually stressed square of grass. Several times Ingold attempted to persuade the former West Virginian to try xeric landscaping, but for him natural beauty came only in water-sucking, broad leaves of green. He was her senior by a few years and would buy almost anything if he deemed the price cheap, and sometimes she was the beneficiary when he bought on sale more produce than he could eat. Except in his friendliness, the landlord was nearly the opposite of his tenant, a Manichaean arrangement that had worked for more than a decade, their association interrupted only a few times, most notably when, after studying the large United States wall map above her bed, Ingold decided to learn more about her country.

She laid out a plan to live for six months in two different towns each year. Carefully placing only necessities in two modest backpacks and six liftable cartons, she sent the boxes ahead — Parcel Post, general delivery — and boarded a bus, taking off first to the Salems, Oregon and Massachusetts; then to Lansing, Michigan; and later to Columbia, Missouri (our paths never crossed). What she carried along was only valued possessions: a portable typewriter, a few clothes, photo albums, and a ten-inch file of significant documents, including her poems ("It's light enough I can carry it out in case of fire"). Additional clothes, utensils, and miscellanea, she readily replaced from thrift shops, donating things back when the time came to move on. It was a good plan, but housing proved considerably more expensive than her limited footage in the morning shadow of the Sacramentos and a panoramic view of the San Andres.

She hadn't driven a car in a dozen years and had disliked driving when she did because "sudden decisions are always in the wings"; even though she was widely recognized — if misinterpreted — in Alamogordo, her operator's license was simply for identification. I have read about people other than vagrants or the institutionalized who subsist on less than Ingold, but I've never spent time with one, excepting a couple of monks whose cells were larger than her room. This Age of American Nimiety had given me a long curiosity about any antimammonist who renders no respect to avarice and acquisition.

(Perhaps this is the place to mention my forty-eight-month deacquisition plan some years ago to get rid of at least one material possession, large and small, every day. It went along easily for a while, some days seeing a dozen things recycled or given to the Salvation Army; I concluded that the program was working when a guest looked around the house and said, "Does anyone live here?" But, once I reached my books, things turned difficult. After three additional months of donations to the public library, the project began to totter. One afternoon it came to me: why not, when my voice in the human chorus at last croaks into silence, consign books — now sifted into useful concentration — to my alma mater? And so I rewrote my will. Q has since argued that a good book is not a material possession but a spiritual one. Nevertheless, *books aside,* I believe every object I continue to dispossess myself of further unencumbers my mind and allows it to think more crisply. Whatever you find muddled in this book, clear-sighted reader, feel free to ascribe its imprecision to the walking stick my great-grandfather made from a limb of an orange tree, or my father's pocket watch, or the medicine stone an Osage gave me, none of which I've yet seen my way clear to give away. And there could be one or two other things, like that 1850 ink bottle from Hannibal, Missouri, Mark Twain might have dipped a pen into. Still, I realize sentimentality does not assist perspicuity.)

Our talk that first evening, Jean and I — as initial conversations often do — hopscotched about, I (and perhaps she) avoiding a sharp focus so that a broader picture might emerge.

Topic: She was reading a library book, *Physics for Dummies,* although she was graduated magna cum laude from American University in Washington, DC (Ingold looked up the Latin before accepting the diploma), and she had also received from the *Wall Street Journal* an award for "excellence in finance courses." (With it came a free subscription to the *Journal,* a gift as fitting as *Mother Earth News* to a Republican.) "In science, I've never been very capable, even though my former husband was a physicist at the Air Force base down the road. He helped develop the lunar excursion module, the LEM. I worked there too as a secretary in the Radar Measurement Division."

Topic: Not long before my arrival, her typewriter abruptly malfunctioned and, beyond reasonable repair, joined the Land of Goners. Within a week, as if miraculous, she came upon another in a Dumpster, but it wasn't *just* another — it was an old machine identical to her earlier one and in working order, down to its ribbon. In demonstration, she pulled it from beneath the bed, opened it, and clicked in a few words of greeting to me. "There's nothing wrong with it," she said, "unless you call being old wrong."

Topic: Food-eating contests were worse than revolting self-humiliations — they were symptomatic of profligate consumption, an encouragement to overeat, to get so supersized one has to jumbo-size one's clothes and car and furniture. The problem, really, was the obesity of all contemporary American life and its inflated desires.

Topic: The night before, there had been a ruckus at the pit-bull trailer; slammed doors, thrown beer cans, shouted profanity. "The woman's voice was animalistic and violent," Jean said. "If I owned a record player — and a record — I'd have put on Brahms's 'Lullaby' to calm them" — pausing — "or maybe the '1812 Overture' to accompany them."

Topic: "Don't you think if *pulchritude,* for example, or *synthesis* or *hydraulic* or some others meant what the f-word means, we'd hear it less often? Most swearwords are just too easy to say." On the other hand, she saw no real use for unpronounced letters: the *w* in *sword,* the *k* and *gh* in *knight,* the *p* and maybe the *e* in *pneumonia.*

"Oh," she said, "did I ever write you that it was pneumonia that brought me from McLean, Virginia, to the Southwest, to Tucson? When I was five or six, I came down with it five times, so my father left a good job as a statistician with the federal government and moved us to the desert air. He took the opportunity to try to become a writer, but it came to nothing, and we ran out of savings. Watching his efforts go nowhere, I have to say, taught me something about the greatest failure — not trying in the first place. *The best angle to approach a problem is the try-angle.*"

Topic: I said her wondrously compressed economy reminded me of a couple of lines from an Emily Dickinson poem:

> *It would have starved a Gnat —*
> *To live so small as I —*

"Her birthday's the same as mine, but I don't think we're very similar. She's terribly cryptic. I'd rather be less enigmatic." Pausing again. "Actually, I don't know how to be enigmatic." Nevertheless, I said, you both have worked intensely and independently but not in isolation. Nodding, she said, "There's no recluse in me" — smiling —

"I'm a woman of the streets." Then another aphorism she liked: "*At low tide, islands may touch.*" Was America at low tide? "Maybe so. Maybe as long as we believe solutions lie in greater efficiency rather than in less consumption."

Topic: A *Newsweek* magazine article saying "the ten pounds Americans gained on average during the 1990s required an additional 350 million gallons of fuel a year," adding that a three-hundred-pound person carries the energy equivalent in fat of about fifteen gallons of gasoline. "How long," mocked the reporter, "will we let this resource go unused?"

Most days Jean walked around in Alamogordo, often carrying a plastic trash bag for the litter she picked up along the route of her errands, each day a small exploration, sometimes crossing paths with someone in need. She said, "A few years ago in Tucson, I came upon a beggar woman, and I didn't help her. Her expression intimidated me, so I kept my distance. That's odd, because I know her side too. Then, not long after, when I was back in Alamogordo, I found a ten-dollar bill on the street, and I thought how that woman should have found it instead of me. So I tried to track her down, and eventually I did and sent her the ten and added another ten with a letter saying I hoped she'd spend it on clothes, and I told her where the Tucson thrift shop was. A month later, I got an envelope with hand-drawn flowers on it. It was a note of thanks. I wrote a little essay about our meeting. 'Investing in a Beggar,' I called it. To my surprise, the money I invested in her — and then some — came back to me from a magazine that published my article."

Were there times when things didn't work out so nicely? "A while back," she said, "a young man with a good physique — I admire a man with a good physique — he saw me picking up aluminum cans, and he offered me a bag of them he had, and I accepted. Then he said he was out of cigarettes and asked a dollar for the cans. I gave back his cans. It wasn't the dollar — it was a dollar *for cigarettes.*"

When I'd kept her long enough from the pines where she would fall asleep to the desert air soughing through the branches and awake to the first squawks of the grackles, I asked about a man she'd mentioned in a letter, a fellow wondering how to retire on an annual thirty-seven-thousand dollars. "Oh, him," she said. "I told him I could show how to live on seven-thousand dollars a year." Thoreau: *Almost any man knows how to earn money, but not one in a million knows how to spend it.*

As I went to the door, she added, "I withdraw sixty dollars from the bank twice a month." That was a little less than fifteen-hundred dollars a year, about four dollars a day. The cost of a franchise burger and fries (neither of which Ingold ate). "Oh!" she said. "*Four* dollars? That sounds like too much. Maybe I should cut back." That might have been a jest.

Tomorrow, I said, maybe you'll show me how you do it, and she answered, "We could start by carrying water from the rain barrels."

⊱ 14 ⊰

After the Fuse Blows

WHEN JEAN WAS SIXTEEN and living in Tucson, she had her hand-writing analyzed, a report she showed me. Its predictive commentary has proven to be remarkably prescient, except for a single evaluation: "She'll develop material ambition later on, no doubt, when she will need to support herself." But the graphologist's last sentence, as enigmatic as a line from Emily Dickinson, should have put the lie to such an interpretation about materiality: "The girl's handwriting reminds me most of the nuns."

Without drawing a comparison too fine, I saw Ingold as a secular and humanistic nun in an order of one, a woman of the cloth — from the thrift shop. Were she to wear a wedding band, her spiritual marriage would be to the Lord of Sustainability and His Doctrine of Simplicity in its eternal struggle against the dark powers of Want-ingness. She once wrote me a few lines about all the ancient wisdoms reckoning contentment as a consequence of reduced cravings. Not long ago, I saw a Sunday-supplement advertisement from a nation-ally known company: THE URGE TO BUY IS GOOD! GIVE IN TO THE URGE! For Ingold, those are eleven words from Hell.

While her views were broadly Christian, her interest was not in some imagined "personal" salvation but in a real and practical planetary salvation marked by husbandry, tolerance, and fellowship, where concern for survival supersedes confession of sin. She was not monastic or ascetic in a religious way, and, because connections were all-important, she was neither an eremite nor suited to a cloister. She belonged to the sidewalks and alleyways of life, once referring to herself as "an independent, walkabout person." A friend of hers said, "For Jean, walking is sacred." She went forth in simple, leather moccasins with the thinnest of soles, her small footprints usually invisible. You knew where she'd been only because there was no litter along her path. A woman of practicality in all things, she once mentioned in a letter another honored aphorism: *The purpose of life is to lead a life of purpose.*

While Q worked on her book in the city library the next morning, Ingold and I planned to take a walkabout through her territory so I could see how she lived on fifteen-hundred dollars a year. At the time of our meeting, the federally recognized poverty level for a household was twenty-thousand dollars annually, but to speak of Jean in terms of "poverty" would be like talking about the poverty of ravens or sparrows or lilies of the field, for how could a woman having all she wanted, with money to share, be thought poor? She drew neither Social Security nor a pension and accepted no welfare. When her mother died some years ago and left her a modest trust fund, Ingold gave half of it to the Nature Conservancy in exchange for an annuity of about five-thousand dollars, more than enough to live as she chose. Still, she had found ways to supplement it without any sort of traditional employment. ("I've read about jobs that slowly kill people so they can buy health insurance.") From a monthly income of no more than six-hundred dollars, she saved about four-hundred to add to the annuity or give or lend to a person or organization in need. To her, money should be at work in the service of others. Lest anyone view her as hoity-toity holy or even irksomely righteous, a self-plumed peahen of poverty, I'll mention her "gift to self," a trip to New Zealand to see a nation she thought might be living sensibly within its resources. (*Righteous,* by the way, Ingold defined as "right use," reflecting the earliest meaning of the word.) She also once considered a face-lift but decided it excessively vain and wasteful.

What would happen were she to become seriously ill? "If it's my time to die," she said, "I'd rather die. Often, it's prolonging a no-longer-viable life that gets expensive and wasteful. A person can be just as greedy for more useless days as for more needless things or dollars." But what if she received a bad diagnosis, say cancer? "Cancer? I'd consult a book called *Eat and Heal.* I have a copy. I'd go on a cleansing water fast and eat lots of raw garlic. When the time came, I'd accept the end. But preventative medicine is the best approach."

Speaking of money reminded her of the sixty dollars she'd received that morning for aluminum cans picked up on recent walkabouts. "Now I don't have to make a bank withdrawal for the next two weeks — depending on how much bread the sandwich franchise gets rid of." Because Ingold found those loaves the best in town, she tried to convince the manager to offer them in the shop at a reduced price instead of wasting them, but still, every Wednesday and Saturday several loaves usually went into the bin at the back door. "Last week he threw out an unopened container of avocado paste, and before that several unopened bags of baby carrots. All of it was in excellent condition." (I had read recently that Americans every year throw away more than forty-five million tons of food; if we ate them, that would be about ten million elephants.)

I paraphrased the French novelist Anatole France's sentence, "It's good to collect things, but it's better to go on walks." I said she did both at the same time, and she answered, "When I travel to other towns, I like to collect good ideas, innovative ones for improvements I can bring back home and try to get implemented here, even though there's usually resistance. But I always believe a better world can happen."

Did any of the food she found ever make her ill? "I rarely get sick," she said. "Maybe a cold, but you don't catch a cold from a carrot. What makes America sick is *too much* food and too much of the *wrong* food that leads to obesity and high blood pressure and diabetes. And tooth decay." Ingold took no medications, needed no spectacles, and had all her teeth, but she wanted to weigh ten pounds more, maybe twelve.

We were talking as we filled a trio of four-gallon buckets from the rain barrels. America grew up on rainwater, I said, from barrels and cisterns, but this stuff looks a little corrupted. "It's not for drinking," she said. "I wash in it after I filter it through an old white blouse. For the table, I take a jug to the corner-store to buy a gallon of reverse-osmosis water. Twenty-five cents." Unless the drought broke when the "rainy" season arrived, her next trip to the barrels would be the last for a while, and she would have to use the faucet in the bathtub.

With the three buckets almost full, we started back, she with one and I with the others. In the desert heat it was labor, but her nearly seventy years and her pail of water scarcely slowed her. We paused once in the shade of a little mesquite, and she said, "Have you read about concerns that all the dammed-up water on Earth could alter the tilt of the axis or the rotation?" I had, and I thought, *How many seventy-year-olds have more concern for the planetary axis than their own aging spinal one?*

We sat awhile in her room so she could pull from beneath the bed a carton of her photo albums, the material possessions having the greatest claim on her. When she looked at an image of her father or mother or daughter or uncle Bill, she seemed to be looking deeply into what time had taken; her fingers lightly touched the pictures, almost in a caress, and she told who each was and about each a story. Her mother's escape from Hitler's Germany, her uncle William L. Shirer and his classic book *The Rise and Fall of the Third Reich,* her daughter in London, to whom she wrote regularly but who didn't reply. Her greatest wish, she said, was for them to find reconciliation.

There were snapshots of her horse, Misca, the one she used to ride into the Arizona desert, and she told of the time Misca stepped too close to a cholla, the "jumping" cactus, and got a bleeding flank full of spines, and how Jean picked up two stones and used them like tweezers to pull the barbs out of the wincing pony.

After college she worked as a "price economist" in the Bureau of Labor Statistics, married, returned to the Southwest, worked various secretarial jobs in governmental and university offices, became a mother, saw her marriage end. ("He didn't care for my environmental views. That was part of it.") She helped him find a second wife, a woman her young daughter approved; but that marriage failed also — another strain for the daughter. Jean went to live and work

on an organic farm north of Alamogordo, learned about xeric hor-
ticulture and wrote the newsletter for the New Mexico Citizens for
Clean Air and Water. As time passed and her independence grew, her
relations with men became more friendships than otherwise; two of
her male friends I met spoke of her warmly. Perhaps the graphologist
saw it years earlier: "Jean would be good in work where she could be
by herself. She has a feeling of sympathy for the human race and for
people in need — but that's not really loving them." The same might
be said of the Buddha or Confucius or Clara Barton or certain holy
figures from the Middle East.

Q came by to take us to lunch, but Jean declined. As Q looked
about the 117-square feet, I said, This is it — this is everything, and
Jean added, "I like the challenge of seeing how little I need to be not
unduly uncomfortable. It's wonderful to feel light." Q, something of
a minimalist herself, said, "I admire that," and Jean, in a near whisper — "Not everyone does."

The following morning I met Ingold on the grounds of the School
for the Blind and Visually Impaired, almost at the center of her usual
purlieus. The campus was lushly green in the desert valley, an oasis
of birds and shrubs and tall pecan-trees that in season provided wildlife and Jean with provender — in that instance, nuts she turned into
pecan butter to put on cast-off bread from the franchise shop.

We walked several streets so she could point out some sources of
her gleanings; at foot level there was purslane (her favorite green),
plantain, salsify, dandelion, mallow, lamb's-quarters, and a wild
sweet potato with a tuber the size of the tip of her little finger. Farther from our route grew other edible and nutritious green "weeds,"
with names to challenge the appetite of even the starving: sow this-
tle, prickly lettuce, ragweed (redroot), and a tumbleweed succulent
when young. She said, "There's a species of prickly pear cactus that
provides a good fruit, but you have to burn the spines off. I haven't
tried it yet."

Overhead, Jean pointed out mulberry leaves for tea, crab apples for drying, and her favorite tree, a Chinese jujube that gave lovely little dates. Even more distant were pears, pistachios, a tiny arbor of Golden Delicious apples ignored by its owners, and a neglected grove of apricots bearing marble-size fruits with a palatable — if potentially toxic — seed she dislodged from the pits by putting them in a sock and hammering them open. "Sometimes a friend gives me government food she won't eat, the healthful foods like dried plums or trail mix. Or dates. She eats the canned meat." No grocery for you? I asked. "Oh yes," she said. "I buy things I'm not going to find on a walkabout. Vegetable oil, rice, eggs, yogurt, buttermilk. Sometimes even produce when it's good and priced right."

That menu suggested Jean was a vegetarian, but she allowed herself "several small bites of meat, poultry, or fish once a day — just enough to sample the flavor and texture." But later she said, "Meat-eating is on a collision course with human population. Increasing human numbers will make every problem facing us insoluble. But it's an unusual organization today that will even mention overpopulation, especially the big environmental groups." On that topic, I said, they've lost their courage to talk about a world populace increasing by more than two-hundred-thousand humans *every day.* Until humanity decides to get a grip on its deadly proliferation, nothing — no other problem — can be solved. She considered, then said, "I'm afraid we're going to let things slide so long, forced sterilization will become necessary."

Ingold was carrying a plastic trash bag folded small; on her return home, she would walk through Alameda Park: "I don't go to picnic — I go to pick up. I like to think, wherever I live, the neighborhood looks better after a few of my walkabouts." That reminded her: "When I was in your town a few years ago, a man in a new car saw me picking up litter, and stopped and tried to hand me twenty dollars. He was terribly insistent." Was he buying off his conscience the way people do the homeless? She said, "Maybe it was just a thanks. I get them sometimes."

Although she would, from time to time, check for forgotten change in the coin return of a public phone, she usually would not accept money offered her. It was more than a matter of pride: refusing money in America gets remembered along with — she hoped — the act of somebody doing a lowly task to upgrade the public weal without being paid for it beyond recognition (even if sometimes of a disdainful sort). Yet in her was no self-congratulation, no sanctimoniousness about a fearless lone-woman stewardship. She was doing simply what she wanted to do.

In spite of her always being alert to her appearance and never looking unkempt, always keeping her thrift-shop outfits neatly coordinated, her litter sack could nonetheless cause people to take her for a bag lady, a judgment making it easy for them to explain her to their convenient satisfaction. After all, where's the pigeonhole for an educated and attractive woman working alone to clean up after the rest of us? Ingold did not mention it, but I saw it: an occasional person deprecating and depreciating her efforts, palliatives against anyone disturbing the smugly comfortable who are incapable of considering two words — *rethink excess.*

At one point, Jean stepped off to pick up a couple of beverage containers — an aluminum one to resell, but the plastic one in Alamogordo was only trash. I watched her small buckskin moccasins leave ever-so-faint imprints in the dusty alley. There was a woman who had walked away — steadily if slowly — from a life of artificial wants made to look like needs. She would never speak of it this way, but I will: Jean Ingold's monkey wrench of nonconformity was tiny, but she never hesitated to throw it into the greased machinery of crapulent consumerism.

I had no plan to live exactly as she did, in part because she depended on the overflow of a prodigal nation. What I saw in her life was an alert to superfluity, a demonstration of the ancient and universal wisdom of controlling material desires by enhancing the life of one's heart and mind, the grand goal of every major religion and spiritual path ever put before humanity. Perhaps I'm unaware of one, but I can't recall any way of the spirit that demands perfection (Matthew's "Be ye perfect" gets a better reading from Luke: "Be ye merciful"). Most of the paths, it seems to me, say more simply, "Wake up! Do better! Connect!" Ingold's habits set a marker to measure how near or far I might be from such a course, how close to a broadly sensible material existence. For me, the mirror she held up reflected not so much her achievement as the distance I believed I had yet to go. Her life was a burr in my conscience, and I was in her debt for it.

Before he died, her father wrote twenty-seven-year-old Jean to urge her to *choose* a life she wanted rather than to merely drift into one. Said he, a former analyst with the Securities and Exchange Commission, "I would not advocate as a supreme goal a comfortable, affluent life in the suburbs. Even poverty itself would not be bad if you were making some sacrifice for an ethical objective. But sheer, purposeless poverty I can't accept." Forty years later, I believe Father Shirer would accept his daughter's walking away from a pampered life and the emptiness of possessions into a fulfilling one of considered and deliberate frugality.

The night before I said good-bye to her, I was up in the foothills near La Luz, with the Sacramentos at my back. I looked across the Tularosa Basin to watch for a new weapon of luminescence to get shot up toward the Oscura Mountains. Somewhere out there under the white gypsum sands was the ancient lake the old inhabitants foresaw one day rising again, and southward was Lake Lucero, now a dusty alkali barren waiting for rain, a withered flat more like a fallen Lucifer than the Morning Star. I was straining to see into the dusk, as if my vision were impaired.

Down there too were Jean Ingold's 117-square-feet sitting on the edge of a vast field of lights and darks, some natural, some humanly made, some of beauty, some of terror. Perhaps it was her proximity to that Armageddon that made me remember another of the adages she liked: *After your fuse blows, let your light shine.* A day earlier, hearing herself say it, Jean looked at me and said, "But do we even have fuses anymore?"

IV.
Into the Northeast

The Northeast

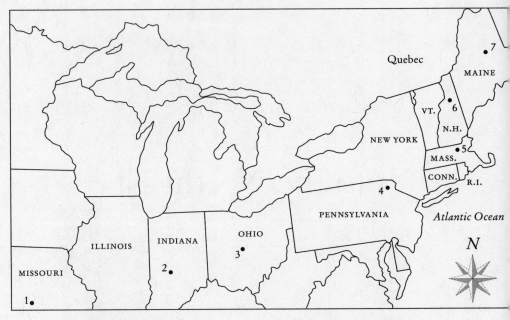

1 Columbia, Missouri
2 Bloomington, Indiana
3 Westerville, Ohio
4 Starrucca Viaduct, Pennsylvania
5 Lowell, Massachusetts
6 Mount Washington, New Hampshire
7 Millinocket, Maine

Into the Northeast

On Motoring

Considering the fixation of the American people upon automobiles
and their use, there has been surprisingly little of what might be
called personal or imaginative writing on the subject. In the first
decade of the century, C. N. and A. M. Williamson delighted the
reading public with a series of novels under such titles as *The Motor
Maid,* and *The Car of Destiny.* But since that time has there been a
novel based chiefly on motoring?

> — George R. Stewart,
> *U.S. 40: Cross Section of the
> United States of America,*
> 1953

❥ 1 ❦

In Hopes Perdurable Reader
Will Not Absquatulate

NOW THAT OUR TRAVELS have reached beyond the halfway mark, perdurable reader, it occurs to me I've not yet said anything about the subtitle of this book and its key word, *mosey*. Maybe you first heard the term from the mouth of a bewhiskered, hornswogglin bullwhacker in some B Western: "I reckon I'll just mosey on."

But you'll note I've turned it into a noun about jogging along literally and figuratively, the destinations little places in the nation or in a notion. It's a mosey because roads to quoz everywhere are posted "reduced speed ahead." To hurry, in space or idea, is to miss obscured signposts, hidden turnoffs, or an exit to Sublimity City (Kentucky), or Surprise Valley (California), or even Dull Center (Wyoming). To go leisurely today is almost un-American, so putting *mosey,* a pure Americanism, into the title of a book about America verges on illogic and invites mocking from any citizen carrying a fastport issued by the Department of Speed in a nation hell-bent for destination if not destiny in the Posthaste Era:

[**TO BE READ** *PRESTISSIMO*] Speedy drive-up window, speed-dialing, speed-reading, speedball, speed freak, speedway, Speedy Gonzales *Andale-ándale,* immediate access, no waiting, call now — don't wait, now's the time, haven't got the time, hasty decisions, hasty pudding, short orders from a fast-food window, quick lunch and make it snappy, quick stops, quick time, quick count, quick-change artist, quick and dirty, a quickie, double-quick, on the double, be there in a jiff, jiffy copies, instant coffee, instant cash, instant winners, instant replay, instant stardom, overnight success, overnight express, nine-day wonder, fifteen minutes of fame, ten-minute manager, five-minute rice, minute steak, a minute's all I got, flash-fried clams, flash-dried potatoes, flash drive, in a flash, greased lightning, like a blue streak, express lane, fast lane, fast track in the rat race, fast-talking hustler, fast freeze, fast breeder reactor, can't hit the fastball, faster than a speeding bullet *Upupandaway*, zip, zoom, whiz, lickety-split, in nothing flat, in less than no time, a rolling stone gathers no moss, don't let the grass grow under your feet, make tracks, step lively, step on it, shake a leg, hotfoot it, hightail it, pick 'em up and set 'em down, get in and get out, get the lead out, pour it on, put it in high gear, put the pedal to the metal, run it wide open, ball the jack, highball it, full speed ahead, full steam, full throttle, full blast, hauling ass, barrel-assing, going like ninety, eat my dust, now you see me — now you don't, Road Runner *Beep-beep,* going like mad, going like a house afire, speed maniac, speed demon, a bat out of hell, hell-bent for leather, only green lights on god's highway, never look back — something might be gaining on you, here today — gone tomorrow.

[**TO BE READ** *ADAGIO MOLTO*] On the dead run until you reach the finish line where six pallbearers will carry you at a funereal pace to your six-feet-under to spend eternity at Dead Slow.

These wanderings into quoz are a mosey because they took three years and four seasons to accomplish their sixteen-thousand miles of journeys to places a goodly portion of the American populace would call "nowhere." But I believe simply *lighting out for the territory,* to crib Huck Finn's words, carries its own sweet justification; to lift another phrase, you might see it as a *because-it's-there* approach to exploration. In a hundred ways, America is where it is because its people can be maniacally destination-bound; America is where it isn't for the same reason. Some of us find that a pleasant circumstance.

I'll add here, also somewhat belatedly, any reviewers attempting to find a thesis in these pages will be summarily barred from their writing machines until able to state clearly and concisely *the* thesis of their lives. Meanings, of course, are another matter. More life happens on the way to the forum than *in* the forum, and there's a word relevant to that phenomenon: *circumforaneous,* the strolling from forum to forum. Whether we like it or not, for better or worse, we all live circumforaneous lives, and that's why this is a circumforaneous book.

The word *mosey,* as does *vamoose,* probably derives from the Spanish *vamos,* "we go." Some lexicographers offer, however, the possibility it descends from nineteenth-century itinerant Jewish peddlers often named (or pejoratively called) Moses; other scholars find its origin in the leisurely and relaxed gait of antebellum, Southern Negroes ("Mose" a not-uncommon moniker) who had little to gain by hurrying to the hot fields. The earliest theory I've seen comes from John Russell Bartlett in his wonderfully jolly (although I think not so intended) *Dictionary of Americanisms* of 1848, which contends the word *mosey* (he termed it "a low expression") derives from an Ohio postmaster named Moses who absconded with considerable federal receipts. But absconding is no longer — if it ever was — at the heart of moseying.

A better term, by the way, for such flight, coincidentally one I learned from Bartlett's lexicon, is *absquatulate.* He cites an illustration of its usage:

> Hope's brightest visions absquatulate with their golden promises before the least cloud of disappointment, and leave not a shin-plaster behind.

(A *shinplaster* here, as Bartlett explains under that entry, is "worthless currency.")

I sometimes read his dictionary as if he intended it to be compendious stories of mid-nineteenth-century life; you need only fill in details between his entries and definitions to see yarns and anecdotes emerge from obscurity like a *mud-pout* (catfish) caught by a *sneezer* (thoroughgoing fellow) lazily smoking his *loco-foco* (self-igniting cigar). That last word carries a five-hundred-word microessay I'm tempted to pass along, but editorial judgments suggest I leave certain things to your own further explorations. Bartlett's citation for *sneezer,* however, I'll give to you because I gave it to Q:

> It's awful to hear a minister swear; and the only match I know
> for it is to hear a regular sneezer of a sinner quote Scripture.

She, who often says more with a glance than with words, thereby making it difficult to quote her, considered that sentence, then looked at me, her silence louder than necessary.

That evening, while we were talking about Bartlett and definitions of *mosey* as a subtitle, she said, "Let me understand — you're going to put on the cover of a book a six-word title, and two of those words are *quoz* and *mosey?*" I was waiting as she took her time to drop the other glossological shoe. "Aren't you concerned that readers, even before you start the book's engine for the journey, will absquatulate?" Ha! said I, feigning certainty, My readers are perdurable, and when it comes to the American language, in them is no absquatulation! (Proof: you are still here, steadfast reader.)

I'll bring this particular notional mosey to a conclusion. In 1850, at the behest of Congress, John Russell Bartlett led an expedition into the Southwest, a journey he was eager to undertake because he wanted to see the territory and its native flora, fauna, and peoples. After three years, his frequent pursuits of quoz had turned a federally sanctioned exploration into a grand mosey, and the politicos in Washington removed him as leader. On his return to the East, he published the next year an illustrated account of nearly twelve-hundred pages that has become one of the timeless books on the Far West: *Personal Narrative of Explorations and Incidents in Texas, New Mexico, California, Sonora, and Chihuahua.* John Russell Bartlett — not to be confused with his contemporary John Bartlett of the *Familiar Quotations* — belongs to that pantheon of Americans who contribute much but in recognition receive little. The last and only reprinting of his great narrative, at the moment of writing this sentence, was forty years ago.

As summer came on, our mosey shifted into cooler territory, with a loose goal of heading northeastward as far as we could without leaving the country. The destination was to be the North Maine Woods, an area about the size of an entire New England state, having no public roads and virtually no paved ones, with the roads that *are* there marked by checkpoints to allow or deny an ordinary traveler permission to enter. Such an apparently restricted space was a land of quoz I'd never managed to find my way into, and I'd not met anyone who had penetrated its perimeter. Most of my knowledge of it came from Henry David Thoreau who traveled through a corner by canoe in preparation for writing *The Maine Woods*.

Again, I must excuse my story for overleaping itself.

A week before the summer solstice, Q and I left Missouri, paused in central Illinois to see the granite mausoleum where William Grayston's slayer lies protectively embalmed and entombed for what he hoped was eternity, where his mummified flesh waits to be arisen, his resting place unlike that of the man he murdered who got put into an oaken box set down into a shallow grave and whose corporeality has long since risen in the surrounding cedars to become scented wood seasonally holding berries eaten by waxwings working the miracle of a sylvan Eucharist so that now a thousand trees grow from Grayston's essence and raise him into the light.

❥ 2 ❧

Hoisting Jack

W E STARTED FOR INDIANA to meet up with one more rara avis, this one a Canary, James Canary, the conservator of a most peculiar and legendary literary American manuscript: a hundred-twenty-foot scroll of typewritten words on what is now effectively a single piece of paper. It may be the only literary manuscript — when displayed fully — that looks like both its title and topic. Readers of foresight may see what's coming, because no other American document exactly matches that description of Jack Kerouac's *On the Road.*

Before going east, I mentioned to a man my wish to see the manuscript, and he said, "I'm with you, buddy. I've read his and your road-reads." The northeastward mosey and its quest for quoz to put into a new road-read seemed to pick up, if not a pattern, then at least a leitmotif of transport: roads, bridges, rails, words. How that came about, I have little idea.

Our mosey, Q and I, from time to time seemed to reveal emerging patterns, although — even if I lived long enough — I was likely years away from perceiving any grand shapes or the wholeness of them. But on occasion I could see a few pieces, perhaps ones of only minor significance, forming a design. When I catch a glimpse of things arranging themselves, I usually call them coincidences.

The more days I put behind me, the more I realize — or maybe *believe* is a better word — the pieces of one's existence seem in due course to assemble themselves into patterns, into different topographies, whether or not we perceive them. Each piece — a word, an occurrence, an object, a decision — creeps along in search of its position. Once a part is there, perhaps we can change its location or coloration, maybe even forget or ignore it, but we cannot remove it any more than we can delete having lived through yesterday. Our hours, with their invisible magnetism, arrange and rearrange the iron filings we, moment by moment, grind off our existence.

Sometimes this happens: a person unknown to you walks up, greets you, introduces himself, and thereafter your life is of a changed order. Or: one Monday morning you leave home at a minute past eight instead of the accustomed eight straight-up only to arrive at an intersection at the same second as a running-the-light delivery van. A moment here, a word there, and our lives suddenly lurch off into some new territory requiring a different map.

Occasionally, when I'm rolling along a two-lane and watching an eighteen-wheeler highballing toward me, I think were it a fired bullet or a slush ball headed my way, I'd be ducking. Yet twenty tons of freight moving at seventy miles an hour an arm's length from my left ear causes no response other than to hold the wheel steady. At that moment, there is no greater wheel of fortune (or, as a Buddhist might express it, Wheel of True Meaning) than a steering wheel — mine and the trucker's. Most of the time I live oblivious to the ontological implications of proximity and their potential to make necessary remapping a life. Yet, at the end of each day — given the universal advisability of not occupying a point in space at the same instant as another something — we all could razz existence with a "Ha! You missed me again!" To age is to become good at either ducking or hiding. The elderly are consummate escape artists, although they know with certainty everybody sooner or later either fails to duck or dodge quickly enough, whether it's away from a speeding vehicle or an even faster pathogen. (Of escapes, I'll say a little more farther along.)

The degree that moseying improves one's ability to duck and dodge, I can't say, but I believe it does generally assist longevity and, even more, in remapping a territory; and it certainly can improve perception and awareness during the consequent survival. Speed doesn't get you more time — it just botches what you've got and makes for inferior maps.

The first piece in this northern leg of the mosey may have been a letter inviting me east to help celebrate the fiftieth anniversary of publication of *On the Road* with an exhibition of the typed scroll that's a veritable symbol of transport; its words are tracks of many kinds — intellectual, spiritual, actual.

In Bloomington, Indiana, we met James Canary, the man who would transport the manuscript eastward, he who called himself "the delivery boy." As conservator of the *On the Road* scroll, he equally self-deprecatingly could have added, "And the fix-it guy." At supper one evening, he talked about his long interest in Buddhism and its writings, especially the tantra. *"Tantra,"* he said, "means *woven together.*" In ways never planned, his life indeed has been woven together with such details as to make him quite possibly the most apropos person in the world for delivering a small, heavy case containing a long piece of paper worth at this moment about fourteen-hundred dollars an inch. Here are some of those threads, many carrying the look of coincidences:

Thread One: As a boy, Jim always kept a suitcase packed and ready for the road at a moment's notice. "I had a good family, but because I was adopted, I could feel maybe I didn't really belong with them."

Two: His adoptive father farmed in south-central Indiana where he occasionally plowed up prehistoric artifacts — stone points and a few grooved axes — that gave young Canary a sense of the depth of the human past and an interest in preserving what remains. Now those points hang on a wall in his home and the axes are in a box nearby.

Three: The man who wrote a beautiful book on prehistoric artifacts in Indiana was Eli Lilly, the grandfather of the man whose library formed the nucleus of the Lilly Library at Indiana University where Jim later became conservator and where the Kerouac type-written manuscript resided when not on the road to an exhibition.

Four: Unusual for an Indiana farmer, Canary's father also repaired typewriters.

Five: Teenage Jim's favorite book was Kerouac's 1958 novel, *The Dharma Bums,* in which a central character, Japhy Ryder (based upon the Beat poet Gary Snyder), expressed literary and spiritual interest in things Asian, which resonated with Canary. Consider this sentence from Ryder, speaking about the legendary poet of ancient China Han Shan: "He was a man of solitude who could take off by himself and live purely and true to himself." Jim said, "My dream became to go off into the woods and practice a craft and translate Buddhist texts."

Six: Although Canary didn't know it then, *The Dharma Bums* manuscript was one of four Jack Kerouac typed out on long rolls of paper he would tape end to end in a kind of weaving together of sentences.

Seven: On his first of a dozen trips to the Himalayas, Jim came upon two Tibetan refugees in India who were making paper in the ancient way for use in sacred texts. Those papermakers encouraged his deeper study of Buddhism, papermaking, bookbinding, and the preservation of knowledge, artifacts, culture, and even the planet itself.

Eight: Jim's house in the woods lies between Hindustan and Buddha, Indiana, the only towns in America, as far as I know, so named.

Nine: The man who bought the scroll of *On the Road* in 2001 happened to live forty minutes north of Canary.

Not a man of especial height, Jim is nevertheless solid and carries the belly of the famous "Jolly Buddha" frequently represented in statuettes, whose rounded abdomen Asians rub for good luck. In his mid-fifties, Jim wore his graying hair in a slender ponytail almost hidden by white sideburns that, as if electrified, reached out into the world laterally from his temples and upper jaw; they were like antennae feeling for cosmic vibrations. Whenever he stood between me and a bright light, his sideburns gleamed in such radiance they took on the aspect of a partial aureola, a nimbus I think he was unaware of.

Canary delivered his words quietly enough to require dedicated attention, and, for an American, he was notably tranquil, that state so desired in Buddhism. He followed the counsel of the Taoist Lao-tzu: "The way of the sage is not to compete but to act."

If Jim was too young to have been a Beatnik, he didn't miss the chance at putting in some time as a descendant of the Beats, although he didn't apply the term *hippie* to days in the '70s when he lived in an abandoned log cabin until one winter a fire took it and his library, a housing predicament he resolved by moving into a teepee. He had also lived under the stairs of an old apartment building. He said, "I wasn't really a hippie — I was just a stair person."

To me, the difference between the young Canary and the thousands who once affected hippiedom was that he was authentic, almost an archetype, and he worked to weave together core values of the later '60s and early '70s into a useful life able to make a difference in other lives. He was a flowering of flower power and of that high promise honestly and constructively fulfilled. If he never became Japhy Ryder, he did weave a well-patterned life Gary Snyder could respect. Not long before I met Jim, he had carried the *On the Road* scroll for exhibition to Santa Fe where he met Snyder, then nearing eighty, and told him how his advice that a young poet should learn a trade had given a controlling shape and substance to Canary's life. Snyder nodded, pleased his counsel had been practicably useful.

In the house Jim built with his own hands in a woods near Bloomington was a small room dedicated to meditation, and in it were the commonly associated accoutrements: a scroll painting, candles, cushions, incense. Also in the house were a cluttered printing and bookbinding shop and a large room with a twenty-four-foot ceiling he managed to construct despite a touch of acrophobia. Under that cathedral chamber, with its half-finished chimney of Bedford limestone (from the same quarry as the facade of the Empire State Building), his domicile in the woods began simply as a bookbindery; but, at his former wife's insistence, over time it grew into a home with additions and modifications — all afterthoughts fitting a perpetual work in progress.

The initial book Jim bound was a first edition of Kerouac's *The Scripture of the Golden Eternity,* a work written in a cabin the novelist shared for several happy weeks with Snyder. The small volume attempts to weave together pieces of the Catholicism of Kerouac's boyhood with Buddhist notions Snyder was opening to him. Here's a single sentence from it: "There are not two of us here, reader and writer, but one, one golden eternity, One-Which-It-Is, That-Which-Everything-Is." Kerouac wrote those words right around the time Canary was born. Jim told me, not with regret but in resigned chagrin, "I should have begun working on a book I didn't care about, something without any value, because I made a clunky mess of *Golden Eternity.*" I said, Don't we all?

Except for his meditation room, Canary's place was still a sprawling workshop with a home tucked into various available corners rather than the other way around. It contained, perhaps, more material objects than a bodhisattva might deem wise, and Canary, looking around, said, "All this could get *totally* out of control." Once or twice he has hired a university student to help sort books, tools, things: sort, mind you, not toss out. As far as I know, Jim's discomfort with discarding is the most un-Zen aspect of his otherwise enlightened existence.

The house, despite a couple of decades of labor, was still enough incomplete that from time to time he would glance up from his work or reading to see above in some unfinished juncture a flying squirrel looking down on him and his plump cat. Rather common creatures not often seen, the squirrels weren't an annoyance but a blessing of harmony between his quarters and theirs, a separation they — and other critters — sometimes failed to acknowledge; but such occurrences were another reason he went into the woods to live.

At the point where his small lawn joined the gravel lane was a shoulder-height tree stump weathered gray, and atop it Canary had placed a concrete figure of a seated Buddha that so blended with the weathered stump, the statue appeared to be an outgrowth of it, as if the Enlightened One had risen from the heart of the old beech to felicitate the home in the woods.

In the 1970s, Canary entered Indiana University to study philosophy but left before his first year was complete to, in the words of the old license plates, WANDER INDIANA. He returned a couple of years later and began study of Asian languages and cultures, especially things Tibetan, and even more especially, ancient Buddhist religious texts and the handmade papers they were set down on. Over seven or eight years, he gathered up enough hours for a doctorate, although his broad pursuits — which some professors saw as unfocused — left him with a more useful bachelor of arts. During those years, he worked on what could have become a dissertation: a translation of a short biography of Padmasambhava, the legendary teacher said to have brought Tantric Buddhism to Tibet in the eighth century.

Canary's interest widened from translation of Tibetan texts to the conservation and preservation of the paper containing the sacred inscriptions, marvelous calligraphy often executed in a liquid-gold ink on heavy sheets dyed indigo to create an exotic beauty that makes even the most mundane utterance appear holy and worth deeper consideration, something the Western World has lacked since monks ceased creating elaborately decorated initial letters in Christian gospels written on vellum. Canary is particularly aware of the demise of that legacy, in part because among the many objects in his home is an old Linotype machine requiring molten lead to cast its letters, and in part because his work at the library sometimes includes restoring damaged figures on medieval manuscripts, exacting work often necessitating use of a microscope.

Among the nearly half-million volumes and seven-million pages of manuscript in the Lilly Library are twenty-thousand miniature books (some that would fit inside a garbanzo bean). There is also a virtually mint copy of the Double Elephant Edition of Audubon's *Birds of America*, a book large enough to be opened safely only by two people — or perhaps one Canary. (The 435 hand-colored etchings in the four volumes, one per sheet, depict each bird life-size — even the turkey and great heron. To display the illustrations in their entirety, two librarians every seven days open the exhibit case to turn a page; just after I happened to see there the last etching, it was time to start again at the beginning. Several citizens had come by once a week for eight and a half years to view all the birds.)

Jim took us into the vault to show treasures: Virginia Woolf's inky corrections on page proofs of *Mrs. Dalloway;* a nicely bound copy of Arnold Bennett's *Old Wives' Tale* that only a close look revealed to be a hand-lettered, working manuscript; a file labeled VONNEGUT, K., REJECTION LETTERS. (I, commiseratingly, read all ninety of them, including a once-crumpled refusal used as a coaster for a highball glass.) There was also a pen sketch of Sherlock Holmes drawn by Arthur Conan Doyle, the creator perhaps wanting to see for himself the face of his creation.

To stand in the narrow aisles of the Lilly vault, containing so much evidence of the labors in making literature, is to be reminded how a manuscript — arduously, haltingly, confoundedly — proceeds from the frailties and unacceptabilities of inception to a finished book able to stir humankind long past those anguished hours of initial composition. In file after file were phrases inked over, sentences crossed out, paragraphs expunged, new words scribbled in only to be lined through with yet another try for the best sentence. Those acid-free boxes held slips of lives revealing someone finding a way through darkness, each writerly mind driven more by hope or necessity than certainty of outcome. On a messed page, in a stain or crumple or angrily scratched-off phrase, we might see the promise of eventual triumph, but the writer would remember struggle. Stopping repeatedly to read labels on the cartons — Hemingway, Conrad, Durrell, Frost, Lawrence, Maugham, Wharton, Synge, Pound — I had to be pushed along. The Lilly Library is a place that can transform a bibliophile — before he can say *Jack Kerouac!* — into a blithering bibliomaniac.

Inside a heavy case inside a locked cabinet inside the vault (I counted seven locks between it and the world beyond the library front door) lay the thing that had acquainted me with Jim Canary: that single paragraph of typed words which, if unrolled on a football field, would reach from one goal line almost halfway to the other, even without the few inches chewed off by Kerouac's friend's spaniel. It is the most famous manuscript of *On the Road* but not the only one. Canary calls it "Jack-in-the-Box."

Q and I elsewhere had seen the front thirty-six feet of it. In the vault, I asked Jim if I might heft the case — why, I'm not sure. Perhaps it had to do with my first book. After I finished the seventh and last draft of it, I stacked them all up on a bathroom scale: fifty pounds exactly. There, before me, were four years of my life reduced to avoirdupois: 1,461 days become eight-hundred ounces. Was that all? It seemed insufficient for the labor expended until I realized the evidential weight of the four years preceding my writing the book, excluding some canceled checks, a few letters, and a dozen snapshots, was zero.

When I hoisted Jack-in-the-Box, I felt the weight of a portion of Kerouac's life — twenty days if we count only the typing of the scroll, several years if we count his notebooks and various abandoned versions, and about a third of a century if we consider the time it took the man to become the writer he was in 1957.

⋟ 3 ⋞

Spontaneous Bop

I WAS EIGHTEEN when *On the Road* came out. I saw the book, I liked the title, I respected what I knew of its contents, but I didn't read it for some time because then I was more in the thrall of the Beat poets, especially Lawrence Ferlinghetti (*A Coney Island of the Mind*) and, in a much lesser way, Allen Ginsberg (*Howl*), works my teachers considered worthless if not trash; to the teenage brain, of course, there is no higher commendation. My sense of language was then too innocent and uninformed for me to see the undigested ideas and hurried assemblage in so much Beat writing, and if I did notice an occasional solecism (rife in Kerouac's novels), I defended it as proof of spontaneous creation — a howling artistic challenge to the rigidities and conformities dulling the '50s. With nescient ideas about the interweavings of form and content, I would argue half-heartedly that the Beats were important for *what* they said rather than *how* they said it. Instinct was of more consequence than crafts-manship. After all, somebody besides musicians needed to do some-thing about that bland, insipid decade.

Nevertheless, I was at the same time suspicious of acquaintances who materially pretended life as a hipster, whose self-indulgence masqueraded as revolution (a confusion perfected in the decade fol-lowing). In a classroom or at a bar, they might spout Kerouac or Ginsberg, but any abiding interest in discovering avenues of mind beyond mere revolt against wearing khaki trousers or spindling and mutilating an IBM card — *that* passion faded quickly. Indeed, soon enough, nearly all of them were headed back toward the faubourgs they had reviled a couple of years earlier. Their return, their capitulation, may have been for the best.

But something not for the best was our miscomprehension of "spontaneous" artistic creation. The more notorious Kerouac's four manuscript scrolls became, the more fables about them increased: he didn't slow down for punctuation; he could write a novel in a couple of weeks while on Benzedrine, cigarettes, and booze; a single draft was all he needed. Those untruths led us to wrongful notions about literary genesis, inspiration, structures, and the role of self in writing. (On those last two, it seems to me, much American poetry still hasn't recovered.)

If only we'd known the truth: Jack Kerouac did not simply sit down at his Underwood typewriter one morning, stick in the front end of a "Teletype" roll, and, over the following nineteen days, bang out a novel that brought him instant fame and challenged the lives of an entire generation.

If only we'd known the truth: Kerouac worked at the book for more than a decade and executed several drafts of *On the Road*, both short ones and long, including a version in French. With remarkable dedication through those years, he also kept notebooks and sketchbooks — words and drawings — to sharpen perception and feed his memory and imagination when he sat down at the typewriter. By the time *On the Road* got into print, Kerouac had written ten other works, one of them published to good reviews if modest sales. We of my age, only a few years behind the big Beats, simply did not understand what Allen Ginsberg called "spontaneous bop prosody." We had no idea of actual writerly methods, and we bought into the bogus "first thought — best thought, first draft — best draft." Today, I'm not sure the Beat writers wanted us to understand; I think they encouraged us to see them, again in Ginsberg's words, as "angelheaded hipsters burning for the ancient heavenly connection." Indeed. Those "desolation angels" got us believing in a divine afflatus waiting to flow out of whoever was blessed. Weren't writers more chosen than made? Genius was inspiration, and to have to toil was proof of one's lack of celestial exaltation. Wasn't artistic conception immaculate? We knew, goddamnitall, you had it or you didn't.

If only we'd known the truth: Kerouac labored hard and he worked long and accepted eminent editorial counsel to make *On the Road* publishable. The title, the author wrote later, came at the insistence of an editor (the value of those three words is incalculable, worth more, some readers have said, than all the other words following them). If John Kerouac (not yet Jack in the early versions) was angelheaded, his was a damned sweaty seraphic noggin that did not simply open to some heavenly tap. The truth is there were more drafts than draughts, and his angelhead was dedicated to rethinking, rereading, reworking, revising, rewriting, reshaping, replacing, removing, rebuilding, restructuring, renaming, reducing, rehearsing, reviewing, and then doing it all again. For those reasons, I must admit now — even considering the affection I hold for him and my appreciation of what he accomplished — I often wish his expression had turned out better, especially his influential *The Dharma Bums.* But then, in *On the Road,* I'll come upon a passage describing some gone hepcat blowing a hot crazy sax, and, oh dad, lay it on us!

The evening of the day Q and I saw the front end of the scroll in Lowell, Massachusetts, Kerouac's hometown on the banks of the Merrimack River, we joined Jim Canary for a tour of some of the taverns the novelist knew too well. In one, the Rainbow Café, we sat at the bar, I on the very spot Kerouac preferred — so the bartender said. A couple of stools away was the only other patron, a millworker, a man in his fifties who cleaned the interior of huge boilers. For a few minutes he watched us intently, listening, then said excitedly, "I recognize you!" and he pointed our way. "You're that guy! That guy in the paper!" Q and Jim looked at me, but I was not that guy. That guy was Canary. "In the paper," the man said with some excitement. "I saw your picture in the paper!"

On the Road meant nothing to the worker, but the celebrity of a man in the news did. To come face-to-face in your very own hangout with a face appearing in print that very day! I did what I think Jack might have done: I bought the fellow a drink, and he soon was telling us about his job. I asked if he knew the name Jack Kerouac, and the workman said, "I think that's one I've heard." Then to the bartender, "Was he in here the other night?" And the bartender said, "He's here every night."

None of Canary's three sons, all in their twenties, has really inquired about the *OTR* scroll, although one of them once did ask a friend of Jim's, "Is Dad, like, famous?" I don't know, but for a fellow who set out for the woods to translate Buddhist texts in quietude, Jim's path has, at least for a while, gone off in a direction of some celebrity, one that often pulls him out of his woody hollow and onto the road — if air travel may be so considered.

Did Kerouac ever imagine a later life for his typed scrolls? Did he ever — in those hours (to use his phrase) "atop an Underwood" of tapping out words a hundred a minute with amazing accuracy, slowing only to check a notebook beside him, once in a while stopping to insert another of the eight rolls of *draftsman's tracing paper,* and all the while hoping his novel would fulfill the promise of his first published book — did he then imagine his words sailing through space, on the road for people to read not his words but to look at his typing? As he assembled his scrolls, was there any thought about icons or artifacts?

What we do know about him then are some of his thoughts just before his first novel, *The Town and the City,* came out in 1950 when he confessed in a notebook, "I gloat more & more in the fact I may be rich & famous soon." But the book sold fewer copies than he hoped, and he later wrote, "Wasn't born to be rich."

I would like to tell him about Jack-in-the-Box. I'd like to say, So now, Ti Jean, your manuscript is clipping along at nearly the speed of sound and soon it will touch down at an airport where security guards will x-ray it in its case, and they'll take it and its conservator aside to have him prove he is not transporting some ingeniously disguised weapon of terror, and as they reach for the brittle paper, he will say, "You can't touch that!" and one of the guards will pause, then light up with recognition and tell his colleague who's also looking closely at the densely typed words, "I know this thing! I saw a teevee special about it! This is a Dead Sea Scroll!" and then he will okay Jim to carry the "holy words" on through to their exhibition. What do you make of that, Ti Jean? Has your afflatus at last become divine?

And what do you make of it belonging to a man, owner of a professional football team, who paid more than two-million dollars for it? At about twenty dollars a word, that's rather more than you made off all your eighteen books published in your lifetime. Or what about a first edition of *On the Road* selling fifty years later for a thousand times more than its original price of a couple of bucks?

The value of the scroll — logging in several thousand miles a year on its well-received tours and traveling farther than did its author — undoubtedly has increased with its own time on the road. But, beyond the monetary, a deeper worth must lie elsewhere — perhaps in its being a unique icon and exotic artifact. Such an interpretation suggests similarity to a grand-master painting, but I believe that would be misleading. Each of those 120,000 typed words has been precisely recorded, beginning with the error in the opening sentence:

I first met met Neal not long after my father died.

down to the final period. (And, yes, the scroll *is* punctuated.) We know today how it differs from the published novel, and we realize it really isn't like a master painting, with layers of pigment some advanced technology may one day examine to reveal new understandings of how the artist conceived and executed the work. Beneath the carbon of the letters Kerouac struck is no pentimento of earlier tries. It seems heretical to say it, but in practical terms, we no longer really need the scroll itself.

But in other ways, ways more profound, we very much *do* need it. If you've ever waited in line outside the National Archives in Washington to climb the steps to get a brief look at one of the handwritten versions of the Declaration of Independence, that one behind bulletproof glass, you know the answer. In an alert human, there can rise from somewhere deeply within, from beyond facile apprehension, a desire to encounter not simply the authentic but *the original,* to stand close to a first thing that counts for something. Is there not a craving in us to witness inceptive force?

Kerouac is gone, and we can no longer hope to look down a bar and discover Jack seated there, waiting for us to blurt out, "I recognize you! You're that guy!" But we can look at the traces he left across yellowing sheets, line after line in a single paragraph the length of a long touchdown pass, and we can imagine what those forty yards of words cost him. If we can no longer see the artist, perhaps we can see his labor and efforts at craftsmanship shaping inspiration: a vision like that, no perfectly printed book can ever quite reveal to us.

The other day I asked Q to hypothesize: In one room is a famous manuscript under glass; inside a transparent box in another room is the embalmed cadaver of its author, laid out like Lenin. Now, if a visitor can enter only one room, which would the majority choose? She took time to answer: "People deeply bookish or people afraid of the dead — which may work out to the same thing — they would choose the manuscript, and everybody else the cadaver."

(In a few weeks, this sheet of paper before me at this moment and on which I'm setting down these words with a fountain pen — and their subsequent typed revisions — will all be inside a box in the Western Historical Manuscript Collection in Ellis Library at the University of Missouri. Perhaps someday you, a distant reader, might see this very manuscript page, and I'll be honored by your curiosity. As for the hand, the arm, and other attached parts directing the pen, they will lie unboxed and nowhere other than wherever, as dust is wont to do. You see, for one who sets some store in immaterial over material traces, it can't very well be elsewhere.)

It is not so with Jean-Louis Kerouac, who rests in Lowell inside a couple of nesting boxes next to his third wife in Edson Cemetery in the part of town known as Spaghettiville. On the warm day Q and I went there, above a worn-down splotch of ground gritty with pebbles and shards of broken glass, was a small, flat, polished-granite marker. At the top was "TI JEAN" and below JOHN L. KEROUAC and the dates of his birth and death. Under that was HE HONORED LIFE. Atop the stone but not covering the inscriptions were a desiccated rose, an unsmoked cigarette, a dollar-twenty-three in coins, a sharpened pencil, and a folded sheet of paper with handwritten words: "Poem For Jack." From the penmanship, I guessed the author was a young male. It was a heartfelt, artless ramble, and at the bottom of the page: "P.S. Please write back. I'll leave you a paper and a pen — all a writer ever needs."

When we stepped under the shade of a large sugar-maple to take it all in, a Lowell woman toward seventy years came along with a friend from New York, who wanted to see the grave. The woman watched quietly while her visiting companion slowly knelt and kissed the stone. The last time I saw a tomb kissed was in Jerusalem at the Holy Sepulcher. The woman of Lowell turned to me so her reverent friend could not hear and said, "I used to see him around. An alcoholic. His writing was gahbage."

I said, Why are we here, then? But I should have said something about legacies and traces. I should have said something about the pentimento of a human life.

❥ 4 ❧

Ten M To B

T HE NEXT THREE CHAPTERS are a story of a dedication become an obsession, a mania become mastery, an absorption promising to become a national contribution, a tale of a lifelong love almost surpassing understanding. It began some years ago in the Patapsco River Valley, ten miles west of downtown Baltimore, in Ellicott City, Maryland, where sits a small chunk of stone against an exterior wall of an eighteenth-century building at the foot of Main Street and beside the old Baltimore & Ohio Railroad bridge. The rock is knee-bone-high to a small woman, has a breadth nearly that of a man's forearm, and a depth commensurate to his opened hand. The top is an arc, giving it the look of a squat tombstone, as some passersby have thought. The gray granite, now noticeably worn on the edges, has been there since about 1798; soon after, the old National Road, the first American *through* high-road with federal sanction, was laid out in front of it. I have no good figures, but I like to imagine the number of travelers who have passed the stone on foot or horseback, or in an oxcart, farm wagon, stagecoach, buggy, horse-car, automobile, bus, taxi, truck, trolley, or on motorcycles, bicycles, roller skates, skateboards, and all those seeing it when a B&O train crossed above it. The total might well match the current population of America.

The letters, simply incised, are still quite legible: 10 M TO B. The first time I read them years ago, they struck me as crypto-mystico-religico-philosophy: or perhaps a slightly scrambled, "O! I Am to Be!" Maybe, on what looked like a tombstone, they were an anagram of *tomb.* I, a ten-year-old, wanted to interpret them as code — covert marching orders to a place to be revealed later.

I wrote the inscription down and for years spoke of it to no one. In time, the stone proved to be something a little different: not only itself a quoz but, in its own way, a tablet of recondite directions to other quoz.

Because of that small monument, Frank Xavier Brusca and I became acquainted a few years ago. His initials could serve to identify a piece of a computer: "My god! My FXB port is on the fritz!" But any link between his initials and his work as an instructional technologist who teaches staff (in Brusca's words) "effective and pedagogically sound use of computers" at Otterbein College in Westerville, Ohio, a few miles north of Columbus, is coincidental as far as he can see. His father, in the early days of digitized information, did work on "a bizarre form of nonlinear analytic thinking," but for his son's name he had in mind not technology but theology. Yet that link too is peculiarly coincidental in that St. Francis Xavier, the Apostle to the Indies, was a roaming priest nonpareil. If Frank's life is about anything beyond his family, it's about traveling, as you'll see. Transportation and transmission, things St. Francis knew well, are to Brusca as sails to a seaman, an airfoil to a pilot, yeast to a baker. They move him, carry him, let him rise to become something else.

The first time we met, at Antioch College in Ohio, Frank spoke of his interest in the old National Road which later became a long section of U.S. Highway 40, sometimes called the "Main Street of America." I told him I'd grown up not far from 40 and U.S. 50, another transcontinental route, about where they crossed U.S. 71, a road running from Canada almost to the Gulf. In the late 1940s and early 1950s, I became navigator in my father's tub of a car, a 1947 Pontiac Chieftain, a machine heavy enough to save his life when a drunk rammed him along U.S. 71. At the nose of the hood was a chromium visage of a Plains Indian I'd shine with my sleeve each morning on the road. For six consecutive Augusts, starting near the center of America at Kansas City, Missouri, my father would pack up the family and strike a course along a cardinal direction down one of those routes we'd follow to its terminus. After a half-dozen summers, those three highways had taken me coast-to-coast twice and to Canada and the Gulf once. By the time I was twelve — all six birthdays of those years celebrated on the road — in my mind was a paved grid of latitudes and longitudes, a geometry useful in visualizing a continent. It was a way to see the face of America. Among the myriad details hidden in that imagined countenance was the Ellicott City stone with its mysterious inscription.

As I told this to Frank, his expression became beatific, and I stopped and said it seemed I'd struck something, and he replied, "You're talking about Number Ten, the milestone along Main Street. It was my first milestone too. I used to live not far away. I'd ride my bicycle fifteen miles down to see it." Brusca also grew up as family navigator. The eldest of five children, he would gather road-maps filling stations once gave away, folding them to fit the top of the beverage cooler in front of him that served as his chart table; from it, he directed the passage, each year of travel giving him increased authority.

The fascination so many people have for maps and nautical charts may come from a deeply buried and often unrecognized sense that we are riding a planetary ship sailing the solar winds under the galactic clouds to who-can-say-where, with no landfall in sight, a voyage to outlast us, the entire way yielding us no more certain idea of our cosmic position than a possum has of its hollow. A map gives comfort because it can say YOU ARE NOW HERE, and that surely is preferable to YOU ARE NO WHERE. Maps, by this line of thought, are ontological documents, because whereness can be central to whoness and whatness. A ballplayer in center field is not the same *who* or *what* he'd be in a cotton field. For FXB and me, Route 40 embraced the plane of America as the equator does the sphere of Earth. From it we could calculate our positions. If he grew up near the eastern tip of the great belt of U.S. 40 and I at the buckle, the distance mattered little because the road bound us, and, to press the metaphor toward the absurd, that highway helped hold up our philosophical pants covering our less public spiritual Skivvies.

(Have I wandered again from the through route of a story?)

At its peak use, Highway 40 was slightly more than three-thousand miles long, running at one time from near the Boardwalk in Atlantic City to the Embarcadero in San Francisco, salt water to salt water. I told Frank, in all those miles, the Ellicott stone was a detail I especially cherished, although I wasn't sure I understood its inscription, 10 M TO B, and he said, rupturing its mystery, "Ten miles to Baltimore. It wasn't so useful if you were headed west."

Except for my years in the Navy, my homes have never been more than a few miles from 40, which, unintendedly, straddles the fortieth parallel which, also unintendedly, is the halfway mark, a useful equatorial line, of the forty-eight states. Frank's abodes throughout his life also have clung to the route like dungarees hanging from a clothesline: Baltimore; Denver; several returns to each; and Kettering, Yellow Springs, and Westerville in Ohio.

On those moves, for the most part, destiny has directed him, although when he was ten, he did his best to take a hand in it. After his family returned the first time from Denver to Baltimore (Randallstown, to be precise), young Frank longed for the Front Range and gave considerable thought to ways he might engineer a move back west. At last, he hoped he'd found a means when he happened upon a book in the public library, a single work that would come to shape his life as the Bible, or *The Adventures of Tom Sawyer*, or *How to Win Friends and Influence People*, have molded others. It was George Stewart's *U.S. 40: Cross Section of the United States of America,* a kind of road narrative in words and photographs compiled from two coast-to-coast trips, one in 1949 and the second in 1950 (the very years I was navigating that chromium chieftain's head over the great highway).

Recognizing some of the images of 40 in both Maryland and Colorado, Frank fell under the spell of the photographs and then realized they might have the same power to create in his parents an irresistible urge to return to the mountains. He checked the book out and took it home to leave on the living room coffee-table, casually opened to a Colorado scene, and then waited for it to work its magic.

The magic failed. His parents didn't catch the hint, but destiny did, and for reasons other than an opened book, the family moved back to Denver, only to return once more to Maryland a couple of years later. Frank assuaged his second loss of the Front Range by tirelessly checking out the library copy of *U.S. 40,* returning it when due, waiting the required hour while hoping no one would claim it, then checking it out again. He did that for eleven years, taking the book home week after week. Then the day came when the library put the worn thing into the sale box and sold it for a dime, and Frank had to soldier on without it for several years. Things ended happily: by midlife, through the Internet, he had found and bought fifteen copies, giving several away to people he met along 40. He knew the book as a priest does the Mass, or Satan and Santa Claus your transgressions. In quest of images and history, Brusca estimated since 1979 he had logged a hundred-thousand miles on that one highway, although he'd never done it coast-to-coast in a single trip, as Stewart did twice for his book.

If the photographs in *U.S. 40* got FXB started, it was a 1973 article in the *Baltimore Sun* about a man, Ned Nye, who was photographing all the National Road milestones he could find, that put teenage Brusca in motion. Dropping the paper, he got onto his bicycle, pedaled to Ellicott City and, with new understanding, studied the incised granite of Number Ten as if it were a Rosetta stone or a tablet dropped by Moses on the way back down the mountain.

Six years later, Brusca began his own search for and recording of the National Road markers once numbering well more than five hundred between Baltimore and Vandalia, Illinois, 760 miles west. Of those hundreds of mileposts (some merely wooden fingers pointing the way), perhaps 350 originals or replicas remained (several no longer at their proper mile), virtually every one of them photographed and described by him.

After he was old enough to drive, using Number Ten as his establishing datum, he began cruising the route, his gaze moving from the side of the road to the odometer and back to the right-of-way; after a mile, if he hadn't seen a marker, he'd stop and kick around in the brush for it. In places, the post was only obscured, but in others it had fallen or, worse, it was vandalized or had vanished entirely. Over the years, he found original markers in museums, reused in a rock fence, built into the foundation of a barn, and one set into the wall of a tavern. Nobody, not even Brusca, knows how many must have ended up in the bed of later pavement.

Between the National Road milestones and Stewart's Highway 40 photographs, FXB's project was born, and from those, if he himself was not quite reborn, he was surely reconfigured. After his family, the point of his days became the methodical documentation of a three-thousand-mile, three-century-old route over which his seven homes along seventeen-hundred miles of U.S. 40 have never been more than fifteen miles distant. When he began, he thought he could complete his documentary survey, his then-and-now pictures, on a single, two-month trip west. Thirty years later, he was still at it.

❯ 5 ❮

Building a Time Machine

F ROM A SINGLE INSCRIBED ROCK that would almost fit into a toy
chest and from an initial idea a child could understand, Frank
Brusca's project developed over three decades into a complex creation yet unseen in this country: a means of going back in time to
travel along what is the most significantly historic cross-country
route in America, one that encompasses an eighth of the circumference of the earth.

U.S. 40 comprises pieces of Indian paths, colonial post roads,
Washington's Road, Braddock's Road, the Baltimore National
Pike, the Frederick Turnpike, the Bank Road, Cumberland Road,
National Road, Zane's Trace, Boonslick Trail, Santa Fe Trail,
Oregon-California Trail, Smoky Hill Trail, Berthoud's Road, Hast-
ings' Cutoff, National Old Trail, Lincoln Highway, and the Victory
Highway. The progenitor of most of Interstate 70 and portions of
I-80 was once a central artery of eight major cities and the Main
Street of a few hundred towns and villages. It intersects every major
north-south U.S. highway and, in one form or another, has been
moving freightage of merchandise, job lots of culture, passels of animals and people, diseases and medicines, food and mail, science and
religion, for a third of a millennium. When the federal government
began numbering highways, there was even talk of making an exception and marking the route as U.S. 1, although east-west roads were
scheduled to have even numbers.

Were a traveler from Rome or London or Tokyo to ask where
to see the most representative sweep of America — from ocean to

ocean; from cornfields to oil fields to goldfields; through the Great Plains into four mountain ranges; from forests to prairies to deserts; from sea level to more than two miles into the sky and down again; where precipitation ranges from sixty inches to five; where lies military history, from the French and Indian War to the latest undeclared war in Whereisitstan (an early use was moving troops and matériel); where travelers can find a meal of blue crabs at one end and Dungeness crabs on the other, Chesapeake oysters or prairie oysters; can see barns, skyscrapers, the largest aboriginal earthwork in North America, the tallest arch in the world, tenements and mansions, neighborhoods of every major ethnicity; can cross four continental rivers (the Ohio, Mississippi, Missouri, and Colorado) or a dozen regional ones, from the Potomac to the Sacramento; can see three great bays (Delaware, Chesapeake, San Francisco); can find capitals of six states, and six former capitals, with another half dozen and the seat of federal power nearby; and can pass within an hour's drive of (by my estimate) about a fifth of the nation — the answer would be U.S. 40. No other highway comes close in significance.

You can recite these facts to a foreign traveler, but just like us, few will undertake the route because not many of them come here to see the commonplace heart and soul of America. Even Europeans can't resist a sham European castle, especially if it's in a drained Florida swamp. When plastic and plaster simulations are easily at hand, who could want a thousand-year-old mound once the urban center of aboriginal America — after all, Cahokia is made of dirt. A number of people living along 40, antediluvians though we be, consider the desire for synthetic America a blessing, and we sleep in contentment knowing U.S. 40 lacks cachet and that it will become a destination for only a dedicatedly curious Parisian or Yokohaman — *or* a fellow Yank.

Rumors of a "Celebrate We Aren't on Route 66" parade are ill-founded because heartlanders understand America needs a half-continental highway of concrete-teepee motels, fiberglass dinosaurs, cobra gardens, and sheet-metal whales. It's been some years since

I heard anyone complain that 40 has never had a hit song (unless you consider the country-western "Idaho Red" one), or that it has no Pulitzer Prize–winning novel, or a classic movie, or a television series, or that it's never been called the "Mother Road" (although it clearly is) by a renowned writer better at fiction than history. The Ur-Mother of American transcontinental highways remains within her limitations, without hype, able to show only history. Forty is to Route 66 as Beethoven to the Beatles, Beowulf to Babar, sponge cake to corn pone. It's true, staid U.S. 40 may be short of goosey merriments, and, as even Brusca will admit, it's a highway requiring a little effort and perhaps some knowledge in order to get your kicks on it.

Of the seven original, uninterrupted two-lane transcontinental highways, all are junior to 40 which can trace one of its several origins back to 1651. It was among the earliest topographical sinews holding America together. With independence secured, few threats concerned George Washington more than the fledgling Union fracturing into separate nation-states. Believing physical communication central to unity and commerce, the perpetually practical Washington worked for and invested in a canal and roadway to link the eastern seaboard with the Ohio and Mississippi valleys. (George, incidentally, lost his first battle along the future path of 40.) In this sober light, the National Road is the Appian Way of America, and it was the central overland-route Anglo-Americans first used to come into the heart of the country.

Frank Xavier Brusca was not Anglo-American. His paternal grandparents arrived here from Priverno, Italy, a village not far from the actual Appian Way. He was raised in Catholicism but through DNA testing later found he may have in his ancestry a few Sephardic Jews forced out of Spain by the Inquisition, some of whom, the *conversi,* converted to the Church of Rome. Ancestors aside, Frank inclined toward Quakerism and also, while not a spiritual path for him, vegetarianism (nothing better than a supper of eggplant Parmesan or mapa tofu). Frank's teenage daughter, Elaine, sometimes accompanied him on his research excursions along 40 or on train trips the pair took simply to see the country. His wife, K.C., not much of an automobile traveler, honored his obsession but did not share it.

He was of modest height and broad-shouldered, and without his vegetarian diet and cycling, he might have edged toward the stocky. He was bespectacled and wore his hair and beard closely cut, but what you were more likely to remember about him was a nearly ceaseless expression of contentment, an evident delight often matched to the degree U.S. 40 was in his mind. With the highway not far from consciousness, his dreams also must have put a smile on him, a result of a requited devotion.

That gift of the old highway (aided by a little tofu and his bicycle) had carried him into his fiftieth year the last time I saw him, but that number was less important than other figures you might want to translate into days necessary to acquire or create them: he had about a thousand U.S. road-maps of the oil-company variety. Of them, he said, "My mother called me one morning after I'd moved to my own place. She said, 'Frank, I finally did it — I threw out all your maps.' I dropped what I was doing and rushed to my parents' house and pulled the maps from the trash bins at the curb. And that was even before I really knew how much they would mean to my project." Frank Brusca without maps was Count Basie without a piano, Bernhardt without a stage, the Bambino without a bat.

He also owned some seven-thousand postcards depicting scenes along Highway 40. But what he had in even greater numbers were documented photographs from his own hand: more than three-thousand high-resolution black-and-white images, nearly the same number of color transparencies, and at least twenty-thousand digital images. From that treasury, he was slowly and methodically assembling electronic files and a manuscript to document sixty years of U.S. 40 as it had passed through alterations, some so slow they looked like stasis, others of shocking swiftness, some that ravaged and others that renewed, all of them across a continent of landscapes sharing a single highway.

Even as dominating as his absorption was, for nearly two years after their wedding he was reluctant to share it with K.C. because of his concern for what she might think of a man who dreams highways as other men dream of picking the right lottery number. Then, on a trip to Indiana along 40, she at the wheel, Frank began making notes in a way he hoped was not surreptitious but simply inconspicuous. A recently wed man, he did not realize then that a husband writing notes on his knee will catch a wife's eye as if he'd pulled a kitten from his pocket. "What are you writing down?" she said. And suddenly, indeed, the cat of proverb was out of its bag, and Frank had to come clean and admit to a passion that dare not speak its name: he was hopelessly enraptured by 3,100 miles of pavement. He awaited her response, and that's when he learned their union was strong. If K.C. thought his interest a touch eccentric, she neither laughed nor discouraged him. Discouragement arrived from elsewhere soon after.

In 1983, husband-and-wife geographers Thomas and Geraldine Vale published *U.S. 40 Today: Thirty Years of Landscape Change in America,* a photographic resurvey of some of the sites Stewart had recorded almost a third of a century earlier. Frank said, "When I saw their book, I was crestfallen someone had beaten me to the project. I was devastated. It took a long time to recover and find my way again. Their work was good, but it was incomplete because they rephotographed only about seventy-two percent of Stewart's hundred-and-fifteen images appearing in the two editions of his book. And their goal was different, especially so after I began to rethink mine. They made trips over three years. My travels now cover thirty years — even though I consider my first twenty-three years as preliminary fieldwork."

FXB did not toss off answers. He weighed a question and framed his responses as meticulously as his repeat photographs. "You could say their book — after I rallied from my dismay and disappointment — I think it helped me clarify and expand what I was trying to do. My project became bigger, far bigger once it was alive again. Then, thanks to the World Wide Web, I realized my interest —

maybe not my obsession but at least my fascination — might be uncommon, but it wasn't unique. There are other Route Forty road enthusiasts out there. Some of them like neon signs or old motels or diners. I love those things too. A lot of people go for roadside architecture or some other aspect of commercial archaeology, but I haven't found anybody else documenting the highway to the degree I am. And here's a big difference — I want to continue documenting Forty till I no longer can."

Using four different cameras — two manual 35 millimeters, a medium format, and a professional digital — Brusca over the years had hunted down and photographed all but six of Stewart's sites, including several that never appeared in *U.S. 40*. Some views were extraordinarily difficult to locate exactly, one of them even forcing Frank to examine half-century-old cracks in a sidewalk to confirm it. After he unequivocally established the location of a site, he would make three types of images, each with multiple exposures, and record the date, hour, and minute, the latitude and longitude, the weather, and the traffic statistics. If an exact viewpoint was no longer possible — like the roof of the demolished President Hotel in Atlantic City — he considered other solutions, such as hiring a boat or helicopter to get his camera in position. If tree growth obscured a vantage, he waited till winter; for one old water-tower no longer in existence, he got permission to climb the microwave tower that replaced it; if a neighborhood had become dangerous for a visitor with expensive cameras, he asked the police to join him. The best repeat photography demands such persevering exactitude, and Brusca was untiring in rephotographing a scene accurately.

On his return home, he made digital overlays of his images with Stewart's to create in stunning precision a deep view into time. The work of two photographers became considerably greater, especially when Frank added his 360-degree panoramas, each of them requiring at least two dozen linked images. "I always wondered what existed beyond the view of Stewart's lens," he said. "What the view was behind him. Nobody will have to wonder that about mine."

George Stewart was a novelist, historian, and professor of English at the University of California, and the man who first gave names to storms (inspiration for Lerner and Loewe's "They Call the Wind Maria" came from his novel *Storm*). Wanting to portray and interpret the typical, ordinary, and commonplace actualities along the Main Street of America, Stewart was not much interested in people or fine scenery or the picturesque. If an image of his does contain an individual or two, it's usually happenstance; if a photograph rises above merely a good snapshot, it was more the result of beautiful terrain than art. Although a friend of landscape photographer Ansel Adams, Stewart was after something else: he wanted his book to say only, "Thus it was when I passed by, in my time." He understood common does not mean trivial. Because George Stewart, the first practitioner of "photographic odology" — the study of roads — chose U.S. 40 before anyone else was documenting a highway as a place in itself, no other route in the world can surpass the continuity of images when Brusca combines his with Stewart's.

Frank said of him, "He was traveling in the golden age of American two-lane highways when U.S. Forty was the major cross-country route. He recorded it just before the interstate system came along and began overrunning it or turning it into frontage and secondary roads. In his pictures and words, you can hear the future coming on fast. But still today, there's much more of Forty left than of Route Sixty-six. Most of Forty is still there, even in places where it no longer has a number. Out west you can sometimes see a defunct strip running off to nowhere."

It's useful to remember that the highway, like the Oregon and Santa Fe trails, was a complexity of intertwined roads, never a single thoroughfare. Not only did it continually change many of its alignments, it also in places had simultaneously several paths: Business Route 40, Commercial Route 40, City Route 40, Truck Route 40, Alternate 40, Bypass 40, Temporary 40, Detour 40, Old 40, New 40, 40 South, 40 North. Trying to visualize its structure across the body of America is like trying to see the circulatory system in your body.

One afternoon I asked FXB to pull from his computer a map of the various alignments over the years 40 has struck across Missouri and through my town. Later I learned what I was asking for: it took him one evening — three decades and one evening. But the result is a lovely piece of cartography just now unavailable in any other library anywhere except Frank's (and mine).

With technology unknown to Stewart — or even to the Vales — Brusca created in his computer overlays a kind of digital motion-picture of the past, as he morphed Stewart's images into his own later ones. It was a time machine allowing virtual travel into yesterday: on a screen, two-lanes become four, an old tavern vanishes into thin air, trees give way to billboards (more rarely, vice versa), a suburb rises from a pasture, a Studebaker becomes a Subaru. But the mountains abide and sometimes also the forest on them, and the prairie is still prairie, and it is those images that give promise we are not yet too late to control the juggernaut of landscape destruction.

If Brusca's work is not exactly time-lapse photography, then it is time-gap photography. His time machine, of course, can travel backward only to 1949 before turning around to come forward, moving across both years and space, but if you believe an image of what is to come can be discerned from what has gone before, then you can see in his work a future emerging.

And from that movement, questions arise: Where is Brusca's virtual highway leading? What will the future learn from us? And about us? Will people of another time judge our quotidian, creepingly incremental changes to be as significant as the cataclysmic ones bound to happen? Is the slow rise and slower collapse of the Colosseum a parallel to the empire that built it? Are the uncounted days of scientific failure preceding a single microstep forward in discovering the plasmodium parasite in the guts of an anopheles mosquito — are those humdrum laboratory hours equal to the brevity of a Presidential assassination or the collapse of a skyscraper? Is Stewart right that the commonplace is not synonymous with the inconsequential? When it's happening, just where is ordinary history?

❥ 6 ❦

Finding the Kaiser Billy Road

B ECAUSE THE NATIONAL ROAD MILESTONE in Ellicott City is for me a quoz of the first order, I appreciate its close escape from being swallowed by the old building behind it as I do its significance, longevity, uniqueness, and the way it sits there with its weather-battered face like a plump way-god to bless all who pass. One October evening years ago, it further imprinted itself into my memory after I overheard personifying words spoken by a woman whose pearls and haute coiffure led me to take her for a Howard County peeress. Atop the marker was a jack-o'-lantern truly giving Number Ten the look of a compact statue. Her gentleman, clearly familiar with the stone, pointed it out to her and, by way of explanation, said, "There's the little chap, my dear," and she said, "Why, Albert! You didn't tell me he's a cute little son of a bitch!"

I suppose he is, and I suppose one person's son of a bitch is another's way-god, but I know Number Ten has enough power to have a life within my life — another attribute of the best quoz. That piece of aged granite has led me beyond its own particular mile into mile-ages and places and people far more distant. A good quoz of a way-god can do that too.

Some time ago the marker began transforming my abstract con-ception of the National Road into a material reality that compre-hension and memory could visually grasp; an intangible notion of cultural transport and transmission suddenly had form and body, and the stone became a synecdoche for the old high-road itself linking the Atlantic seaboard with the great central rivers leading to the Gulf.

Number Ten is a piece of infrastructure that once helped build the Union and maintain it against rankly greedy men who plotted to fragment America for personal gain. (Consider the likes of conspirator Aaron Burr wanting to "detach" certain territories, or James Wilkinson scheming a personally lucrative secession of Kentucky and Tennessee to Spain; General Anthony Wayne called him "the worst of all bad men," and a business rival said Wilkinson was "a mammoth of iniquity . . . the only man I ever saw who was from the bark to the very core a villain.") For reasons of fragmentation alone, I believe the Ellicott City mile marker meant almost as much as their own hearthstones to Washington and Jefferson and Madison, all of whom may have ridden past it. As arteries of tissue and their supporting structures are to a heart, so are arteries of communication and their components to a democracy.

From the Beyond I hear my old stiff-backed American history professor, a sarcastic avatar of negativism, scolding, "Hold on there, Socrates!" (We all were Socrates, women too.) "Is a single hunk of rock of real societal significance compared to something like an atomic bomb or an analgesic to ease an arthritic joint?" Today I'd answer him in my blue-book with: *When Number Ten was set in place, America needed transport more than either an atomic bomb or the easing of the President's lumbago because the ready movement of a national economy and its culture — for better or worse — was of greater import than nuking Indians or easing the movement of George's spinal column.* (Socrates could then take his C minus and go home in good conscience to sleep the bliss of a baby.)

When I met Frank Brusca, I had no idea how many other National Road mile markers existed. *But he knew.* In fact, he knew more about the mileposts — whether in granite, sandstone, cast iron, wood, or replica fiberglass — than anybody else on earth, and he could show me his photographs of every one he'd found, which was nearly every one still in existence. (I admire such unquestioned expertise in a field because I have no unquestioned expertise in any area except in my own history, about which I can say, without concern for contradiction, I am the sole authority and will likely remain so; that, however, does not mean *my* version, to pick one example, of what happened between me and a throw pillow and a lamp shade fifteen New Year's Eves ago cannot be gainsaid.)

Frank knew Ellicott City took its name from three founding brothers, one of them father to surveyor Andrew Ellicott who in 1798 (the time Number Ten was set) laid out and oversaw the physical cutting of a boundary between the United States and Spain, a line today visible as the Florida border below Alabama and Georgia. (Ellicott, coincidentally, became a chief witness in the 1811 court-martial of General James Wilkinson.)

These are some of the reasons, forbearant reader, that brought Q and me to Westerville to visit Frank Brusca in his home eleven miles north of Old Highway 40. One Wednesday morning we were all in his van with the license plate ROUTE 40 as he drove us east through southern Licking and Muskingum counties, the whole way narrating, at first concentrating on sandstone markers still standing at the side of what used to be the National Road before it became U.S. 40. In places, the highway was just shy of being chockablock with them, and a resident here or there had turned the 170-year-old posts into little gardens with a surround of flowers, while other people had whitewashed them and blackened in the inscriptions to make them easily legible from a vehicle. They were a kind of secular road shrine, like those little wayside, wooden crucifixes once prevalent in the Tyrolean Alps or the carved-rock *dosojin* protecting travelers in old Japan. These American stones, though, honored not deities but history and continuance, things only now and then accorded respect along a U.S. highway.

For each one, FXB could give a story or detail; he even knew particulars about virtually every mile missing its stone, and his narration bespoke his life as a chantey does a sailor's. At one of the spots lacking a marker, he told of a man of wealth and some national recognition (whom he didn't want named) known to send out a crew to dig up a loose milepost for his collection, only to lock it in a warehouse. Frank was disturbed by such questionable removal of public property and responded in several *legal* ways, one of which was to buy at auction for two-hundred dollars a single Ohio stone and return it to its original place. Brusca does not have enough hundred-dollar bills to protect the remaining markers in Ohio, let alone in four other states, and that's another reason his thorough documentation is important. "In England," he said, "there's a Milestone Society to look after their markers. We need one here too."

Ohio is notable in having so many markers still in place, as it is also in having so many miles of the National Road and early Route 40 still extant, a number of them yet open to travelers forgoing parallel Interstate 70. In some locations, Old 40 remained a thoroughfare even if it had lost its federal number; in other segments, the road was a forgotten piece of pavement serving only farm machinery or as a court for a basketball game. Across those rolling hills, the outliers of the middle Appalachians, U.S. 40 was concrete here, asphalt there, but in its finest permutation it was well-laid bricks shined by eighty years of rolling tires.

Along the way were the old stone-arch bridges known for their configuration of a stretched S as well as a recent concrete-bridge in the shape of a Y, the fifth with that design at Zanesville. A mile south of it, we stopped near the Muskingum River for lunch at Nicols, a café from the age of FRESH HOT NUTS machines, the one at Nicols still functioning with heat furnished by a twenty-five-watt lightbulb. Over our sandwiches, Frank continued the stories and histories, never detouring from U.S. 40 or doubling back or losing his way, the whole time smiling as do people who have found passionate purpose; happily for him, his was taking him years to express in its fullness. Even when he talked of police who, in the age of terrorism, would stop to question why he was photographing a bridge or even a stretch of road in the middle of some vacant nowhere, he smiled. If he had more difficulty than Stewart in getting permission to climb a tower or grain elevator or to stop along a four-lane to take photographs, even those tangles of red tape made him smile because they were U.S. 40 red tape.

Frank said, "Stewart's road notes don't help me much in locating people who appear in one of his photographs, but I enjoy trying to find them. There were never many, of course, and only a few are still around. After almost sixty years, finding them is harder than identifying some of his locations, but by using the Internet, I discovered one person living in India, and she remembered Stewart. But the most recognizable faces of all, two small boys, cute little guys, in front of row houses on West Fayette Street in an African-American section of Baltimore, I haven't even come close to finding out their fate. I showed the picture around the neighborhood but learned nothing."

"Of all the miles along your beloved highway," Q said, "which are your favorites?" Frank closed his eyes as if he were watching U.S. 40 unreel in his head. When he'd reached San Francisco, he said, "Kansas. The openness of the prairie, I just love, even though a patrolman in Wamego — a different one every time — seems to come along whenever I stop there to photograph that site. And Berthoud Pass over the Rockies west of Denver is special. And there are a couple of dozen diners along the way I really like. The S bridges. A decommissioned section in Reno. Should I keep going?" She asked what he didn't like, and to that there came no ready answer, but finally he said, shaking his head, "Out west, rattlesnakes. They like rocky outcrops that are also good places to take a photograph."

We rolled on eastward to the location of the purported first highway fatality in Ohio, in 1835 (surely somebody went down before that), then on again to a splendid eighteen-foot-wide section of old brick pavement ascending a sweet curve up a hill, the road transformed into a country lane by the interstate a mile or so south. While I was kneeling to run my hand over the smoothed bricks, a weathered fellow paused in his pickup to nod at my admiration of the paving men's skill. He understood my response but spoke not a word as he watched. I asked when the section was put down, and the man said, "Nineteen and eighteen, right after the war. Somebody thought the Army might need a good surface to get somewhere — in case some kaiser decided to come on over here and try to put a gun under somebody's snoot. I call it the Kaiser Billy Road."

A decade later, those bricks, solid things without lightening holes, became a section of U.S. 40. They were so well-set, their joint lines still more straight than warped despite the steep slope and braking vehicles and the pull of gravity. Each brick weighed ten pounds, and a square foot required exactly four and a quarter of them, and that meant every mile, minimally, held more than four-hundred-thousand bricks. If you've ever laid a walkway or patio using ordinary perforated, wall brick half the thickness of those heavy pavers, your hands, knees, arms, and back may give perspective on what it took to get an American flivver out of the mire and across the countryside.

At the hilltop village of Norwich, Ohio, Frank pointed at a small monument to the librarian and scoutmaster Rollin Allen who in the 1970s formed a preservation committee of one and took a seat on top of a mile marker to prevent a construction crew from removing or harming it. His perch, an original stone, still stands, although no longer does its savior.

Not far from the short and narrow S bridge of 1830 over Fox Creek, once a hiding spot for slaves escaping along the Underground Railroad, we left the old route to take up a few miles of an even older one following a ridge to the south. From Zane's Trace we could look across a creeked valley to the clear delineations of the National Road, the old B&O tracks, U.S. 40, and Interstate 70. Frank said, "The Trace was a real labor to cut through the forest in here. One traveler commented, in the early days it was 'a tight fit for a fat horse.'"

Beyond the Trace, just before sunset, we turned back toward Westerville and entered the interstate clogged with traffic, traffic exhaust, and exhausted drivers doing their best to contain their exasperation. Frank said, "I love driving. Maybe not on a highway like this but on the kind that Stewart called *equal*. He wrote about *dominating, dominated,* and *equal* highways, the category determined by how well a route is integrated with the countryside it passes through.

A multilane tends to dominate because you're more conscious of it than the land around. In a city, the highway gets dominated by the surroundings. But on an equal road, you're aware of the road and also what's beyond it. That was his ideal type for motoring."

Brusca believed the scholarly work on U.S. 40 surpassed that of any other American highway, including Route 66, which has spawned numerous glossy picture-books repeating images of the same defunct gas-stations, rusting EAT signs, and tawdry motels. I tossed in that Route 66 is epitomized by an alleged piece of the Blarney Stone displayed along it — another synecdoche. A traveler can pay to kiss a bit of Blarney Stone or, without fee, rub the smooth belly of milestone Number Ten. Q, considering the choice, said, "I've been able to whistle Bobby Troup's tune since I was fifteen-years old, but nobody ever told me about the National Road or all that Highway Forty has — everything except a catchy tune. And I grew up along Forty." To her challenge, I took Troup's song and tried to substitute route numerals and towns (Columbus is a bear for a lyricist); the rhythm and rhyme failed utterly, and I returned to the original, but Q noted only my fumbled word: "Did you just sing 'Get your kitsch on Route Sixty-six'?"

"Forty is one of the highways Jack Kerouac drove on the five trips he compressed into three in his *On the Road*," Frank said. "The novel doesn't contain a whole lot of identifying landmarks except in the cities along it where he stopped, but I've got his routes mapped out pretty well now, I think."

Over a good supper of hummus and pita, olives and feta, Frank talked about another photographer inspired by George Stewart's landmark book of the landscape. Soon after *U.S. 40* appeared, William Price, a World War II pilot, decided to pay homage to Stewart by taking aloft a war-surplus four-by-five aerial-reconnaissance camera and flying the length of Route 40 in 1954 and again the next year. Although there were long gaps without pictures, he still came home with almost two-thousand images — about twice the number Stewart made — the best of which he hoped to put into a book.

"I'd heard of his photographs for some time," Frank said, "but I didn't believe they really existed. I dismissed stories about them. Then I got a call out of the blue from a man telling me about Price's work. Right away I drove to Mister Price's apartment in New York City to see them. He was up in years and a little frail, and he had trouble identifying the locations of some of his images, although I could help with that.

"I liked him. I respected his conscience — his belief in social and economic justice. He had a good heart, it seemed. He was a progressive thinker who spoke openly of being in love with America. But he still got blacklisted by McCarthy and those people, and I think it harmed him. Stewart also had an encounter with McCarthyism when the University of California tried to force teachers to sign a loyalty oath. He refused and wrote a book about it. *The Year of the Oath*."

A careening tractor-trailer rig interrupted the conversation, but Brusca responded only with his smile momentarily flickering, then he continued. "Here were two men dedicated to preserving the landscapes of America, and they're accused of disloyalty. But for Price, even worse than McCarthy's blacklist was a fire in his apartment. All of his negatives, every one of them on hundred-foot rolls of film, were burned up, and all he had left were his contact sheets. There went his hope for a book." FXB shook his head. "Price's experience impressed on me the fragility of images. I do everything I can to stave off perishability, but it's still my biggest fear."

The last evening I was with Frank, I asked about the financial costs of his project. I think I knew the emotional ones. He said, "Even if my Highway Forty work gets into print and becomes a wild, financial success, I still wouldn't break even. The expenses and getting time off from work force me to go slowly." And then, as if to clarify, the smile disappeared. "But then I'm not in it for the money."

I told him about years ago when I was struggling along writing my first book, a road narrative of sorts, and how I often imagined the manuscript never finding a publisher and ending up in an attic where somebody would come across it a century later. A readership of one, but one seemed better than none, especially if that one would say, "So that's how the hell it was in 1978." My lone imaginary reader kept me going on those dark nights of a writer's soul.

"If I never get mine published," Frank said, "fifty years from now I hope someone at least will find my virtual-reality panoramas, those three-sixty-degree images, and realize how they're a window into a past time. I keep reminding myself I'm trying to put something together for later generations. I believe that." And then his smile, which again had vanished for a moment, returned, and he said, "I have to believe that. Otherwise, what am I doing?"

❥ 7 ❧

A Tortfeasor
Declines to Take a Victim

As one of the ways I may pass time while waiting for an auto mechanic or dentist or barber — when I'm without a book — I'll draw faces I see near me, or I may draw up a list (often a mental one) of just about anything. Like a scent from the past — Proust's madeleine — a list can provoke memory, mine often working backward: instead of reminding me what I'm to do, my enumerations may recall things I've done.

A couple of years ago, on a gloomy day of repeated vexations, I sat waiting in the barbershop and, finding myself bookless, I started a list titled "Six or Seven Times I Nearly Died." Even before I was summoned to the chair, I gave it up because I realized the number was greater than six or seven. The close calls were, if not infinite, certainly innumerable: stumbles on stairs or spills from bicycles and one motor-scooter failing to break my neck; a rifle-range ricochet grazing me above the heart but not hitting it; a ship's hawser snapping in my hands but not cutting me in half; my appendix going awry at home rather than on a hike in some remoteness. So on and so forth. Think of your own list. Every moment alive is a chance to die. That last sentence went through my head as I watched the barber's straight-edged razor, a half-inch from jugular veins, glide down the neck of a relaxed customer laid back in the chair; to him, "close shave" meant only a smooth chin.

At the moment I put a period to that sentence, I've been alive for

375

some two-point-one billion seconds, and that means more than two billion times — *and counting* — I've escaped death. Even if most of those instants can't be termed hairbreadth escapes, there remains perfect assurance one particular future second will halt the count to fulfill that consequent and lone certainty of having been born. But it is about a particular grouping of those seconds, an incident occupying only a small cluster of them, I want to relate to you; it's a story I told Q when we were winding our way across the rippled landscape of northern Pennsylvania. In the anecdote are tracks of a different order, ones leading to other tracks farther along.

I remembered the occurrence when I looked down from a high bridge over the Allegheny River. As you'll soon see, bridges are relevant to the place we were headed. The event I was speaking of happened years earlier but only a few months before I took off on a long journey I described in my first book. Had things gone the way I advised on one October night, it's highly unlikely I'd have been around to write that book — and three that followed. In other words, a woman's rejection of my advice on the night in question made possible this sentence now before you. (There may be a sour reader or two who has just uttered, "Damn her rejection!" Perhaps in thinking that, I'm recalling a letter of some years ago from a man who disliked my books and assured me his opinion was sound because he had pressed on, reading *every word* in each one. Q recommended I reply — although I didn't — with a note saying, "Dear Sir: Today one can find effective treatments for obsessive-compulsive behavior.")

In the late '70s, I was finishing up work for a (post-Phud) degree in photojournalism at the University of Missouri; the culminating project of our class was visual documentation of life in the rivertown of Glasgow, Missouri, population about twelve hundred. The other photographers were talented, and competition for space in the book we would publish was intense because those who produced good pictures had a chance at the best jobs. I've long believed what I lack in natural gifts in a field, I might overcome with dedicated diligence laced with a dollop of audaciousness, efforts once called by a senior family member "harebrained schemes." Since I, by a decade, was the oldest in the class, I was the most in need of a job, which is to say I was the most desperate.

The broken topography of Glasgow makes getting a good photograph of the townscape difficult. The lone place for a panoramic riverine view was from the railroad bridge across the Missouri, an old span blocking visibility from a parallel highway-bridge. I calculated no one else would go to the halfway point of the aerial trackway because — besides the question of trespass — just to look down between the open ties at the swirling currents sixty feet below had to discourage anyone whose brain, well, was not that of a hare. But, to be certain I'd have no competitor for the photograph, I planned to make it after sundown when the opolis lights would reflect off the black river; darkness, of course, would also help cover trespass. (My solicitor, Q, assures me Missouri statutes of limitations make this confession, a generation later, impossible to prosecute successfully.)

Once I got the idea, I was incapable of escaping it, and I figured I was doomed to execute it. I even spoke of it in those very terms. I believed the maxim "No guts, no glory," which to a journalist means "No guts, no story." So, one moonlit night in October, I set out for the *long* and *narrow* bridge, two adjectives I should have given more attention. With me was a classmate, a young woman innocent of the risk involved and lacking any real knowledge of what sudden immersion into a cold river can do to the capacity to draw a breath, unaware of the speed with which water half the temperature of the human body can incapacitate it. At her insistence, I agreed to her joining in.

A prudent journalist would have learned the train schedule beforehand, an easy thing to do. I did not. I simply drove us to the bean fields in the bottoms on the west bank where we climbed up the high grade and onto the long, raised trestle leading to the bridge. We started a cautious stepping from tie to greasy tie, watching our feet, inescapably seeing below the swirling currents shining in the moonlight. At the center of the bridge, I stopped and began struggling to secure the tripod atop the slick ties. Because the antiquated bridge had only a single track, there was no place to work except right in the middle of the rails. I worried about my camera slipping between the ties into the river so unnervingly visible beneath, and I mentioned my concern. She replied, "You might worry about one of us falling through. I guess I forgot to tell you, but I can't swim." Yes, she had forgotten that fact, and yes, I too had thought of falling — every step of the way out. We were above the barge channel where the cold water was deepest and swiftest. (The bridge deck was later rebuilt, and the gaps narrowed.)

I should declare here that part of my naval training entailed an abandon-ship exercise beginning with a jump off a twenty-foot tower, followed by a long swim, followed by fifteen minutes of treading water. A large buddy whom I had to help — that is, push off the high platform — whose sorry swimming barely got him to the treading, had to keep an underwater hand clandestinely locked to my hip to stay afloat. We made it. I should also remark, as a sixteen-year-old I completed a Red Cross water-safety course called Junior Lifesaving.

Those professed qualifications, unfortunately, did not ease her mind as she kept fixed on the river below. They didn't much ease mine either, and I had to remind myself not to rush the work while she, holding to a girder of a bridge without any safety rail whatsoever, tossed out distractions about dumb ideas and her stupidity in not watching from shore. I suggested she stop looking down. She said, "If a train comes along, there's no place to go *except* down. I'm saying my life right now is all about *down*. D-O-W-N. It rhymes with D-R-O-W-N." A moment later she added, "Of course, there's also back the way we came, but I doubt even you, Mister Hotshot, can outrun a train."

You don't try to outrun a train, I said. You drop between the ties and hang until it's safe to come up. "Or," she said, "until you fall into the Missouri." That's better than being greased by a locomotive. It was about then I accidentally dislodged a piece of something, and we watched it drop to the river. The splash was not so unsettling as the time required to get to the splash.

My artistry, as you can see, was bedeviled by useless reminders of precariousness. What the hell, a photojournalist whose first thought is safety needs to shift to copyediting. I calculated exposures and framed different compositions, and I managed to click off several frames as I became almost oblivious to anything but the photographs.

She poked me. "Did you hear that?" What? "There it is again." The third time, I heard it, and it was a sound more dreadful than a cornet of God calling a sinner home. Maybe it *was* a cornet of God calling home a sinner — he who has failed to gain forgiveness for his trespasses. Or maybe it was just the horn from a locomotive. *Just?* Surely an impossibility on a line of such light traffic. We all know getting caught on railroad tracks happens only to fools or inebriates whose names you read in the paper the next day.

Because of a curve in the track and a large grain elevator near it, the east end of the bridge revealed only comforting darkness. Nothing there. Then suddenly something *was* there: a large, bright, single beam emerging from around the bend and freezing me in disbelief. *Impossible!* I felt my arm being pulled, and I yelled we couldn't outrun it. Get down between the ties! "Are you crazy?" she shouted and gave a hard yank and began jerking me and my tripod over the black gaps. "I can't swim!" she was crying out. "I can't swim!"

Especially if a locomotive is behind one, hopping on open-spaced railway ties is injudicious, but that's what she was doing, dragging me along. We're not going to make it, I yelled, even though I had the daft hope we might reach the high trestle on the far shore before dropping between the ties. Neither of us looked away from the decking to glance back. Surely we'd first hear the engine snorting down our necks.

If you've ever tried to run from something in a dream, you know the feeling then in my leaden legs. The west end of the bridge remained invisible in the darkness, and I thought, *If it weren't for her, I'd right now be hanging out of harm's way. Why did I wear such heavy shoes? If I'd climbed up a truss for the picture, I'd be safely clear. Is that as fast as she can go?*

Then, for the first time, I could see the end of the bridge where the trestle began, and I started to think we might make it, and I slowed to

look back. There the big, blinding light was. But it seemed to be holding steady. I got yanked forward again, on toward the trestle, until
at last we got off it and jumped to the side of the earthen approach.
Lying in the cool dust, squinting at the light, we waited for it to reach
us. We listened for the horn to blast me for stupidity and trespass.

But there came no horn. There came nothing. There was no sound
except two people panting, then laughing the laughter of the temporarily insane. We watched the light, still waiting for it to come on and
rocket past. We watched, we waited. It just held steady. Either the train
was moving dead slow or it wasn't moving at all. Then an impossibility:
the light began to recede. It got smaller, smaller, smaller, only to vanish as if the train never were. Had it stopped partway across the bridge
only to back up out of sight? Whoever heard of a train reversing itself
on a bridge on an active, single track — and doing so in the dark?

That's when I realized: *No wonder I can't run properly — I'm
dreaming. In a moment, I'll wake up and discover it's the night before
I'm to go out onto the bridge. This dream is nothing but anxiety. I
just need to force myself awake.*

I couldn't do it, and the dream went on: I found myself driving
us back over the river to town, and at that moment I came up with a
second possibility, one more probable than a train reversing itself off
a bridge. I told her it could be we were dead — maybe that's the way
death works: you think you go on and you believe you're still alive.
"I saw a movie like that," she murmured. I added how surprising to
get run over by a locomotive and feel no pain. If people only knew
how easy death —

"Look at that," she said as we came up to the bend in the tracks on
the east side. Obscured from the bridge, just where the road crossed
the rails, was a huge white light, the kind some people who survive
cardiac arrest report seeing as they start to slip away. Proof! The
Great White Light truly exists!

That particular Great White Light, however, was attached to the
front of a dieseling locomotive. She whispered as if to keep higher
powers from overhearing her, "I think we're still alive." If we are,

I gloated, then I've escaped with half-a-dozen photographs. "The photograph out there wasn't of Glasgow," she said. "It was your face when you saw that big light coming our way." She was a bit smug in offering that, but I suppose her having rejected my plan of hanging like baboons from the creosoted ties warranted smugness. Her evaluation, of course, assumed we were in fact yet among the living.

Evidence of reality and improbability — instead of a dream — came the next day when I developed the film: On six negatives were clusters of black spots that were the lights of Glasgow reflecting off the Missouri River. One of those images got selected for the book until a sensible kid hired a plane on a sunny afternoon and went aloft for an aerial photograph of the town, and my death-defying picture went for naught.

Yet, it seems to me, there continues the possibility I'm having one hell of a long dream (or, less likely, the Other Side does indeed exist and even admits those who deny its existence and — to stretch credibility to the breaking point — allows them to have a spanking good time there). Only you, fortunate reader, in hearing this story, will ever know for certain: dream or not? But please don't write to assure me: if you enter my consciousness, then you could be part of a dream, and I prefer the other conclusion — that one about actuality.

Initially, I intended the bridge misadventure, evincible as I now believe it to be, to occupy some miles across Pennsylvania, but it turned out to have potential for an additional purpose after Q and I arrived in Lanesboro on the Susquehanna River in the far northeast corner of the state. Her first glance at what we'd come there to see told me the incident on the Glasgow bridge had been for her mere entertainment. (I'm speaking of a woman, her left leg carrying a four-inch scar from a cycling crash, who had said recently as she whizzed along on a slick-riding bicycle I'd just given her, "It's so smooth, it makes me want to get reckless on it.") She was looking up at the historic Starrucca Viaduct, probably the least-known great bridge in America, a marvel of nineteenth-century engineering.

Where is the traveler who has never experienced arriving at a destination only to find anticipation surpassing reality? If the worth of the objective depends on expected awe, then one's disappointment may double. How many times have you heard "Is that it? Is that all of it? Isn't there more?" The gorge wasn't deep enough, the mountain high enough, the famed roller coaster frightful enough.

But for the Starrucca (Star-RUCK-ah), the first time I came upon the 1848 masonry railroad bridge, it was unquestionably enough, and the longer I looked, it became more than enough, both at that moment and in recollection: its age, height, length, and solidity, its unembellished grace, its beauty of plainness — qualities residents living in its shadows almost take for granted. If they cherish it, to them it's still just "the stone bridge."

The Starrucca Viaduct at Lanesboro, Pennsylvania, circa 1880.

Q and I arrived beneath it one morning when the sun had about finished turning the eastern face of the viaduct into seventeen golden portals. Surrounded by interrupted woodlands, the tall arches of big blocks of bluestone appeared to be a rock wall of massive doorways opening into some country beyond America, a land that finds use and beauty in structures of yore. A few old two-storey houses with backyards extending right up to the big stone piers introduced a dollop of reality and a sense of scale. Atop the sharp peaks of their steeply pitched roofs was space to set a seven-storey building which would reach only to the level of the viaduct parapets edging the deck carrying the tracks that, when first laid, were a section of the longest railroad (at less than five-hundred miles) in the world.

By the time of completion of the span, thirteen years before commencement of the Civil War, the surrounding hills had been heavily timbered off, and the bridge stood better revealed than today. It looked even longer and higher, much in the way a closely cropped head makes ears look bigger. Pieces of opened forest had returned to beautify the valley while somewhat minifying the span, although it could still call to mind a great, multiple-arched, classical Roman aqueduct, especially the one of the first century A.D. called the Claudian.

A ten-storey-high bridge a thousand-feet long is big enough to reach across most American rivers, yet under it, a child could toss a pebble over Starrucca Creek and in many places wade to the opposite bank without wetting more than a shirttail. To say this another way, the span is about forty times longer and a hundred times higher than necessary to get over the stream. Because the Susquehanna River is less than a half-mile west, a visitor can be forgiven for thinking the contractor built the bridge above the wrong waterway. It was, of course, not the creek but its rather deep Appalachian valley that the old Erie Railroad — on a route from the Hudson River to Lake Erie — needed to cross. Even though Starrucca Creek is a fraction of the width of the Mississippi, its valley is deeper than anything the big river flows through in its two-thousand-mile descent.

America has other huge bridges. Only twenty-five miles southwest, to name one, is the great Tunkhannock Creek Viaduct, a splendid 1915 monument of reinforced concrete. But, beyond that, since alterations to the rebuilt High (or Aqueduct) Bridge over the Harlem River north of Manhattan, no longer is there a span anywhere in the country (and few in the world) of such size *and* age as the Starrucca. Designed to support fifty-ton engines of the mid-nineteenth century, its pure and scarcely modified masonry, 160 years later, carried two-hundred-ton locomotives with monstrous loads behind them, and until not long ago might bear two trains at once. The Starrucca Viaduct, in architecture and undeserved anonymity, stands supreme.

Q has been known, on a slow Saturday afternoon, to go down to a switchyard to watch locomotives rumble around, and she's dreamed of tucking her hair under a cap and dressing like a hobo and hopping a boxcar for Arizona. Such a woman, looking at such a bridge, is almost bound to say "What do you think about walking across it?"

Because Q is counsel licensed to stand before a judge's bench, I assumed she was referring to the issue of trespass. She corrected me: "I'm not asking about the legality of it." Oh, I said, you mean the sanity of it.

She knew my long record of misdemeanor trespasses, all of them probably brought about by the version of the Lord's Prayer drummed into me as a child: "Forgive us our trespasses as we forgive those who trespass against us." Yet what she said was something else, something devilishly alluring: "A writer writing about quoz would have an interesting chapter if he got tossed into the clink for pursuing a quoz. Readers love complications. A writer who takes things right to the edge."

Edges: telling her about the Glasgow bridge had been bootless, and worse, my earlier mention of the death-defying, one-legged bicyclist who allegedly rode across the Starrucca Viaduct *on the narrow parapet* had only encouraged her. Trying to counter with my fractured understanding of jurisprudence involving torts of trespass, I repeated a phrase I'd heard her and my father say, a tenet students of the law cannot escape: a tortfeasor takes his victims as he finds them.

Q pointed out, while my quoting the law sounded good, it was more amusing than accurately applied. Thinking how much I also would like to see the view from the top of the viaduct, I reminded her of putting another woman's life at risk on another railroad bridge as I remembered my vow never to do anything similar again. But my brain was calculating risks against rewards. To slow it, I said, Let's go to lunch.

❥ 8 ❦

Forty Pages Against a Headache Ball

WE WENT INTO LITTLE LANESBORO to Joe's Country Store. It had the look of an old village-grocery, an institution seriously diminishing across America but perhaps less so in the Northeast. It still contained the standard meat-and-cheese counter at the rear where once a Bert — now more commonly a Betty or their grand-daughter — could assemble a lunch of ingredients you select from a slant-front glass case. My fare in such a grocery is often the sandwich of several names: in western Pennsylvania people may call it a zeppelin (after the shape of the stubby loaf), but in the eastern corner, it can be a hoagie or a bomber, and a little farther on eastward, it becomes a grinder. The rest of the country, generally, has seen other names vanish in the corporate campaign of attack submarines, even though a franchise sub is to a well-filled grinder from a grocery as shaken milk is to a milk shake. In Joe's, Betty was Patricia, the third in a line of four females who have assembled hoagies and rolled out homemade pizza dough, the fifth generation soon to enter the throng of Planet Earth.

Of all ingredients, none exceeds bread as key to the quality of the finished whole, and into my short loaf Pat stuffed green peppers, banana peppers, pepperoncini, pimiento olives, Greek olives, sliced tomatoes, chopped lettuce, two kinds of sharp cheese, and a good shot of black pepper held in place with olive oil and vinegar. My running commentary on why those were necessary ingredients turned a transaction into a conversation leading to details of a recent irruption the Susquehanna made through Lanesboro.

"You might be interested in this," she said, and handed me a pamphlet of historical highlights of the village. "We've got pictures too, if you want to see them." I expected the customary, personal archive a visitor may find in hinterland America: an album of blurry snapshots or a folder of yellowed news clippings, one of which always seems to be an article about the place published forty years ago in the *Saturday Evening Post*. "Sarah," she said to her daughter, "run home and bring back your laptop."

About the time Q and I finished our hoagies, Sarah returned and sat down with us in one of the four wooden-booths. While Mama rolled pizza dough, the daughter opened her computer to run a video she made of Old Man Susquehanna coming into town and, with neither invitation nor a wiping of his feet, slipping into parlors to leave behind mud and stink. To everyone's sorrow, that's what he did in the historic hotel, the lone building once giving Lanesboro the appearance of a village rather than a mere collocation of several houses around a general store.

Coming is the day when a curious traveler asks a question of a resident of someplace and gets treated to a digital album of moving history. To see the Susquehanna *flow* through town was a different experience from seeing its motion held forever static in a photograph. What if we could watch the great viaduct rising, men climbing scaffolds, donkey engines hoisting stones, could hear the chink of hammers, Irish brogues and Yankee twangs calling to each other? The future will surely view us, at the forefront of the personal-video age, in ways we can never see our nineteenth-century ancestors who got held rigidly still by portrait photographers' head-clamps. "Good god!" we say. "Were they really that solemn? Was existence so hard it washed out even a flicker of joy?" To judge by the old tintypes — incapable of catching a chuckle, a wink, a nod — the answer would seem to be yes, but stories reveal it wasn't. As the means of recording history change, so will the appearance of history.

Following Pat's directions, Q and I headed on down the highway a mile to Susquehanna, the whilom railroad town that had turned its defunct switchyard into a small shopping-center below the main commercial street. Q went to the library while I looked around downtown and uptown — the latter several actual feet above the other — for the Lanesboro historical pamphlet and any other information on the viaduct. I came up empty. That proved fortuitous because, had I found anything, I might have ceased my hunt there.

The highest form of travel for me is a wandering into a quoz and the subsequent search for its quintessence and a try at elucidating its mysteries. Investigative journeying brings you quickly into a local milieu and gives you a handful of new acquaintances, some of whom may become friends. I've grown old with people I met perhaps only a couple of times in distant places — Kankakee and Kyoto, Kennebunk and Killarney, Manhattan and Mantua. To receive from an acquaintance an occasional letter with a photograph, to see them move through time as I do, to share that time *across space* is a great thing, and slowly and inevitably to lose those faces makes death not so much a state of nonexistence as just another stop on a long itinerary.

The temporary citizenship a questing visitor may earn, beyond lending meaning to travel, grants the privilege to ask questions without (usually) being considered intrusive or getting told to get the hell on down the road. Not *all* people a traveler meets want to give up their stories or relate the history of the town pump or explain why the Podunk up the road is called Toad Suck or Hot Coffee. But, so goes my estimate, ninety percent (under the right conditions) will discover they are happy to teach you. Being a teacher, being considered a master of certain knowledge, is a pleasure. Proof of that is the number of times when — in a formal interview with a tape recorder — I reach to shut off the machine and the master says, "I've got more time if you want it." Never have I heard anyone say, "Are we about finished here?" The single thing a master native asks from the traveler is nothing more than genuine curiosity.

And — if you'll allow one last notion on this topic — entry into other lives can turn a forgettable locale into indelibility, your recollections forever inscribed with faces and words and times shared. To deepen memory may not be the major goal in a human life — at least not one we're usually cognizant of — but as our days proceed to stretch out ever more behind us, it seems to me deepening memory has got to be no lower than second place. And, beyond that, to bring a quoz to life, to bring it into your *own* life — now *that* surely, ultimately, is the highest end of exploration.

I returned to the library in the former train yard. A gleeful Q stood at the checkout desk, and in her raised hands were a pair of booklets, neither the one I was looking for, yet her expression said, "Bingo!" One was about the Tunkhannock Viaduct, the other about the Starrucca, both written by the same man. I took the histories to a corner of the library. The author, William Young, clearly had done detailed research, and information in his booklets raised questions until that moment I didn't know I had. Bingo.

The librarian said the booklets were out of print and the copy machine wasn't working properly. I asked whether she knew Mr. Young. "Not really." Did she have a local phone directory? "Well, of course! This is a library." She called him, introduced not me but my quest, and handed over the receiver.

Perhaps, I asked him, he had a copy he'd sell? No, didn't think so, he said, but even if he did, he couldn't bring it into town anytime soon. Might we come to him? "I'm way out." How far? "About nine miles." Your books, I said, are worth more than nine miles — if we could stop by just long enough to ask a few questions about Starrucca. Maybe borrow a booklet to photocopy — paying full cover price, of course. "Let me look around," he said, and gave directions.

William Young lived in the old family place on a slope above Starrucca Creek, where he learned to swim, eight miles east of the grand bridge. His white-clapboard, Greek Revival house, fronted with big lilac bushes and surrounded by hard maples, was of an age commensurate with the building of the 1848 viaduct. His people came into the forested valley in 1815, but Young was born in Brooklyn and grew up in New Jersey. In his retirement he had made himself the sixth generation to live in the two-storey house. His grandfather knew a fellow who had watched the building of the span, and an even earlier forebear may have worked on it.

A cottage behind the house was made of the same bluestone as the bridge, rock from a quarry not far across the creek. He said he was counting down to his seventy-ninth birthday, although a sixty-ninth seemed more credible. Like the Starrucca, he had weathered well, part of the happy return for his seventy-thousand miles of cycling (not one of them across the viaduct), and his face radiated pleasure in talking history. After losing a beloved woman years ago, he had never married.

Young knew the stone arches from the ground up; that is, from the valley they crossed on upward a hundred feet to the tracks atop them. Beyond that knowledge, he was a student and writer of American rail history, and he could tell you what a Mallet Triplex 2-8-8-8-2 was (a huge locomotive with twenty-eight wheels in a certain arrangement), and he could say when one last went over the valley. He enumerated the eight railroads that have owned the viaduct during its long existence, and he explained the corbels mysteriously projecting from each pier (to support wooden scaffolds to complete the construction of the arch).

At age sixteen he went to work as a printer's devil, where one of his duties was filing rough edges off Linotype lead "pigs," a job that for him turned the smell of ink into a sweet cachet. After two years in the Army during the Korean War (he was stationed in Germany), he returned to work as a printer and occasional news-reporter in New Jersey and South Carolina. When he retired to the home place in the Starrucca Valley, he gave his time to research and writing about railroads.

Education after high school was largely of his own creation — he read history and authors whose styles he admired: Mark Twain, E. B. White, and, more generally, other writers in *The New Yorker* "as it used to be." Former jobs and research allowed him to write his illustrated histories, compose their pages, produce the booklets, and at each stage keep an eye out for errors. "I can do it all in my way," he said, "and that helps to keep the price down in an economically depressed area." If his chronicles weren't a major piece of income for him, they were still a significant source of satisfaction. I asked whether his histories were his highest achievement, and he said, "I suppose they are, but there's always the next book which I hope will be even better." The next book was to be about the Unadilla Valley Railway in central New York.

We sat on the side porch. Propped on a chair were his two booklets waiting for us; he hoped to have out soon the sixth edition of *Starrucca: The Bridge of Stone.* Young did not say it — he would never say it — but I would soon learn he was *the* authority on the viaducts, his knowledge the result of some forty years of research and a boyhood partly spent along Starrucca Creek. He belonged to the valley by chance of family settlement, but he belonged to the bridge by dint of learning. Early immersions in the stream and later immersions in the history of the span over it had turned a long avocation into an even longer contribution. How much of the past he alone had preserved, even he did not know.

When I told him he wrote a good sentence, he said, "I wrote nothing good until I was forty-eight." That was about the time *Starrucca,* then titled simply *Bridge of Stone,* first appeared. For a third of a century thereafter, he had continued to accumulate facts and to find forgotten historic photographs while taking new ones of the viaduct. Longevity taketh away, but it also giveth to those who persevere. Although never his intent, he had made himself over time, if you will, the Star of Starrucca and had carved his name not in its bluestone but in works even more durable. (Gus Kubitzki once said, "If the worst part of death is the thought of oblivion, then leaving behind something of worth makes it a little more tolerable.")

I mentioned to Young how much we'd like to cross the viaduct in a passenger train. "The last one," he said, "was forty years ago, but you might have a chance again, because I hope the bridge will be properly maintained and will see more trains as part of the railroad renaissance that appears to be coming on. The line is underused now, but the Starrucca route has potential value, especially as a bypass for freight traffic that's beginning to choke other routes. Although there's only one now, there used to be dual tracks on it, and someday there could be twin tracks again."

Q confessed our urge to trespass our way across the viaduct and asked whether he had ever walked it. "I've been over it a few times on a train," he said, "but never all the way on foot. I was inside one of the arches once, and I've taken pictures from the top. And an acquaintance claims he rode a bicycle across." I asked about suicides. "None I know of. But somebody did jump from the Tunkhannock Viaduct just last year. For suicide, people seem to prefer a bridge down at Scranton. I don't know why. Closer to home maybe."

What if use of the bridge should come to an end? "It's been a National Historic Civil Engineering Landmark for years," he said, "but that still doesn't give it much protection. It's also on the National Register of Historic Places, but that only means federal money could never be used to tear it down. Should it ever be abandoned, though, I think preservation would be certain." Especially so now, I said, with your research serving as a kind of eighteenth supporting arch. He said only, "I hope what I've done is positive."

Had there been a William Young in the valley in 1900, how much greater our comprehension would be today. The past everywhere is a huge chunk of murky ice perpetually melting in the heat of the moment, and the great drain beneath leads straight down to the River Lethe. He said, "I started collecting material about the bridge when I was twelve — just basic information then, some of which turned out to be wrong. In all those years, I've never learned how several silly legends got started, like the one about every train that crosses having to pay a fee to the descendants of the builders. Then there's one about the first locomotive to cross the viaduct going over unmanned because nobody dared trust the bridge."

If the total population of the Starrucca Valley for the initial 150 years of the viaduct was — and I'm just guessing a number to make a point — ten thousand, then Young is the only one of ten thousand people who has had enough concern to dedicate himself toward preserving knowledge of the span, which, after the structure itself, is the most important aspect of its survival.

Years ago a civil suit was brought to tear down the Brooklyn Bridge as a navigational hazard on the East River. If such a beloved icon can be threatened, then what future perils await an isolated viaduct — never mind its beauty and historic significance? It's possible one day, the sturdiest thing standing between those massive bluestone arches and a wrecker's ball will be the forty pages of Young's pamphlet. After all, America is not Italy where the great Claudian aqueduct has been allowed to remain for two-thousand years to inspire generations of engineers, architects, artists. For two millennia it has bridged not just the two sides of valleys but two sides of time, one of them the future. If William Young's niche in American history is narrow, it also is deep.

❯ 9 ❮

No More Than a Couple of Skeletons

T‌RAVELERS BOUND FOR RURAL NEW ENGLAND can see they've
arrived when villages fill with houses having front-door fan-
lights and Palladian windows, churches near a green are pedimented,
porticoed, and pilastered, ferns grow just about anywhere untrodden
by man or beast, and dry-laid rock walls enclose a burying ground
having two or three slate markers attesting MY GLASSE IS RUN.

Q and I made our way toward Mount Washington and the North
Maine Woods via a hot-dog wagon in Connecticut, plates of clam
fritters and steamers along Narragansett Bay, and bowls of chowder
in Massachusetts. We passed through Franconia Notch where, until
just four years earlier, the Old Man of the Mountain, that famed profile in rock, the Great Stone Face, kept watch over things.

After a night of heavy rain, it — he — broke loose and fell from
the sheer cliff to get smithereened several hundred feet below. Up
on the mountain, the yet-fresh scar — pink like a healing wound — was a sorrowful thing to see; the New
Hampshire route markers, still depicting his silhouette,
were continual reminders of mutability, even for men of
stone. Said Q, "A regrettable loss of face."

Never by any method — foot, horse, auto, rail —
had she made the ascent of Mount Washington, the
tallest peak in the Northeast, a six-thousand-foot-
high rocky island of arctic plants and home to some of
the worst weather on earth. Over the course of a year, the summit
will average hurricane-velocity winds two out of three days, and at

least once a month, they hit 150 miles an hour; one night it was 231. Beneath the crest, permafrost reaches down two-hundred feet to hold ice unthawed since before the last continental glaciation. Not many visitors, of course, make the trip up for violent winds and ancient ice — it's the view or climb they want. When I was on the mountain a few years earlier, visibility was three feet, but under a rare clear sky, you can see the Atlantic seventy-five miles east. So I've heard.

Train buff that Q is, she was elated to take the antique cog railway to the summit. Few are the places in America where you can cover *exactly* the same route as travelers of 140 years earlier, and even fewer are those (at the moment I can't think of another) where the conveyance is by the same vehicle, or one nearly so. Behind our coach, the little coal-fired, steam locomotive pushing us up was 135 years old, albeit replaced piece by piece over those years; perhaps somewhere in it was still an original brass knob or lever. After a few hundred yards of ascent, as I looked down the steep trestles that carry the entire track once it starts climbing, it was comforting to think not of antique bolts and gears but of replaced parts. Less reassuring was to see that the coach was unattached, except by gravity, to the engine, had only the locomotive and tiny tender between it and the bottom of the mountain.

Judging from the other passengers, one of whom refused to look back down the cogged tracks, the little pufferbelly was either "decrepit" or "cute," the latter more commonly heard *after* we reached the summit about an hour later — a rise of 3,600 feet over three miles. The angle of climb in one place was nearly thirty-eight percent (in a hundred feet forward, you rise thirty-eight feet; only a cog line in the Swiss Alps was steeper, and merely by a degree or so). At that pitch, a seat at the front end of the small coach is fourteen feet higher than one at the rear, although the difference didn't appear that great. The plump boiler sat tilted so that during ascent it was parallel to, say, the Atlantic Ocean but not to the mountain slope, thereby keeping water from draining off the steam tubes. One of the delights of passage was to notice how one's brain began to adjust to the extreme incline by seeing the world beyond the tracks as horribly slanted: I was certain several spruces — in truth growing perfectly vertically — were leaning almost forty degrees toward Vermont. On a disturbingly canted maintenance shed — one appearing ready to slide down the mountain — was a sign: THIS BUILDING IS LEVEL.

In the 1860s, the plan to get up to the top on slick steel-tracks got mockingly called the Railway to the Moon, in part because it was the first cogger in the world to try to climb the face of a mountain. Today, the ascent up the rails begins with great remonstrance from a smoky locomotive — seemingly of a size to fit a kiddie zoo. As the engine starts up, it whistles and spouts, sputters, shakes, shivers, shudders, knocks, and rattles in racketing, clanking, clanging, groaning, grinding, screeching, squealing, squeaking, spewing, hissing, smoke-belching protestations suggesting you have just boarded a train that can only transport you to singing hymns in the Angelic Choir. Although the little, green engine looked like something out of a child's illustrated story, no one could possibly hear in its puff-puff-chug-chug, *I think I can, I think I can.* The noise was more the classic lament of seniority: *Oh, not again! Not Again!*

After Q entrained, she said with some expectation, "This is better than a carnival ride. We'll actually get somewhere. We'll arrive in another place." Jerkily, snortingly, blowing hot cinders, the locomotive began pushing us up. If years before I'd seen only as far as thirty-six inches will allow, the legendary Mount Washington weather fulfilling itself, for Q the sky opened, and from the summit — if we didn't see quite to the Atlantic — we did see deeply enough to get an aerial sense of the White Mountains, sometimes called the White Hills. Below in the forest it had been almost too warm; but on top, the wind — no breeze, that gusting — required a jacket or a run for cover. Mount Washington rises near a nexus of three major storm paths, and their collisions often produce weathers so unendurable only a polar ice cap in winter can equal their vehemence. If the wind blows at two-hundred miles an hour and the temperature is twenty below, what's the windchill? Lethal.

When the time came to go back down, I looked down the winding cogs (I mean to give some emphasis to the *down*s in that sentence). I'd read about a method used by nineteenth-century trackmen to return to Base Station faster than ambulation allowed. Sitting on a narrow three-foot-long board straddling the cogs centered between the rails, relying on the crudest of friction brakes, workers could toboggan toward home on what they called a Devil's Shingle. One fellow reached the station, a descent an engine requires about an hour to make, in two minutes and forty-five seconds. Not everyone did it quite so fast, and not everyone did it without injury, and Devil's Shingles were outlawed in 1906.

But what I found most remarkable about the cog railway had to do not with speed but with distance: even in living memory, a traveler could once board a coach in beachy San Diego (to pick a place) and just by changing trains disembark two days and more than three thousand miles later into the arctic world atop Mount Washington.

The portion of the northern Appalachians called the White Mountains, square mile for square mile, may have the most extensive shelf of relevant books of any range in America, a literature beginning in the late eighteenth century. The nearest comparable topography around is the Green Mountains in Vermont, but for every word they have evoked over the years, the New Hampshire range can show, so I'd guess, five times that. It's as if some travelers come into the country through one of the three great notches and thereupon get imbued with an urge to describe the territory, to tell *its* tales or tell *their* tales about it. Were the White Mountains in the South, that land of natural tale-tellers, the stories might fill American literature and leave little room for the rest of us. And perhaps a reverse is true: were the range in Minnesota, we would not yet have heard about them.

Beyond beauty and their proximity to a populace of generally well-educated citizens — Harvard Yard is only 120 miles away — the bookish attention to the White Hills is much the result of a national forest established there in 1918, a protection that helped keep out early-day rapacious, liquidating, timber operations to create a future of tourists, hikers, climbers, hunters, skiers, and artists who replenish themselves somewhat faster and spend more on lattes than a stand of spruce. That wisdom of long-lasting prosperity for the many over short-term profit for the few set up my expectations for the North Maine Woods lying, geologically at least, not far from the tail end of the New Hampshire range.

We left the mountainous forest and followed broken hills northeast to Skowhegan, Maine, where one cool and gloomy morning we came upon the Empire Grill. We were drawn to it not so much by the old red-neon Indian glowing in profile as by two simpler signs also suggesting another era: HOT MEALS. BOOTH SERVICE. Inside was that unmistakable and memory-releasing scent unique to an American breakfast café: vaporing coffee, toasting bread, hot maple syrup, a wisp of eggs-over-easy. On a morning of thorough Maine dismals, I suddenly had reason — beyond eventual necessity — to have gotten out of bed. I heard, as if an addendum to my remark: "A reason to get out of bed? How about why you're alive? When is it you don't hear the Empire Grills of America calling?"

Before going again to the road, we walked worn Water Street with its shop windows of dusty merchandise. In one hung a sign: WE GOT 'EM! BUG SUITS! (Q: "Roaches dressed fit to kill?") If you've ever put yourself near trees or water in northern Maine in early summer, you know the reference is not to bug toggery but to a collection of winged things, from the invisible (midges) to the whining (mosquitoes) to the silent (blackflies) and on down to crawlers (ticks). Some people refer to the North Maine Woods as "uninhabited," but an estival stroll anywhere near water or timber will disabuse anybody of that description, for the place is fully inhabited, and the habitants are nature's first line of defense against the sprawling of humanity into one of the last great, forested realms in the Northeast. To be sure, Americans owe a debt to the blackfly, for without it we might have Six Flags Over Moose World and its attendant parking lots, tract housing — well, you know the story.

As we rolled on northward, the territory thinned of humanity and its contemporary disfigurements. At the old mill towns of Millinocket and East Millinocket, the highways at last shied away from the northwest corner, the so-called Unorganized Territory, the North Maine Woods still largely owned by timber companies feeding paper mills, although ownership was changing (about that I'll say more shortly). From Route 11 on the east and south, the Woods lay unintruded upon except by privately owned logging roads and some fish and hunting camps. With the exception of Baxter State Park, for a hundred miles west and more than that north, there was no entry without permission of the corporations calling themselves the North Maine Woods, Inc., as though they were the forest itself. (I'll use that term to refer to trees, not companies.) In area, imagine New Hampshire without pavement and population. An expanse that size in the Far West would draw scarce attention to private enterprises controlling open access to it, but in New England, a million square-miles is a significant piece of realty to lie beyond unrestricted public purview.

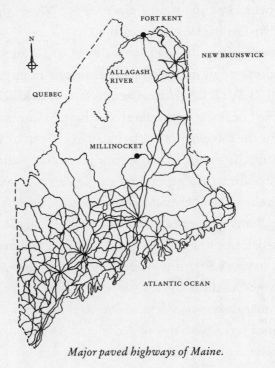

Major paved highways of Maine.

To enter that domain, you approach a "checkpoint," answer a few questions, pay a fee, agree (readily) to give timber trucks right-of-way, and express hope of finding your course over continually changing gravel roads and one-lane bridges, where signposts are as rare as those on the Road to Hell, and the way is not paved with even so much as a good intention.

That is not a complaint. I am generally comfortable with limiting the sprawl of exurbia by keeping certain areas tucked away so at least a little effort and commitment are necessary to enter. Because there is hardly a place in America I would not go to see at least once (well, I did skip that so-called museum of ceramic figurines of angels and another one "proving" the concurrent existence of *Homo sapiens* and brontosauruses), a partially forbidden territory carries something of an added allure of trespass.

[**DIGRESSION ALERT:** A man in North Dakota, an Assiniboin, told me years ago when I asked if I could cross a fence to take a picture, "Every white or black man and woman in this country lives in trespass. How could you make any difference?" I take his point, but I still honor fences except on occasion when the deed holder is an absentee corporation whose board of directors couldn't distinguish "their" north forty in west Texas from a national park in Oregon. As the man explained, "Five hundred generations of footprints and burials give possession — not some goddamn piece of paper in a courthouse signed ninety years ago."]

For three decades I'd wanted to enter the Unorganized Territory, sometimes simply called, after the river running through its heart, "the Allagash." Reading Thoreau's *The Maine Woods* intensified my wish to see it, and the urge gained strength from my oldest highway atlas depicting the territory and labeling the unimproved roads there with five come-hither words: PRIVATE RD — OPEN TO PUBLIC. Weeks previous, when I mentioned to Q the time had come at last to head out for the Maine Woods, she who at the drop of a suggestion will go anywhere (including, candor compels me to say, an "Elvis

Lives!" exhibit) was mentally packed in less time than it takes to read a Thoreau sentence.

Counter to my usual approach of just wandering into a place without advisement from others, I thought — because of Q's presence — getting local counsel before entering the Woods a sound idea. In Millinocket, in the shadow of Mount Katahdin, in a downpour, I began asking questions in offices, cafés, the library, and, later, even the town tavern, one of those places commonly known for misrepresentation, misinterpretation, misinformation, misguidance, misconception, misdirection, misestimation, misunderstanding, and misbegotten notions leading to misadventures, mishaps, mistakes, misfortunes, and (worst of all should Q overhear any of it) misgivings. But, outside of legislative chambers, where else can one hear such a pile of dreck and drivel, dregs and dross, duff and dung, all for the price of a pint?

In everything I learned during the day, only one discovery surprised me: I found nobody who had ever done what I proposed doing — looping along on logging roads through the forest to gain a real sense of it — south to north, east to west. To make such an irregular ambit without long backtrackings would require slipping into Quebec and out again to reenter the Allagash and end up eventually along the St. John River at the Canadian border. The route, marked on my map, looked something like a grotesquely misshapen S.

Even though informants could not account for its name, they all had traveled the Golden Road, a kind of southern boundary and the last stretch of pavement for many miles north, east, or west. If natives went into the Woods at all, it was to fish or hunt, perhaps even to canoe, although canoes and kayaks were mostly for outsiders. But just to "wander around up in there" — *that* was pointless if not wacky, a view expressed most concisely by a fellow to whom comb, razor, and soap apparently were anathema: "First question," he said. "Why?" I wanted to respond, *Quoz, man, quoz!* but with my sanity already at issue, an introduction of arcane vocabulary into the conversation could not possibly help.

Of more use was the man who said, "Just south to north — *if* you don't make any wrong turns — that's a hundred-sixty miles. I've been up in there a couple of dozen times, and I've gotten lost three times that many times and ran out of gas twice. One damn wrong turn late in the day, and you'll spend the night with bears licking your hood and blackflies sucking your blood. A couple of wrong turns down to a dead end, and you'll be out of gas." He let that sink in, then tried to get helpful. "Got a CB?" No. "How about GPS?" Just a compass. "Shit," he said. "And you're taking the blonde?" Q heard that one. "I'm not the blonde," she said. "I'm the mechanic!" (Her riposte was more warranted than accurate.)

The range of opinions from his view went on down to a couple of culinary references by a woman quoting her husband: "He says it's a piece of cake. Easy as pie — *if* you can tolerate getting lost now and then." As I went out the door, she called out cheerfully, "You be sure now to take water and food. And extra tires." Her last words were more ominous: "Let us know *if* you make it!" My thought was, *How easy can pie be if it requires extra tires?*

Later, in the Blue Ox Saloon, a man used his wetted finger to draw maps on the bar top. Watching his directions evaporate, I realized I'd neglected to ask the most fundamental question: could an ordinary, low-clearance automobile handle the roads? "Sure," he said, "*if* you go slow." All the advice had in it somewhere a damn *if*. As he calculated, he apparently noticed Q's necklace, a small brass compass I'd given her and had engraved with, *I am your guide.* Turning back to me, he said, "They don't usually pull more than a couple of skeletons a year out of the Allagash, and only a few of them are wearing a compass." She didn't hear him, although moments later she said, "You know, going down the Allagash River has an advantage." Which is? "It flows only out."

With that, I proposed a toast to Dr. Benjamin Ball. "Who's he?" she asked. A Boston physician. In 1855 he decided to climb Mount Washington. After he arrived and saw the thing, he decided to borrow a pair of boots, a warm cap, and an umbrella, and in late October, Doc started up. Alone. The boots were too big for him. "Did he make it?" No. "He died?" No. "So what happened?" Three days later a search party found him and helped him down the mountain. "And?" He spent the next three months in recovery. She said, "Did you bring an umbrella?"

❧ 10 ❧

What Raven Whispered

As SOUTHERN FLORIDA IS THE SOUTH only by proximity, so northern Maine is New England, lacking as it does village greens, old liberal-arts colleges, Paul Revere bells hanging in belfries, preserved homes of honored poets, and tended graves of eighteenth-century statesmen. It's a harder, tougher place, with a pedigree not of letters and quaintness but of timber mills and potato barns, where the past looks not so much historic as just beat-up. The true proximity shaping it is both more primitive and primeval, and lies northward, in the opposite direction, toward the boreal forest and chains of lakes and ponds, bogs and fens, that mark the courses of glaciation after glaciation having their way with the terrain and shaping everything in their paths.

Following the flows of linked streams and lakes — called quick water and dead water — a dedicated canoeist could paddle from near the center of the state to the Canadian border almost two-hundred aqueous miles north over a route of portages short and somewhat longer to reach the St. John River. At the heart of the Woods is the Allagash, four decades ago designated a Wilderness Waterway, perhaps an accurate description by current standards, but certainly not in terms Thoreau would accept. If *wilderness* means untrampled by humans other than those once living with stone tools, then the so-called Unorganized Territory may no longer quite match the description Thoreau wrote in 1846 after his initial visit there:

What is most striking in the Maine wilderness is the continu-
ousness of the forest, with fewer open intervals or glades than
you had imagined. Except the few burnt lands, the narrow intervals on the rivers, the bare tops of the high mountains, and the
lakes and streams, the forest is uninterrupted. It is even more
grim and wild than you had anticipated, a damp and intricate
wilderness, in the spring everywhere wet and miry. The aspect
of the country indeed is universally stern and savage, excepting
the distant views of the forest from hills, and the lake prospects,
which are mild and civilizing in a degree. . . . These are not the
artificial forests of an English king — a royal preserve merely.
Here prevail no forest laws, but those of nature. The aborigines
have never been dispossessed, nor nature disforested.

On the first morning of summer, Q and I set out early to have
every minute of extra light the planet could collect even in that land
of long summer days. The Maine glooms obscured sunrise, but by
the time we neared the Golden Road, the dreariness lifted to reveal
clouds in such variety they created a veritable primer of nephology.
Staring skyward, the navigator (he) missed a turn, and we had to
backtrack, the very thing I conjectured would be the biggest hin-
drance to maintaining a sensible course through the Woods. Q: "Is
one tank enough to do the miles twice?" Probably not.

We were outfitted with a pair of compasses, the two most-detailed
maps I could find, and *The Maine Atlas and Gazetteer;* maybe I also
should count my old hubris of almost always being able to match
routes on paper with those on pavement. Entry to the Golden Road
was marked by a wordy sign perhaps meant to discourage the timid;
in my interpretation it boiled down to this:

THESE LOGGING ROADS ARE FOR MOVING LOGS,
NOT YOU, SO KEEP THE HELL OUT OF THE WAY
OF TIMBER TRUCKS AND REMEMBER
THERE IS NOTHING IN HERE YOU CAN BUY.

Fair enough.

The initial thirty-five miles were on two-lane asphalt through unexceptional woodlands, and for the first ten minutes we followed a large trash-truck I would have preferred seeing — if at all — going *out* of the Woods. The route was an alley of mixed forest, the trees younger than I, a place of regrowth without a tincture of wilderness, and fully unlike Thoreau's description — including his sentence about the nondispossession of "the aborigines."

We crossed a little bridge over the West Branch of the Penobscot River at a stretch called the Abol Deadwater, and there, at last, the timberland opened: five miles east rose Katahdin, its south slope set into splendid relief by the low angle of the morning sun, and on its north a jam-up of clouds evaporated while trying to find a way around the mountain. The customary mantle of weather around Katahdin had always before prevented me from seeing much of it. We stopped and walked to the stream to get an even better view, and there a couple dozen cliff swallows flittered and chittered about a puddle as they beaked up goo for their mud-jug nests. They gathered so fearlessly around us, I felt like St. Francis, and my hopes rose for more wilderness where nature might see humans as just another creature: stand still, hold out an arm till Raven flies to your perch and whispers secrets of the earth.

Near the top of the broad arc of the Golden Road, we left it and the pavement at Big Eddy just below Ripogenus Lake, from there to head northward on what locals call "dirt" roads but which are in fact graveled. A few miles beyond was the Telos checkpoint formally admitting us into the North Maine Woods. I went to the small office to pay sixteen dollars for passage. At about a dime a mile, it would be a bargain of ruts and chuckholes, loose rock, and muddy sloughs or dust clouds (depending on whether it had rained on a spot an hour earlier or the night before). Inside, I opened my marked map to show the gatekeeper our proposed route. She glanced at it and said, "That's not possible. Not anymore." Why not? "They say a couple of the Nine-Eleven terrorists entered the country through one of those checkpoints on the Canadian border, so all the private-road crossings are closed now. You can't hook over into Quebec on one road and come back into the NMW on another. You can go up to the border, but then you'll have to turn around and come back the way you came."

Five sentences, and there went my itinerary. I stepped outside to mutter over to a picnic table where I spread out the maps, weighted them with rocks, and began to refigure. Q said, "Why didn't anybody tell us yesterday those border checkpoints have been shut down?" Because they never use them. They go into the Woods to hunt or fish, not to pass through. If they want to go to Fort Kent, they take Route 11. Only cabbageheads tour on the logging roads.

As I calculated a different route northward to get us into as much territory as possible without retracing miles of it, I came up with a course generally following the Allagash River, but I couldn't shake my disappointment, at least not until the breeze slackened enough to let blackflies find me. I continued figuring, slapping, measuring, slapping, marking, slapping, cursing, slapping, slapping, and finally going back into the cramped office. If those little botherations can drive a half-ton of moose to near frenzy, why should a man feel unmanly by retreating behind screen windows? "Got to you, did they?" the gatekeeper said. "Now you'll scratch for a week."

I pointed to my redrawn route through the heart of the Woods to the mouth of the Allagash. What do you think? I asked. She looked at it and said, "I've never been up that far, but I can tell you that even we get lost in there. The roads change all the time, or some of them do anyway. I'd say you're in for a little adventure."

She called over a log hauler who had just stopped by. He looked at the map and said nothing. What do you think? I asked. "About what?" Let me ask it this way, are the roads marked? "Some of the main ones got names." But are there signs on the roads? "I seen a few. They got signs to the fish camps up." What about closed bridges? "Yeah." The hauler, a crackerjack of taciturnity, was the kind of chap you hope is seated next to you on a transcontinental night-flight. I pointed out the window. Can that car make it? "*If* you don't get on the wrong road." Ah, that little conditional again.

It was time to call up my favorite Quaker apothegm: proceed as the way opens. Off we went, slowly, giving wide berth to log trucks — though few — and their trail of airborne rocks. After puzzling through a couple of crossroads, Q said, "What do you think? Onward?" It's trickier than I'd imagined, I said, but Daniel Boone and I have never been lost, although — as he admitted — we've been once or twice confused for a couple of weeks. All I need to do is keep us from going too far west or east and hitting a dead end. "Won't the compasses keep us straight?"

The problem was this: some northering roads had portions running east or west, and in one place, even south. When a change of direction happened at a junction, the correct road might head off for a few miles in the wrong direction and the wrong road in the correct direction. I had new comprehension of what the first cross-country automobilists faced in the days before highways and route markers.

Q was at the wheel and I at the chart table of my lap holding the two maps, both of which I quickly put aside because they left the roads unlabeled. But *The Maine Atlas* did show some names, and when an intersection actually had a sign, I was able to fix our position. At several crossings or forks, I hopped out to hunt in the brush for an overgrown or knocked-down marker, one of which I picked up to match the post to its broken base to see which direction it formerly pointed. Those hunts could last until the blackflies found me.

Except from the little bridges, trees blocked long views, although occasionally I could look fifty or sixty feet into the trees to see more trees, many of which I assumed were only a screen masking a clear-cut a few yards on beyond. It was as if we moved in a tunnel cut through heavy fog. (Whoever first uttered that old platitude "Can't see the forest for the trees" may have been then in the Maine Woods.) Yet the forest I saw wasn't the ancient and mossy giants of spruce and fir I had hoped for; rather, it was deciduous trees mixed with scrawny conifers and much scrub. The lack of sight lines, of course, is part of the experience of the Maine Woods, and our moving half blindly did give a sense of remoteness, even if more imagined than actual. When we came upon an occasional unscreened clear-cut, it was *almost* possible to be grateful for the longer — if unnatural — view it allowed of the roll in the landscape.

In a way, navigation was easy — that is, useless — because other than turning back, there was only one direction to go until we came to a junction where finding the way was a matter of reading a text of three letters, a little alphabet of decisions: an X, a Y, a T. After an hour, it became clear many crossings differed one from the other as does dawn from daybreak, your right thumb from your left. At nondescript intersections, I would hop out to drag a heel into the gravel. And, amazingly, at one place, I discovered my mark ten miles farther had somehow migrated to the opposite side. I said, How could this crossroad be Cyr Road if we're *on* Cyr Road which, according to the map, we have to be? Q: "Maybe a prankster moved the sign." (It must be said here, should you ever visit the North Maine Woods and come upon a log hauler who welcomes your presence, who will slow down to give directions, you have met a Samaritan indeed. I would not want it otherwise: part of my reason for going in was to see whether — relying little on human assistance — I could find a course all the way through and out again with mind and marriage still intact.)

At one Y intersection, a mirror of three others, I got out to scour the brush for a fallen marker. When I climbed aboard again and pointed straight ahead, I heard, "You found a sign?" No. "How do you figure it then?" In the scrub there's a skeleton with a bony finger aimed more or less north-northwest — I think it was a wife. "How about a bite of lunch?" Q said.

On an overgrown trail, once an old timber "tote road," we pulled up and, using the hood for a table, laid out raisins, peanut butter, and crackers. On came the blackflies whose notion of a bite of lunch was Dracula's, preferring as they did blood to a banana; if they failed to find my neck, a knuckle or eyelid would do. Not once, for reasons unknown, did they nip Q.

As we ate in the car, she said, "Do you think there's a single square meter here a Euro-American foot has never trod upon?" At the bottom of a lake, perhaps. I held up the atlas showing the forest filled with dashed and dotted lines indicating "unimproved roads" and bulldozed skid trails, old and new. They were all but everywhere. Yet twenty miles west of the Woods lay Quebec and its grid of highways and half a hundred villages named after Christian saints. Across the border was an agricultural economy as different from that of the timberland as a monsieur is from a sir, a baguette from a bagel, Grande Rivière Noire from Chemquasabamticook Stream.

We proceeded on. At the margin of a T juncture, as I started to mark it with my boot, I noticed the damp shoulder already designated with fresh footprints of a black bear; a half mile on, there it was, shambling along, avoiding the dense and infested wet underbrush. The bear heard the crunching gravel in our slow approach and turned to look; if a bear is capable of a shrug, that one shrugged and ambled onward until reaching a narrow gap in the understory where it disappeared. Its nonchalance suggested a degree of wilderness — or maybe its belly was full with the last wanderer stopping to mark his way.

Some miles farther, a moose slipped from the trees, took similar note of us, and trudged off with the same nonchalance as the bear. I assumed they both had encountered just enough loggers to have no curiosity about humans and just enough hunters to know to keep moving, even if only grudgingly. They seemed certain of their territory and not so much fearful as simply undesirous of human company, a response expressed in their insouciant road moseys until a convenient opening allowed them to vanish.

Q had never seen a moose before. She said, "It's a funny name — *moose*. It has no sharp edge to it like *tiger* or *catamount*." As we watched it, Q added, "You see a helicopter fly, and you've got to say, 'How could that thing get into the air?' You see a moose, and you have to say, 'How could that creature happen?'" I explained that evolutionary process long ago had taken a few infelicitous turns, an easy thing to do in the North Maine Woods. Or it could be, out on the Great Plains a bison had eyes for an elk. "That," said Q, "explains the humped back and beard, but what about the flat nose?" Did I not mention the sporting platypus?

Creatures came and went: a snapping turtle, spruce grouse, flight of robins, another of evening grosbeaks, a loon, and, yes, a lone raven — plump, shiny, guttural. Finally, we came to a crisscross, an X in the forest no amount of interpreting could match to the map. No wonder I struggled — this wasn't navigation, it was algebra: if Y is your former location, and T to the left is the wrong way, then what does X equal? A night with the flies.

Patient and trusting, Q waited quietly as my facade of competence vanished faster than blue sky in Maine. Having a twenty-five percent chance of guessing the way to Clayton Lake correctly, I said to angle right, and she did, and after three miles, we found the decision was clearly wrong. Let's go back and angle left, I said, happy the odds were improving. After all, this was not open sea where the difference between a heading of ninety degrees and ninety-two degrees, after a while, is to arrive in Yokohama instead of Hong Kong.

The direction leftward *felt* good, almost as good as the wrong one. And it felt even better when we happened upon a man precariously backing a big backhoe off a flatbed truck. I hollered over the engine noise to ask if we were on the road to Clayton Lake, and he was courteous enough to pause, somewhat dangerously, midway in his descent to say what I heard in his heavy Slavic accent as "*If* you take the next left." (That clinched it: know, venturing reader, without the word *if*, accurate directions cannot be given in the Maine Woods.) Q asked, "What did he say?" It sounded like "Next left," but it might have been something else, maybe a curse for endangering his life. "Wasn't he smiling?" Q asked. Yes, but for all I know, in Zagreb curses and misdirections are delivered with a grin.

Beyond the left, we did get to Clayton Lake, but then I needed two tries to find the right road out, and from there we rolled on nicely in a direction that felt right until it began to feel wrong. If we were where I feared we were, we might reach the Atlantic but we weren't going to find the mouth of the Allagash, and it was already late afternoon.

We came to a lumber camp, only the second we'd seen, and Q stopped. I walked about, looked around, knocked on a door, peered into a window, hollered to no response, and found nobody anywhere. Then I heard something from behind a building: a man loading firewood into a pickup. Yes, we were on the right road, but there was a nasty trick of a junction ahead. "You can follow me if you want," he said, and got into his truck and roared off. Unwilling to crash along as fast as he, we soon lost him in his dust trail. Then came the problem intersection. We paused so the map could have another chance to mock me. With little hope of a solution, I got out again. Signs none, clues zero, nothing. Then, as the dust settled, I saw him in the distance, waving us left. "If we happen onto him tonight," Q said, "I'm standing him a round." Let's make it the next payment on his truck.

The road got worse. For an auto, it was a ten-mile-an-hour veering away from potholes, ruts, and ridges, and bouncing through everything inescapable. If language can represent it, our passage was a spell of humps, bumps, thumps, chunks, clunks, and thunks. But it wasn't festered with forks and cross points, and so we banged onward in hopeful spirits. Then the Allagash, the beautifully *wide* Allagash, revealed itself, and we knew its union with the St. John wasn't far.

About forty years earlier, the people of Maine called for and helped underwrite the establishment of the Allagash Wilderness Waterway, thereby giving nature along its shores and tributaries a chance to recover from a century of aggressive logging and dam building. By the time we were in the North Maine Woods, timber-products industries in the region and elsewhere were faltering. Before a recent bankruptcy, the pair of mills in the two Millinockets once employed four-thousand people, a figure that had dropped to four hundred.

Companies realized that selling off their timberlands in million-acre deals returned greater profit than cutting the timber. Two years earlier, a U.S. Forest Service report, *Forests on the Edge,* estimated an area the size of all New England over the next thirty years would likely undergo a "dramatic increase in housing development," almost all of it in the eastern half of the nation.

As I write these words, anyone sharing in a group pension plan likely has some stake in the wholesale realty divestitures of eastern forests from Maine to Florida, and it is not easy to step away from complicity in the deforestation that divestment encourages. If a portfolio contains a TIMO (Timber Investment Management Organization) or a REIT (Real Estate Investment Trust), it is almost certainly taking hefty profits through selling not trees but the lands they grow on to high-bidding companies ready to bulldoze forests for vacation homes, golf resorts, waterslides, tract housing, and the whatnots that go with such things.

By preserving an ecological core and lumbering only on the perimeter, it may be possible to manage large tracts of timber for both "sustainable forestry" and the native diversity underpinning the survival of species, including the human. With a central wilderness to support them, moose and black bear and their associates may be able to withstand the aftereffects of chain saws, but against the asphalt and concrete world of franchised chains, they haven't a chance. A cutover woodland in time can often recover, but a built-over forest is forever lost. For a while, in the North Woods, land ownership, even more than invasive species, will be *the* issue deciding what future men and moose, realty agents and ravens, will find there.

Near the joining of the Allagash River with the St. John on the border of New Brunswick, we left the forest about sundown and headed to Fort Kent for the night. By then I knew a better way to see the North Maine Woods, at least for now, was from a canoe on a lake or the Allagash River, and that was as it should be: in this era of cushioned travel, wilderness needs to be earned. Our passage through the great Woods had been too easy, but it was still sufficient to reveal the potential loss of something priceless getting priced out of existence by short-term profiteers.

We hadn't seen much of what Thoreau reports in *The Maine Woods,* and for a while I thought the place one more I had reached too late. But then I considered travelers a generation or two hence: What would they find there? Would it be disastrously reduced even further? Or was there a possibility they might see a returning forest to surpass what we saw?

When we went into the Woods, there were still many people alive who knew the Allagash country before there was anything like a state park, a game preserve, a protected reserve, or a conservation easement in or adjacent to it. Take those changes away, and what would remain there today? The question of how much more will be allowed to remain — which direction the teeter-totter future will tip — has been passed on down to us, and Thoreau offered a solution: "Cast your whole vote, not a strip of paper merely, but your whole influence."

A couple of months prior to his first journey into upper Maine, he spent a night in jail for refusing to pay a poll tax. There's a well-known story, perhaps doctored, that nevertheless makes a point: When his friend Ralph Waldo Emerson visited the jail, he asked, "Henry, why are you here?" And Thoreau is said to have answered, "Why are you *not* here?"

That evening at supper I told the waitress her crimson blouse and lavender headband helped brighten a night turned again to drizzle, and she said, "I grew up across the river in Canada. Canadians don't do gaudy — we do genteel." Pointing out the window toward the terminus of U.S. 1, the other end some two-thousand miles south in Key West, she said, "But I lived for a while just down the road — down in Miami. I guess Florida de-genteeled me." Q said, "You traded the Maine Woods for South Florida?" And the waitress said, "Not for long."

After she brought our supper, she asked what we were doing so far from home, and I explained how we'd taken the entire longest day of the year to drive the hundred-and-some miles from Millinocket up through the Allagash to arrive at her table. "Why would you do that?" she said, then, catching herself, "Oh, by accident — you got lost." Q said, "That's half right."

The next morning when I was transcribing notes from my memoranda pad into my logbook, I came upon a notation I'd made in Maine two days earlier when I saw a sign in front of a house where dilapidation was about to yield to collapse: *GOD STILL PLANS TO MAKE FARMINGTON HIS NEW JERUSALEM*. Reading my note, I realized I'd been remiss in not stopping to talk with someone who knew the mind of God. I might have learned whether the Divine Plans include a review of the original purpose of the North Maine Woods. If not, it looked like it would be up to us. I think that's what Raven whispered.

V.
Into the Northwest

The Northern Plains & Near West

1 Columbia, Missouri
2 Kansas City, Missouri
3 Last Chance, Colorado
4 Buffalo, Wyoming
5 Orofino, Idaho
6 Bicknell, Utah

Into the Northwest

"May No One Say to Your Shame
All Was Beauty Here Till You Came"

Beautiful as the transparent thin air shows all distant objects, we have never found the great western prairies equal to the flowery descriptions of travelers. They lack the pure streamlet wherein the hunter may assuage his thirst, the delicious copses of dark, leafy trees; and even the thousands of fragrant flowers, which they are poetically described as possessing, are generally of the smaller varieties; and the Indian who roams over them is far from the ideal being — all grace, strength, and nobleness in his savage freedom — that we from these descriptions conceive him. Reader, do not expect to find any of the vast prairies that border the upper Missouri or the Yellowstone rivers, and extend to the Salt Lakes amid the Californian range of the Rocky Mountains, versant pastures ready for flocks and herds, and full of the soft perfume of the violet. No; you will find an immense waste of stony, gravelly, barren soil stretched before you; you will be tormented with thirst, half-eaten up by stinging flies, and lucky will you be if at night you find wood and water enough to supply your fire and make your cup of coffee; and should you meet a band of Indians, you will find them wrapped in old buffalo robes, their bodies filthy and covered with vermin, and by stealing or begging they will obtain from you perhaps more than you can spare from your scanty store of necessaries; and armed with bows and arrows or firearms, they are not unfrequently ready to murder, or at least rob you of all your personal property, including your ammunition, gun, and butcher knife!

— John James Audubon & the Reverend John Bachman,
The Quadrupeds of North America,
1854

Only to the white man was nature a wilderness and only to him was the land infested with wild animals and savage people. To us it was tame. Earth was bountiful and we were surrounded with the blessing of the Great Mystery. Not until the hairy man from the east came and with brutal frenzy heaped injustices upon us and the families that we loved was it wild for us. When the very animals of the forest began fleeing from his approach, then it was for us the Wild West began.

— Ota K'te (Luther Standing Bear),
Land of the Spotted Eagle,
1933

❧ 1 ❧

Out There Beyond Last Chance

A s a physiographic region, the Great Plains are — by an archaic
description — a land of little topographical relief; but for me,
as a topography of the mind, they are forever a place of considerable relief. Entering from the east, I come into them relieved of ever-
increasing human congestion, and entering from the west, I reach
them pleased to leave behind horizons congested by mountain roads
impeded with twisted curves. When I see the grand openness lying
immensely ahead, my response is: And now for some *plain* sailing!
Crossing the Plains is like reading a nineteenth-century Russian
novel: you begin hopefully only to reach the end (if you do) muttering weak huzzahs and vowing once is enough.

So, as always, I looked forward to the Great Plains when Q and I set
out a few days before the arrival of autumn. We made a stop in Kansas
City to attend the fiftieth reunion of my class of '57, one event held
at Southeast High School where I'd not set foot for half-a-century. It
was happenstance during my teenage years that Gus Kubitzki lived
only a couple of blocks away and directly in line with the front doors
of the school. Having heard on our excursions enough about Gus to
feel she had met him somewhere along the way, Q wanted to see his
hand-built bungalow in order to have a sense of the man beyond
my stories of him. I have waited until this moment to tell you, road-
worthy reader, a few facts about him so that he might first emerge in
your imagination fleshed out with your colorations. All I want to do
now is top those off, perhaps expand and refine them a smidgen for
you and let you see that he is not an anonym.

Gus Kubitzki in 1955.

To clarify any misperception of his Slavic surname, he described himself — unequivocally — as of Prussian descent. Although born in Ohio, he often tossed at me simple old-world phrases, a bold thing in the '40s, when the Third Reich was still fresh enough in all our minds for German words to send a chill. He was tall for his time, broad-shouldered, with strong arms and large hands. In the early years of the twentieth century, he was a pitcher for a semiprofessional baseball team in Cleveland, if I remember correctly. When he was born, home plate was not a pentagon but a simple square, a batter got four strikes, a base on balls counted as a hit, and catchers wore no shin guards.

As we would toss a baseball back and forth, Gus often told me about games he played years earlier, about crazy plays, lucky bounces, a "home run" he hit no farther than three feet but that the catcher pounced on and threw into a cabbage patch beyond right field. Especially, he talked about striking out a pitcher named George who swung a good stick: "He never got the bat off his shoulder on the first strike. Strike two was a big curve the catcher couldn't even handle. And, on the third pitch, down he went on a slow ball right over the plate." I knew each throw, and I'd mouth the result along with Gus, but I wasn't smart enough to pick up why he kept retelling the story, especially since the kid, a pitcher, was eight years younger. But after a while I began to suspect there was something behind the repetitions, a detail I was supposed to discover. One day he called the player Herman, and I said I thought his name was George. "George Herman," Gus said.

On a warm August afternoon in 1948, as he threw me a few dawdling curves, his Sunday cigar in a holder clenched between his teeth, he once again told the strikeout story but concluded it this time with "Herman died yesterday. It made the front page." *Yeah, yeah,* I thought. That evening I pulled a *Kansas City Times* from the box where we kept them for the annual Boy Scout newspaper drive. On the front page was a small headline, something like: BABE RUTH DIES. Great Scott! I'd been catching curves from an arm that once whiffed George Herman Ruth.

Perhaps because of that feat — or maybe because Gus's name was also William — he was the only person other than an aged Sunday-school teacher I allowed to call me Billy. And why not? Here was a Nestor who could pop a boy's catcher's mitt.

Once again, abiding reader, I've let my story tumble forward too fast, eager as I am to tell it to you.

A few years after the death of my maternal grandfather — a man who tossed out not curves but tales of the Spanish-American War — Gus, a widower, wedded my grandmother, a marriage we all honored. My mother and her sisters loved him, although he had a habit, said one aunt, that came straight from Satan: at the supper table, during our standard-to-the-point-dozen-word-plus-*Amen* grace, Gus did not bow his head. He looked directly forward as if staring something down. At age eight I loved that moment because I was sure heavenly remonstrance sooner or later would happen right there over the Sunday chicken and dumplings — probably nothing dramatic like his forehead suddenly sprouting horns, but maybe a warning shot, like his pupils turning into vertical slits. Such flagrance in the face of Powers Eternal, *that* just had to be asking for it. Then again, a man who could whiff the Babe might also be able to slip a fast one past a deity or two.

The way things turned out, nothing at all occurred, and Gus's years exceeded those of all but one of my blood ancestors; what's more, as he of generous heart aged, I saw the grip of the Devil loosen in my brain until I no longer believed there was a Devil to grip anybody's brain. So you see, had young William Kubitzki not one afternoon fanned the Bambino, my theological notions might today have quite a different cast, and this book might be a tract about sin and redemption. But then again, maybe it is.

I tell these few things about Gus because Q once said I traveled as if he were in the backseat. I don't believe his revenant ever was, but he indeed has done many miles in the back of my head, including more than I can account for in crossing the Great Plains by each of its major auto routes, a number of those passages made solo, a condition almost necessitating voices in the back of one's head. It's good for sanity to traverse the Plains with a companion (even if your own memory) who can tell stories. Should you have ever crossed with children (in the days before electronic distractions), you may remember the value of a tale, no matter where it ranged on the whopper index: my father once got me through two Kansas counties (and into a hell of a nightmare) with one about a boy forced by Old Man Grimsley to bury Mrs. Grimsley's severed arm which for months afterward would drag itself from the grave each Wednesday night to hunt for the soft throat of the boy who could chokingly tell the appendage where the rest of the body was. A shrewd parent knows monotony is not a physiographic fact but a mental condition, something the Great Plains teach, as does the open sea.

On one eastward crossing, I stopped near the western edge in Last Chance, Colorado. At the café counter was a woman heading to her home along the Front Range. When I asked how the town got its name, she said, "It used to be the last chance to fill your tank or get a soda pop, but the real reason if you ask me is that it's your last chance to turn back before you get way the devil *out there.*" With the last two words, she waved her arm eastward all the way to Missouri. I said I liked it *out there.* "So do I," she clarified. "It always reminds me how much I love trees." Here was a woman who might like a bald man just for making her thankful for a hairy husband. Her point, nevertheless, stands: who can doubt deprivation being a keen intensifier of appreciation?

The Great Plains seem destined to be misperceived and consequently misunderstood by any traveler arriving with assumptions and myths rather than with eyes and mind open. If we've at last gotten beyond the early description — the Great American Desert — we've still not entirely escaped a frequent conflation of two homonyms: *plain* and *plane*. The expectation of finding a realm of two dimensions (which at times can even look like a place of one dimension — that of *across*) is likely to fulfill itself, because the third dimension of height often seems measurable only with a micrometer.

In truth, no matter how difficult we find them to perceive, there are assuredly three dimensions *out there*. I would even argue there is also a fourth: rare is the traveler who can cross without occasionally tapping a watch to see if it's stopped.

The other homonym, *plain,* is also misleading, tinged as its dozen or so meanings are with inaccuracy and negativity: (1) unobstructed; (2) uncomplicated; (3) unmixed; (4) undecorated; (5) unpretentious; (6) neither beautiful nor ugly; (7) not hard to comprehend; (8) not unusual. Only the first term has a tincture of accuracy, and I think it's the meaning white Americans had in mind when they first encountered the vastness some two centuries ago. On a clear day — even in the pollution-dimmed skies of our time — if you are on a rise (like the back of a pickup), you may be able to see forty miles around. Were you on a horse or behind a team of oxen heading westward in 1848, you could see all the way into your next week.

I'm speaking here of the *view* being unobstructed. To set foot onto the Plains is to find obstructions beyond measure: rocks, cacti, gullies and gulches invisible until you reach their edges, quicksand, and rivers too dry for a raft and too damp for feet. But the greatest obstruction is not on the ground — it lies in the mind where the potential for a collapse of resolution is there at every moment, as the traveler sees ahead only more of what lies behind.

Walt Whitman said the Plains were a land to "test propositions," such as (say I) the proposition that your desire is sufficiently strong to reach the other side of a place comprising about a fifth of the forty-eight states. Other propositions also have been tested there, with failure the result as often as otherwise. An institution carried beyond the ninety-seventh meridian is certain to get changed, often vanishing through either withering or transformation: plows, crops, hats, laws, faiths, attitudes, words. The Plains are the greatest terrestrial transformative force within America, and they are the only region to broadly defeat us: we succeed in leveling mountains and forests, in damming rivers and killing lakes, but the Great Western Plains frequently best our tries at mastery. Like no other landform, they teach humility: they are a place to put hubris in *its* place. And because wisdom requires the vanquishing of vain pride, it is possible to love the Plains for that.

Walter Prescott Webb, in *The Great Plains,* wrote in 1931:

> East of the Mississippi civilization stood on three legs — land, water, and timber; west of the Mississippi, not one but two of these legs were withdrawn — water and timber — and civilization was left on one leg — land. It is small wonder that it toppled over in temporary failure.

I question only that penultimate word. It isn't failures that are temporary but rather many of the successes.

Americans first came onto the Plains with a sense of beauty influenced by European Romantic painters who revered verticality — the Alps, the Highlands, castle towers, church steeples, gorges, waterfalls, cliffs — and they demonstrated little appreciation for long and uninterrupted horizontals. Those explorers and traders couldn't see that the Great Plains were to become a distinctively diagnostic American landform, nor could they realize then, compared to a grand savanna, the coasts and mountains of the world were common as tenpenny nails.

Show a German or Japanese two pictures: one of a windmill against a long and level horizon, and a second of, perhaps, the New Jersey shore, and ask him which photograph "says" America.

I'm not representing myself as a plainsman, because I'm only a passer-through that territory: my longest stay has never exceeded a month, but I've been there in heat and blizzard, drought and flood, I've been there in storms of lightning and thunder, wind, rain, hail, ice, snow, and dust. Authentic American weathers. I've walked the ground, photographed a prairie fire from the inside, ridden the Plains on a horse, slept on them, and studied on them, and I cherish them and do not want to live there.

For me, the High Country is a broken wilderness, although in places it remains wilderness enough. When I make a crossing now, I no longer look glumly on abandoned and dessicated barnyards, schoolhouses, churches, gas stations, and sometimes even an entire Main Street overgrown and all but gone — like Kanona in north-western Kansas where my mother came from (a tree growing inside the old vault of the unroofed bank). In county after county across the Plains, the American economic experiment failed within a gen-eration or two, yet the tribal peoples there have lasted for more than five-hundred generations, in part because they understood the Plains demand either nomadism — like the totemic bison — or provident moderation, especially in the use of water. The place challenges Amer-ican economics because it will not long tolerate overload.

The dust bowl years were a result of a ten-foot-deep carpet of grasses getting torn loose and the great engine of the Plains — wind — picking up and hauling Kansas and Oklahoma and eastern Colorado elsewhere. In the late '80s, I spent seven years writing a book about a single county on the tallgrass prairie of Kansas. In one interview, a woman rancher said, "Rip out the carpet, and the boots are soon wearing a hole in the parlor floor." If farmers today turn the soil more wisely, they drill ever deeper into it to suck the aquifer to grow crops properly belonging in Ohio or Mississippi; if ranchers have seen the consequences of overgrazing, they neverthe-less run cattle on land barely capable of supporting skinny-legged pronghorn. The injudicious American "experiment" on the Plains is not yet over, and young citizens alive as I write these words will see even more of it continue to fail until our goal becomes not voracious mastery but circumspect harmony.

Some inhabitants live on the Plains out of necessity, some out of inertia, but others abide because they want to dwell under a sky so deep on a clear night you can still see all the way to the beginning of the universe, and it seems then you can breathe in the cosmos directly; they are people able to tolerate winters that look not like a season but extinction.

Those natives must lead the rest of us in comprehending the Great Plains, that seemingly boundless and distinctive place (to return to homonymic meanings) of mixed and innumerable complications, often decorated (especially in spring), frequently beautiful *and* ugly, always difficult to comprehend spatially and temporarily, as ready to excel at obstructing human passage and plans as they are to bring forth some of the most pretentious cloud formations on earth.

Primitive societies recognize, for one reason or another, forbidden lands, but in America, such a concept can be the very reason for intrusion or invasion, and in a landscape appearing limitless, to speak about limits can turn some citizens choleric. If a place exists in nature, so they believe, then it's out there for the taking. But the *plain* fact is, the Plains foil and stymie, and they are always ready to make a fellow run for cover where there is none, and that's why they are great.

I meet Americans elsewhere who think the Plains are emptying, and perhaps that's true in Thunder Hawk and White Earth and Haydraw and Windhorst and Circle Back (five miles from Needmore), but in Lubbock, Oklahoma City, Wichita, Bismarck, and dozens of other cities *out there,* populations continue to rise. People aren't leaving the Plains so much as they are clustering, concentrating, redistributing themselves into sprawl around urban edges. Even Wyoming of the great vacancies has more residents than a decade ago. Across the grand American champaigns, Plains folk are doing what their cattle do in the face of a storm: rambling to a place to hunker down. Maybe you make it through the night, and maybe you don't.

⋎ 2 ⋏

The Widow's Man

WERE TRAVELING CHILDREN TO HAVE an encompassing conception of space, time, *and* a capacity for patience, then that eternal question "Are we there yet?" might scarcely exist in their instantaneous world. For an adult air traveler, arrival is clearly defined and the *yet* has the promise of termination: you get in a machine, it moves, you get out of the machine, and you're there — or nearly so. For a long-distance land traveler, even an adult, arrival is not only more drawn out but more problematic: if it's not an address, the exact location of *there* can become a question without certain answer. Like our march toward earthly finality, arrival by road comes only incrementally, with a mile here, an hour there, a night someplace else. Approach is more than just the last phase before arrival — it's at the heart of a true journey and one aspect separating real travelers from mere arrivalists whose highest wish is for destination.

When I'm on the road, I often measure distance from my journey's end not in miles but by indicators. I've already mentioned or implied geographic lines of black-eyed peas and green chile and corner-grocery grinders, but of course those "lines" are even less than imaginary because territory changes gradually like a seaward-flowing river losing its freshness to brackishness before becoming salt water in another realm.

Those three indicators all happen to be culinary, but intimations, of course, can appear in other ways: the shape of a barn roof, the style of a pasture fence, what's considered a weed, what's taken for granted, the length of a vowel, or whether an *R* appears where it shouldn't be or disappears where it should remain. And certainly, there's that loveliest of signposts: the native willingness to chat with a traveler.

On the Great Plains, I always know I'm entering the West when I see a recumbent horizon of 360 degrees. But there are other signs too: sagebrush, tumbleweed, mounted jackalopes in taverns, loping pronghorns (called by Westerners *antelope,* which they properly are not any more than a bison is a buffalo or a chile pepper a chili). Even more totemic to my eye, though, is a crooked juniper fence-post topped with a magpie. If magpies could truly speak (instead of just garbling along in mock English), and were I to ask one of them, "Are we West yet?" it would say, "You bet your boots, brother." (About the magpie, I'll say more anon.)

You'll note in my Great Plains identifiers nothing remotely culinary. If we exclude beef and potatoes and possibly pie, the Plains are a great American desert when it comes to the table. The nineteenth-century necessity of stretching out a supply of coffee beans to get over the Oregon Trail, for one example, apparently permanently affected and infected not just a cup of joe but also most of the comestibles. Beer? On the Plains, the only hops you'll find are on a playground. Mixed drinks? Order a cocktail (if you dare) in Broken Bow or Lusk, and after the bartender dopes out how to make it, you'll need to explain why a nightly martini is doctor's orders and that you don't mind if it's in a beer glass; you may then want to stare down anyone who heard you. Other than putting tomato juice into Budwater beer, a manly fellow drinks only what's taken straight out of a bottle, and if his potion is distilled, it will have to come from a grand selection of four or five choices behind the bar; in the northern Plains, two of those will be schnapps, regular and flavored (expect butterscotch).

In certain agricultural areas, the recent influx of Hispanic labor has raised possibilities of a toothsome meal, but beware: so-called Tex-Mex lends itself to victuals coming from a box or carton. If the sign outside does *not* use the word *authentic,* if the salsa was made that morning in the kitchen and includes fresh cilantro, and if the only blue eyes in the place belong to customers, then there's a chance of good eating. Often I have to cross the High Country on big breakfasts and milk shakes.

After three days on the Plains, Q and I had passed through Nebraska and on into Wyoming where we found our way to Buffalo and the Occidental Hotel of 1880 right on Main Street and smack along Clear Creek. The Occidental was a long, brick building — actually three linked ones — of two storeys and a lobby with a hearth, a mounted elk-head, a framed Navajo blanket, and a wooden-cabinet radio wafting out Guy Lombardo. It was one of those places a visitor will later describe with a sentence beginning, "It was one of those places."

Down a short hallway from the lobby was the saloon which, even without a stuffed jackalope, made this clear: "If it's the West you're after, bub, then you're there." Although needing none, a bonus in the Occidental Hotel was a well-stocked, second-floor library of real books — not condensed novels or broken sets of cheap encyclopedias or official state-manuals or thirty-year-old textbooks. Just down the hallway and around the corner was our room (in fact, a trio of small linked rooms ending with a claw-foot bathtub). On the radio, a model that likely announced the death of Franklin Roosevelt, the Sons of the Pioneers warbled out "Cool Water." Later, from the tub, I heard a warbling Q:

> *All day I face*
> *The barren waste,*
> *Without the taste*
> *Of water, cool water.*
> *Ol Dan and I*
> *With throats burned dry*
> *And souls that cry,*
> *For water,*
> *Cool, clear water.*

Her Ol Dan invited her to quench a thirst down below at the brass rail in the saloon and across from the player piano and under the glassy gazes of twenty-one mounted trophy-heads or skulls. In a far corner was a poker table covered in green felt and, above it, bullet holes requisite in such a room.

Q said, "Well, Ol Dan, are we there yet?" We were so much *there* we decided to stay a few days to walk around Buffalo, population something more than four-thousand souls, hang out in the library, walk down Main to the soda fountain, hang out in the library, walk up Main to a plate of chop suey, hang out in the library, and at sunset join the menagerie of taxidermied ungulates for conversation with whatever cowpoke — genuine or sham — wandered in for a toothful of Old Tickler. On one of those evenings when no one wandered in but an osculatory twosome, I told Q a Wyoming story that for a while disturbed her.

About a decade earlier I'd laid up a few days at a former sheep-ranch in the northeast corner of the state where I'd hoped to find a little isolation so I could figure out the organization of a book I wanted to write about the tallgrass prairie. On that count my progress got slowed because I met Max Dwightman (as I'll call him). What I set before you now comes from notes I wrote after two evenings with him, the first in a parlor corner where a body could find a taste of Admiral Foghorn 1843, and the second on a long, wooden porch good for listening to coyotes and owls, with a glass of diddle at hand. The dark remoteness promoted reflection.

Because it would not have been appropriate — as you'll see — to jot down notes and also because I was slow to realize the quozzical import in Dwightman's words, I could only soon afterward outline memos. What I write now is my close paraphrase of his story, minus his repetitions and stumbles as he found his way along. I'm going to put some of his words inside quotation marks with the understanding I'm re-creating his voice as accurately as I'm able. I've changed all the surnames and avoided most place-names.

Around the ranch were a few old cabins, each with a sagging porch, sagging floor, sagging bed, sagging divan, and sagging and dusty curtains; the only thing without sag was a hard chair and, from an old hotel lobby, an ink-splotched oak escritoire once stocked with imprinted stationery, envelopes, scratchy pen, and ink pot. In all the cabins, it was the only desk. I hoped the antique drippages might encourage a few creative dribblings into my notebooks. Trying to scribble at the table, I studied its stains as if they were little Rorschachs holding clues to creative patterns; I stared out the window, read on the divan, walked into the dry hills thick with the scent of ponderosa resin warmed by the afternoon sun. In other words, I did what I could to *act* like a writer. When the old word magic isn't going well, sometimes it can help just to pretend.

In the evening I'd go down to the former ranch-house for a seat in a corner, and from somewhere a Shoshone woman soon would come forth unbidden and, saying not a word, wait for my request for a Bourbon and jigger of water. I do not ever try to write alongside alcohol, but of an evening I may take a peg and let my mind graze in green pastures as if words were woollies. Sometimes a notion gets legs and stands up like a newborn lamb ready to gambol. Sometimes, but not then.

My second night there, a man came in and sat unnecessarily near. He wasn't a handsome man, but he had stately features: with a bleached rag mop on his head, he could have stood as George Washington on the American Legion float in a Fourth of July parade. He was wearing denim pants with sharp creases, his boots were shined, his white shirt in a Western cut and perfectly pressed right down to the fraying cuffs. His thick hair was at midpoint between dark and silver. He was slender, clean-shaven, and the nails on his fingers were immaculate and trimmed short. He was — as I was to learn — nearly seventy, and he had served with the Army in Korea during the war and been wounded there. After years in the Southwest, he had recently returned to Wyoming to look for a couple of acres where he could set up a house trailer.

When his whiskey arrived, he rolled the glass to warm it, then put it down and, ignoring my fake scribbles meant to show I was occupied, spoke that dreaded sentence: "I hear you're a book writer." Not now, I said. It's not going so well. "I'm writing up my life," he said. I thought, *Oh god! Please don't ask me to read your manuscript.*

He continued, "I haven't actually put the words down on paper yet, but I'm writing it in my head. Once I figure it all out, that's when I'll find somebody to type it up. I mean, anybody can write a book." *(You bet — now see how anybody does getting anybody to publish it.)* I nodded and, my own manuscript struggles making me churlish, ungenerously said that a manuscript was not a book. Nevertheless, he turned his chair toward me. It would take open rudeness to discourage this man.

"My dad told me on more than one occasion, I'm quoting him, 'Your old pa wasn't never nothing but a no-count nobody. But don't you be one too.' I've worked hard not to."

With that, I made a real note — setting down exactly his father's advice. Taking notes without permission can sometimes silence a talker. The further he went on, though, the more my resistance failed.

He had grown up a hundred miles from the Wyoming ranch, attended public school nearby, and gone off for a year to a Colorado college to study physical therapy before returning home to help his family after a steer made his father a virtual invalid. Dwightman took a job in a Main Street hardware run by an elderly man (let him be Mr. Morgan) whose health was failing. Capable and honest, he soon won Morgan's trust and earned greater responsibility as the proprietor observed Dwightman's knack for satisfying customers, even those who came into Morgan's Hardware and Supply with a complaint. After a year, the trade was up by several hundred dollars, although a heart condition forced the old fellow to work less, doing only what he could from home where he was not recuperating but simply declining.

Dwightman began going by the Morgan house after work to report the day's custom and to see how he might help with whatever needed attention: hanging storm windows, taking down storm windows, trimming the hedge, the lawn, everything but Mrs. Morgan's roses. His presence seemed to steady the couple. At both the store and in their home, he became indispensable.

One spring evening, pulling Dwightman aside, Mr. Morgan explained he wanted him to take over the business. Max said to me, "I told him I was about to get married, and even without that I didn't have enough money to buy the store. And he told me, 'I'm not selling Morgan's Hardware — I'm giving it to you.' He told me to sit down so he could explain. It would come with a proviso, and that proviso was, after he was gone I was to share half the net with Mrs. Morgan and help her in any way I could. 'Whatever she needs,' he said. 'You understand? *Whatever.* You be her angel.'"

Dwightman took a couple of days to mull it over, to talk to his fiancée, before agreeing to accept the emporium with its proviso. Three weeks following the wedding, Mr. Morgan died. Each evening thereafter Dwightman continued to go by the house, and every two weeks he made the proper deposit to Mrs. Morgan's bank account. She was then in her early seventies and in good health, other than failing eyes and a little lumbago that a hot bath eased, but her progressive views and sardonic humor limited friendships in a small, conservative Wyoming town. Her opinions amused Max, and his amusement amused her; it was a good relationship.

On afternoons when there was no outside task for him, she served a cup of chamomile tea which, weak though it was, he didn't care for, but his respect for her led him to feign enjoyment. One day a few months after Mr. Morgan's death, as Dwightman was about to leave the house, he asked his usual question, if there was anything else he could do, and she said, "Yes, Maxwell, if you will." *Surely, Mrs. Morgan. Just name it.* She had slept in a position that had put a crick in her neck, and she could hardly turn her head to the left. With his training in physical therapy, maybe he could ease the stiffness. He folded a wet washcloth to make a warm compress and placed it on her neck, held it there for a few minutes, then, while she sat upright in a kitchen chair, gently kneaded her left trapezius until she could turn her head freely.

"It was tight as a guitar string," Dwightman said to me. "From then on, sometimes she called me 'Maxwell the Master.'"

A few months later, the local newspaper ran a piece about a big cut-rate mega-retailer beginning construction on a building a few miles away in an old pasture, and the next year the business opened. "We all saw it coming," Dwightman said, "but we didn't see how fast it would hit. That very first month, our trade was down, and it did nothing but go on down until we had to put our store up for sale. The price, when it finally came, it wasn't too good because everybody had lost faith in Main Street property." Mrs. Morgan received her half. Dwightman's share didn't last long, and he counted himself lucky only in that he and his wife had no children. "That was the first time I ever saw my Korean War injury do any good for me."

Once his money was gone, making his three years of invested work seem fruitless, he went to the megamart and came out with a job. "I was assistant to the assistant manager in the automotive and hardware section. Having to wear that blue jacket just plain shamed me. The worst was, with it on, I had to face my former customers. I'm talking about a lot of people who quit our store to save a penny on the dollar. I used to ask myself how I could feel shame in front of people who left me high and dry."

After a year in the blue coat, he came home one night to find the kitchen table bare and his wife sitting stiffly at it. He thought someone must have died. She said — when annoyed she always called him by his surname — "Dwightman, I can't go on like this. There's no money, the town gives us nothing but pity, and those are the same damn people who caused you to fail. And on top of it all, I have a half man. What do you expect?"

He said he'd been looking into a job at an airplane plant down in Kansas, and she said, "Like hell I'm moving to Kansas." *Then what if* — "It's no use," she said. "I want out." The next morning she was gone, and his letters suggesting this or that to her she ignored, and at last he realized the main thing she wanted away from was Max Dwightman.

Over the succeeding three months, his distracted performance almost caused him to lose his job, and he probably would have had not Mrs. Morgan steadied him as he'd earlier steadied her. She told him several times, "Maxwell, keep the hinges oiled, and the door one day will swing open." She continued to pour him chamomile tea, and he even began to enjoy it, or maybe it was just the conversation along with it, conversations unlike any he'd ever had with his wife. "Mrs. Morgan came to know me well," he said. "Even about my war disability. And when I'd mention my dad saying he wasn't never nothing but a no-count nobody, she'd tell me, 'Don't you believe it about yourself, Maxwell. Honesty and faithfulness have never been not nothing.'"

It took him almost two hours to relate those events, even though I had the feeling it was only half the story. Then, without warning he drained his second glass and said, "I'm getting stiff in the knees. Time to get up," and he did. He looked at me, his first close look. "You're a polite listener," he said, and left.

The next morning when I went out for a walk, I noticed by the door a rock holding down a slip of paper, and on it was "I'll be on the porch tonight. If you want, I'll tell you how the hinges got oiled. Your glass is on me."

3

How Max Oiled the Hinges

MAX DWIGHTMAN WAS A STORYTELLER lacking vivid turns of phrase and humorous twists (other than a few inadvertent double entendres), having only a gift of methodical clarity, yet in his words and even more in his face were hints of something beyond a tale of divorce and job loss. Having come to believe perhaps I should listen to his tale rather than study ink splotches on a desk, that evening I went to find him on the porch. The Indian woman appeared — again unbidden — and stood in her usual wordless wait until Dwightman asked her to bring us two whiskeys, but he said nothing more until she returned and he thanked her in Shoshone, yet still she did not speak. Then to me he said, "Her name means 'Talk-Talk Girl.' And her nickname means 'Little Magpie.' But what I call her means 'Pretty Night-Woman.'"

He lifted his glass. I mentioned I'd seen a couple of pronghorn that morning, and he answered, "There are more now than when I was a boy. I love antelope. In Wyoming, wildlife is called game — you know, Game and Fish Department. I could shoot you before I could take one of them. They have the most beautiful dark eyes — those long lashes. A lonely sheepherder could fall in love with one. And I'll tell you this — take a look at that backside. Sweetest rump in the West. There's a tale for your next book."

I said I had the feeling last night he had a story that went beyond afternoons with Mrs. Morgan. "She was a fine woman," he said. "If she'd been younger —" He stopped, lifted his whiskey, and took his time before saying brokenly, "When I was in Korea — that injury —

438

it was a groin injury. I didn't lose any body parts, but I lost some function in some parts."

Again he stopped. I think he was deciding how — or even whether — to go on. Then he continued, uncertainly and at times fumblingly. "Mrs. Morgan was thirty years older than me, but I think I might not be around today if I didn't ever get to know her. I don't mean her financial help so much, because it was more than that. She was a pretty woman, the kind that a few age lines in a face seem to improve. Whenever I said hello or good-bye, I gave her a heartfelt hug, and sometimes I wanted to hold her longer. And I think now she wouldn't have said no. But to risk disrespect or scare her — that, I couldn't do.

"She knew my history, all about my crappy marriage and the way the Korean War messed it up. And I've got to tell you this — I told her my injury made me a master in other ways. I mean, I *did* have training in physical therapy. But that didn't matter to my wife."

He called out something in Shoshone, and the woman appeared, and he raised his empty glass. He sat quietly until he had a new whiskey, then he spoke again in Shoshone to the woman, words that pleased her. "Excuse me," he said, "but I need some courage to talk about some of this stuff.

"Where was I?" Therapy, I said. "Therapy, yes. One evening after I rehung her screen door and oiled the hinges, she said, 'See what I mean about doors?' I don't know if it made much sense then, but I agreed. And she called me in to tea, and we sat down, and she said, 'Try to follow me here, Maxwell. Mister Morgan' — she always referred to him as Mister Morgan around me — 'his health emasculated him in his last years. He was never difficult as he declined, but he just wasn't really here. Now, not every woman needs a man — especially in her later years — but more of us do than young people realize. It's sort of a national secret.' And she stopped there to give me time to catch on.

"Then she told me how her bridge ladies — they were all widows — how they talked during the game about their health and how a couple of them mentioned looking forward to their annual women's exams. You know, for women's health. There was a doctor over in Sheridan that seemed to understand all that, and he always some way added a few extra movements with his hands and sort of stretched out the exam without ever really crossing the line. She said he was good but had retired."

At that point, Dwightman took a swallow and commented how it was a warm night for the season. Then he said, "I should have told you before — my neck massages had more or less progressed to back and chest massaging, even though she was always seated in a kitchen chair and was clothed. She was always fresh out of a hot bath to loosen her joints. You know, to relax her muscles. She smelled of lavender soap. Her housedress was always fresh too.

"On one afternoon as I was working on her shoulders, she said, 'Maxwell, stop for a moment. I want to talk about something.' So I did. She got up and went to the sofa and sort of reclined out like a lady of leisure. She said, 'Let me tell you more about us old gals. You listen up now. You men die on us, and before a lot of you die, you're already dead from the navel down. Where does that leave us?' "

Dwightman began struggling to express to me all that Mrs. Morgan had said, but what it came down to was this: After a woman loses her husband, she may find herself living somewhere between loneliness and relief at his passing. She can miss his contributions and at the same time be happy to be shut of his male stuff — obtuseness, poor listening, self-gratifying sexual demands *or* sexual incapacities attendant with age and disease. Some of those widows, once free, did not want a second or third marriage to someone else who would only end up dying on them. Between the burden of a man and a no-man's-land, there should be another choice. I don't think Dwightman was punning when he said, "Mrs. Morgan made it clear there was a gap to fill."

To a coyote howl, he called a Shoshone word into the darkness, and there followed a silence, then a yipping of several voices, and he smiled. "They speak Shoshone. Around here anyway."

He returned to his story. "When Mrs. Morgan finished what she wanted to tell me, she asked, 'Do you know what I'm saying?' I was afraid to answer. She said, 'Speak up, Maxwell,' and I said I didn't know, and she reprimanded me. 'Sure you do. You've told me many times you'd do whatever you could to help out in this house, and now I want to call in that pledge.'

"I was scared all to hell. She said, 'It's all right,' and she sort of motioned me toward the sofa. 'Come over here to the couch and put your hand under my shift and continue your very effective therapy.'

"I just stood there. She said real sweet, 'Come along now. You're a professional, and you have a patient.' She was as cool as could be, but I was shaking so much I thought I might have to leave, but I made it over to her. She pointed to a jar of unguent and closed her eyes, and I — you know — I reached up under her housedress, and I closed my eyes too, and I did as she asked."

Here Dwightman again fell silent, and I dared not speak until the silence became uncomfortable. I said so softly I'm not sure he heard me, And? "Oh," he said, "the therapy was successful, and it continued more or less weekly for the next couple of years, even after her eyesight was almost gone. At a completion, I'd pull an afghan over her to leave her to a comfortable nap. I did everything I could to make it professional.

"Then she began to fail. It happened so fast there wasn't even time for a nursing home. When they put her in the ambulance, the last thing she said to me was 'Maxwell, you're the best of men.' She didn't make it through to morning."

He cleared his throat and said he'd like another whiskey, but he'd better not, because there was more to tell and he didn't want to muddle it. I hadn't touched mine. The sky in that remote piece of Wyoming was a carbon black letting even the most feeble starlight shine through from far corners of the galaxy.

Dwightman said, "A week later Mrs. Morgan's lawyer called to tell me she'd left her entire estate to me. It wasn't big, but it was big enough I could do what I'd wanted for a while. I turned in that god-damn blue coat and went out and bought a pickup and put a camper shell on it, and I took off. I needed to figure out two things — what I was good for and where I could live to be good for something and not be a no-count nobody."

For six months Dwightman roamed around the West — this town, that one, none of them ideal. When his money was about gone, he became less finicky and settled on a place in Arizona where he found a house trailer for rent to satisfy his second question. The first was more difficult, but he thought he might have the answer.

"I love kids. I wanted to start a school, a day care. Early-education centers, they call them now. One for disadvantaged kids. It would focus on nature education, with several Indians as teachers. We would get the little ones outside and make the natural world a part of their lives. They'd learn the names of flowers and cacti — in fact, I wanted to call the center Kactus Kids, spelled with *K*s shaped like saguaros. They'd learn about spiders and lizards. And in the class-room they'd learn how to use their hands to make things like an Indian drum and how to imitate birdcalls — things Indians would teach them. Then later, as the school developed, they'd learn Span-ish — or English, as the case might be. But they'd never be allowed to forget the dirt under their feet. If you asked one of my kids where corn came from, he'd never say, like I heard a little boy one time, 'Out of a can, you dummy.' I wanted to reach city kids clueless about nature. I had a million ideas and about zero dollars."

To make friends, Dwightman joined a small, progressive church group with a weekly meeting led by any member willing to give a devotion or perhaps a talk without any particular religious focus. When it came his turn, he told them about his dream of Kactus Kids. By then, he'd found an empty lot for sale on the edge of the city, and he showed some snapshots of it: a weedy, rocky, ugly place but with open access to the desert behind. After the meeting, a woman came up to invite him for coffee the next morning.

"We talked about our histories. Mine was just no-count stuff, but hers was pretty colorful until she lost her husband, and her life sort of turned drab. She was especially interested in how I'd come to think up the center. She knew a Zuni man who would be perfect to teach elementary weaving, including to the boys too. You know, Zuni men do the weaving. Or they used to, anyway."

Several days later Dwightman received in the mail papers indicating she'd put down in his name a payment on the lot. There was a note from her saying now he had something tangible to lend credibility to his fund-raising. "I was fired up and went out and after a couple of months of soliciting, I made the first payment against the principal. But then things got tougher. The easy contributions were gone.

"The lady and I became friends. I helped her with chores, and she would bring me groceries. She said if I had to put on a blue coat again I'd never get the center built, so she'd make sure I had time to work on it. The next year, she had enough confidence in my plan to pay off the mortgage, not that it was all that much. And she paid for some dental work for me too."

That December she asked Dwightman to accompany her to a Christmas party. He liked the request because he had come to feel more comfortable with women his senior, and he enjoyed hearing about their lives. Most of them had stories. And for them, here was a handyman who could rewire a lamp or trim toenails or get a rattlesnake out of a garage.

He said, "I guess it was inevitable, but she and I got involved in a way something like with Mrs. Morgan. And like Mrs. Morgan, she was as generous as she could afford to be. She even paid a local builder to draw up blueprints for the center so I'd have another means to attract contributions — small as they were. On my birthday she said she might pay to start the building, but she thought, despite our age difference, maybe we should be married. I asked for a little time to think about it. I had nothing but bad memories of marriage, and I told her so. She said to take my time, she'd leave the offer open. So things went on. Then at dinner one night she told me she'd had a bad diagnosis and a worse prognosis. Now, marriage wouldn't be fair to me."

Dwightman paused again, collected himself. "Her treatments really flattened her, and the damn things didn't do one goddamn thing to help. She was just very sick from them. Then I lost her."

Putting everything on hold in Arizona, he went off in his pickup again, but the second time, his question had sharp focus: how could he make Kactus Kids a reality? "I knew the answer all along," he said. "I knew about oiling hinges to keep doors swinging open, but I didn't really like the answer. I mean, would you?"

I said I didn't think I knew what the answer was, and he said, "I could offer something people wanted, and Arizona has quite a few childless widows with estates they'll never use up. So why let bureaucrats and politicians get it? It's called escheatment, but it ought to be cheatment. And if it's not the bureaucrats, then it's some evangelist who's going to take the money and give not one damn thing in return except more requests for contributions, and that money will go to buy them a Cadillac. That dough's not going to help a little kid whose mom is a crackhead or whose dad is beating the family up."

He looked directly at me, I think to ascertain my response. "Sure — by then I knew the answer, and I knew without doing what I could do so well, the center wasn't ever going to get built."

Somewhere in California, Dwightman wheeled his truck around and returned to his trailer in Arizona and laid out his criteria as if they were part of a business plan: each widow would have to have some means but no children or at least no close contact with her children. "Everybody knows," he said, "a widow's kids watch her money like it's theirs." He would avoid anyone who no longer had concern for problems of this world, and there would be no spinsters because they had too little experience with men; romantic involvement would be verboten because each woman would have been told of his other "house calls." He had learned both his "Korean dysfunction" and the resulting mastery at physical therapy were assets giving him the equivalent to professional qualifications, and a woman was safe with him, and transmission of disease was impossible.

Dwightman had come to understand how loneliness can be deadly and how he could treat it. He developed a short list of clientele. He said, again intending no pun, "I never let there be more widows than I could handle. I knew their birthdays, favorite flowers, whether they liked to dance or play cards." Dwightman could sing a heart-tugging tenor rendition of "Danny Boy," but above all he knew what could make a woman smile. "For certain widows," he said, "I don't mind telling you, I was a dream come true."

He stared into the Wyoming night, and then, without a word, he pulled himself up slowly from his chair and walked off. I sat waiting. Then I figured, *That's that,* and got up to leave, when I saw him coming back. Even before he sat down again, he said, "One time a client referred to me as her 'escort,' and I told her that an escort uses the money for himself — or herself — but mine was going for a school for kids who needed a leg up. Oh, sure, I had to take some of the money to support myself, but living in a trailer and driving a ten-year-old pickup pretty well showed I wasn't spending much on me.

"My hope, of course, was always for significant contributions for the school — money that went beyond any rendered services. And that happened sometimes. I'd show the ladies the architectural sketch and take them out to the site, but some of them only cared about self-gratification, and if I saw that, I'd move on. And if I heard somebody complain about 'these damn kids today,' I'd close the account, so to speak. Understand, not every situation was what you might call intimately personalized.

"I believed there would come along somebody to step up big and build the school and endow it and let me put her name on it, and then I could give all my time to the real work. I had a couple of teachers lined up. I wrote up subject outlines. You should see the one I called 'Thinking Like a Hopi.' Everything in it was about balance, and nobody can teach that better than a Hopi, and I had the teacher for it too."

One September Dwightman met a woman, notably attractive and somewhat younger than usual but with the means to take the plan all the way. They got on well, oddly well because she was agreeable to everything, even to the point of immediately paying for a concrete understructure. The cement had hardly dried when she told him if her deceased husband's name was on the building and hers on the mortgage, she might underwrite the cost of the entire school.

At that point, Dwightman stopped once more. He motioned toward the sound of owl hoots, and he said, "Beautiful, but I don't think they speak Shoshone. Magpies do, though. I've heard them dress me down in Shoshone — from a safe distance."

And then he continued. "If the land title wasn't in my name, then I'd just be a blue coat employee again, so I had to question the offer. I mean, it looked like a little concrete got poured to hook me. Maybe I made the mistake of being too direct about my hesitation, because she got mad as hell. I'd never seen her like that. She walked out, accused me of manipulating *her*, and the next thing I know, she's threatening me with a lawsuit. Accusing me of being a grifter."

It was the first time I saw Dwightman show bitterness, and he had to take a moment to settle himself down. "Hell," he said, "even if I'd had the money to match her high-priced lawyer, my defense would be full of details no judge would accept. Who would understand my special line of work?" Here he repeated part of his story before finding his way back. "She sued me for the cost of the concrete, and I ended up having to hand over the lot. Six years of work — my whole dream — gone because I'd miscalculated one person's character.

"A month later I found out it had been a scheme all along, ever since plans for a new road that would go in down the hill got announced and suddenly gave that property real value. She was a front for a real-estate bunch. If only — *if only* I could have held on just a little longer, then *I* could have sold the land and somewhere else built the finest kids' center in the Southwest. If you go past my old lot sometime, you won't see any school. What you'll see is a big condo and a bunch of fat-cat snowbirds living there for a few weeks every winter. Some of them are widows, and I'll tell you, I've had ideas about starting again, but I'm too old. But I'll tell you this too — that woman slammed a door with oiled hinges the hell in my face. She broke my dream, and I failed my dad. I mean, what's the goddamn truth? I've never not been nothing but a no-count nobody, and now it's too late."

He stopped. The coyotes were really at it, and we listened. Then, so quietly I had to lean forward to hear him over the yipping, he said, "There for a while, don't you see, there for a while I came damn close to doing something."

Dwightman lifted his glass toward the sky and said, "Beware deceptive bastards out there," and he drained his whiskey. "Knees getting stiff," he said. "Time to walk," and walk off stiffly he did.

The next morning, under the rock doorstop was another message: "The story's yours if you want it. Maybe it can help somehow. But wait till I'm gone."

Did he mean *move on* or *die?* I went to his cabin. He'd moved on. Over the next several years I found no place for his story, but sometime later I phoned the ranch to get a lead on him. A woman said, "He checked out not long ago." I asked if he left an address. "I mean," she said, "he checked out for good. Cashed in feet first. I heard he's buried over west in the Bighorns."

⋋ 4 ⋌

Querencia

O N A FINE AUTUMNAL MORNING, Q and I left the Occidental Hotel to take up a wandering route into the Thunder Basin National Grasslands and on beyond. I was counting pronghorn as they appeared here and there, and she was turning in her mind legal aspects of Max Dwightman's life. She said, "I admire his goal of wanting to educate children in ways so many of them are missing out on now, but, I'll tell you, his method of raising money troubled me until I decided his means weren't *malum in se* — like murder, robbery, rape, arson, you know. They were closer to *malum prohibitum* — jaywalking, an uncut lawn, an overdue library-book." Raising her finger as if before a jury, she added, "By his testimony, he deceived nobody, and all activity was both consensual and mutually beneficial. So maybe it's just the unorthodoxy that bothered me."

She interrupted herself to point out a pronghorn on her side of the road. "How many does that make?" she said. Seventy-seven. "Their bodies seem too heavy for those skinny legs." They do indeed, but those bony gams, carved by generations of wolves' teeth, under a three-day-old pronghorn, can outrun the fastest human on earth. I told her what I'd read in the Occidental library: prior to the arrival of whites, there may have been forty-five-million of them, but by 1924 there were about fourteen thousand. Today, the estimate is a half million.

"I have a question about Max," Q said. "What did he mean when he told you maybe his story might help in some way?" I said I didn't know, but I was sure the answer had more to do with educating children than ministering to widows.

. . .

Bill, Wyoming, despite its highly excellent name, could serve as a lexicographer's illustrative definition of either *windblown* or *godforsaken* (the only "town" within four-thousand square-miles), although the lone store/tavern/café there did put together a good sandwich. North of Bill, Q asked, "What's it like to be a classic Don't-Blink-or-You'll-Miss-It?" (Story of my life.)

We entered the Thunder Basin and came upon gigantically awesome coal pits, one of them three-miles long and deep enough to bury a twenty-storey building without having to tip it over. We stopped alongside a railroad to watch two miles of coal hoppers roll past, trains so lengthy they frequently go uphill and downhill at the same time. One large power-generation plant in Georgia burned up two-thousand miles of coal every year, or to say it another way, that plant — five days distant — would consume ten-thousand linear-feet of sixty-million-year-old Wyoming in only eight hours. Over a year, that was thirty-four-thousand miles of Wyoming to be paid for not just in quick dollars but also in promissory notes for a warming climate generating violent weathers, rising oceans, and mass extinctions.

Along the road, I often try to visualize a landscape as it appeared a century or an aeon or a cataclysm ago, but in watching the coal move past us in almost morsel-sized pieces (if they were chops, a couple on a plate would make supper), I just couldn't imagine the ancient ferns and cycads and other Paleocene boscage they once were. I couldn't see their past. What I *did* see rolling along was the end of a current era: not ancient carboniferous Wyoming but rather chances measured in expiring time to reconfigure an economy — a way of life — not foreordained by its own principles to collapse.

[TO READER OF THE FUTURE — IF YOU'RE THERE: Let no one tell you otherwise — the word was out. We knew what we were doing, and as a society we went ahead and did it anyway. When it came to whistling past graveyards, we were talented.]

· · ·

Beyond the Thunder Basin coalfields, we came into the shallow valley of the Little Powder River rolling, as were we, toward Montana. At a distance, the grasslands were beautiful with the buffy colors of fall, but a closer look showed mile after mile of Wyoming chewed by cattle down to dust and broken rock. When the shoulder of a highway looks more naturally abundant than a thousand acres beyond, something is out of whack. Anyone who may have doubts that cattle-raising is an extractive industry — at least as it's widely practiced in eastern Wyoming by corporations, some of them foreign — should consider a little tour along Route 59. A popular chamber-of-commerce slogan at that time was "Wyoming — Open for Business!" (The Administration of intellectually incapable George W. Bush and his Wyoming-raised Vice President had recently proposed selling public lands to underwrite "deficit reduction": to pay for its corporation enrichments and its calamitously ill-conceived Mesopotamian war.) A more accurate slogan — should I say epitaph? — might have been "Wyoming — For Sale!"

Crossing into Montana changed things. There the land was less eaten up, and the state flat-out looked less molested than Wyoming, cursed with its rich basement of combustibles. Montana didn't often need a soft-focus lens to make its high plains beautiful.

A family van with an Illinois license plate overtook us at a good clip, the face of the driver scowlingly tense. "The GPS must have gone on the blink," Q said. "Maybe that's why Mom's on her cell phone." Two of the three children in the rear were attached to wires: a boy bobbed his head to some MP3 beat, a girl stared up at an overhead DVD screen, and the other child — of indeterminate gender — was bent over what I took for an electronic game. Clearly, there were enough virtual realities available in that vehicle to entertain a small ship's crew for months.

As all old travelers know, inventors of whizz-bizzles (Gus Kubitzki's word for electronic parts — transistors, diodes, silicon chips) are not at fault for such disconnections. The blame for such youthful electronic translocations lies with farmers who, years ago, ceased putting colored-glass-ball lightning rods on their houses and barns for traveling children to tally; and it lies with Burma-Shave for giving up on roadside doggerel to keep tykes chanting for miles; and also with highway engineers for cutting down all those road humps called kiss-me-quicks that gave a child a chance to watch the roll of the land in order to urge a driver to take the next KMQ faster: "Come on, Pop! Get her airborne!" You geezers out there from the twentieth century can add to this list.

Only the retro-minded side of my brain would venture to suggest that passing time — one's days — in a place other than where one *actually* is at a particular moment can have disjunctive spiritual consequences reaching beyond the individual. For me to say so could also be hypocritical, given the hours (although not in an auto) I've spent reading literature and history and even some science, all of which require entering realms other than one of the moment. Such retro-notions remind me of Vivian Woodmiller — her mortal coil long ago shuffled off — a beloved librarian who once said to me, "When I see nine-year-olds, I envy them. Not for their youth but for their chance to read for the first time *Treasure Island* or *Alice's Adventures in Wonderland* or *The Wonderful Wizard of Oz* — maybe even old miser Silas Marner with his gold coins. I remember the first time sixty years ago I heard a teacher read aloud 'The Raven.' How beautiful a virgin mind in the world of books!"

Poor retrorse Miss Woodmiller. She surely would have raised the question whether an electronically driven virtual-world can ever create the same response as an imagined realm. Presuming to speak for her, I think she would argue that imagination — the supreme requisite for reading good books — can allow transforming ideas to arise. With voltage-powered entertainments, imagination is taken care of for you. On a screen, your Long John Silver looks precisely like mine, and my Alice wears the same pinafore as yours because it *is* the same one.

The Illinois van had added a conversational dimension to a few miles of Montana for Q and me, but for that to happen, of course, we first had to *see* the family in the van. Q said, "Those plugged-in kids remind me of little P.C. and your scheme to rewire him and cure his videosis." P.C. — his actual initials and the name he went by — had come to spend time with me a few years earlier. He was nine years old, skinny, small for his age but mentally quick, of sweet disposition, possessed of the gift of gab, and still uneasy in the dark, especially in a strange house surrounded by woods. At that time he was engaged in writing a novel about a sleight-of-hand magician — not a wizard but just an ordinary boy much like himself for whom a thick woods held unknowns better left to themselves. He'd gotten his manuscript to page three.

P.C. was largely schooled in his home by his grandmother who thought a few days in a distant place with his "uncle" in Missouri would be of benefit. My plan was to take him on the road, open territory new to him, walk him through my woods, show him the dark sinkhole and tell him a tale of the man trapped down in it; I would lay before him my hand-drawn, 1950 map of two Kansas City blocks centered around 74th and Flora Avenue, illustrating every fruit tree and grape arbor planted by an earlier generation and ignored by postwar supermarketing neighbors. I'd try to demonstrate how cherries or a pear picked and eaten while perched like a bird *in the tree* was fruit sweeter than any from a grocery. I'd give a recounting of Hellcats and Messerschmitts and Zeros built of balsa and tissue paper that, sooner or later, would be taken up to an attic window, a match put to them, and set off on a flaming glide to earth. World War II redux. I, a Svengali, would open worlds young P.C. hadn't found on any screen and therefore couldn't imagine.

On our road trip, as I pointed out quoz of the territory, he dutifully would raise his head from his handheld electronic-game to look out the window and say "Oh," and then return to his screen to vaporize into a digital ether various fell creatures — some furry, others well-muscled, and still others deranged machinery, but all

452

intent on mayhem. To travel his world, he didn't need two legs — a pair of agile thumbs would do. So we gave up the road to try another approach: hands-on construction.

I bought a 176-piece Erector Set with directions for eight possible models of "Super Flyers." P.C. chose the ultralight — a small, quirky, one-pilot aircraft a nine-year-old (or sixty-year-old) might wondrously fly in his sleep. A winged dream-machine. I set him up at a table. An hour later I returned to find two pieces bolted together and P.C. thumbing away at his video screen. The ultralight directions were entirely in pictures requiring close examination to interpret, so I sat beside him as counsel. After all, it was his first airplane. Three or four bolts later, he slipped away to the bathroom. When he didn't soon return, I went to see about him; from behind the door I heard a tattoo of highly pitched beeps and blips and "Polly Wolly Doodle" played on what sounded like a tiny, tinny carousel.

The solution (thought I) *is to let him see a finished plane to inspire him.* So I took up the bolts and nuts of a size a nine-year-old can see, and over the rest of the afternoon squintingly assembled the plane, down to its spinning propeller and cockpit where P.C. might imagine himself piloting safely above a perilous reach of dark woods and over deep sinkholes lying just beyond his bed. As he looked at it blankly, I, knowing the allure of dismantling to a nine-year-old male brain (especially one dedicated to amusements in which things must be etherized before they get you), suggested he take the ultralight apart to make another model, maybe the biplane or crop duster. He said, "That's a lot of work."

During his visit, all I accomplished was a return to my own ninth year, and I altered not at all his progress toward his eventual study of computeristics leading to improved games he hoped to design. Q said, "Maybe a raft trip with a GPS would've made a less radical transition." Erector Sets, I said, are now radical?

The truth is, I should have minded my own business, but then, of course, I wouldn't have that swell little ultralight sitting on a bookshelf and continually reminding me how I'd like to fly a bigger one treetop high across America to see how the surface fits together. Might be a book there. Maybe a transforming idea.

To love children must also be to love their future, and any future that impoverishes connections to the grand dominion of the natural world is endangered even before it's born. It may also prove to be a future impossible not to produce but to sustain. To tolerate separation from spiritual links to the imperium of nature is to hang on the edge and wait for cataclysm. Any religion or science — the two priestcrafts most often posing that ultimate question *Why is there not nothing?* — unwilling to embrace and enhance spiritual ties to the mysterious and miraculous existence of all Being can only hinder human fulfillment and its very continuance.

I know a woman in Connecticut who served as navigator on her honeymoon. Her duty was to watch the dashboard GPS screen and to listen for the electronic voice and match its bidding with exit signs along I-95 all the way to Florida. Her groom was a man for whom the heart of navigation was not territory but time. The briefest travel was the best travel. Over their fourteen-hundred miles, she performed admirably, keeping them en route flawlessly, with never a sarcastic word from him about a missed turn, and they arrived in Fort Lauderdale almost on the dot of his ETA, their marriage well-begun. She said, "My image of South Carolina or North Carolina — oh hell, the whole way down — is a little glowing screen on the dashboard and a thousand, green exit signs. I told him, the next time, either we get on a jet or you watch the GPS."

I should say in defense of my implications here that I *do* recognize how new instruments have put the lie to millennia of intelligent but incorrect theories about things, from stars to staphylococci, and I do credit machines (like the telescope) which have exposed the bunk in much theosophy and philosophy. I also recognize the possibility that one day mechanisms might reveal dimensions of existence we can now only hypothesize. And certainly it's evident new technologies require time to learn how to use them wisely. Maybe that's it: the instance at hand is nothing more than not knowing how to let electronic navigation bring us *into* a new territory rather than merely directing us *through* it, because we've not yet sufficiently distinguished between being told where we are and comprehending where we are.

Nonetheless, for me, twenty-five square-inches of pixels cannot ever deliver the same sense of location as can fifteen-hundred square-inches of paper road-map — a document capable of suggesting a traveler's place in a greater landscape embracing heart and soul. Isn't allowing whizz-bizzles to create geographic illiteracy — which is to say, a disconnect between mind and territory, body and sources, spirit and its longings — a misuse of technology? There is, of course, the possibility the entire vast and unstable, carbon-fueled infrastructure undergirding the creation of whizz-bizzles may of itself terminate such mechanistic botherations.

Had I not so flatly failed young P.C., I might have been able to help him discover the difference between virtual and experiential travel, the latter that great and timeless metaphor of passage down through the corridor of one's own days, the deepest journey we undertake. To him, most topographical places were just locales out there somewhere. They were nothing he saw any need to belong to.

I failed to evoke within him the slightest recognition of querencia (from the Spanish *querer*, to love), a term vaqueros of old Texas used in referring to the location where a longhorn was born. For travelers, no matter the distance traveled, a querencia can be a place of recognition and recrudescence. They are not difficult to find: like connections, they lie over the land as if stardust. And, one way or another, we've been there before.

⍚ 5 ⍚

What the Chatternag Quarked

EASILY ASTOUNDED — or at least readily perplexed — by the world as they are, children are small-scale specialists at turning up quoz as they go forth daily to expand their querencia, and some remarkable few of them retain their expertise for years long past childhood. Art, in its broadest meaning, is the oldest and perhaps most sublime human endeavor to represent the existence and promise of quoz that can reawaken any of us spiritually nodding off.

Recent inquiry has shown humans are not the only creatures to make or use tools; we must look for our defining characteristic elsewhere, and one elsewhere is cavern walls painted with pigments thirty-five-thousand years old. Whatever else depictions of aurochs and ibex and mammoths may reveal, those beasts and the handprints often attendant manifest a Cro-Magnon sense of connection and belonging, memory and awareness. Who makes an artistic image lacking a name and an attached meaning? It's in our nature to participate in a place and its events by rendering it into images and words, and thereby coming to belong not merely to it but *within* it.

All wild creatures recognize their native querencia — knowing it as a child does its mother — because that's where they can thrive; take them from it, and they are more likely to wither than adapt. For the past half century, I've spent much time in trying to extend my querencia to make it somewhat contiguous with the borders of America so that I might belong in a few ways to Maine and Arizona, Montana and Alabama (the path into some querencia is easier than others). You, foreseeing reader, may have already reckoned that it is quoz that comprise querencia, and to discover the one, a traveler must find the others.

On occasion I wish I were Mark Twain, writing in a time when an author could dance around a faulty memory — or notebook — and slip past even a surveillant reader three short sentences like these about a smart Australian bird he claimed could outtalk a parrot. In *Following the Equator,* Twain says, "I cannot recall that bird's name. I think it begins with M. I wish it began with G or something that a person can remember." Comic genius, you see, lets a writer get away with — what's the word? I think it begins with *M.*

Bird names beginning with *M* bring me again to a quoz of the West sometimes called a magpie. If in crossing the Great Plains you've seen one, has it been nothing more than a long-tailed thing gliding gracefully and iridescently from fence post to sagebrush or maybe picking at a hare flattened to the asphalt? If so, reconsider the magpie and a few of its six-dozen names in English: mockapie, rudder-bird, Madge, pegpie, tellpie, maggotpie, hedge-mag, egg-lift, long-tailed Nan (its pied coloring suggests *nun* might be more descriptive, but then, it was once thought to carry a drop of the Devil's blood). The name I like is chatternag. People have described some of its natterings as wheezes, whistles, screeches, squeaks, squawks, rasps, guttural *quarks,* and even ringing cell phones.

North of the Yellowstone River, just beyond where Sunday Creek comes in, I saw two magpies (they often are in pairs), a good omen to anyone remembering certain versions of an old folk rhyme:

> *One magpie for woe, two mags for joy,*
> *three for a wedding, and four for a boy;*
> *five for a pearl, but a flock to get a girl.*

A child's bird-guide my father gave me when I was twelve allowed me to redefine "some old black bird" into *Pica pica,* the black-billed magpie, and the magic associated with names transformed a heretofore assumed commonplace into a High Country quoz. But one boy's quoz can be an adult's vexation. Western farmers and ranchers once set out poison for magpies, and maybe that still happens, even though later ornithological research has shown the birds contribute more than they take — except in animal traps from which the mags are adept at stealing bait, an event now not entirely unwelcome to some of us.

During winter storms, their big domed nests — up to eight feet high, among the grandest built by North American birds, and far out of proportion to the nestlings within — provide shelter for other creatures. And there's one more magpie gift: it will pick insects off of an ungulate, and it will clean out a mess of maggots as if they were, well, pie.

If the issue is man versus magpie, we also might want to consider just who the hell it was that came into the territory first. The Euro-American taking of the West, as we know, has been an ingress leaving almost nothing as it was — rivers, prairies, deserts, forests, bison, native residents. The white man is a Noah riding in on the flood of his own numbers and technologies, and inside his ark of invasively destructive species is also a library of formularies and covenants to purge, like an angry god, all flesh that offends his economy so that it might be repopulated with species selected to offer quick monetary gain. The consequence there (to continue Old Testament locution) is the fear of man and the dread of him upon every beast of the earth, and upon every fowl of the air, upon all that moveth upon the earth. So on and so forth.

Almost as old as the Genesis account is folklore saying magpies were the sole critters aboard Noah's ark to refuse shelter under the roof during those forty days and nights of deluge. Instead, the hardy pair perched atop the roof to *quark-quark* about the iniquity of humanity that had brought on the Flood and to give a good round of cussing to the wicked cities as the water covered them. Considering the reason for the inundation, the magpies appear to speak the mind of God. (Let no animal showing it wants no truck with humanity be called dumb.) If global climate change does indeed produce rising coastal waters, one day there may be moguls, magnates, mugwumps, and muckety-mucks on Wall Street and Pennsylvania Avenue who will complain, "The goddamn magpies had it right all along."

A few years ago when I was sleeping out in a stretch of low hills in northern Utah, I was awakened every morning just past dawn by a dozen or so chatternags (such a congregation is called, appropriately, *a tidings*). Their incessant chattering nagged me awake, so I lay there listening. Meowing and purring, they tried out on me the language of the house cat; yipping and growling, they essayed the tongue of dog and coyote, then somebody's budgie, then in desperation came what I can only describe as an imitation of a running lawn-mower. I called to them, Damnit! I am a man! And I do believe one answered with what sounded not like *quark-quark* but *jerk-jerk!* as if commenting even yet from Noah's roof.

For supporting evidence of that possibility, I offer to the skeptical reader the ancient eminence of Pliny the Elder who died observing the Vesuvius eruption that buried Pompeii. In his *Natural History,* he writes of magpies repeating favored words and then pondering their meaning; and, says he, should a mag fail to comprehend a particular word, it might die of disappointment. (He also offered that buzzards are impregnated by the wind.) If the ancient Roman encyclopedist is too credulous or too much of a fabulist for our view of nature, the truth remains that a fledgling magpie — when taken into our society of (to use Plato's mocking definition) "the plumeless genus of bipeds" — can let loose fifteen different vocalizations, some of which mimic human cadences. A chatternag is no taciturn raven croaking nothing more than "Nevermore."

In our time, one ornithologist has demonstrated magpie intelligence (beyond its notable curiosity and its wise wariness of us) through a clever experiment proving they can recognize themselves in a mirror: when the scientist shined a dot of red light on a magpie, the bird discovered it by looking in the mirror but knew to try to pick the dot off itself rather than off its image. Run that experiment on the smartest puss you know.

As they ascended the Missouri River through what is today the Dakotas, Lewis and Clark were the first to record formally the existence of the magpie in North America. Fascinated with the "parti-colored corvid," they made cages of sticks and sent a living quartet of the birds (along with a few prairie dogs, another garrulous Western resident) downriver and on east to the President. One of the magpies — and a lone "barking squirrel" — survived the two-thousand-mile journey and the loss of their querencia to become the first creatures to bring a living voice of the far plains to Washington. I toy with history here as I imagine Clark wanting to communicate to the President advance *spoken* tidings of the great expedition: in his study, Jefferson leans close to examine the magpie, and like an avian recorder, it quarks what William taught it: "Hello, Tom!"

❧ 6 ❧

A Smart Bike

I N THE SUMMER OF 1975, evidence was accumulating that my life as an academic was about to come down around my ears and leave no significant aspect standing. Between vain hopes and denials, I knew I should begin looking for an exit leading not merely to another room but to a different life. There was no place for me in the towers of ivory. Desperation steadily obviated any need to weigh risks against rewards, and futility left me looking for almost anything other than where my thirty-six years had ended up.

One morning I sat on a deck I'd built out into a cluster of trees, a place of natural repose; before me was the *Kansas City Times*. In it I saw a photograph, a four-by-four-inch picture of a bicyclist riding through southwest Missouri, and he was doing it atop the tracks of a short-line railroad, his bike propelled by an old one-cylinder washing-machine motor. *Putt-putt-putt* he went across the counties in the company of a friend chugging along behind. Their contraptions were balanced upright by an outrigger with a wheel rolling atop the opposite rail. *Putt-putt-putt*. The sound of their washer motors awoke me.

Hubba-hubba! An exit. Why not? I'd convert my bicycle to ride the rails right across America! At once I had a motto — *Shore to shore and maybe more.* And I'd need no motor to do it. When I returned — if I did return to my calendar of failures — I'd write a book about the trip. Such an eccentric jaunt would be unique in American letters. In a mobile nation where everyone has ancestors who traveled here from the other hemisphere, a journey book is the most endemic of literary motifs — *Moby-Dick, The Adventures of Huckleberry Finn, The Grapes of Wrath.*

All the better in my mind that American pooh-bahs of literature — and I don't mean writers — would dismiss as they have always done a book of travels no matter its depth and facility. I'd been trained by those watery-blooded, supercilious men (and males they were) to sniff at and disregard such stuff. But, once turned out of the grove, I was free to take off for the nearest railroad — the hobo express. Of course, were I to write up my travels as fiction — a *novel* might allow "a serious writer" readmission to the enclave of literati. Who could say? Who cared? Call me Ishmael. I'd light out for the territory on a bicycle atop steel rails.

I never did it, and today I regret I didn't. Instead, three years later, standing among the candle ends of my flops, I struck out in a small van with a homemade bunk in the back and the remnants of a low three-digit savings-account to travel back roads for a full season. But I did write about that jaunt, and I didn't cast it as fiction. When it became clear the book, despite being called a "travelogue" (reviewers, please check the definition), had found an audience, a New York literary mandarin who critiqued novels but did not write them, a man whose certainty of opinion was exceeded only by his pomposity, took me aside in a Fifth Avenue bookshop to say, "Now that you've got that out of your system, perhaps you'll try to step up to the novel." Remembering the standard U.S. Navy shipboard advice, I said I'd give thought to it if he'd consider taking a flying fuck at a rolling doughnut.

That 1975 news clipping, now yellowed, is still in my files, and I've never come across it without a twitch of regret always superseded by a twinge of hope I might yet bike the rails across America, whether or not I ever wrote about it. I understand now — as I didn't before — the journey would have to be done in total trespass; but then, by law, a tortfeasor takes his victims as he finds them.

I set these words before you, valued reader (a number of you making possible that escape from academia, for which I give you deepest thanks), as preface to another photograph, one I saw not long ago, of a man pedaling a bicycle atop a railroad in the Nevada desert. The picture stopped me, allow me to say, in my tracks. I wrote a letter to the rider, and he soon responded with an invitation to see his Railcycle in operation. His name was Richard Smart, and he was a dentist in Coeur d'Alene, Idaho. He suggested we meet a little farther south near a scenic, abandoned line running from the Clearwater River up toward the crest of the Bitterroot Range. When we spoke on the phone to confirm plans, the last thing he asked was, "Are you afraid of heights?" Because we were talking about an old logging railroad, I said no; after all, how high in the air can a hundred-ton locomotive get?

Q and I met him and his longtime fellow biker of the rails, Kenneth Wright, on the western slope of the Clearwater Mountains just outside Orofino and at the edge of the Nez Percé Reservation. Our plan for the next morning was to haul four Railcycles of Smart's design up along the Camas Prairie Railroad which followed Orofino Creek descending from the western reaches of the Bitterroots. The line, once used for carrying out virgin white-pine, had recently been removed from service and, within a week, the question of pulling up its steel and sleepers for salvage was to be answered. We might be the last people ever to ride those miles.

That evening, Q and I joined the two men for supper at a Mexican café in Orofino, a tiny county seat in a narrow valley opening to the Clearwater River nearly where the Lewis and Clark Expedition on its westbound leg stopped for twelve days to recover from gastrointestinal discomforts possibly brought on by a diet heavily laced with camas tubers which, nonetheless, had kept starvation at bay during the harrowing trek through the Bitterroots. In his inimitably solecistic and perfunctory style, Clark wrote in his logbook:

Indians caught Sammon & Sold us, 2 Chiefs & thir families came & camped near us, Several men bad, Capt Lewis Sick I gave Pukes Salts &c. to Several, I am a little unwell. hot day.

While the men recovered, they hewed out with hand axes too small for the task several dugouts to carry them onward to the Pacific. Boats, locomotives, Railcycles — transport was all around us.

Railcycle is a name coined by Richard Smart to describe specifically one of the ten models he had made over the preceding three decades. *Railbike* is the generic term, although in the mid-nineteenth century such a vehicle was usually a velocipede; but even earlier, that older word denoted a two- or three-wheeled cycle, sans pedals, the rider pushed forward with his feet.

It was an antique photograph of a railroad velocipede Smart happened upon in a public-library book that started him on a changed life of pedaling atop tracks on three continents. Although the pictures were different, as were our lives, we shared the experience of a single photo of a two-wheeled, rail-riding contraption that propelled us into an altered life. Coincidentally (I assume), a half continent apart, we'd come upon the images at nearly the same time and at a similar age. Hearing his stories of railbiking was like listening to a book I never wrote.

The photograph that set him forth was of a stout man in a baggy suit and vest strung with a watch fob, wearing a black fedora and standing by a bicycle attached to an outrigger connected to a steel wheel the size of a pie plate. Hanging from the handlebars was what looked like a lunch pail, and behind him were a water tank, a steaming locomotive ready to move, and six workers, one of whom might be mocking the rider. The man could have been a track inspector, although some early trains also carried in the baggage car such a velocipede the conductor could ride for help in case of a breakdown out in some to-hell-and-gone. In its fundamentals, the machine reflected the Railcycles we would ride the next day. Dick said, "When I saw the picture of that contraption, I wanted to ride it so bad I could taste it. But you just don't go out and buy one. I knew I'd have to make my own. That was thirty years ago."

He started with a standard, wide-tire American bicycle and began experimenting and tinkering with outriggers and guidance wheels to keep the bike atop the rail. His first model used a steel rim from a small boat-trailer, a wheel not unlike the one in the old photograph. Smart had no special mechanical training, unless you consider making a dental bridge mechanical. He did not then — or when we met him — know how to weld. "Persistence is the key to discovering what works," he said. "With inventing, things get complex before they get simpler because a lot of little inventions go to make up bigger ones." He paused. "And I have to say, there are a million Americans more mechanical than I am, but I'm the one who wanted the patent so much I wouldn't give up."

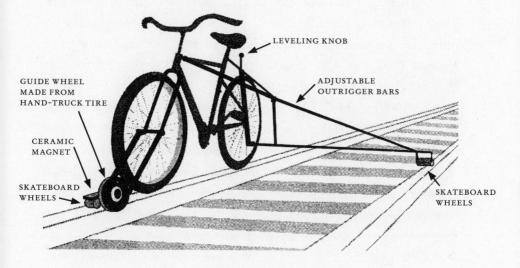

LEVELING KNOB

GUIDE WHEEL
MADE FROM
HAND-TRUCK TIRE

ADJUSTABLE
OUTRIGGER BARS

CERAMIC
MAGNET

SKATEBOARD
WHEELS

SKATEBOARD
WHEELS

A basic Railcycle.

In the large, pine-studded backyard of his home on the west edge of Coeur d'Alene, Smart built a small train precisely modeled on the Little Engine That Could. His version, of course, was pedal-powered and just large enough to carry in its coach or caboose his children or those of neighbors around a four-hundred-foot wooden track, through a covered bridge, and across a trestle over a swale. A close look at its construction revealed parts made from a salad bowl, pizza platter, pie tin, flowerpot, wastebasket — all of it assembled with simple hand tools. "The Little Engine That Could, that's who

I am," he said. "I always think I can. Not to mention at heart, I'm a sixty-year-old twelve-year-old, and for that I thank my mother. She was an elementary-school teacher who taught us to play."

Smart is an ectomorphic six-footer, fair-haired and blue-eyed, quiet-spoken, kindly, generous, and fascinated by hoboes, at least one of whom he has befriended with free dental care. Over the thirty years of designing and building his Railcycles, he had ridden them almost forty-thousand miles on seldom-used or dormant or abandoned tracks to become the leading proponent of what he once called "America's slowest-growing sport." On the eve of our ride, he wondered whether it had become America's fastest-disappearing sport. The steel and ties and bridges, often formerly left in place after rail abandonment, had come to have too much salvage value to be ignored. Dick said, "Our happiness is two rusty ribbons of steel, but they're becoming ever harder to find."

Ken Wright added, "They've torn up our playground, and these days we have to drive three hours or more to reach out-of-service tracks. I saw figures several years ago that there are more than forty-thousand miles of abandoned trackage in America, but I think that number is diminishing. The big railroad abandonments of a few years ago are about over. And today, even if the steel isn't salvaged, thieves sometimes tear out ties to sell to landscapers."

There was also the life span of dormant tracks: it doesn't take long for nature to reclaim a grade with saplings and heavy brush and fallen trees that thwart passage. Smart carries a small bucksaw to administer short-lived maintenance. Bridges can be more of a challenge: he and Wright have crossed over creeks on tracks lacking an understructure, the rails drooping as if melting. In such an instance, his Railcycle has an advantage over many other versions in that Smart's machines quickly convert for road travel or getting around impassable sections of tracks.

The doctor had a collection of photographs he'd taken of wildlife frequently failing to hear his approach: unlike footfalls, rubber tires on steel rails allow silent movement. When animals did notice the man-machine, they seemed not to recognize it as a threat; on sun-warmed ballast, he'd come upon dozing coyote pups, sitting bears, and even rattlesnakes coiling to strike at his front tire.

Wright said, "The farther we get toward our favorite goal of reaching the end of steel, the more wildlife we encounter — things you're not likely to see from a car or on foot." For one expedition, the men hired a bush pilot to fly them deep into remote British Columbia to a rail terminus. Not sure they could get through to a highway far down-country, they nonetheless pedaled off on the defunct line, camping as they went. After eleven days and 250 miles, they came out again. "I always want to see the world where nobody else goes," Dick said. "And I'm always after serenity and beauty."

Ken Wright was a newly retired professor of chemistry and environmental science and, like his friend, a student of American railroad history. He met Dick when he went to him for dental work and noticed train artifacts in the office. Smart, who connected affably with his patients, told Ken about Railcycles rolling along ghost railroads. "I saw right off all the places we could go," Ken said. "Another world, one hidden away." For the last twenty-five years, the pair had traveled together over some fifteen-thousand miles of ghost lines. Dick said, "If we're away too long from the smell of creosote, we get withdrawal symptoms. It's a good escape from a high-stress profession."

The men called each other "Boss," and Wright said, "The car wash, Boss." Dick smiled. "Dentistry is like building a ship in a bottle while standing in a car wash," he said. Ken prodded again: "The abscess." To that, Smart frowned. "People will put off going to see a dentist. A patient came in with an abscess he'd let go way too long. When he opened his mouth, the muscular strain caused it to burst all over me. That kind of foul vomica is unpleasant in all ways." Far more so, he meant, than a broken railbike miles from assistance.

Dick was a believer in the HPV movement — human-powered vehicles — and as such he pedaled to work in a peculiar, three-wheeled, futuristic-looking machine that enclosed him inside a fiberglass and carbon-fiber canopy with a windshield and a wiper, a headlight and air scoops; on the interior (not for claustrophobes) were a stereo and deep-cushion seat. More than once, somebody watching him raise the pod and climb out had asked, "Where's the mother ship?" He bought the velomobile from Leitra, a company in Denmark where human-powered vehicles receive serious consideration. The thing looked like the front end of a light plane that had lost its wings, or — from another angle — a daisy-yellow, streamlined, high-top hiking shoe with spoke wheels. It had twenty-one gears, weighed seventy pounds, and on a downslope Dick could reach almost fifty miles an hour. He said, "It stops at a gas station only for the air hose."

Roads, rails, I said, you've got the types of travel covered except for hulls and wings. Ken smiled; he knew what was coming. Dick said, "I've read that a few months after the Wright brothers first got off the ground in North Carolina, an Idaho man up this way invented a pedal-powered biplane. I haven't pedaled aloft yet, but I do have a pedal-powered canoe. I pull it on a little trailer behind one of my bicycles and take it out on Lake Coeur d'Alene. A small propeller drives it along at a pretty good clip, especially into the wind. It has a rudder I control with bicycle handlebars." Q said, "A canoo-cycle."

Then she asked how people react when they encounter him with one of his HPVs. "Oh," he said, "I think there's a third who don't even see me. Then there's a third who write me off as Doctor Gyro Gearloose. But the last third — they want to join in."

That final group Smart tried to reach in the 1980s with Railcycles in three models he assembled and sold, all made from standard mountain bikes. For a while he also offered twelve sheets of plans showing how to build a Railcycle. He wrote a newsletter and approached anyone able to advance preservation of abandoned tracks or assist in opening seldom-used lines for occasional railbiking. To all who would listen, he pointed out how a rider was safer on a dormant or even infrequently used railroad free of fast-moving autos and trucks driven by drunks or of late, cell-phone inattentives.

For a while, he said, "I was married to the idea, and sometimes it was tricky balancing dentistry and a family with four children. But Ann, she's a wife who helped me pursue my passion even when it was hard on her. I used to connect Railcycles so all of us could ride together, and once I hooked up six to see if it could be done. It could, and one person could easily pull all of them."

In 1980, four years after his first Railcycle, *Sports Illustrated* published a short piece about the bike, and much publicity followed, although most of it was small notices ("Ripley's Believe It or Not!"). Dick wondered briefly whether he could afford to give up dentistry. His company — and even more his advocacy — drew the attention of a few railroad corporations that chose to believe he was urging people to ride active rail lines, "live steel." One morning Dick came into his dental office to find a railroad detective waiting to talk to him, and not about an abscessed tooth. "Evil letters" began arriving from rail executives, but among them was one concluding politely:

I apologize for the firmness of this letter but, as a professional yourself, I am certain you understand the necessity of our challenging those individuals with no legal right to be on our property. Your cooperation in discouraging others from participating in such a dangerous and unlawful pastime will be greatly appreciated.

The litigiousness of Americans, so implied the corporations, made the sport impossible for the railroads to countenance.

Along with other advocates, Smart believed indemnity waivers could be signed by riders on either dormant rails or tracks active only periodically or even ones opened just on Sundays when many railroads don't operate, an idea he suggested to the Secretary of Transportation, who said she'd have her staff "look into it." Nothing happened because the big railroads refused to consider the useful reverberations from corporate generosity and goodwill. Nor would they, seeing no big-dollar profit, discuss selling passes to ride unused lines.

With each Railcycle, Dick required a signed sales-agreement containing a sentence in capital letters: BUYER SHALL ASSUME SOLE RESPONSIBILITY FOR SELECTION OF TRACKS ON WHICH TO USE THE RAILCYCLE AND ONLY ON ABANDONED TRACKS WITH PROPER PERMISSION. But industry flacks did not let up, one of them calling railbiking "a deadly activity" and citing Smart's own warning that "A single train can ruin your day." Another accused him of "playing Russian roulette with the lives of his customers."

The truth was that there had never been an accident involving a railbike and a train. Unless we count the time a black bear looked at Smart and licked its chops, the closest thing to a close call he'd ever had occurred while *walking* across a trestle on a low-use branch line. Time and again he explained the greatest danger in sensible — call it smart — railbiking is in derailing. Mastering a Railcycle, he guessed, was about twenty-five percent more difficult than a street bike on good pavement. (Since we were to ride the next day over a line called the "Railroad on Stilts," that percentage was rather higher than I wanted to hear. Q has the envious trait, born somewhat out of inexperience, of not becoming edgy even when standing on a high edge. In her words, "When it comes to acrophobia, I guess I fell off the turnip truck." I've not been so lucky to have that tumble.)

In Sweden there are a good many miles of defunct trackage maintained for railbiking; you can even rent a stable, three-wheeled velocipede called a *dressin*. Smart once came upon a Swedish elementary-school teacher and her entire class on a rail-riding nature excursion. In Finland, there are annual televised contests for vehicles Finns call *resiina* which travel the rails from one corner of the country to another. In Switzerland, that mountainous country, there is a yearly competition for HPVs of several types, and at one of them Smart, widely respected overseas, won a trophy for his Railcycle in the "practical vehicle" category.

He said, "Whatever we can do around the world to promote increased use of human power has to be of benefit. It has to be good to curtail use of fossil fuels and obesity — two things with clear connections. On a railbike, you leave no carbon footprint. In fact, you don't leave footprints of any kind. It's now the least disturbing and quietest way we have to reach isolated places of incredible beauty and solitude."

The safety record in proper railbiking is strong enough for proponents to offer it to the blind who ride in four-wheeled machines (as with a locomotive, the tracks do the steering). And Dick, using a side-by-side tandem model and turning the pedals, had taken a paraplegic friend on outings. (Another paraplegic, a machinist, helped make parts for one experimental Railcycle.) The mother of a child with cerebral palsy, after a ride in the East, told a maker of four-wheeled cycles, "That's the only way my daughter can ride a 'bicycle.' If those corporate presidents and their lawyers knew what it means to a child to experience something the rest of us take for granted, maybe they'd rethink the issue. Riding a bike is an American rite of passage."

Smart said, "In this country, abandoned and dormant tracks are a huge resource we've never really realized or utilized. Right in front of us are thousands of miles of linear parks. The infrastructure is already there, and so is the need." (Pogo, of the great Okefenokee: "We stand here confronted by insurmountable opportunities.")

In 1999, the London Underground, Bakerloo line, bought eight heavy-duty Railcycles Smart designed for track inspectors and maintenance crews to use during off-service hours. Twenty years after his initial experimental model, he figured the way at last had opened, but when we met him in Orofino, the Underground experiment seemed to have withered. He guessed the problem was a guidance system not then perfected and the requirement of several "weird English safety features" making the cycles somewhat heavy and unwieldy. Nevertheless, he'd heard that following a terrorist attack in the London Underground, the bikes had been put to good advantage.

After a quarter of a century, he gave up making Railcycles to sell, concentrating instead on machines for only himself and friends. At the time we were headed toward the Camas Prairie line, he was working on a lightweight, collapsible model that would fit into a suitcase he could put on a train bound for the end of steel — say, in Bolivia or on the Old Patagonian Express where sidetracks are abundant and unencumbered by corporate self-interest masked with persiflage blaming litigious Americans.

"I decided I'd pushed the business of making Railcycles as far as I wanted. In twenty-five years, I built fifteen bicycles for myself or friends or family, and I built another forty to sell. Even though I've never heard of a railbike-train accident, I got tired of worrying where people might ride my Railcycles." He was speaking slowly. "I came to see it was rich, older men who bought the bikes, and most of those guys didn't have much time to ride. The people with good opportunities to go out and explore the nooks and crannies couldn't afford a Railcycle."

It was discouraging for him to say that. "I made very little money from sales, but while it lasted, it was an energizing dream. But, to tell the truth, after nearly thirty years, I began to feel imprisoned by the whole concept. So I simplified my passion. When I retire next year, I just want to enjoy biking the rails. Enjoy it while I can. While the old tracks remain, I'd like to ride more than my usual thousand miles a year."

≫ 7 ≪

Railroad on Stilts

THE 1902 SEARS, ROEBUCK CATALOG offered for $8.50 an outrigger "railroad attachment" that could transform an ordinary bicycle into one capable of riding the tracks; the description claimed, "We have found this device to be very popular with railroad and telegraph men, particularly in the West, although it is adapted for use by anyone, and the parts will fit a lady's bicycle as readily as a man's bicycle." The attachment was essentially similar to all successful later conversion devices, and (like Smart's renditions) it could be removed to allow the bike to travel "on the wagon roads." No railbike, apparently, has ever succeeded without employing an outrigger — not a surprising result since the width of the top of a standard-gauge rail varies only from two-and-a-half to three inches, the surface both slightly convex and often canted. Riding a full-sized bicycle atop a rail raised four to six inches above the ties gives a rider a near sensation of being a cyclist on a circus wire.

Saturday came on sunny — rain-slicked tracks would have canceled our plans — and Q and I headed out with Smart and Wright, a pair of names to give confidence as we drove up into the mountains toward an isolated and abandoned stretch of the Camas Prairie Railroad (the prairie lay elsewhere). We were at the base of the Idaho Panhandle, on the edge, as it were, of the skillet. The Orofino Creek section of the CPR, built in 1928, was the "Railroad on Stilts," its nickname deriving from an original fifty-nine bridges in its forty-mile length; nearly all those wooden trestles remained, and they were the reason Dick had asked earlier if I was afraid of heights. The night before our ride, he lent me an illustrated history of the CPR, and in the book was a photograph of a big locomotive on its side below a trestle. *If a dozen heavy wheels can career off into Orofino Creek,* thought I, *then what about a mere two, each weighing about the same as my skull?*

Never more than a logging railroad, the Headquarters branch of the line carried no passengers other than timbermen, a sad circumstance given the beauty of the terrain it penetrated. Several miles west of the erstwhile gold-mining town of Pierce and about fifty miles from the spine of the Bitterroots to the east, we rumbled down a rough rock-road to the rusted tracks, where we assembled outriggers to four Railcycles, the models slightly different and each once experimental.

Between the tracks grew ferns and daisies and also a few conifer seedlings that all too quickly would rise to obstruct passage, although nothing then was big enough to require cutting. Dick rubbed his shoe over a rusted rail and said, "We'll have good traction." I was happy to hear that, even more so because of my concern having to do not with traction but with impaction and compaction: bikes, riders, locomotives. Q popped out with a faux Confucianism: "He who rides rail with shine, soon makes headline." After a moment I answered, If rail gleams, I'll listen for your screams.

Although the tracks had been in place almost three-quarters of a century, the rails themselves were a hundred-years old (every length of steel carries the date and place of manufacture), and that meant they were low (good news to a novice) as well as narrow (not so good); another way to express riding old rails is to say derailments are usually more frequent but less consequential in outcome. Nonetheless, a front wheel falling off a six-inch-high rail (if the rock ballast reaches the tops of the ties) is like hitting a half-foot-deep pothole in a street, and that's why to railbike is to sooner or later make a trip over the handlebars, one's cranium leading the way. Such somersaults can also come from braking too fast; from steel encumbered by debris or slicked by rain, frost, or cow pies; or from failing to notice damaged tracks. The worst injury Smart had witnessed happened when a rider did not see a spike a vandal had pounded between a gap in adjoining rails. The good doctor bandaged up his friend's cut head with what was at hand (a clean diaper), and on they rode. (He once bound up another noggin with a spare inner tube.) His own most serious somersault left him with a cracked eye socket that didn't keep him from continuing, even though he was, as usual, far from assistance. "For the first twenty years," he said, "I didn't wear a helmet. I hope you remembered yours." Q and I looked at each other. "Well then," he said, "try to stay on your bike."

Richard Smart's innovations to the guidance device in front of the forward wheel were sophisticated enough to have earned a patent: the current Railcycles employed magnets — made of rare earth and strong enough to lift two-hundred pounds — to keep in place the guide wheel which in turn kept the front wheel atop the rail; under an experienced rider, the rear wheel followed along like an obedient dog on a leash. The outrigger and its roller held the bike upright, and in Smart's ingenious system its height could be adjusted to prevent the cycle on banked curves from leaning too far to one side and derailing. The leveler knob, back of the seat, necessitated a rider reaching behind to adjust it, and learning the optimum degree of incline required experience. Twisting the knob beyond what was needed would assure the bike of falling off the rail to land either between the tracks or, more disturbingly, outside them. No chalkboard instruction here: you learned to avoid derailing by derailing.

Because of the low friction between tires and tracks, railbiking is often a hands-free coasting or effortless pedaling through forest or countryside at eight miles an hour, although a veteran rider on well-laid track can do safely more than twice that. A cyclist who neglects to lock the brakes after dismounting and steps away for a moment may turn around to see the bike, quite on its own, heading for the next county.

Except when passing through track switches, a Railcycle did not really need to be steered, and the gentle gradients necessary for heavy trains meant a single gear-ratio could serve, leaving hands free to fiddle with the leveler knob, take photographs, point out bovine-beshat rails, or make the sign of the Cross.

There was one additional variable to be reckoned with: the standard American measure between rail centers is 56½ inches, but that distance varies (the source of sway a coach passenger feels) because of shoddy track construction, poor maintenance, or an expansion or contraction of steel caused by changing temperature. Such variations increase chances for derailments, and for those reasons mastering a railbike was more difficult than riding a street bike.

We set off, going down the grade first, with Doc on point and the Prof at the rear and Q behind me so I could serve as an early-warning device for the neophyte. Dick called out, "We're going to gain speed! Avoid braking hard!"

A year earlier Q and I had biked the old towpath of the Chesapeake and Ohio Canal in Maryland, an almost two-hundred-mile run from the Appalachian front at Cumberland down to virtual sea level at Georgetown. Failing to remember that between locks, a canal consists of pools — *level* water — I expected an easy coasting down to Washington, but the whole way was dedicated pedaling over rock surfaces of various finish, some requiring us to walk the bicycles. A week later, my thighs were almost capable of leaping a small bike in a single bound. On the Camas Prairie line, which rises from 925 feet at Orofino to 3,521 feet near the eastern terminus, I'd prepared my mind for serious exertion on a machine thirty pounds heavier than my lightweight bike at home.

Holding the Railcycle down onto the rail as I mounted *up* — a preposition not to be ignored when balancing almost four feet above the ballast — I released the brake, and without a single turn of the pedals I began rolling along, although the trackway looked level, and within a minute I was slipping into a speed probably beyond my facility to handle. From behind I heard Ken say, "Is it like riding on glass?" Never having ridden on glass in any sort of vehicle, I agreed it was, all the while thinking how comforting would feel a touch of bituminous friction. My memory, either to taunt or warn, kept flashing that photograph of the giant locomotive on its side down in Orofino Creek, a stream then with more boulders than water.

Only a hundred yards from our start was the first trestle — not one of the little, straight and quaint ones but a long and curving and banked monster sixty feet above the rocks, and on it was not an inch of guardrailing. Elevated steel on an elevated railroad. *Well, Stanley, here's another fine mess you've gotten yourself into.*

I began adjusting my leveler to match the canted tracks, giving it an extra turn or two to make sure a derailment would toss me not over the edge but to the centerline of the bridge, and that's just what it did. I managed to land on my feet on the ties — those blessed ties — but I let slip a loud utterance more blasphemous than prudent, should it prove to be one's last words.

In my head was this: if I'd nearly gone over the side of a trestle in the first three minutes, what did the rest of the day hold? Q rode up and calmly asked, "What happened?" I explained with further graphic embellishment. Here was a fellow who once was going to bike three-thousand miles of trackage across America, a plan as feasible as his earlier one to bicycle from Alaska to Tierra del Fuego. No guts, no story — sometimes better rendered as no brains, no story.

On foot, Dick came back across the bridge to check on the situation. "Overcorrected?" he said. Then, gently, "A lot of beginners aren't ashamed to walk the bike over trestles." It's nothing, I lied. Dick said, "The first time I rode my first Railcycle, I didn't make it more than a hundred feet." Were you on a trestle? "No, but the early bikes were even harder to get the hang of."

I set the cycle again atop the tracks, and just before we rolled on, Dick added, "It's good that happened early so you can see derailing isn't all that bad." (He was out of earshot when I mumbled that going over the edge of a six-storey building seemed to me a little bad.)

We continued, I making a mental note to remind Honored Reader that western Kansas is a good place to learn railbiking. Then another long, curving, banking, high trestle, and again came an overcorrection of the leveler, followed once more by a blurt of billingsgate. (The phrase "straight as a rail" may describe a fence but it surely doesn't fit the Camas Prairie tracks through the Clearwater Mountains.) Q, rolling up calmly if not cocksurely, commented, "Did it again?" I vowed, on the next trestle, I would kiss the boulders before giving that damned knob one cautious turn too many.

Doc, ever solicitous, came back again, and I asked him how Q was able to stay atop the steel. "She's on a London Underground model," he said. "It's heavier and more stable." Q volunteered to switch machines. As have we all, I've met a few people I'd gladly have swapped bikes with as a public service (not all of them legislators), but to put Q on my wheels of death — now, that would have been wrong.

Forward once more to another set of stilts, but that time I made a successful if uneasy crossing. Between the trestles, I was enjoying the silent rolling through the national forest; the movement was that in a dream where gravity doesn't exist.

To reduce apprehension and enhance the ride further, on the next trestle I forced myself to lift my arms from the handlebars and coast across (the old stratagem — *Do what you fear*), and Q, who had not seen the photograph of the fallen locomotive, did likewise but with bravado, as if she were on a boulevard. (The retentive reader will recall she once practiced flying with her mother's kitchen-broom.)

Where the tracks entered a deep rock cut high above the creek, we stopped and unpacked lunch from a tiny single-wheel trailer Dick towed behind his cycle. I got my camera from a backpack tied to the poles of my outrigger which served as both counterbalance and a means to get the burden of camping gear off one's spine.

While we ate sandwiches, I mentioned the news article I'd seen in 1975 and the washing-machine motors propelling those railbikes, and Dick said, "Sooner or later, everyone we meet asks why I don't put a motor on a Railcycle, and I explain how engines would destroy the serenity we go into the backcountry to find." Ken said, "Anyone who doesn't mind motors and uproar and fumes would be happier in

a speeder club." Speeders are small four-wheeled vehicles with gasoline engines once used by track crews; they're a motorized version of
a handcar. (Today it's more usual for crews to ride in "high railers,"
a pickup with an undercarriage allowing it to clip along atop the
steel.)

In the United States, there were some seven-hundred speeders
and a couple-of-dozen railbikers. Happily for the HPV corps, speeders require a well-maintained line where the heavy, cumbersome
machines have assured passage. A Railcycle can go wherever a bicycle
can go, but a speeder travels only where a locomotive can. Ken said,
"In a speeder, you might as well be in a car with a bad muffler."

"On one trip," Dick said, "we came upon apples hanging right
over the tracks, so we picked a few on the fly. Never got off the bikes.
Experiences like that — that's what we hope to find. And wildlife.
I've encountered wolves, cougars, black bears, weasels, badgers,
marmots, skunks, elk, deer, beaver, moose, coyotes, mustangs. I
can't recall all of them."

On tracks not completely abandoned, Doc and the Prof had also
occasionally encountered trainmen and laborers. "They're curious
about a Railcycle and some even want to give it a try," Wright said.
"They don't have any interest in running us off. That comes from a
corporate office, the leaders, guys who haven't set foot between the
rails in years, if ever."

When he and Smart rode a seldom-used or closed-on-Sunday line,
they reported any track damage they saw, picked up litter, and considered themselves not threats or impediments to the rail industry
but contributors. Yet getting permission to ride any route was difficult. "Even on defunct lines with bridges out and telegraph poles
fallen across the rails, lines where no train could run anymore," Ken
said, "we've been denied permission by somebody eight-hundred
miles away who's never seen the tracks we're talking about. To tell
you the truth, on lines like that, it's easier to seek forgiveness than
seek permission. After all, we know better than anyone else you'd be
crazy to ride live steel."

I said that the federal government granted railroads most of the land their trains run on, especially in the West, and when that ground is abandoned or used only seasonally — as on an agricultural short line moving a wheat harvest — it ought to be open other times to the public granting the right-of-way. Railbanking, the preservation of defunct rail corridors for possible later use, is a sound economic idea, especially in a nation already in need of increased efficiency in transporting things and people, and steel-on-steel is as efficient as transport gets. To surrender shuttered rail-corridors or tear out infrastructure is manifestly shortsighted.

If Smart had a million dollars, he didn't think he could improve his Railcycle except to make it smaller, lighter, and more portable. How about putting the leveler, I said, up where I can see it? He smiled. "Ken and I have been over the handlebars more times than we can remember. Riding two wheels of any kind means you're going to eat dust now and then. Ken even did it once off a trestle. Not a high one, but still a trestle."

"The jar of pickles, Boss," Wright said. Dick nodded: "When I was three or four, my mother accidentally dropped a jar of pickles at the top of the stair above where I was sitting. She screamed, and I saw the pickles coming down at my head, and I reached up and caught the jar. My point is, I've been lucky so far, even on bridges."

We packed up and turned the bikes around for the climb eastward. Going up the grade, I was relieved to discover, felt less like a high-wire act because pedaling against gravity held the bike to the rails. On some trestles, I even closed my eyes for a few yards as part of my therapy.

Along we rode, quietly, usually talking only when stopped to look at something — a view, a marmot, or a spread of syringa, also called mock orange or arrowwood (Indians made shafts from the stems). Syringa thrives near the Bitterroots and is the Idaho state flower partly because of its lovely white blossoms and partly, so I'd guess, because a healthy patch of it can send out a sweet fragrance a considerable distance. We weren't far from where Meriwether Lewis, who first recorded the species for science, gathered a couple of sprigs, pressed them, and eventually sent them on to Philadelphia. Against probabilities, those frangible, brittle, ephemeral blossoms are two of the very few things any expedition member actually touched still with us today.

Dick spent his first years in the remote corners of the Bitterroots where his father worked for the U.S. Forest Service. The family's major link with the world beyond was the Milwaukee Road, and along its tracks Dick watched pass through "fancy people" seated in dining cars with white tablecloths and cut flowers. A Christmas present, no matter how fine, was even more enticingly exotic because it came to him not by a reindeer-drawn sleigh but by a baggage car behind a locomotive. He could only dream of places along the tracks then, places where gifts came from. He said, "Right from the start, I always wanted to go someplace, especially if I could do it on a railroad. To reach the far end. That hasn't changed at all."

It was the Milwaukee line that also brought in another exotic for him: hoboes. "Except for being short of money," he said, "hoboes seemed to an eleven-year-old to live a dream life — camping out, fishing, traveling to far places. We thought they had complete freedom, and riding the rails, that's how they did it."

On westward we climbed, the steady ascent requiring only modest pedaling. The route passed through wooded hills, many of them recovering from prior logging, and signs of the old timber camps were overgrown or gone altogether, except one at a former lumber depot called Haley (not to be confused with the Idaho ski-area town of Hailey) where a squatter had taken up residence only a few feet from the rails in a shack hanging to the edge of a cliff above Orofino Creek. Junked machinery cluttered the weedy clearing. Dick and Ken knew the man from other rides and had brought him a few packets of food. He, a long-term trespasser, had put up a sign: *WARNING! TRESPASSERS WILL BE SHOT. SURVIVORS WILL BE SHOT AGAIN.* The alert was intended not for us but for any Seventh-Day Adventist in search of converts or any federal employee in search of anything.

The squatter was Ed. Coming out to greet us, he talked and talked as isolates may do when human ears happen along, and he delighted in any question I asked. I could have inquired about his gender denominator, and he would have joyfully discoursed on that topic. Ed was almost seventy-years old, and his eyes were bright and his manner lively, and his movement spry if not nimble. He showed us around the overgrown clearing, offered to trade me a rusty saw blade from the old timber yard for my cap, all the while explaining he was living there only until he could get to another place more defensible. Who was he defending himself against? Surprised I wouldn't know about such an apparent enemy, he grumbled, "Why, the feds!" and he explained how he'd seen black helicopters, and he spoke about the federally mandated reintroduction of wolves intended "to drive people away so the government could take the land." Wasn't he living in a national forest? "Well," he countered, "you've got them Seventh-Day Adventists too. I've driven them off a couple of times." Whatever could they want with somebody so far from everything? "They know about the gold in here. They know I've found the original Pierce mine. I should've kept my mouth shut. But I guarantee, they ain't nobody going to get me." While he talked, he interjected frequent biblical citations, each attached with chapter and verse.

Ed had been an alcoholic. None of that "recovering" stuff for him. "I did it," he said. "I am *recovered.*" He was a conscientious objector during the war in Vietnam. If he was willing to shoot somebody for trespassing on land not his, on what grounds did he refuse induction? "That's all bygones," he said, and invited us inside.

The floor of his shanty had a decided bias toward the edge of the cliff, and it may have been the stacks of faded *National Geographic* magazines older than Q that furnished the counterweight to keep the place from tumbling down into the creek. He knew their contents well and quoted details from half-century-old articles almost as often as biblical passages. It was "the wisdom of the good book" and "several hundred yellow books" holding him steady in the vicissitudes of existence — not to mention on the top of the cliff.

Ed was eager to show his larder of organic oats, wheat, flax, dates, nuts, raisins, cranberries, and five gallons of fresh raspberries, and an equivalent amount of honey. "Bears are the strongest animals in the forest — that's why I eat what they eat, except I drink better water. I treat mine with an electrolytic solution I cook up from colloidal silver. You ought to be on it too."

His health, given much attention, he additionally aided by mixing into his hand-rolled cigarettes crushed mullein-leaves picked from the clearing, although he would have preferred menthol, had it grown there. "Indians used to smoke mullein," he said, "and look how strong they were."

How did he manage to pay for his food? "Social Security checks," he said. Isn't that from the feds? "Look," he said, "I worked as an auto-body mechanic for a lot of years, and I paid my taxes." Then, touching my arm lightly so I wouldn't miss his insider's tip, he said, "The best car ever built was the fifty-nine Cadillac. If you see one for sale, snap it up." And where was his?

"Hellfire," he said. "Look at me. Do I need one? I got no debt, no credit cards, my clothes got holes in them, but I own them free and clear. I ain't wearing any undershorts owned by a credit-card company." He stopped for me to respond, and I vowed that my shorts too were without a lien. "I'll tell you what I do have," he said, "and that's gold in the ground."

When we got ready to pedal on up the line, he asked us to come see him again. "You know," he said, "I ain't went into that Big Back Room yet." Off we went, I in hopes ahead were no trestles leading to that Big Back Room. When we were some distance along, I asked Doc about Ed's gold, and he said, almost sadly, "I've flushed more gold down the drain in putting a crown on a tooth than Ed's ever found."

Late in the afternoon we turned back for a glassy glide down to the place of our morning departure. When we arrived and had detached the outriggers and rolled the Railcycles up into Dick's camper-shell pickup, he looked off toward a distant bend in the line and said, "There are people who are never satisfied until they see what's around the next curve, and I'm one of them, and there's always a next curve. And it makes no difference if I've been around it before because the curve's never the same."

Sometime later after I was home again, Dick wrote, "When I'm riding the tracks, I think about the incredible effort it took to build the tunnels and bridges when there was little heavy equipment available. On tunnel ceilings, old smoke stains from the coal burners make me think about all the people who traveled that line and how many died or were injured during construction.

"I like to look closely at the rails to see the date they were made. The oldest I've ridden was 1873 — three years before Custer's Last Stand. And once I found some railroad china in the brush — it was barely chipped. I think an overworked porter might have deliberately left it behind. It's things like that, when I'm riding steel, that make me feel in touch with things."

❧ 8 ❧

Printer's Pie

U NTIL ONE EVENING IN BICKNELL, UTAH, population about what would fill a couple of crosstown busses, I'd not known pickle pie existed or that it could be agreeably eaten by something other than a scavenger or the deranged. It was, however, the word *pie* itself (rather than the pickles) that led me to compare it with a book: miscellaneous contents presented between two coverings. In that way also, a pie suggests a life: our assorted ingredients tossed in between a beginning and an end.

Q and I had spent the day by driving the largely aerial and twisted highway numbered Utah 12. Winding through the south-central portion of the state, 12 is a half-circular course into the plateau-and-mountain country of the Escalante River, a land of exceptional terrain; as a scenic route, the road may be matchable in another place or two, but I don't believe it can be surpassed. It's only a little more than a hundred miles long, yet to travel it is to go deep into a time when Earth looked like some other planet, a bare-bones world trying to mantle itself with life. The national forest along parts of the road, even where seriously mangled and manured by cattle, revealed by contrast how far the great stony expanses had yet to go to overcome their extraplanetariness. With the Southwest returning to greater aridity after more than a century of atypical precipitation, the native beauty of sereness would recur to be further enhanced by the reappearance of the ancient climate.

Once we'd taken quarters and I'd spotted a phone-directory ad for a promising café at an opolis on down the road, we set out for the

place. In the window was a painted sign: HOME OF THE FAMOUS
PICKLE & PINTO BEAN PIES. Another sign, a flickering red-
neon OPEN, suffused the interior with a glow like a campfire just
barely keeping a desert night at bay. The air was redolent with cinnamon and baking pies, and near the center stood a tall glass-case "pie
fridge" holding ten different kinds, both whole and sliced. Among a
half-dozen with standard ingredients and the two of self-proclaimed
fame were also ones of oatmeal and buttermilk.

We ordered a lone bowl of green-chile stew to share so that we
could later take on a few slender wedges of pie. I waited for the supper by walking around the café. In my eyes, the '60s building was
neither old nor quaint, but it did have an austere honesty. On the
notice board was the usual array of business cards and penned notes
offering well-drilling, cattle sales, pest control, babysitting (different people), and one from a man wanting to buy antlers, and another
announcing a charity Haircut-a-Thon.

In a booth, a couple of tough road characters, the bigger with a
thick wrist tattooed TRY ME, seemed to take a low view of my note-
taking, but they didn't challenge it, and they nodded to my greeting.
(When the men left, Q whispered, "Tell me there isn't a load of some
contraband stashed in that van.") They ate cheeseburgers, and to the
young waitress's suggestion of some pie, they shook their heads, but
when she had stepped away, one made a smutty remark about pie of
a more physiological sort.

It was that reference, unseemly as it was, that got me thinking
about the nature of pie, and I challenged Q to name a dozen pies not
on the menu, which she did, although I felt obligated to question
"boiled braunschweiger pie." I added onion pie, eel pie, funeral pie,
and printer's pie, the last of which she forced me to define: a jumble
of assorted and unsorted type of various fonts and sizes a hard-up
compositor may hunt through to find letters to complete a story.

That's when I saw the metaphor: we arise each morning to begin
looking for a few letters among the ems and slugs and dingbats of
our lives so that we might spell out a couple of words or, on a good

day, a complete sentence to fit the longer story of our existence. Is your life to be set in Bodoni or Bembo, Caslon or Clarendon? Does its size belong in four-point gem or ten-point elite? Should we printer's devils in the Great Cosmic Printery put forth our tales in full-face or blackface, chapel text or old style, condensed or extended? Is your tale in serif or sans serif? If the type at hand has been used many times before to spell other words in other lives, if it's worn and chipped, nevertheless it's what we have, and so, journeymen all, we compose our stories that we might publish them in hopes they'll not too soon go to the fishmonger to wrap a mullet.

In making anything — a book, a suit of clothes, a journey — not every item can be profitably used, because some pieces seem not to fit readily the pattern at hand. In a more frugal time, neglected fonts and rejects weren't discarded but went instead into a hellbox, a term used by pressmen, tailors, and old-style quilters. I descend from such a line, two of whom you've already met: the slain William Grayston's first wife who was later a tailoress (as the term was) on the border of Indian Territory; you'll also recall the great-grandmother who delighted in making quilts in the turkey-foot pattern.

Perhaps here a mindful reader says, "Are you, or are you not, going to get to the pickle pie?" Very well: its crust was flaky. With that, a reporter who tries for accuracy must stop, for to describe a taste precisely is no more possible than to write the final decimal of a transcendental number. Gustatory sensations simply cannot be well-conveyed in words, and odd it is that two functions of the human tongue are so unavailing to each other. To speak of a taste, we must do it obliquely, impressionistically, metaphorically, comparatively. For someone who has never had sight, *perhaps* I could convey the appearance of an apple, but for a person who has never tasted, I could not describe the flavor of even something so simple as salt. Texture, consistency, temperature, and our own response ("Delicious!" "Awful!") do not convey taste. Describing the flavors of food is verbal sleight of hand.

I can, though, when it comes to pickle pie, give you something of considerable accuracy and usefulness: I can pass along Cula Ekker's recipe for it as served in the Sunglow Family Restaurant in Bicknell, Utah. *"But,"* the insistent reader cries, *"is the pie any good?"* You tell me.*

We tried pinto-bean, oatmeal, and pickle pies, and I liked the latter two well enough that they led me, before Q could get out of the way, back to my metaphoric recipe for printer's pie.

This chapter, as it turns out, is a found text selected from what I've come upon in the printer's pie of my travels. The hellbox holding the pieces is notebooks composed to a considerable extent of things overheard or said to me during the last two decades of the twentieth century. I began the practice of recording certain chance utterances one afternoon when I found myself wishing for a book by a Shakespeare or a Brontë or a Hawthorne that would contain nothing other than what they heard on their daily rounds, words set down but not otherwise expanded, a kaleidoscope of ordinary quartz-sand. What picture of a vanished day and place would emerge? What was it the cobbler said when Will brought in a shoe beyond repair? What words made Emily smile as she stepped into the tilbury?

Time turns the commonplace uncommon: Archaeologists study the thousand-year-old coprolites of the Anasazi; believers buy and enshrine a dusty hair once attached to the pate of St. Polycarp. The seventeenth-century Japanese pilgrim-poet Bashō traveled for twelve-hundred miles over five months, writing prose and verse about landscape and history and passions and death, and still, maybe the most memorable haiku in his *Narrow Road to a Far Province* is about being kept awake all night by fleas and lice and a horse pissing close to his pillow.

---

* Pickle Pie: 5 eggs; 2 cups sugar; 1 tsp each of cinnamon, nutmeg, and lemon extract; 2 tbsp cornstarch; 1 cup and 2 tbsp light cream; ⅛ cup melted margarine; 12 ounces sweet pickles, drained and ground; 2 pie shells. Beat eggs and sugar until lemon-colored and thick; beat in spices, extract, cornstarch, cream, and margarine. Stir pickles into mixture and pour into 2 pie shells. Bake at 350 degrees for 60 to 75 minutes or until a knife into the center comes out clean. [Q tip: Add a soupçon of *diced* sweet pickles for crunch.]

What follows is a selection taken down beyond the hundredth meridian, a congeries Q sportingly calls "Heat-Moon's Concise Oral History of the American West." I think of it now more as a printer's pie of memories. Some of its pieces with their attached stories, its pickled ingredients, helped carry us through the Rockies and across the Great Plains and on home again.

"Lady, I don't believe in no God. I ride Harleys."

———

Old fellow to a young man: "You look more like I used to look like than I ever did."

———

On a woman at her estranged father's funeral: "I've seen dried salt-cod with damper eyes."

———

"Sure he was a commodities trader, but when it came to his own investments, he wore both a belt and suspenders and maybe two pairs of shorts."

———

"I got you a date tonight."
"Who?"
"The guy down at the phone company."
"Well, he'd better not be cheap."

———

"When Mike and I went to clean out Mother's apartment, we emptied the stinking refrigerator first. I set to one side a can of congealed skillet drippings while we did the rest of the rooms, and when I came back to the grease, it had melted, so I took it out to the yard to dump it. Inside the can was a smaller one, and rolled up in it was thirty-five-thousand dollars. That was her entire inheritance to us."

———

From a young man: "I don't live according to who I am. I live according to what I pretend I am. It's working out for me."

———

Woman on cell phone: "I'm tired of this, Ray. You've been allowed one phone call one too many times, and this time I'm not coming down."

———

To a man behind a piled desk: "You ready to do some fishing?"
"No, I got to waller these papers around for a while."

———

"What's wrong with you now?"
"I'm just hungry."
"You're a whole lot worse than hungry."

———

A daughter to her mother in the home center: "Oh, come on! You're saying the best wallpaper is books?"

———

"She just sort of sat up in bed and looked around and stared at me and said, 'Well, so long, Jim,' and she laid back down again, and she was gone. I'm telling you, she went so easy, I think she'd been rehearsing it."

———

"That boy's had too much solo love in his own closet."

———

"When I was in the Pacific during the war, for some reason two things I missed most were my mother's burnt-sugar cake and the smell of honeysuckle. One time she sent me a cake wrapped and pad- ded around with honeysuckle leaves and blossoms. The flour sucked up that smell, and the cake wasn't edible. I had to toss it overboard. I cried like a baby."

———

"No, goddamnit, sweetheart. I will not go camping out there with all the creepers great and small!"

———

"Mother's present to Dad on his birthday was an eye tuck so she'd look better to him."

———

Rancher to a Denver tourist driving a big and gleaming pickup truck: "If you ain't going to work that machine, then you ought not be driving it."

———

"You're so negative about people, if you ever become mayor of San Francisco, you'll put diving boards on the Golden Gate Bridge."

———

To a clerk in a bookstore: "I'm looking for a runner's guide to running for nonrunners."

———

"Every Sunday in his church it's the same thing — concoctions about concoctions."

———

"Your problem is, you think too much."
"I don't think that never crossed my mind."

———

He: "I thought you were going to wear your glitterati coat."
She, opening her coat to show the spangles turned outside in: "I don't feel too glitterati tonight."

———

"Look at you. Life's been wasted on you."

———

"You know, Son, a little mileage of thinking isn't going to wear the tread off your brain."

———

Earnest advice to a writer at a cocktail party: "You want a good subject for your next book? I've got one for you. You can have it — *Ten Great Ways to Die.*"

———

"Don't tell me I've got no faith. I've got great faith in skepticism."

———

From a hardware-store clerk: "We don't get much craftsmanship today. What we get is crapmanshit."

———

Senior fellow: "You say the story of your life could be called *Almost*. Well, you're ahead of me. Mine would have to be *Nothing Much.* Or, better, *Whoosh!*"

———

"Quit squirming! What's wrong with you, boy? You got a cockchafer beetle in your shorts?"

———

"That preacher's so self-righteous he'd reform Heaven and heal God."

———

"*Father-in-law*'s a mouthful. *Mother-in-law* too. They got all those dashes in there. We need better words, like fatherado. Motherina."

———

An elderly man leaning on his cane: "My axles is holding up okay, but my rims is worn down pretty good."

———

"This is her last year teaching grade school. She's had it with a bunch of whining, self-centered brats. And their children aren't much better."

———

Same man: "One parent complained that telling her kid to stop running in the hallway was 'too militaristic.' And there are people who say we don't need the draft."

———

"Fred's appetite isn't voracious — it's predacious."

———

"How's Mister Wilson?"
"I guess you didn't hear? Last Friday he got initiated into the fraternity of death."
"Oh, I'm so sorry. He was a good man. Well, I guess we're all pledged."

———

"Mother taught us it was bad grammar to end a sentence with a proposition."

"I don't know about that, but it could be bad manners."

———

"That bunch up there at X Ranch ain't nothing but underbrush that needs to be grubbed out."

———

At a gas pump after petroleum reached one hundred dollars a barrel: "Do you remember when we called these places 'service stations'?"
"I do."
"The only service here now is the kind the bull gives the cow."

———

"My wife has long, dark hair. Beautiful hair. When she doesn't want any hanky-panky, she pulls it down over her face like a drawn curtain, and that means No Show Tonight."

———

Following a lecture, a man wearing a cross came up to the writer and said, "You speak from the pulpit of deviltry."

———

"After Walter began recovering from his stroke, he wanted to be of help again to regain a little self-esteem. One night he brought me in a tray of milk and cookies. He stood there holding the tray very formally. He hadn't tied up his pajama bottoms properly, and they fell to the floor. Poor man was trying to demonstrate recovery, and right there, almost in the macaroons, was his, you know."

———

Man: "Will you please stop kicking me under the table?"
Woman: "I did not kick you. I was just gesturing."

———

On a man seated at a bar, whose face suggested he had stories: "Forget it. That's Charles. His closet is invisible, but you won't get him to open the door."

———

"I can't stand his religion or his politics or his lodge hall or the shoes he wears. You name it, we're diabolically opposite."

———

At a reunion: "Bob, where the hell would we be today if we'd stayed in this little stinking town?"

———

"You complain about her too much. Here's one dude who'd like to put the clamps on your old lady."

———

From a man named Schluckenbeyer: "My grandmother almost didn't marry Pop-Pop because of names — his *and* hers. Before him, she could spell her whole name with three letters — Hannah Ann Hanahan."

———

Father to daughter: "If your dear dad didn't do everything he didn't want to do, he wouldn't have done much. And you'd have starved to death."

———

"My ex was honest to a fault, and that was her biggest fault — telling me the truth when I didn't need the truth just then."

———

"He was mean, and he didn't get along with his kids. They told me he had big pockets stitched into a shroud, packed them with rolled-up hundred-dollar bills, and had his lawyer see to his cremation. By god, the old bastard took it with him."

———

"My dad was a preacher, and he didn't give us an inch. You'd step out of line, and right there in your face he'd open his Bible like a switch-blade and cut you down."

———

"When I moved to Utah, I couldn't believe how ignorant these Mormons were about Jews. One woman asked if I celebrated Thanksgiving. I said, 'Of course.' And she said, 'But it's not in your Koran, is it?'"

———

"Before the divorce, I got to hating him so much, I'd leave the wrapping on cheese slices in his sandwich. Maybe he'd choke on it."

"That's not so bad. You probably remember both my kids were born at home. Randy never knew I kept their placentas in the freezer in case the boys ever needed a skin graft or something. When things turned south before our divorce, one time after he hit Jason, for dinner that night I cut off a slice of placenta and mixed it in with that meat-loaf Randy loved."

———

"No sir, I'm not paying for another night in your fancy four-letter hotel."

———

From a man showing scars on the backs of his hands: "I got caught in a prairie fire in about fifty-six. All I could do was lay out in a low spot, unzip, and pee up in the air, and wet myself down. Of course, that meant I had to keep the wet side up, so I covered my face with my hands."

———

"The thing I like about the ancient Greeks is they had so many gods, they couldn't force just *one* on people. The people had a choice."

———

A worried student to a writer at a book signing: "Where's climate change or jihadism or species decline in your books? What's the use of a book today if it's not about survival?"
A woman, unknown to either of them, overhearing: "What's the use of survival without books that go beyond survival?"

VI.
Down an Old Waterway

The Southern Atlantic Seaboard

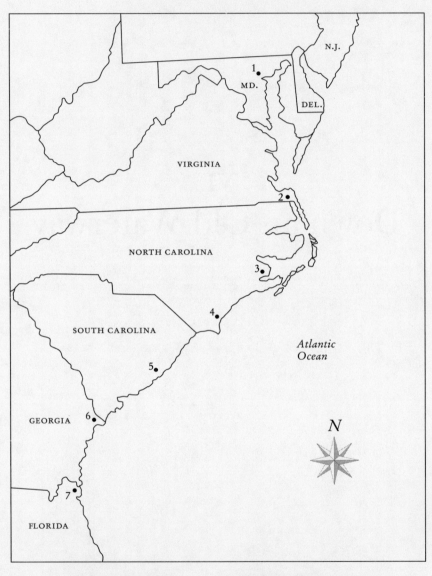

1 Baltimore, Maryland
2 Great Dismal Swamp
3 Oriental, North Carolina
4 Wilmington, North Carolina
5 Charleston, South Carolina
6 Savannah, Georgia
7 Fernandina Beach, Florida

Down an Old Waterway

On the Beach

The beach, in many ways, is an extremely unpleasant place in which to live. The soil is unstable, shifted by each tide, thoroughly churned by storms; anything projecting from the surface is given a sand blasting with each high wind. The landward edge is saline desert because occasional spring and storm tides bring sea water that evaporates, leaving its salts behind. The plant life, therefore, consists of only a few succulents just above high water. Paradoxically, fresh water is also a danger; for a marine animal may find the rain soaking its precious salts away if it ventures too far up the beach. Without plants to break the winter gales or provide shade from summer sun, the beach can also be very cold and very hot. But animals live there in large numbers.

There are some advantages. Food is concentrated there by the water. Flotsam collects along the high-water mark. Waves furnish a constant supply of fresh sea water for filter feeders, without any effort on their part. Finally, some animals may be able to make a living in a marginal environment who couldn't stand the competition in more favored places.

— Mildred and John Teal,
Portrait of an Island,
1964

❥ 1 ❧

Following the Magenta Line

THE FIRST DRAFT of one of the great adventure stories was in watercolor. Robert Louis Stevenson, stormbound for several days inside a cramped Scottish cottage in 1881, took up a brush and his stepson's shilling box of paints to idle away some hours. Rarely has a writer idled himself into such masterfully unexpected creation, for what first came to his mind was neither words nor even a picture but rather an outline, or more accurately, a shoreline of an imaginary island that Stevenson was soon filling with invented topography. His sketching further brought forth characters and details to fill the landscape — a peg-legged sea cook, an eye-patched buccaneer with a parrot on his shoulder, and even a chantey ("Yo-ho-ho, and a bottle of rum") — all elements that would become virtual requisites in subsequent pirate tales. At its completion he labeled his chart TREASURE ISLAND and thereby set children for a century to drawing their own maps, each containing the sine qua non of such topographs, an X-marks-the-spot above hidden booty.

Whether children today — given their pixel-driven, binary disconnect from a real world — draw such maps, I don't know. But surely a number of us from years gone did, and we did it in much the same manner with an irregular outline filled in with a few common features: deep woods, dark valley, dismal swamp, and stony outcrops resembling something threatening (Coffin Rock, Deadman's Jawbone, the Gallows).

Years removed from my versions of such charts, I see now I never quite escaped them. If Stevenson drew a novel from his, from mine

I've drawn a life. Virtually all I've done of any possible consequence has proceeded from imagination confronting printed maps and nautical charts. Maps were — and still are for me — catechism. Place-names pose the questions, and I hunt the answers. To discover in an atlas, say, Dagsboro, Delaware, the questions follow: *Have I been there? What's it like? Any hidden booty?* But this catechism has no prescribed responses, for the catechist is only an imagined chorographer and I a secular catechumen.

In my study I have a 1966 U.S. road atlas wherein every roadway I've ever traveled is highlighted in yellow. Except for a couple of mountain valleys in Nevada, those yellow centerline routes have taken me within at least twenty-five miles of nearly every place in the forty-eight states, the nation constituted as it was in 1947 when I drew my first treasure map. Far more than has any classroom or textbook, crooked map lines connecting place-names have directed my life. Route Whatever between Puddleton and Podunk, betwixt St. Joe and San Jose, Watertown and Waterville, between me and a land of quoz.

By the time Q and I were bringing to an end our several seasons of quozzing, the evidence of a warming Earth was no longer in question, and we began to change the way we traveled: more canoes and rafts, bicycles and trains — even boots or moving along with a group. That's how the final leg of these journeys came about.

In November we made our way to the Inner Harbor of Baltimore to meet up with a small boat for a run southward. I echo what a fellow traveler, a Bostonian, would soon answer when I asked what he hoped to see: "I'm just the bear that went over the mountain," he said. So Q and I too were wanting only to see what we could see on the Intracoastal Waterway, a nine-hundred-mile voyage on inside passages to Fernandina Beach on Amelia Island, Florida, just north of Jacksonville. It may not have been happenstance that the route, indicated on government navigation charts by the so-called magenta line, was a passage into the erstwhile territory of eighteenth-century pirates and their treasured islands.

The day before departure, not far from the dock, we took quarters in a hotel at an intersection where once stood the Indian Queen Tavern antedating the Revolutionary War. The *History of Baltimore City and County* says it was "a place of great celebrity in its day, and many of the most distinguished men of the past were entertained within its walls." Q believes William Clark stayed there on the way home from his river-and-sea voyage of 1798 that she was writing about. The Indian Queen, while long vanished, exists in my imagination as a portion of my interior map of old Baltimore.

French visitor Moreau de St. Méry stayed at the tavern a generation after the Revolutionary War and noted "an enormous collection of large slippers to which one helps himself on going to bed so that he may find, on waking the next day, his cleaned shoes or boots outside his door." Finding a shine in Baltimore has today become rather more challenging, perhaps an indicator of greater prosperity and racial equality.

From the corner of Baltimore and Hanover streets, we walked to Lexington Market. Although we'd devote the next two weeks to remotenesses along the Waterway — town-bred fellow that I am — I wanted to get a solid shove off from the culinary docks of Baltimore, the city H. L. Mencken said in 1910 "has the frowzy, unkempt, out-of-the-elbow, forlorn air of a third-rate boarding house." Only a native can utter such talk without yielding his place of honor; yet, were the old curmudgeon to see downtown Baltimore today, he would have to account differently for all the glassy high-rises surrounding the rebuilt waterfront from where the frowzy, unkempt, and forlorn disappeared a generation ago. No other American city harbor, to my eye, has the pleasing curve of a bent inlet ending in a watery cul-de-sac that baffles rough waters so that even pedal boats can glide about in it.

The market, embracing the natural slope of the hill, was full of voices and the clunk of chopping cleavers and the sizzle of griddles, the scents rising from iced fish, baking dough, and frying oils — a Baltimorean hubbub redolent and cacophonous. Signs everywhere:

neon signs, painted ones, signs advertising rabbit, pigs' feet, scrapple, fried chicken, oysters raw or steamed, clams, fresh grated horseradish, bean pie, greens (turnip, mustard, rape, kale), and a sign labeled *RACCOON AND MUSKRAT IN SEASON* and another, *HEADQUARTERS FOR FRESH HOG MAWS AND CHITTERLINGS*. The offerings (suggesting here were no votaries of Levitical dietary law), as much as the speech and faces, revealed the importance of Baltimore, sitting almost atop the Mason-Dixon Line, as one of the important urban stops on the Underground Railroad. By my reckoning, Baltimore is the southernmost northern city in no small way because of its significance in African-American life. (The NAACP national headquarters is here, and on its grounds, in a nice ethnic mélange, lie the ashes of Dorothy Parker who, in admiration of Martin Luther King, left her estate to the association. Her marker, in addition to some usual commemorative words, includes her chosen epitaph: EXCUSE MY DUST.)

The jumbling of ethnic foods sharpened my appetite and cleared my mind for the voyage as we strolled about, assembling a meal of Chesapeake crab cake, "Jewish corned beef," and a side of Korean bibimap (wokked vegetables topped with a fried egg). Gus Kubitzki long believed it an evolutionary injustice that a slow-witted bovine would end up with four stomachs while humankind gets only one (but then, to consider the girth of so many size XXXXL citizens, perhaps evolution knows best). In expiation, we spent the rest of the afternoon in walking downtown Baltimore.

In the hotel room that evening, I sat back to scan the Yellow Pages to help fill in a mental map of the city. There were listings for Accordion Players, Anchors (Marine), Clammers' Supplies, Crab Houses, Davits, Luncheonettes, Nautical Charts, Naval Architects, Oceanographers, Parrots, Quill Pens, and Yacht Brokers. Predictably, accordion players, oceanographers, and parrots combined were far outnumbered by 104 pages of lawyers.

⫸ 2 ⫷

At the Temporary Edge of America

T HE NEXT MORNING we went down to the harbor to board our boat — with a length of only 165 feet, it hardly seemed a "ship" to me who first went to sea on a nine-hundred-foot aircraft carrier. Our vessel was tied up across the pier from the sloop USS *Constellation* — not the first one of that name but the one of 1854, the only Civil War vessel still afloat. The presence of the sloop was apropos to the voyage we were about to undertake, because her initial duty was off the African coast to interdict slave ships commonly headed for southern ports we'd see or pass near. Outdoor speakers at her pier wafted out sea chanteys, and a fair breeze set one's spiritual sails for two weeks of following the southern half of the Atlantic shores on an engineered inside-passage first proposed by Albert Gallatin in 1808. Abundant with history — human and natural — the Intracoastal Waterway is the backside of the American front door, a route far too little-known, in part because no one has yet written a definitive history of it.

On the dock, I couldn't pick up the vapors of Baltimore that I remembered from earlier years, the drift from factories making soap, sugar, and spices (including the spice without which Chesapeake cuisine would literally pale — the rusty grains of Old Bay Seasoning). Instead I smelled the old bay itself into which we soon headed, briefly accompanied by a school of small fish, down the Patapsco River lined with wharves and warehouses and behind them enough pointed steeples and spires near Fell's Point to make it appear bristled. Baltimore — the third-busiest port on the East Coast — is about fifteen miles from the open water of Chesapeake Bay and almost two-hundred sailing miles by the southern route from the Atlantic.

We passed the anchorage from which Francis Scott Key got an early-morning view of the immense flag that was still flying at Fort McHenry following a night of British bombardment. Some years before, I was inside the fortification one evening when, helping five others to fold the huge replica flag, I got a true notion of its size (no wonder Key could see it); a view from his anchorage would have revealed more banner than bastion visible, and that raised a question with Q: "Wouldn't a spangled flag that big help an enemy direct bombs bursting in air?"

The Atlantic Intracoastal Waterway, in its most limited definition, begins 180 miles due south of that banner, virtually at the mouth of the Chesapeake. Our voyage was to be a sailing through backwaters and into waterside villages — some reachable only by boat — all the way paying little attention to the few cities along the route. In my mind I wanted to hear the electronic voice of one of those automobile satellite-navigation systems cautioning: "You are entering an unverified area."

The prefix *intra* is crucial to the history of this interior passage because the Waterway came about as protection from seas dangerous with storms and, during several wars, British privateers and German U-boats. Following Gallatin's formal proposal, construction of a route *within* the coastline — behind the peninsulas and outer islands — took more than a century. The Inland Waterway System, of which the AICW is a portion, offers almost four-thousand miles of sheltered passage from Boston to Brownsville, Texas, only a few of those miles open to the sea. At the time of our voyage though, survival of the Waterway was not assured, in part because of enormous expenditures for a war in the Middle East. I'd been aboard just a couple of hours when I heard that funding for the Army Corps of Engineers to maintain the route was insufficient, despite urgings from the Atlantic Intracoastal Waterway Association. Should you, peripatetic reader, enjoy sailing inland waters, wait no longer to travel this passage unless you are a long-distance canoeist.

I'd have preferred following the route in my own small boat on my own schedule, one accommodating quixotic quests and over-night anchorages in the creeks and guts and gunkholes where I could snub a cockleboat to a tree to await the clapping of a Virginia rail or hear against the hull the clicks of snapping shrimp, or catch a glimpse of a little mouse-sized native, its name longer than its tail: the Southern marsh rice-rat. After several years of hoping, I decided such an independent expedition was unlikely and settled for travel on a small motor-vessel with a name so chauvinistically vainglorious I won't mention it. But, unlike my imaginary skiff, the real boat rose high enough above the water to give good viewing over bankside trees into territory otherwise veiled from a smaller craft. Our tub had its advantages, some of which came from a few fellow travelers who had knowledge to share. In my notes I rechristened her the *Bog Trotter,* an old name for that peculiar bird of wetlands, the American bittern, about which I'll say more when a moment of quiet in the voyage arrives.

It was past midday by the time we reached the open water of Chesapeake, and the early November sunset further shortened vis-ibility so that we would sail half the bay at night, a loss acceptable only because it wasn't the Chesapeake we'd come for. After dark, trying to keep the estuary before me, I pulled from my satchel of books about territory along the Waterway William B. Cronin's *The Disappearing Islands of the Chesapeake.* Disappearance and van-ishings are a significant aspect of the ICW because the Atlantic has moved its shores eastward and westward, back and forth, for mil-lions of years, perpetually shifting the sea-edge across hundreds of miles. Greenville, North Carolina, to pick a place, today about seventy-five miles from the ocean, would have been a coastal town forty-five million years ago; Atlantic City, to choose another, only eleven-thousand years ago would have been more than a hundred miles from the beach. Even now, longtime residents along the southern shores have numerous here-today, gone-tomorrow stories, and the engineering effort to keep the Intracoastal open is an unceasing battle to deny the Atlantic its ancient grounds and defy its nature. Perhaps more than any other thousand miles in America, this southeastern coast and its attendant islands are continually being remade at a rate humans refuse either to conceive or concede.

Cronin says that some five-hundred islands have slipped beneath Chesapeake waves in historical times, implying a pattern that not merely augurs the future but guarantees it. While most of the now vanished lands — once the Indians were pushed off — were without later residents, a few currently inhabited islands, such as well-known Tangier and Smith, are today effectively dissolving. In the last century and a half, Tangier has lost an average of almost nine acres each year, and Smith has had to be, quite literally, shored up with dredge spoil, a "solution" (so say I, not Cronin) that will last only somewhat longer than a cake of ice in Lexington Market.

The great engine — in addition to shifting tectonic plates — behind this change is climate. Polar ice-caps melt or enlarge, and the consequent heat-exchanges create storms that cause submergences and risings, erosions and depositions, a metaphor, if you will, for the engines that drive our lives: our past submerging, our memories eroding here, perhaps depositing something over there.

A hat on the head of a five-year-old child standing at the edge of the shoreline at low tide on Smith Island is equal to its highest point, scarcely enough elevation to accommodate erosion or a storm surge in a bay rising two inches every decade. Given the transience in so many aspects of American life — jobs, marriages, housing, first place in the National League — we should do better in at least acknowledging temporariness other than by disbelief, surprise, or irritation; of all nations, we should grasp ceaseless comings and goings.

So, with those ideas, Q and I descended the temporarily present eastern edge of the American continent, an intricate terrene-marine realm.

❥ 3 ❧

Where the Turkey Buzzard Won't Fly

By dawn the *Bog Trotter* had left the Chesapeake and crossed Hampton Roads — the historic waters of the battle between the USS *Monitor* and CSS *Virginia* (built as the USS *Merrimack*), where neither vessel could do in the other but did do in the era of wooden warships. We tied to the wharf in the "refurbished" Town Point section of Norfolk, Virginia, just long enough to allow a walk through the rebuilt heart of the city, now tidy and clean but purged of much history, including the barnacle-back haunts I remember from my naval days there in the early '60s. I don't want to argue for the preservation of dives and boozers and juke-joints, flophouses and fleshpots. Nevertheless, isn't there a middle ground between those places and vapid, disinfected high-rises or the new massive mall that not only obliterated history but seemed to drive out humanity after five p.m.? Was this Norfolk, Norwalk, or Norwich?

For us just then, it mattered not, because our boat was again soon under way toward the promise of unverified areas lying in a slender strip of creeks and cuts and canals and channels, islands and islets, shoals and sounds, the corridor of the magenta sailing-line, places where dwelt wood storks and manatees, and fish that drum, shrimp that snap, birds that clap, and not a few chefs who cook up Low Country cuisine of utterly silent oysters living in a cavalcade of waters once coursed by Indian dugouts long before Britons began cutting sarsens for Stonehenge.

Our tacks during the next two weeks would be alternations from due south to southeast to southwest, to get us not only nine-hundred miles south but more than two-hundred miles westward, directly below not Baltimore but almost due south of Cleveland. At the mouth of the Elizabeth River, between Norfolk and Portsmouth, Virginia, floats a buoy called Mile Marker Zero. The Intracoastal Waterway begins there, not far from the encounter between the *Monitor* and *Merrimack* and in the shadow of some of the facilities for the largest naval-base in the world.

How is it we are to know our pasts? One approach is to stand where significant pieces of it unfolded, and there to imagine the place as it was then, its colors, weather, sounds; at Mile Zero, to hear the Dahlgren guns of the *Monitor* and smell the burnt powder from the *Merrimack* is to become a kind of witness to a battle that saw no winner except warfare itself. Giving our recall of history a physical setting — its own actual stage — improves memory and deepens travel and provides one more reason to rise and go forth. (Incidentally, the guns and history-changing turret of the *Monitor* recently had been brought up from the Atlantic and were on display — temporarily in a tank of water — just a few miles from Hampton Roads, and that makes imaginative re-creation easier: you can at last see big pieces of that infernally fascinating engine of war.)

The lower Elizabeth River was a corridor of naval ships large enough to hoist aboard the *Monitor* and *Merrimack* as if they were dinghies. The riverbanks, initially lined with piers and naval cranes, gradually changed to industrial wharves and fuel tanks and piles of construction materials, then changed again to a wooded shore on the west, the east side splattered with rusting hulls, an abandoned tug in collapse, a few moored small boats. Several of the bridges raised for us, revealing waiting autos with drivers whose faces wore not curiosity but annoyance, thereby disproving my notion that to see a moving boat, *any* moving boat, was of necessity to wonder where it might be going and wish to be aboard. Are there truly souls so numbed by contemporary life that a passing vessel with waving hands will fail to rouse an entrapped motorist?

South of Norfolk, two water routes, both canals, run along the

edge of the Great Dismal Swamp; the one we didn't take cuts a generally straight southerly course while the other — somewhat newer,
wider, and deeper — heads east before turning south. They rejoin
below Elizabeth City, North Carolina.

I was hoping we'd follow the older Dismal Swamp Canal because
its narrower channel gets a boat closer to shore and wildlife. Q had
told our captain, "He's an old sailor-boy who likes to get on water so
he can see the land," and the captain said, "So do I." He, nevertheless,
chose the Albemarle and Chesapeake Canal of 1859 that sees some
fifteen-thousand boats annually, most passing through the only lock
on the main line of the ICW and moving on along what's left of the
eastern side of the Dismal Swamp where draining for a naval airfield
and pockets of suburban sprawl had been significant, although a deep
fringe of canal-side trees created an illusion of sailing through a less
overrun wetland. Both canals allowed quick exodus from an urban
world to a wooded one, the A&C merging with the North Landing
River flowing into Albemarle Sound at the North Carolina line.

Years ago, after hearing for the thousandth time that "there are
two kinds of people in this world," I started a list for a short story
(never written) about the follies of a man who sees only two sides of
existence, a limitation that makes him judgmental beyond his capacities to judge wisely, his dichotomizing turning things into opposites
rather than revealing them as strands in a complex web beyond full
comprehension. My list wasn't a high-toned thing of good versus
evil or magnificent against miserly; it was of a much lower order,
duos like Anglophiles versus Francophiles. Lovers of dry barbecue
or wet. Fountain penners versus ballpointers. Sinkers or swimmers.
List makers versus the sane.

Here's one I might have included: inland boaters or blue-water
sailors. My days with the Navy gave me a lifetime fill of an unbroken
ocean-horizon forever beyond, so that in 1964 when I left my ship
as a seaman, I became a mere boatman who prefers voyages with visible bounds, trips that carry a traveler *into* a landscape; the narrower
the water and smaller the boat, the better for my passage. That, as

you can see, means my environmental ethics sometimes bump into my love of canals, since the two don't always harmoniously cohabit. The unnaturally uncurving banks of the Albemarle and Chesapeake, however, didn't destroy the pleasure of gliding quietly along the swamp margin. To sit on the deck in the warm autumn sun and watch America slowly slip past, no semitrucks on your bumper, no weary motel clerk to deal with, no gas tanks to fill, was just plain damn sweet. And then, to be able to study a chart or a text *while moving* through a territory allows one to link symbol with its actuality, a significant boon to remembering a place.

The prospect of seeing the Great Dismal Swamp led me to carry William Byrd's *The History of the Dividing Line Betwixt Virginia and North Carolina,* his narrative of surveying the border in 1728 through the swamp and on westward to the shadow of the Great Smokies. My belief that human voices of the past are also characters in a landscape allowed me to keep traveling the Dismal even after sundown and made me eager for sunrise to see the reality of what I'd been reading about the night before. (You especially understand this last part, envisioning reader, because it's what you're doing at this very moment.)

William Byrd, born in 1674 in Virginia and educated as a barrister in England, returned to America to become a legislator, a naturalist, and a closeted man of letters. He was a cosmopolite in the brambles, he could turn a phrase, and he wasn't overly decorous about describing earthy aspects of life in the colonies a half-century before the Revolution. His narrative is history one rarely encounters in school, as he answers questions anyone but the priggish can delight in. On that second evening I read about a place just seven miles east of where we were at that moment:

On the south shore not far from the inlet dwelt a marooner that modestly called himself a hermit, though he forfeited that name by suffering a wanton female to cohabit with him. His habitation was a bower covered with bark after the Indian fashion, which in that mild situation protected him pretty well from the weather. Like the ravens, he neither plowed nor sowed but subsisted chiefly upon oysters, which his handmaid made a shift to gather from the adjacent rocks. Sometimes, too, for change of diet, he sent her to drive up the neighbor's cows, to moisten their mouths with a little milk. But as for raiment, he depended mostly upon his length of beard and she upon her length of hair, part of which she brought decently forward and the rest dangled behind quite down to her rump, like one of Herodotus' East Indian Pygmies. Thus did these wretches live in a dirty state of nature and were mere Adamites, innocence only excepted.

It was Byrd who firmly affixed the adjective *dismal* to a swamp so challenging penetration by his surveying crew that he, a gentleman, circumvented most of it and concluded it was lifeless to the degree "not even a turkey buzzard will venture to fly over it." Yet, thirty-five years later, George Washington, ever the land speculator, spoke of the Dismal as "a glorious paradise" that could be improved by draining. Whether such drainage might kill paradise didn't cross his mind. Indeed, over the next few generations the greater part of the swamp was drained and logged until 1973 when a portion of what survived became a national wildlife refuge. Even still, continued ditching at its margins allowed agriculture and the sprawlation of Norfolk/ Virginia Beach to continue consuming the Great Dismal until more than two-thirds of the swamp Byrd knew have vanished.

I will risk your patience with a further comment from Byrd suggesting one aspect of such terrestrial loss. About the extinct passenger pigeon, he writes:

The men's mouths watered at the sight of a prodigious flight of wild pigeons, which flew high over our heads to the southward. The flocks of these birds of passage are so amazingly great sometimes that they darken the sky, nor is it uncommon for them to light in such numbers in the larger limbs of mulberry trees and oaks as to break them down. . . . In these long flights they are very lean and their flesh is far from being white or tender, though good enough upon a march, when hunger is the sauce and makes it go down better than truffles and morels would do.

Reading Byrd made me curious enough to leave my bunk and go out on deck and try to see by moonlight whether anything from his world was yet visible. At Troublesome Point we'd left the swamp behind, and I had to imagine rather than see, so I returned to the cabin and Byrd's account of a place once not far from where we were at that moment. In describing his visit with his weary and deprived crew to a Nottoway settlement, he speaks frankly about practices usually ignored or hidden by other writers and implicitly reveals the important role of women in Indian-Caucasian relations not just there but across America:

Though their complexions be a little sad-colored, yet their shapes are very straight and well proportioned. Their faces are seldom handsome, yet they have an air of innocence and bashfulness that with a little less dirt would not fail to make them desirable. Such charms might have had their full effect upon men who had been so long deprived of female conversation but that the whole winter's soil was so crusted on the skins of those dark angels that it required a very strong appetite to approach them. The bear's oil with which they anoint their persons all over makes their skins soft and at the same time protects them from every species of vermin that use[d] to be troublesome to other uncleanly people. We were unluckily so many that they could not well make us the compliment of bedfellows according to the Indian rules of hospitality.

After fourteen miles of dark Currituck Sound, the *Bog Trotter* entered a cut across a low ridge in Maple Swamp to reach Coinjock, North Carolina, where she tied up at a small wharf. I got off for a walk. The place-name is likely an altered Algonquian word for *blueberry swamp,* but the locals have been good at creating more lively (if predictable) and less believable variations. A truculent and weary dockside storekeeper said to a well-meaning woman, "Someday somebody's going to come in here and not ask that question," then answered with a solution involving how much specie he would have in his underdrawers if given a dime for every question about the meaning of Coinjock.

At the wharf stood an old Rhode Island mariner, a slender, angular salt whose sharp-cornered shoulders were wearing holes in his shirt and who spoke in a rusty, mechanical voice in need of oiling. He was taking a rest from moving his motor sailer south for the winter (yacht transit is a common use of the ICW). The most frequent question among those traveling the Waterway, frequent because it's of such significance in making headway, is "What's the draft of your vessel?" He asked, and I said about six feet.

"This is my eighth trip," he squeaked, "and I've learned that for two weeks of transit I'm going to touch bottom about every other damn day and twice on Monday. My goal isn't not to touch, it's not to touch hard. I had to get towed off a shoal my first trip down, but I learned since how to use a rising tide to get free. Those boys who call it a 'damned ditch' don't know how to sail inland waters. If they don't have five fathoms under their keel, they mess their britches. They don't read the day boards and range markers, and they got no clue about the floaters."

Floaters are temporary channel markers, a necessity in waters continually washing up new shoals. Range markers are paired signs separated north and south, so to speak, that a pilot brings into a bow-with-stern alignment to keep his boat in the channel. Cleverly simple but requiring perpetual vigilance. He said, "If challenge isn't a pleasure, then you need to hire some guy to bring your boat down. And that's what a lot of them do."

The Army Corps of Engineers has a mandate to maintain a twelve-foot-deep channel from Norfolk to Miami, but seldom is it that depth, and novices on the ICW are surprised to discover even vast expanses like Albemarle or Pamlico Sound are, at the deepest, rarely more than twenty feet, and in many places of a depth a tall wader wouldn't wet the brim of his hat. Were those big sounds in Holland, I have no doubt they would have been diked and farmed years ago.

The old mariner, whose solar-radiated nose proved his seven decades on glaring water, said, "I don't think there's anything like this protected coastline in terms of mileage — not to mention scenery — in the rest of the world. I mean, the whole route, Boston through the Cape Cod Canal, on behind Long Island, and on to south Texas. It's got just enough use, probably, to keep it open, but not enough to congest it." (I think he was correct: the Inside Passage from Seattle to Alaska is only about a thousand miles, and the interior of the Great Barrier Reef in Australia but a couple-hundred miles greater than that.) "There's some open water on the Gulf in Florida, and that inside route down the New Jersey Shore is only for shallow-draft boats," he said, "but if the government would fix the Delaware-Raritan Canal across the neck of Jersey to Trenton, those miles on the open Atlantic wouldn't be needed."

He looked at me to weigh my attitude, then said, "Hell, the Corps of Engineers can't — or won't — keep this lower section properly dredged, so I don't think they'll take on more. But of course they could if they weren't trying to dam up every stream out west."

Now weighing not me but his cocktail, he said, "Or you can see there'd be money for maintenance if that Bush wasn't trying to undo ten-thousand years of Middle East history to give cover for his taxpayer rape. People along here are Bush supporters, but they have no clue what his war is costing them personally. The commercial fishermen yelp about insufficient maintenance of the canal, all the while they're putting a **SUPPORT THE COMMANDER** magnet on the back of their pickups."

(At the moment I report this conversation, George Bush's Babylonian war was costing Americans three billion dollars a week —

about four-hundred million dollars a day. That meant enough money to bring the ICW back to standard got spent on the desert sands in about the time it takes to brush your teeth and gargle. I leave it to you, sagacious reader, to consider other pieces of broken or endangered America you could restore with seventeen-million dollars an hour. Further, your project, whatever it is, would not likely include four-thousand — and counting — fallen Americans and a hundred-thousand or more Iraqis.

❧ 4 ❧

He Is Us

THE ATLANTIC SHORE OF NORTH CAROLINA has something of the shape of a drawn bow, the arrow tip at Cape Hatteras aimed at the Strait of Gibraltar. Because of dangerous shoals, currents, and winds, the sea beyond the inshore route there is the Graveyard of the Atlantic, a name explaining one of the reasons for the ICW.

Unlike regions above and below it, the upper-half of the North Carolina coast is shaped, predominantly, by Pamlico Sound, a shallow sea allowing winds to gain a good fetch that, in combination with currents and rough water created by the shallow bottom, can make a hell for boats. Still, for a small craft, it's safer than the Graveyard.

The *Bog Trotter* was moving again at dawn, most of the three-hundred miles of Intracoastal in North Carolina before us. The country of Pamlico Sound and its characteristic wetlands called pocosins have produced a different sort of development from that of the beaches just to the east or from places with deepwater harbors supporting a city, so that the Waterway through the state is a traverse past villages, a few towns, and many miles of what, not long ago, were semiwilds. But, as was evident in the morning light, superfluous structures half the age of a grammar-school child were beginning to fester along the magenta line. Those houses were peacock places serving more for display than function, since many got used for only a few weeks. Most of them had two-hundred-foot docks running over a marsh to reach the Waterway, thrusting into it like pikes, devices to impale a careless navigator. For some miles the route felt more like a suburban avenue where docks replaced driveways, and plastic boats, autos. Q: "Everyone wants a Tara."

Of the several books written about traveling the Waterway, the classic, at least in terms of seniority, is Nathaniel Bishop's *Voyage of the Paper Canoe*, describing his 1874 paddle from Quebec to the Gulf, mostly on waters that were then an early version of or were to become the Waterway. His vessel was truly made of treated paper over a wooden frame. To read Bishop is to see what we've lost and maybe to consider whether the gains of unbridled commerce are sensible and equitable compensation for the resulting natural diminishments.

Another voyage book, a cult favorite of sailors, is Henry Plummer's *The Boy, Me and the Cat.* In 1912 he sailed (often actually using sails) from Massachusetts to Florida in a twenty-four-foot cat-boat (the titular cat is a feline), returning in it the next year. The book has some charm, although it's a self-conscious boat log written in elided sentences, many of which only the dedicatedly nautical will follow: "Kept the two reefs on her only settling peak for several sporting jibes." Plummer admits, "I have used all the nautical terms I could think of and some I couldn't think of." He's always more interested in sailing than what he's sailing through because, as he says, "There could be nothing more dreary than just a-setting still and being taken through these twisting rivers that lead for miles and miles through the never ending rice marshes." Not a man in quest of quoz in unverified areas. Still, of the several father-son American journeys presented in books, his is a capable one, even with forced attempts at cleverness in almost every sentence; but then, to be fair, the book has probably grown beyond the author's original intent: Plummer ran off a few hundred copies of the 1913 "first edition" on a stencil machine and hand-stitched them together with fishing line.

These voyages of yore reveal how far we've come from it all and thereby raise the question of where the urge for luxury housing is taking us. Perhaps those shuttered châteaux would have struck me differently had they not looked like ghosts in fresh paint; doesn't a house require actual human habitation to be a home instead of a billboard for one's portfolio? And when did it become necessary for a vacation dwelling to be bigger than one's real house? The pattern often showed clearly: a bungalow or cabin designed by a carpenter as it went up — dwellings now called teardowns — stood partially dismantled on a waterside lot between two châteaux nouveaux. Off and on for some North Carolina miles, I kept hearing in my memory Kurt Vonnegut's character Eliot Rosewater: "Grab much too much, or you'll get nothing at all."

The role played in that unchecked development by the Outer Banks, just beyond a narrow peninsula to the east, has to be significant. After a quarter of a century, I'd recently returned to the Banks. I had myself prepared, so I thought, for emotional surgery without anesthetic, but then, perhaps I'd be pleasingly surprised and my dark view about the American capacity for restraint prove to be fallacious.

I went out to Nags Head, then northward beyond Kitty Hawk. Nathaniel Bishop, who spent the night in 1874 in a new hotel on the Banks, wrote, "Nag's Head Beach is a most desolate locality, with its high sand hills, composed of fine sand, the forms of which are constantly changing with the action of the dry, hard, varying winds. . . . A few fishermen have their homes on this dreary beach, but the village, with its one store, is a forlorn place."

What I recalled from years earlier as two-lane road through open expanses with some wooden houses (easily rebuilt after a storm) had become five congested-lanes of stoplights leading to hastee-tastee tacos, outlet malls, go-cart speedways, realty offices (will sell mother's burial plot), miniature-golf courses with plastic mountains hunted by vinyl T. rexes, high-tension lines, martini bars, all-you-can-eat obeseterias, massage emporia (CALL FOR YOUR RELAXATION NEEDS), and condos so jammed up a guy could toss a wet sock from his window and stick it to the neighbor's. A Floridated shore atop leveled dunes. My antediluvian notions could not comprehend how it was that the very things people ostensibly came here for — the ocean, the beach — were hardly to be seen, obliterated as they were from view and ready access. Prepared? Pass the anesthetic!

Slowly it came to me: no longer were people truly coming for the sea. They were there for what the sea had, in effect, washed up. Not sand dollars and whelks but greenbacks and car wheels. One of Q's favorite quotations is Dorothy Parker's "What fresh hell is this?"

I climbed the now "stabilized" dune the Wright brothers called Big Hill and from which they launched some of their flights, the knoll today across the highway from an SUV dealership. Other than the few acres of the national monument, the openness that helped bring the Ohioans here was gone. Spread out below lay a distension of people for whom moderation seemed meaningless. Gluttony was all. How long would it be until that storm-aligned place would cost taxpayers a whole lot of money? To a man standing near, I said I couldn't see much beach or sand, and he answered with pride, "Isn't it something!" I realized I was beating a dead horse — or maybe it was just the nag's head.

The *Bog Trotter* crossed Albemarle Sound in easy breezes, the rip currents that can bedevil boats just then in abeyance, and we entered the estuary of the Alligator River, a surprising name, given that we were at the latitude of, say, Oklahoma City. But it was true: we had reached the northern limit of gator country, one of many definitions of the Southern border. The Waterway narrowed to the shallow river itself, with banks of cypress swamps closing in until we entered the Pungo Canal where a heron seemed to denote the channel. For a pilot, herons are useful two-legged markers requiring no maintenance other than fit habitat. "The prudent mariner," said my chart book, "will observe both sides of the canal are foul with debris, snags, submerged stumps, and continuous bank erosion caused by passing boats and tows." The "debris" was entirely from nature — mostly branches or pieces of tree trunks — and the other natural "foulness" happened to be the vegetation that fish and many aquatic critters require. The Waterway there — and generally elsewhere — ran remarkably free of human litter. Some credit for the cleanliness surely belongs to that little denizen of waters farther south, Pogo of

Okefenokee Swamp, and his mordant quip "We have met the enemy and he is us."

Along the Pungo lay a reach with reintroduced red wolves, but without a boat on the order of a paper canoe, I wasn't likely to see one, and I didn't, yet it was pleasant to imagine a hidden wolf watching our passage into its domain. Against probability, however, I was hoping to see a clapper rail, a secretive bird built like a skinny leghorn and often called a marsh hen. I understand that listening to a clapper is one of the delights — an ever more rare one — in wild America. Their decline is the result of the usual culprits — habitat loss and human intrusion. We have met the enemy.

Even in the mid-nineteenth century, John James Audubon, who himself brought down a tidy number of wildfowl, wrote in 1840 of people hunting rail eggs in coastal New Jersey:

> It is not an uncommon occurrence for an egger to carry home 100 dozen in a day; and when this havoc is continued upwards of a month, you may imagine its extent. The abundance of the birds themselves is almost beyond belief; but if you suppose a series of salt marshes 20 miles in length and a mile in breadth, while at every 8 or 10 steps one or two birds may be met with, you may calculate their probable number.

Of hunters in South Carolina, Audubon — with his amanuensis — wrote (in prose not admissible today among some of our spindle-shanked, dare-nothing stylists, those insistent practitioners of the unadorned declarative sentence):

> On a floating mass of tangled weeds stand a small group [of clapper rails] side by side. The gunner has marked them, and presently nearly the whole covey is prostrated. Now, onward to that great bunch of tall grass all the boats are seen to steer; shot after shot flies in rapid succession; dead and dying lie all around on the water; the terrified survivors are trying to save their lives by

hurried flight; but their efforts are unavailing — one by one they fall, to rise no more. It is a sorrowful sight after all; see that poor thing gasping hard in the agonies of death, its legs quivering with convulsive twitches, its bright eyes fading into glazed obscurity. In a few hours, hundreds have ceased to breathe the breath of life; hundreds that erstwhile revelled in the joys of careless existence, but which can never behold their beloved marshes again. The cruel sportsman, covered with mud and mire, drenched to the skin by the splashing paddles, his face and hands besmeared with powder, stands amid the wreck which he has made, exultingly surveys his slaughtered heaps, and with joyous feelings returns home with a cargo of game more than enough for a family thrice as numerous as his own.

A traveler preferring plowed fields to wetlands will like the big, bulbous peninsula separating Albemarle and Pamlico sounds. Although a thin scrim of trees had been left along this section of canal, most of the flats for miles beyond them on both sides had been ditched for agriculture. Still, free of domestic obtrusions and billboards, the route through pocosin country was enhanced by a few wildlife refuges, one of them containing two bombing ranges. In its simplest form, a pocosin is a slightly raised pond or bog that overflows onto surrounding flatlands to create swamps and marshes. They are an earmark of the peninsula and a landform considerably more rare than a mountain — and consequently worth saving. A soybean can grow almost anywhere in the contiguous states, but a terrain capable of sheltering overwintering tundra swans fresh from the Arctic is less common.

The *Bog Trotter* left the cut and entered the Pungo River to follow it downstream to its juncture with the big Pamlico, four miles wide where it enters the sound. Cape Hatteras lay sixty miles due east, the distance entirely the open water of Pamlico Sound. Take a paper map of the United States and cut out Rhode Island and place it over the sound, and you'll see a pretty fair fit. To look across that space is to understand how Giovanni da Verrazzano, exploring the eastern coast in 1524, could conclude that Pamlico Sound was the presumed great Western Sea — separated here from the Atlantic by only a narrow isthmus of the Outer Banks — stretching to the Orient. If his error seems woeful, consider that Columbus on his deathbed only eighteen years earlier still believed Mexico to be fabled Cathay, or John Cabot thinking Labrador was Asia.

Because Europeans discovered America piecemeal and because the role of Columbus dominates our current view, other contributors such as Verrazzano have remained shadow men. He deserves more. His voyage up the coast comes to us through a single surviving, brief chronicle, the Cellere Codex, that is considerably more enlightened — as was his behavior — than most other commentary by Europeans in the Americas. His report, a truly significant firsthand narrative of the exploration of sixteenth-century North America, remains the earliest-known description of the inhabitants of the Atlantic coast above Florida. Nearly two-thirds of Verrazzano's account depicts the natives he encountered, and his detailed view is sympathetic — a kidnapping notwithstanding — and marked by comprehension of significant variations among tribes. Of one meeting, he writes (Kathryn Wallace translation from the Italian):

> They have at the ears various whimsical pendants as the Orientals customarily do, not only the women but also the men, on whom we saw many sword-blades of wrought brass, more highly prized by them than gold, which for its color they do not esteem; indeed, of all colors, that is the one considered by them to be the ugliest, they exalting blue and red above all others. What was given them by us they prized most were little bells, little blue crystal beads, and other trinkets to wear at the ears and neck. They did not prize silk cloth or gold more than any other kinds, nor do they care to have any; the same with metals like steel and iron, because often, showing them our weapons garnered no admiration, nor did they ask to have any of them, showing

regard only for the way they were made. With mirrors it was the same — quickly looking at them, pushing them away laughing. The people are very generous, giving away all they have. We made great friends with them, and one day, before we came into harbor with the ship, being a league out to sea in adverse weather, they came in a great many of their little boats, their faces painted and made up with various colors, showing us it was a sign of joy, bringing some of their food supply, making signs to us where, for the safety of the ship, we should come into the harbor, and continuing to accompany us even as we put down anchor.

Another engagement, farther north, was less amicable yet still without bloodshed. Had more explorers possessed Verrazzano's sensibilities, one wonders how differently the European peopling of the Americas might have proceeded.

The great naturalist Rachel Carson described this latitude of the coast — where the Labrador Current collides with the Gulf Stream — as "the Mason-Dixon Line of the marine world." Things change at sea, and those changes change what happens on land. Down East, one eats mackerel; down South, it's mullet. For us, the thermometer was climbing, the South deepening.

❧ 5 ❧

The Gift of Variant Views

O F THE NECESSITIES OF TRAVELING with others, variant view-points, depending on one's openness and tolerance, can be annoyances or gifts. The latter can be recompense for the first. The only fellow voyagers I avoid are those who find every trip they've taken preceding the present one to be superior and who enumerate why — at length. Those people are often AWPs (Authorities Without Portfolios), and their distracting blather is rich with opinions not likely to be amended by differing evidence or variant reasoning. In an automobile, you are trapped, but on a boat, there's always the rail on the other side; it is, happily, other sides and different views they most wish to avoid.

One morning while I was on the sun deck and looking over tree-tops, I had to find refuge at the other rail when a woman wanted to recount her voyage down the Rhine with its "far superior scenery." Said she, "This is just swamp — old mucky swamp."

Later that morning, two other passengers stopped beside me to see what I had the field-glasses locked on. I was sorry to report it was nothing in particular at that moment. He, a Southern Californian, said, "I had no idea of the complexity of this coastline. When we came aboard, I thought we were just going down the Atlantic — outside, along the beach. We'd never heard of the Intracoastal Waterway. I guess I'm not ever going to get too old for my ignorance to amaze me." Southern Californians, to generalize, are not uncommonly dis-inclined to discredit regions lying to their east, a turn of mind that seems concomitant with living in a mild climate, as if the absence of any snow not on a ski slope somehow confers topographical superiority. So his next few sentences surprised me: "There's nothing like this on the West Coast. If you sail from San Diego to Seattle, you're in the open ocean the whole way. I mean, the West Coast is nothing but cliffs — beautiful cliffs — for thirteen-hundred miles." A moment later he said, "I still can't get used to the sun rising over the ocean instead of setting over it."

Even without measuring the multitude of embayments and inlets of the indented and sunken Atlantic coast, its three grand bights between Maine and Florida make it considerably longer and its longitudinal variation twice that of the geologically rising West Coast. I said the differences sometimes seemed as big as those between California beaches and the shores of Japan. The man's wife said, "But all this water and no sushi." Then, perhaps to tone down what sounded like flippancy, she added, "It's a lovely place though. This morning, weren't those big houses something? But where was everybody?" Her husband said, "Out looking for sushi."

The *Bog Trotter* entered the Goose Creek Cut through Gum Swamp on the way to the shrimp-boat docks at Hobucken Bridge where there's an annual blessing of the fleet. Since leaving the Dismal Swamp, we'd been traveling the country of the first English settlements in America, attempts that began with Sir Walter Raleigh's failed Roanoke Island colony. The Waterway, in fact, threads among much initial and superlative American history: in addition to the inchoate efforts by Raleigh, there's the first successful English colony at Jamestown; oldest preserved "American" vessel (Georgetown, South Carolina); last occupation by foreign troops of the American mainland (St. Marys, Georgia); oldest surviving artificial waterway (portions of the AICW); first shot of the Civil War (Fort Sumter); first battle of iron ships (Hampton Roads); first sinking of an enemy ship by a submarine (Charleston outer harbor); home port of first steam-powered ship to cross the Atlantic and the first nuclear cargo ship (both named after that port, *Savannah*); first powered flight (Kitty Hawk); first successful wireless transmission of speech (Cobb

Island, Maryland); and first swig of Pepsi-Cola (New Bern, North Carolina). And, I suspect, current archaeology along the Waterway will reveal eventually a few firsts from Spanish exploration and colonization.

We had come into a locale good for the presence of the real bog trotter — the American bittern — so I sat watchful on deck, beneath a mild Southern sun working to put me into a doze. As I played the binoculars over the edge of the marsh, I realized a transference had happened: my rechristening the boat had brought with the different name a different perception of the vessel, and my attitude toward it partook of the curious bird itself. Nicknames exist for several reasons, perhaps the highest being the intimate approach they allow to the secret nooks within all of us.

[**READER ALERT:** The passage below, like earlier excurses I've set out for you, I intend not to delay the journey; rather this ornithological one is to speak of a bird and to give you a notion how the voyage went in quiet moments attendant with water travel. Freeway-speed readers may whip on down three paragraphs.]

Because it can appear in all the contiguous states, the American bittern is truly a national bird, although nowhere abundant or readily encountered. It's of some height, even if not notably tall for a heron, and possessed of an amusing and meticulously deliberate gait through a marsh. Modestly plumaged in cryptic vertical browns and duns, a bog trotter striking its classic pose — erect stance, uplifted head, long and narrow bill pointed skyward like a reed — can scarcely be distinguished from its sanctuary among the bulrushes and cattails; and when wind moves the flags, the bittern sways in rhythm as if a tule itself.

Remarkable as that behavior is, something else sets it off from the some seven-hundred other avian species in North America. For its so-called song, an accurate word only if you can hear a couple of bass notes from a cello or from a mellifluous gargle as "song," the bittern seems to take a swallow of swamp water in order to sing of it, gulping, charging it within, pumping it up, burbling it, and releasing it as haunting notes that in the dark can shiver your timbers. Of other marshland critters giving voice to a swamp — wrens, woodcocks, rails, snipes, soras, toads and frogs, bobcats and gators — none seems so perfectly distilled from the bog itself. If flat water could sing, the notes of the bittern would be its song.

These are facts, it seems to me, making it natural to humanize the bog trotter. In 1874, the great naturalist and Western historian Elliot Coues wrote of it:

No doubt he enjoys life after his own fashion, but his notions of happiness are peculiar. He prefers solitude, and leads the eccentric life of a recluse, "forgetting the world, and by the world forgot." To see him at his ordinary occupation, one might fancy him shouldering some heavy responsibility, oppressed with a secret, or laboring in the solution of a problem of vital consequence. He stands motionless, with his head drawn in upon his shoulders, and half-closed eyes, in profound meditation, or steps about in a devious way, with an absent-minded air; for greater seclusion, he will even hide in a thick brush clump for hours together. Startled in his retreat whilst his thinking cap is on, he seems dazed, like one suddenly aroused from a deep sleep; but as soon as he collects his wits, remembering unpleasantly that the outside world exists, he shows common sense enough to beat a hasty retreat from a scene of altogether too much action for him.

That afternoon the marshy shore kept hidden all its bog trotters, deepening the mysterious: a phantom unseen has more power than one revealed.

The Neuse River, six miles across at its mouth, is the widest river in the country, say local folk, although to me it appeared more an estuary there than a river. The boat moved up it, rolling a bit, then in the dying light she reached Oriental, North Carolina.

By that time in the voyage, our several boat mates had sorted themselves out not by age or gender but by, in Q's word, inquisitiveness. On one hand were those trying to comprehend and remember what they were seeing, and on the other was a complement for whom the *Bog Trotter* was a floating bridge-table or a large water-bed or a reading room for perusing any paperback having nothing to do with water, coasts, marshes, or boats (unless a murder was committed on one). You get the idea.

Because Q and I were loath to leave a couple of topside observation posts we liked, we were often the last to be seated at a meal, which meant we got put wherever there was an opening. We didn't mind usually, but honesty obliges me to say on one occasion that wasn't the case. I ended up next to an always *en grande toilette* woman who, by my count, was on her fourth romance-novel (I judge from the covers) and whose expression, when turned on me, unquestionably said, "Sir, I shall wake from your presence at any moment." I'm indebted to her, for without her conversation with a man on the other side of me, I could not that night have entered into my log something I might want to use someday: *Without her grievances, Mrs. Y's life seems nearly without purpose. "Wrongs" against her must be enumerated. They are her lifeblood. As inspiration is to a sculptor, so disservices are to her, and those she carves into forms for the hurtful world to acknowledge.*

❧ 6 ❧

Hardtails and Crankshafts

ORIENTAL, NORTH CAROLINA, emerged from the dawn mist as a small harbor with a mix of anchored pleasure craft and docked shrimp boats, the latter dominating not in number but in fishing-port authenticity furthered by potent crustacean-odors from the wharf. To see a fishing boat of any sort along the eastern seaboard today can be to wonder whether you're witnessing the end of an era: my conversations with commercial fishermen about their catch seemed to contain the same sentence — "It's not what it used to be." (A prediction I recently read phrased it this way: "Year by which the world's seafood will run out, at current rates of decline — 2048.") The few species that have risen from possible extinction give more fragile hope than real promise for improved harvests.

While Oriental yet remained a fishing port, it now had three times as many pleasure boats as people and called itself "the sailing capital of North Carolina." The village name — I believe the only "Oriental" in the United States — came from the founder's wife who (on the beach at Cape Hatteras) chanced upon the nameplate of a ship gone to grief in the Atlantic Graveyard. Her enlightened refusal to yield to superstition about naming a settlement after a sunken vessel had seemingly proven itself in the renewed local prosperity.

Q and I went ashore to walk onto the high bridge to get an aerial view of the harbor, then we came down to hoof about and look into a chandlery (marine hardware to me is as jewelry to a pirate). At the former edge of the village, before it began to spread, we found the Hardtail Saloon. It wasn't the name that drew us in; it was the structure itself and what proved to be one man's attempt to do something about the widespread American practice of abandoning the detritus of some entrepreneur's failed dream. Although a municipality may require an owner walking a dog to pick up after it, many Americans consider the abandoning of a building (lasting somewhat longer than dog droppings) not as irresponsibility but as an ungovernable right, a mere consequence of capitalism. A few years ago in the Desert Southwest, where derelict structures not only show up over considerable distances but can last for several centuries, a visiting Englishman said to me, "Roadsides in the States are the place where old buildings go to die. Crossing this country is often like driving through an architectural graveyard."

The owner of the Hardtail, Miles Shorey, was having none of that ethic when he bought a pair of unused, steel grain-bins, each thirty feet in diameter and twenty-five-feet high. He took them apart panel by panel, bolt by uncountable bolt, and hauled them out of a field thirty miles from Oriental, then reassembled them in the same necessarily punctilious, labor-intensive fashion. He linked the round bins with a narrow frame building, turned one bin into the tavern, and was at work converting the other into the Southern Palace Restaurant.

We sat at the bar on what was now a second floor, ordered sandwiches, and imagined the bin full of ten-thousand bushels of soybeans. The food was good, one of the reasons a dozen "Orientals" (no Asians these) were also taking lunch. Among them was Shorey and his wife and business partner, Janice. He was of moderate height, with a shaved head and chinstrap beard à la mode for his generation of thirty-year-olds. Only some months earlier, he was mowing grass for a living. Most of the interior wooden portions — floors, ceiling, stairs, bar top — came from timber he'd cut right on the small roadside plot where he'd moved the bins. His rush to use the unseasoned lumber caused a little shrinkage here and splitting there, but his workmanship — he and a friend had done all of it — was excellent, including the tricky double-angles in the conical roof.

Shorey said, "With a bin, you build the roof first, then put the sides under it and raise the roof a tier at a time." For some years he'd lived among the growing number of derelict grain-bins marking the flat fields of Pamlico County. "I've always wanted to do something with them," he said. "Finally, a year and a half ago, this restaurant idea and the right time came, so I did it. Everything in my life has changed since then."

I asked what a *hardtail* was. "People think it's dirty, and that gets their attention. That's why the sign on the women's room says HARDTAILS and the men's is CRANKSHAFTS."

"Don't evade the question," a woman said.

"There." He pointed across the room to a dusty and worn and engineless — call it derelict — motorcycle frame. "I bought it a long time ago with the idea of rebuilding it. But I never had the money or time. Never even put an engine back in it. Instead, I've ended up rebuilding grain bins."

"Tell him," the same voice repeated.

"That bike's a hardtail. Look, no rear shock absorbers. Harley doesn't make them like that anymore."

The voice to me: "Hey, dude, tell me where there's another bar named after shock absorbers."

Here was a young fellow who couldn't find the wherewithal to rebuild a motorcycle yet could dismantle, move, and reconstruct two large farm-buildings and thereby rebuild his life. A down-home definition of *imagineering*. "There's a book," Q said. "*101 Uses for Abandoned Grain Bins. Item One: Rebuilding Your Life.*"

◢ 7 ◣

Veritable Poverty For Sale

Once again under way, the *Bog Trotter* left the Neuse River to enter the southernmost peninsula of North Carolina, that thrust of land tipped by Cape Lookout. She went along the estuary of Adams Creek, a zigzag leading to six miles of canal through more drained agricultural land. Cherry Point Marine Corps Air Station was ten miles west and Morehead City dead ahead on the far side of the bay of the Newport River, and there the boat tied up to an industrial dock until the next morning.

Q and I took a bus across the river to the third oldest town in North Carolina, Beaufort. (It might have slipped your aural memory that this name has a long *O:* BO-furt; the town in South Carolina, perhaps to vex the French, is BEW-furt.) On Front Street, fronting Taylor Creek, were clapboard and shuttered two-storey houses of a distinct design: roofs sloping down from the peak, making a slight shift in angle toward the obtuse, then continuing until they covered second-level porches. Ship carpenters built some of the places, purportedly after seeing such architecture in the Bahamas. The west end of Front Street manifestly expressed the South, but the other end, the commercial stretch, was of the early twentieth century: small brick buildings that might have been lifted from a main drag in Nebraska. In one shop window, a sign: BUSINESS SUCKS SALE.

Beaufort was the home of two men noteworthy in their earthly conclusions. There was privateer Otway Burns, his pursuit of English merchant-ships during the Revolution earning the respect of Andrew Jackson who appointed him in his later years to keep light on a nearby island where, says one history, old Otway "sank into anecdotage." And in the Old Town Cemetery lay a man who died at sea, his name lost, and who was buried "in a drum of spirits" that had kept his body from putrefying on the return voyage to Beaufort (perhaps a better end than sinking into anecdotage).

Once a fish-factory town, Beaufort renewed itself with gentrification from tourists and yachters. The fish was primarily the Atlantic menhaden, a herring about a foot long harvested largely for manufacture into many products or used as crab-pot bait. Menhaden go by other names, depending on where on the Atlantic coast the fisherman is: bugfish, hardhead, fatback, greasetail, yellowtail, alewife, mossbunker, pogy, shad. In Beaufort, in years gone, a social order developed around the menhaden, a not-surprising system in which African-American men (primarily) brought the fish in to black women (primarily), who processed it; bossmen and owners were whites (entirely). But declines in the number of menhaden — mostly from overharvesting — and improved environmental regulations, and the tremendous rise of recreational boaters, served to a degree to unite the disparate orders while creating a new division between them and the latecomers. If the racial elements have changed, questions of free enterprise versus sustainability, ownership against labor, wealth confronting welfare, remained.

In my interpretation, the history there for the last couple of generations was still about menhaden and its transformation into many products: lipstick, marine lubricants, fertilizer, and more — nearly everything humanly inedible. But it was evident in Beaufort that Front Street — once a place in the shadow of the tall masts of shad boats topped with their signature crow's nests, once lined with groceries, fish houses, and chandleries — had become a street of gift shops, bookstores, restaurants, hostelries, and an excellent museum. The former waterfront of wharves, fuel docks, and huge fishnet reels was now a marina.

In colonial days along the Atlantic coast, menhaden kept many people from starvation, and for plantation workers in the Caribbean and elsewhere, it was a staple. Yet Washington Irving, speaking of Knickerbockers eating menhaden, wrote that "no true Dutchman will admit them to his table"; perhaps his view was influenced by the meaning of the word in the tongue of the Narragansett — "that which manures" (you'll recall Squanto showing the Massachusetts Pilgrims how to fertilize their corn by planting a fish with each kernel).

At the northwest end of Front Street, we came upon a tall black man in his seniority who spoke in a melodious, precise, and Latinate way — *return* for *come back, appear* for *show up* — yet his pronunciations were fully regional: *oyster* was *arster, yesterday* was *yahstudy,* and *they* was *dey.* James Chadwick was resetting a wooden post meant to keep automobiles out of a small public-garden at the end of the street. His shovel chunked hard against old mollusk shells which create a richness in the soil, and that's what we discussed until I asked about menhaden.

"We call them mammy shad," he said. "Mens would split them and remove the interns and then charcoal them." The female fish provided roe, the real treat, but the flesh too, with the right preparation against the oil and bones, made good eating. The only place for a traveler to find them, he thought, was in season in somebody's home. "You'll just have to return," he said. "We can provide."

On the way back to the *Bog Trotter,* I saw a poster announcing the Blackbeard Fest, a celebration of the pirate who used Beaufort as a haven for his infamous flagship, the *Queen Anne's Revenge.* In my home state there's a celebration of Jesse James, and elsewhere around the country I've run into Dillinger Days, D. B. Cooper Days, a cafeteria honoring cannibal Alferd Packer, a Billy the Kid Invitational Fast Draw Shooting Competition. When a Business Sucks Sale isn't enough, what can a strapped Main Street do but to honor villainy to turn twisted history into a buck?

As the boat made its way down the coast and deeper into the former marshy retreats of pirates of the early eighteenth century — local historians call it the "Golden Age of Piracy," which raises the question whether our descendants will one day refer nostalgically to the "Golden Age of Terrorism" — contemporary emblems of the piratical became more evident: T-shirts depicting eye-patched rogues or sporting aphorisms (SURRENDER THE BOOTY), restaurants with names like Pirate's Cove, *AARRHH* scratched in ragged letters on a dock, Jolly Rogers flying above luxury yachts. (This latter manifestation may appear incongruous unless one considers where recent looters of retirement plans and education savings accounts and widows' pensions have spent some of their plunder, all of it accomplished without a single cutlass or musketoon.)

Somewhere nearby, divers had been working for several years to prove a submerged wreck was indeed Edward Teach's flagship, the *Queen Anne's Revenge.* Should it in fact be so, we can expect soon thereafter to see a Six Jolly Rogers Over Blackbeard's World. In another time, attitudes toward piracy on the high seas were different: English pirate Thomas Goldsmith's tombstone is carved with

> *Pray then, ye learned Clergy, show*
> *Where can this Brute, Tom Goldsmith, go,*
> *Whose life was one continued evil,*
> *Striving to cheat God, Man, and Devil?*

Sailing inside a coast of tricky inlets and shoals once providing brigands escape and hideouts, we moved down Bogue Sound, a narrow strip of water behind a skinny barrier island called Bogue Banks (rhymes with *rogue ranks*). Except for one "state natural area," it was entirely given over to side-by-side vacation housing that is to a hurricane as a school of mullet to a shark. Q said, "How much do you think it took to trash this place?" Less than it'll cost after the next Category Three.

Along that portion of the Waterway, unused pleasure boats hung in hoists, their Jolly Rogers furled for the season. On transoms were their home "ports": Vail, Las Vegas, Fort Worth, Nashville. For every cruiser or yacht under way, there were a hundred serving mostly to decorate a dock the way two-storey columns may do for a contemporary house, the message the same. I began writing down names I saw on transoms: *Good Judgement* (except in orthography), *Swagger, My Booty, Pay Dirt,* and (is there a marina without one?) *Wet Dream.* I was not likely to see the *Preposterocity,* or the *Good-bye 40l(k),* or the *Leveraged.* Eighteenth-century pirates, not usually noted for a sense of irony, at least had a way with ship names: sailing the high seas were the *Most Holy Trinity,* or the *Childhood,* or *Happy Delivery, Good Fortune, Black Joke,* the *Merry Christmas.*

I was watching from my favored lookout on the *Bog Trotter,* a wind-sheltered nook at the stern, a high perch often attended by a passel of laughing gulls elegantly airborne and sweetly graceful until some sort of tidbit rose from our wake; then all aerial hell broke loose as the birds dived for what I think were small fish stunned to the surface by the prop wash. It may be such swarming that has associated gulls with greed. Once filled, the birds would chortle to shore, *Hah-ha-ha-ha-ha-hah,* more mock than mirth, the fed gulls laughing all the way to the bank, and there they would take up a mooring post or a yacht mast and duly squirt it with digested fish.

The Waterway passes the eastern edge of Camp Lejeune, a portion of it near the Marines' firing range which can shut down the Intracoastal but has also kept that stretch free of franchises and vacation housing. A coast anywhere may draw martial operations, and the Atlantic inshore route — itself a product of war — passes numerous historic fortifications and militaried sites, from the sixteenth century to the twenty-first. At Camp Lejeune, so I heard, weapons "exercises" cease during wildlife breeding seasons. (Were the moratorium applied to humans as well as muskrats and toads, perhaps humans could begin fornicating weapons of war into silence.)

Our run past the narrow and marshy Topsail Island was, on the west shore, several miles of enlarging Wilmington, but on the east bank a cordgrass marsh had defended itself with squelchy, uliginous ground. Nevertheless, stuck in the morass were a pair of signs in fading letters; from a distance I read one as VIOLATED PROPERTY

FOR SALE, and I thought the second was VERITABLE POVERTY
FOR SALE. What truth in realty was this? As we closed in on the
signs, I raised the binoculars, trying to steady them against the
movement of the boat, and then I made out on both: VACATION
PROPERTY FOR SALE. (A more accurate offer would be FEMA,
HERE I COME.)

We had reached the country of the Cape Fear River which termi-
nates that long coastal bight and takes its name from a 1588 storm of
such ferocity that a ship of hardened English sailors fell into panic.
The *Bogger* left the inshore route and ascended the river for the night,
docking under the protection of the old sixteen-inch guns of the battleship *North Carolina* berthed across the channel. For riverborne
travelers, the city had a pleasantly accessible and historic downtown
where, on a deck at the edge of the Cape Fear River, we found a pint
of handcrafted beer and a bowl of spiced shrimp, sausage, and mush-
room stew, but we were too late for the collard soup.

8

Ob De Goole-Bug

DESCENDING THE RIVER AT DAWN and returning to the Water-way, the *Bog Trotter* turned sharply west at Southport and began a run past forty miles of more vacationers' shores, notably Long Beach, a lengthy and solidly compacted grid of houses. Q joined me topside and, surprised to see the sudden change in landscape, said, "What fresh hell is this, Dorothy?" Preparation for Myrtle Beach not far distant.

About midday we entered South Carolina. Horry County (don't pronounce the *H*) is the site of the final construction work in 1936 on the Waterway, and difficult work it was, cutting through eighteen miles of fossiliferous-limestone ledges now known as the Rockpile, one of the few places on the route where stone crops up and provides several miles of excellent scenery different from the marshes. But before the *Bogger* reached the Rockpile, she tied up across from piles of rock of a different sort, three ten-storey condos under construction opposite Barefoot Landing a little west of *the* beach at Myrtle Beach. It was a good wharf but for the other end being attached to a shopping center of low-end franchises. On the Waterway, it's a maxim rarely gainsaid: "Sail on the rising tide." Because of the Rockpile, that's what the boat was waiting for.

We went ashore to walk. I was just killing time when I stepped into the Bible Factory Outlet, because I wasn't interested in buying a Bible factory. Assuming an outlet store sells only merchandise discontinued, overstocked, or damaged, I told the polite clerk I was looking for a discontinued Bible. He considered and said, "All our stock is current, but we have a New American Bible for Catholics that's a little shopworn." I said being a fellow of old-time religion, I really couldn't settle for anything less than a discontinued Bible. "I have one with the Book of Revelation torn out," he said. "Would that do?"

I also passed up a T-shirt with a big yellow Smiley-face and the proclamation I LOVE GOD! as well as GOD BUYS UGLY LIVES, because I was sorry to learn at long last the face of God was the Great Smiley (although relieved to hear about His checking account). Next door was a shop offering Ts with a different cast: EVER RIDE A FAT BOY? And for the ladies: GIVE HORSES A BREAK — RIDE A COWGIRL. And: MESS WITH ME — MESS WITH THE WHOLE TRAILER PARK.

The Rockpile, though appearing dim in the darkness by the time the *Bog Trotter* reached it, came as relief. When night overtook us, I went to the cabin to read a book lent by a fellow traveler, a memoir about South Carolina rice farming, once the major crop of the Low Country. In his *Seed from Madagascar,* Duncan Clinch Heyward wrote in the late '30s of a ripening rice field:

> Some days it changed as constantly as the colors change on the surface of the sea. . . . Over the fields a breeze often blew, thus the crop was kept in constant motion, swaying in one direction and then in another [and] the whole field, as far as one could see, appeared to be alive, shifting with the wind, the sunshine, and the shadows of passing clouds.

By first light, the boat was beyond the Waccamaw River, an especially beautiful (said the captain) if short stretch of the Waterway we'd traveled in darkness in order to catch the tide. The *Bogger* passed Georgetown and left Winyah Bay to enter the Minim Creek Canal and its subsequent cuts that link with rivers and gutters and marsh, forty-five miles through the unbroken beauty of wildlife refuges all the way to the outskirts of Charleston. Even the shrimpers' opolis of McClellanville did no disservice to the beauty thereabouts.

When I travel, I have a phrase I hope to utter at least a couple of times: *It's for this I've come,* and I said it along that stretch of the magenta line.

The most rigorous definition I know of the South Carolina Low Country says it runs from about Winyah Bay to the Savannah River and as far west as the tidal reach, some thirty miles broad in places. On westward lies a portion of the great coastal plain, an area that in previous travels has led me almost to despair over the poverty of the people and the consequent degradation of their land and resources. Along the Waterway in South Carolina, almost none of that impoverishment appeared, and a voyager might erroneously conclude that the remnants of slavery and sharecropping were at last gone, but the truth was that the fallout of human-chattel history was still quite visible from highways west of the tidal waters.

Several times I'd talked with a chipper woman of pith and vinegar, born a North Carolinian but long a resident of South Carolina. Frances Pierson answered my questions, her responses informed by eighty years of experience, never afraid to say she didn't have an answer, often showing wit touched with irony. We talked as we approached Charleston where development became heavier but appeared less conspicuous than what we'd been seeing. She said, "We know the value of a tree here. We don't cut down all the trees to build a house," her implication being there were fewer vulgarian places. And true it was that the adventive homes and the natural selvage along the Waterway fused in lovely accord and with less ostentation. She said, "Since air conditioners, some people have forgotten about trees."

Despite its name, the sylvan harmony vanished with the Isle of Palms, a barrier island adjoining Sullivan's Island, the setting for Edgar Allan Poe's "The Gold-Bug," a story about finding Captain Kidd's buried treasure. From 1827 to 1828, Poe was stationed there at Fort Moultrie and spent time in walking the open land, saunters he drew upon when he later wrote the story and described the place with a pile of negations now having a positive ring:

This island is a very singular one. It consists of little else than the sea sand and is about three miles long. Its breadth at no point exceeds a quarter of a mile. It is separated from the mainland by a scarcely perceptible creek oozing its way through a wilderness of reeds and slime, a favorite resort of the marsh-hen. The vegetation, as might be supposed, is scant, or at least dwarfish. No trees of any magnitude are to be seen. Near the western extremity, where Fort Moultrie stands and where are some miserable frame buildings tenanted during summer by the fugitives from Charleston dust and fever, may be found, indeed, the bristly palmetto; but the whole island, with the exception of this western point, and a line of hard, white beach on the sea-coast, is covered with a dense undergrowth of the sweet myrtle so much prized by the horticulturists of England. The shrub here often attains the height of fifteen or twenty feet, and forms an almost impenetrable coppice, burthening the air with its fragrance.

Pieces of his description are still recognizable, and the fort yet stands, but much of the island today is driven by a commercialism that makes the words (in coastal dialect) of Poe's character, the manumitted Negro servant Jupiter, seem prophetic: "Dis all cum ob de goole-bug!"

As the *Bog Trotter* motored around the hooked point of the island, Fort Sumter appeared a mile distant, a narrow shadow on the horizon. In April of 1861, secessionist troops of General P. G. T. Beauregard began bombarding Sumter before dawn, but Union soldiers inside the fort didn't engage until after sunrise when the first Federal shot of the war was fired by none other than Abner Doubleday of later baseball renown. One report says Doubleday succeeded in putting two rounds into a hotel near Fort Moultrie. (Charleston itself just then took no Union shells, a good thing since men in top hats and ladies in crinolines were cheering cavalierly from the waterfront.) Doubleday, in his *Reminiscences of Forts Sumter and Moultrie in 1860–61,* says, "Our own guns were very defective, as they had no breech-sights. In place of these, Seymour and myself were obliged to devise notched sticks, which answered the purpose, but were necessarily very imperfect."

With the surrender of Sumter thirty-four hours and four-thousand rebel shells later, Federal commander Robert Anderson ordered a hundred-cannon salute before lowering the flag; exactly halfway through, the cannon discharging the fiftieth round exploded, a "friendly fire" that killed a Union soldier who became the first of more than six-hundred-thousand casualties, the color of their uniforms of no consequence.

Not far east of Sumter, three years later in 1864, a contraption made of an old boiler became the first submarine to sink an enemy ship when the Confederate *Hunley* took down the *Housatonic* — and somehow itself — in another history-remaking battle between ships of alliterating names. Like the *Monitor,* the *Hunley* had been found recently and retrieved, its entombed sailors reburied, and was being readied for display. Such was the topic as we entered Charleston harbor. A North Carolinian, who had lent me several books, said, "Warships on display and prettified battlefields feed warmongering, but if instead we put up wax replicas of dead and mutilated people, maybe the history of wars would have less jingoism. Let kids see the reality of blood and spilled intestines. Don't show a bronze soldier charging forward — show him bloated and rotting in the mud, his eyes pecked out by vultures."

Five miles up the harbor, on the Ashley River, the *Bog Trotter* tied to a dock at the city marina not far from the heart of the old town, and there most of our fellow passengers departed to be replaced the next day by some new, happy lubbers. We were six-hundred-fifty miles out of Baltimore, the upper South now above us, and below lay the nether Southland of Low Country cooking, tidal rivers, cabbage palmettos, yaupon holly, and those invisible biting insects called flying teeth.

❥ 9 ❦

The Oysters of Folly Creek

O F THE PASSENGERS DEPARTING were two South Carolinians, both attorneys, who shared our interests in history and good food and, by happy chance, had an apartment overlooking the city dock. When I first saw the passenger manifest, I reversed their genders, not a difficult error to commit in the South. Garland McWhirter, the daughter of Frances Pierson, was married to Pat McWhirter whose given name, Harrie, also didn't clarify at first who was who. When I learned Garland was named after her grandfather and he after an aunt, my error seemed less Yankee. For our layover in Charleston, the McWhirters and "Miz P" offered a long excursion from Sullivan's Island to Folly Beach, in pursuit of the place historically and culinarily.

Just before sunset, they drove us southward out of the city. I had hopes of at last finding some Low Country pine-bark stew. At an END COUNTY MAINTENANCE sign, we ran out of paved road and followed a packed-dirt lane to a lumpy parking lot, where leaving one's car in the wrong place while inside the eatery could mean returning to find the tide had turned your vehicle into an aquarium.

Behind large heaps of bleached oyster shells was a consecution of connected, low structures, hodgepodge sheds looking more like a transmission shop or recycling center than a restaurant. A few yards distant, Folly Creek was ebbing. A splintery, ramshackle pier wobbled over marsh grass to the edge of the redolent gumbo, a substance here called plough (pronounced *pluff*), a Land of Cockaigne for oysters.

An old fellow who looked like a dishwasher stood near the door. I asked, Oysters fresh tonight? He glanced at me to see whether I was stupid or simple. "Fresh?" he said. "Hell, junior, they ain't out of the crick yet."

Somewhere in this nation in love with contests and records, there must be one for the Most Cluttered Tumbledown Cookshop. I put forth Bowens Island ("Since 1946"). After trying a couple of mishung, locked doors, we found an open one marked with a cardboard sign: *ENTRANCE FOR TONIGHT.* The ceiling was so low that from the stilled ceiling-fan a coat hanger dangled as warning. It's possible there were actually walls behind the thick graffiti rather than simply more graffiti layered into stratigraphies of names and dates. Like a spring tide, inscriptions rose up the walls and overflowed to the ceilings, drained down onto the blackened windowpanes, rose again to cover stacked boxes, signs, framed pictures, and — I'm sure — right across the forehead of any diner sitting still too long.

Against a wall was a stack of ten televisions (when one gave out, it served as a base for the next) and four busted radios (crumbling antiques that had once carried war news from H. V. Kaltenborn and the shadowy voice of Lamont Cranston and the creaking door of *Inner Sanctum*); nearby was a partly melted jukebox (the Inkspots, "To Each His Own") and a hair-dryer frightfully like some primitive electrocution machine. On a cola case I could make out a graffito: *THIS PLACE IS PLUM WORE OUT.*

The tangle of objects ceased at a doorway labeled in large letters over darkened scrawlings, *OYSTER EATERS ONLY.* Inside sat a cadaverous man, shaggily bearded, pulling meat from a barbecued carcass that was slowly becoming skeletal to match his appearance. Covering the dining tables were newspapers and in the center were holes to shove the remains of a meal — bones, oyster shells, shrimp carapaces, that pouty kid — into buckets below. At the other end of the room, a slender, elderly black man tended three bushels of oysters under wet burlap steaming atop a sheet of steel heated by bottled-gas flames. The air, full of Old Bay Seasoning, stunned my eyes and throat until they translated the fragrance into appetite.

We were there for "roasted" oysters, shrimp and grits, and Frogmore stew. (No luck on the pine-bark version.) The Frogmore was a toothsome mix of boiled shrimp, chopped kielbasa, potatoes, and a few cuts of corn-on-the-cob in a broth infused with Old Bay Seasoning (but without amphibians — Frogmore is a Low Country settlement). The shrimp and grits were a *pot au feu* of the titular ingredients with diced sausage, green peppers, celery, sweet onion, and — all together now — Old Bay Seasoning. (I once heard of a Low Country vanilla pie made without that Baltimore elixir, but that's only rumor.)

As good as these dishes were and as heartily as we shared them, what we'd come for arrived last: oysters from Folly Creek right outside the back door via the wet burlap on the grill. They were piled on an oven tray with oyster knives and heavy towels alongside. The sharp shells were still cemented into fist-sized natural clumps that made opening them a puzzle of how to find a way into the cluster without letting one's blood (second Old Bay rumor: its color is to hide lacerations from inexpertly opened mollusks). The oysters — small, sweet, and fresh — had elicited a testimonial graffito above our heads: THEM OYSTERS PUT THE GUMPTION BACK IN ME.

A meal in a place like Bowens Island can make up for days of forgettable, traveler's fare and even help atone for one's sin of dining at somebody's Chez Somebody, and that meant I owed the Island a few more visits to clear my slate, a penance to be looked forward to. Some months later, Pat McWhirter sent me a news clipping: Bowens Island had burned to the ground. So now atonement would have to rest on a few bowls of pine-bark stew.

≫ 10 ≪

Meeting Miss Flossie

SOUTH OF CHARLESTON the magenta line twisted through marshes, estuaries, rivers, and creeks with jolly names for those who love vowels (Toogoodoo, Wadmalaw, Ashepoo, Coosaw), on a generally southwesterly course all the way to Beaufort where the *Bogger* anchored for several hours. The town, almost encircled by handsome marshlands, shows off to best advantage from its riverside of antebellum houses and live oaks that form a scene either classic or clichéd, depending on one's Southern experience or sense of the sardonic. Bay Street was empty of all but the Sunday quiets broken only by grackles rattling from moss-strung oaks and the crunch of quintillions of fallen acorns breaking crisply and loudly under every footfall as if in remonstrance.

Embodied Southern history today often comes down through restored mansions and manicured battlefields that, taken alone, become distortions feeding Northern perceptions of the people. A South Carolinian bookseller said to me, "We exist in the Yankee mind somewhere between *Gone With the Wind* and *Tobacco Road*." There was a little of both in Beaufort, although along the river the former was ascendant.

With our only transport shank's mare, we walked till — to mix the metaphor — our dogs barked, and we took rest in an antiquarian shop where I added to my book satchel (beginning to overflow into a carton) a Low Country history and a cookbook with a recipe for Egg Pie but nothing about pine-bark stew.

In the afternoon, the boat raised her hook and ran due south down the widening Beaufort River, past the Marines at Parris Island and on into Port Royal Sound before jogging westward to get behind shoe-shaped Hilton Head Island for an anchorage there off Harbour Town; being neither town nor harbor, it was as authentically American as its spelling and bogus lighthouse.

We went ashore but got caught in a drizzle and dodged into a shop selling beach hats and T-shirts. From Baltimore I'd been keeping in my notebook a page of slogans on Ts, thinking a progressing list of them would reveal certain aspects of the territory; there I copied down two: OLD GUYS RULE and LET'S GO SHOPPING. When the rain stopped briefly, we walked on among the landscaped acres but again had to duck into another place, this one a clothing boutique where I could have bought a rabbit-fur sweater for twelve-hundred dollars. (Hilton Head was once home to a Gullah community of freed slaves who ate rabbits rather than wore them.) By the door was a flyer advertising an ENVIRO-TOUR! to try to spot a manatee or perhaps glimpse some other fauna whose querencia had been flattened by twenty-five golf courses and an annual load of more than two-million tourists, of whom we were a guilty — if reluctant — pair. A peril of group travel.

On the return to the boat, we cut through a marina hoisting several Jolly Rogers. Coming ashore was an affluent yachtsman wearing not a blue blazer and skipper's cap but the new dress of the line: pressed denims and polished loafers, head wrapped in a bandanna. He saw Q and gave a one-eyed, Long-John-Silver squint intended as a wink, although it looked more like a nervous twitch that she acknowledged with an "Aarrhh."

Respite from such excess lay only a mile distant and across the sound called Calibogue (four syllables, the final two as if one stroke over par), on the north end of Daufuskie Island, the Waterway forming its entire western shore. Large marshes have thwarted a bridge there, and the only access to Daufuskie (rhymes with *the dusky*) was by boat. Isolation of the island before the recolonizing of Hilton Head by realty privateers was measured not by miles but by topography: it's surrounded by two rivers, one sound, an ocean, and the salt marshes. Such impediments helped enhance and preserve local Gullah life — with its distinctive blend of African and American ways and languages — until our time brought relentless real-estate agents. On the day we were there, only about a dozen Gullahs remained on Daufuskie, average age about seventy, all descendants of slaves who worked the indigo and, later, cotton plantations. Agriculture disappeared, and much of the island had returned to woods, although development from Hilton Head was creeping across the sound.

The *Bog Trotter* made fast to a narrow dock near the Cooper River Cemetery. At the small store there, I met the owner, a large fellow with amusing takes on local history, Wick Scurry, who invited several of us onto a school bus to show us Daufuskie stem to stern. The island had become known as the setting of Pat Conroy's *The Water Is Wide* (and a couple of movies made from the book) about his year there in 1970 when he taught grammar-school children who allegedly didn't know the name of the ocean on their eastern shore. Scurry believed the book exaggerates the naïveté of the Gullah: for years they had been making boat trips to Savannah — only eleven miles away by water — and by the '70s they had television and had seen local men return from a couple of overseas wars. While myths of such innocence are always a lure to city people, it was still true that the Daufuskie Gullah were distinctive in several ways, perhaps none more intriguing than their speech. The island was a place I'd long wanted to visit, so when Scurry ended his little tour, I stayed back to talk with him about the people because it was clear he, a white man, for some time had moved easily between well-heeled tourists of Hilton Head and the Gullah on Daufuskie. Above all I wanted to sit down with a senior resident who knew the island as it once was.

Scurry made it clear, in a way politely Southern, that for years the Gullah have been the object of journalists and academics bearing tape recorders and cameras to conduct invasive and tiresome interviews. My curiosity edged toward guilt but got a reprieve when he at last offered inexplicably, "Would you like to meet Miss Flossie?" For his store, she sometimes made her rendition of the celebrated Daufuskie deviled crabs, a couple of which Q and I had just polished off. "I don't think she'll say much or be comfortable unless I'm there," Scurry said, "and I've got to leave here soon, but I'll take you over for a few minutes." I understood I was to be a mere button on his shirt: two eyes, nothing more.

In his electric cart, we followed a sand lane a short distance into the trees where we came upon a clearing with a pair of small frame-houses. We climbed through a fence to enter by the back stoop, Scurry calling her name as we went, Miss Flossie appearing at last in the doorway, portable phone in her hand, the flicker of a television coming down the darkened hallway. So much for isolation. She led us to her dining room, a place made even smaller by a big table piled with papers and mailed flyers, in a corner the glowing television screen, her easy chair pointed at it. Atop the set, beneath a picture of the *Black Madonna*, was a photograph of her late husband, placed so she could see him during commercials.

Miss Flossie, I guessed, was in her seventies, tall for her generation, thin but straight in the spine, wearing a long dress, her hair tightly bound up in a red kerchief. She could have stepped into the Savannah of 1890 and gone unnoticed. Scurry made small talk, seeming rather uncomfortable for having brought unannounced strangers into her home, although she was cordial and apparently content to be interrupted. He declined her offer to sit, so we stood, and I just tried to absorb her words, her speech, to imagine what it would have been had she slipped into full Gullah dialect. As it was, her sentences had the lilt one hears from African descendants in the British Caribbean islands, and it was fast enough I missed some words. Scurry would later tell me that she could have lost me in a flash had she wanted to; I asked could she lose him (who wasn't native to Daufuskie). "No," he said, "but I can't speak it."

Only rarely on my travels do I stumble into crevices in the wall of time, openings one briefly can enter into another era before it evaporates like morning miasma. There she stood, surely from generations gone, looking away as if we weren't really present, her words sweetly rolling forth, she who knew stories that I would never hear, some that nobody would hear ever again. Her age — not in years but in experience — seemed beyond anything I had seen before. I almost believed the moment wasn't truly happening, that I'd not really found a crevice, that I was merely dreaming. But we *were* there, voyagers looking in from a time no longer hers.

Several days after our voyage ended, I phoned Wick to see whether he'd be able to arrange a longer visit he'd suggested, but I think his heart wasn't in it, and it didn't work out, and now, weeks later, I'm not sure I really wanted it to. I like the mythic Miss Flossie whose evanescent appearance has given me a perception of the Gullahs that may outlast their time on the island, her face emerging whenever I happen onto the name Daufuskie.

Once Q and I were again home from the Waterway, an antiquarian-bookshop owner showed me a scarce item, Marcellus Whaley's 1925 *The Old Types Pass — Gullah Sketches of the Carolina Sea Islands.* Much of the narrative is in that creolized dialect. Here are two sentences I take at random:

> "Him ole 'nuff fuh know nuffah do sishaz dat," declared Lizzie, in hearty accord. "Gal en boy all two, en man en' ooman fuh sich 'uh mattah haffuh know ef dem git outtuh bed on de wrong side dem gwine bex 'tell dem guh sleep dah night."

Spoken quickly with a certain lilt, it was something like what I heard in Miss Flossie's dining room, but to read a whole book of it, despite the lure of its yellowed pages, demanded more than I could give.

When we got under way the next morning, I noticed on the chart how the remarkably shoe-shaped Hilton Head (should be Hilton's Foot) seemed to be drop-kicking the little deflated football of Daufuskie westward. Scurry had told me of improved ferry-service across Calibogue Sound he would soon offer, his boat to run from the toe to the ball, but where Daufuskie will land, who could know? My guess is on the drop edge of yonder. Maybe its only hope is the curse a Negro conjurer years ago placed on the island: *Lay no why mon nebba mek no dolla heah nebba.* For a while, the old malediction had worked.

⇥ 11 ⇤

Fanny Kemble Speaks

FOR A FEW MILES the *Bogger* wound her way through a marsh-land of wide reaches of spartina — cord grasses — matured to the color of a wheat field ready for harvest. She crossed the Savannah River as if it were a roadway, entered Georgia, and headed southward below the slightly elevated land atop which sits Savannah, and there the magenta line further contorted. Of the four Waterway states below Virginia, Georgia has the fewest Intracoastal miles, but because it yields its leagues slowly, the distance seems greater, and, for those who find curving lines more interesting than straight ones, it's an excellent run. Were a direct sailing line along the Georgia route possible, it would be about a hundred miles, but because the Intracoastal there makes extensive use of rivers and creeks, the distance increases by a third. Names color the passage: Ogeechee River, Bear River, Front River, Old Tea Kettle Creek, Little Mud River, Jekyll Creek, the Narrows. All of the encumbrances encourage powerboaters wanting to make time — those whose wakes rip the banks and can swamp small boats — to "bump outside" to the open Atlantic. But for those staying inside as we did, the shores are near and the requisite slower progress allows a deeper acquaintance with the territory.

To the traveler in quest of a human hand laid lightly onto nature, the Georgia coast is a sublime example in its almost total protection through a wedding of private and governmental ownership. Although the sixteenth-century Spanish probably had the opposite in mind when naming those outlying lands the Golden Isles, people who visit them in November, surrounded as the islands are by vast spreads of harvest-yellow spartina, will find them — at least in here — auriferous indeed.

Of the Georgia islands, only St. Simons and Jekyll have direct road connections to the mainland. While the former is widely developed, Jekyll, despite its resort amenities, must remain sixty-five percent in a "natural state" according to a decree Georgia declared when it bought the island for a park in 1947. Wassaw, Ossabaw, Blackbeard, Sapelo, and Wolf islands are all wildlife refuges of various sorts; a zoological foundation owns St. Catherines; a homeowners' association controls Little Cumberland; and Little St. Simons, with its single road, is the last family-owned island in the Georgia chain. The National Park Service oversees the largest one, Cumberland.

Some of the islands — where an acre of tidal marsh is ten times as fertile as the richest one in Iowa — have been brought back from heavy human use and returned to nature. The exhausted cotton fields of Ossabaw began changing when it became Georgia's first heritage preserve, now a place for scientific and educational endeavors — further evidence that profits from land need not be concomitant with depletion of the underlying resource. The result of the innovations is that Georgia, even while allowing public access to all beaches up to the high-tide line, today has miles of coast that, if not pristine, still suggest what its shores looked like when Europeans began surveying them for military and mercantile enterprises. To excursionists arriving from the almost unbroken development of the Florida beaches, the change along the Georgia coast is stunning.

As the *Bog Trotter* made her way behind the Golden Isles and crossed the Altamaha River, I asked a man I'd often seen along the rail, his binoculars always at-the-ready, whether he'd picked up any noteworthy birds or beasts. The scowling fellow, whose attitude happily did not match his expression, said, "Slim pickings. I thought I'd see many more birds, even though the big migrations are pretty well completed now. But it's been mostly cormorants, herons, and some pelicans. A couple of kingfishers." I mentioned that early travelers along the inside passage spoke of large populations of many species. He shook his head. "The Christmas bird counts in lots of places across the country show numbers holding up, but I think that's because these days more people are out there counting. I mean, how could numbers possibly stand steady along the ICW with all that new development?"

Only eight miles up the Altamaha was a different disappearance. On Butler Island in 1839, English actress Fanny Kemble (Mrs. Frances Butler) made her first visit to her husband's rice plantation operated almost entirely by slaves. Her several weeks there and a couple more a few miles away on St. Simons Island exposed her to the realities of agricultural bondage. As a youth, Fanny took up the boards out of financial necessity, but she never lost hope for a life in letters. To help herself come to grips with the appalling conditions of the slaves — especially the women — she wrote and wrote, describing in precise and poignant detail a system largely kept hidden from outsiders. But after she left, for eighteen years she too considered publication of her forthright account a "breach of confidence" intolerable to her spouse, and she didn't change her mind until 1863, long after her marriage was dissolved but soon following final proclamation of the Emancipation Act. In her *Journal of a Residence on a Georgian Plantation,* her keen percipience and exactitude raise it from a powerful documentation of slavery (its accuracy now widely accepted despite earlier Southern challenges) into the canon of American historical literature. If you've ever toured an antebellum mansion, here's something you may not have heard. While on her husband's St. Simons estate, she wrote:

> We skirted the plantation burial ground, and a dismal place it looked; the cattle trampling over it in every direction, except where Mr. K had had an enclosure put round the graves of two white men who had worked on the estate. They were strangers, and of course utterly indifferent to the people here; but by virtue of their white skins, their resting place was protected from the hoofs of the cattle, while the parents and children, wives,

husbands, brothers and sisters of the poor slaves, sleeping beside them, might see the graves of those they loved trampled upon and browsed over, desecrated and defiled, from morning till night. There is something intolerably cruel in this disdainful denial of a common humanity pursuing these wretches even when they are hid beneath the earth.

Today, the chattel system is gone, Butler's plantation with it, but the rice-field levees and cemetery, I've heard, remain as witness.

✎12✎

Turn Left at the Fan Belt

O N OUR LAST MORNING aboard the *Trotter,* a small pod of bottle-nose dolphins broke the water ahead of her bow to lead us toward the wide and choppy St. Marys River bringing down the tannic waters of the great Okefenokee Swamp thirty-three miles west. Not far south lay Fernandina Beach, Florida; for us not the sandy strand of vacation cabins and condos but the old commercial and industrial section that had partly recast itself to accommodate tourism. As if to welcome the boat, a dozen pelicans perched atop pilings, their prodigious beaks resting on their breasts, their eyes alert to our approach. If you cross a heron with a goose, you get a pelican, a bird ungainly in all it does (notably backward crash dives for fish) until it takes up its low and lovely flights just above the waves, its big wings creating a cushion of air substantial enough to support its bulk.

The boat tied up at the city dock just down the Amelia River from one of the pulp mills. Under a dismal sky, we went topside, saluted farewell to our doughty little tub, disembarked, stashed our bags, and began walking down Centre Street with its refurbished shop-fronts and a capably restored courthouse. We made our way toward Route A1A — the old snowbird highway — which begins or ends there. The breeze was out of a quarter that brought with it from a kraft-paper factory an effluvium not really nostril-plugging but a bouquet making it seem, under the dark sky, we were walking inside a damp grocery sack.

A woman had told Q that locals liked breakfast at an eatery in an old filling-station still pumping gas but with its grease pit turned

560

into a café. We followed the alphabetized, tree street names south until we saw a station with parked cars and a sign for gasoline but nothing for food, so I asked a couple of pert gaffers sitting outside the station — as is the Southern custom — if we'd found T-Ray's Burger Station. "You're there," one said, the other adding, "Turn left at the fan belt."

In what was formerly a double-bay garage, under a picture of an inexpertly painted hamburger captioned with time-bleached letters — STOP IN AND KETCHUP — we took a rickety table with chairs out of somebody's 1946 kitchen, and ordered up eggs, french toast, and grits. Next to us sat a young couple, hands linked, praying long over tomato omelets and toast but eating faster than canines, then bolting for the door so she could fire up a cigarette, inhale rapidly, puff her cheeks almost maniacally before exhaling smokelessly. She'd gotten all of it, and, after a few drags, she appeared to settle down as if calmed by the hand of her Lord. If you've witnessed modern anesthetics delivered, then you've seen her performance. It seemed to me their earlier, celestially directed gratitude "for what we are about to receive" might have been more honestly spoken over the tobacco than over the tomato omelet.

T-Ray's father stopped by the table to ask how our food was — it was good and honest and reasonable — and I asked about his forty years of business along A1A. He spoke of old north-coast Florida, the shrimp boats, the menhaden fleet. "We used to have a trolley," he said, pointing outside to the intersection of A1A and Beech Street. "It ran right past there and on to the beach. That's why the street's named that." (Someday I'm going to encourage Q to write a history of America as it gets reported in cafés and taverns and churches, versions that shape local understandings. A woman the other day had told me Queen Isabella had Christopher Columbus executed for torturing Indians: she got the torture right, but as for his demise, he died wealthy in his own bed.)

South of Fernandina Beach, the Waterway is another kind of voyage, I hear, a route of so many excavated stretches it's popularly called "The Ditch," a place that reveals the nature of contemporary Florida and its daily throng of arrivals; once there, one in twenty new residents will operate a watercraft of some sort. Use of the ICW in the state is heavy enough to warrant a special agency to oversee it with specific regulations. Instead of rivers and sounds and creeks and marshes, there are concrete seawalls backed by even bigger walls of tall buildings blocking the Atlantic. It's for that place — the last miles called the Gold Coast — most Intracoastal boaters are bound.

Still, I confess, had I come upon a vessel of any sort going farther south, I'd have signed up for much the same reason I'll go once into a Bible Factory Outlet store, which happens to be the same reason the bear went over the mountain.

I won't argue that the local promoters who've dubbed Route A1A the "Paradise Highway" are no longer correct, most areas now more verified than otherwise, but I will say, to each his own heaven — or fresh hell. Sometimes it's a choice between a congestion of vehicles or flying teeth, city black rats or marsh rice-rats, spartina or sports bars, gunkholes or eighteen-hole golf courses. Youse pays your money and takes your choice.

My choice, my Happy Isles, was three-thousand leagues of ragged and sometimes submerged coastal plain, a country sometimes called Low, a tidal world of blackwater rivers, muddied creeks, rank flats; a soggy, stormbound border cursed in at least one place to keep whites from ever making a dollar off the land, a widely unverified area of brackish water where terra firma is more the exception than a given, a spongy maze of runnels and gutters that defy roads and concrete foundations; a slender realm of fluvial and marine emergence where the controlling, inceptive sea usually lies beyond, unseen although eternally there as the intricate isles are not. To travel such a forever temporary continental-edge is to enter a few leagues of a kingdom come, a land of quoz rich in native booty.

Valedictories

An Infinity of Sundry Forms

In a day to come, world weary, people will no longer regard Creation as entitled to admiration and reverence. The unexcelled All, which is goodness and the greatest of what has been, what is, and what shall be, will slip into danger of perishing, for then people will consider Creation a burden, and they will no longer revere the Whole of the Mystery — this incomparable work, this glorious construction made from an infinity of sundry forms, each part an instrument of the Cosmos which without bias pours forth favor on each of its works from whence is assembled entireties in harmonious diversity. Within every one of them exists everything worthy of veneration, praise, and love. And in that grimness to come, then darkness will be preferred to light, and people will think it better to vanquish than to seek harmony, and they will turn their eyes away from Creation, and the generous-of-heart will be thought fools, the intolerant rational, the destructive brave, and the self-serving clever. And all that attaches to the indefinable soul of Creation will be scorned and reckoned nonsense.

> — *The Asclepius of Hermes Trismegistus*
> Third Century A.D.
> (Free translation by WLH-M)

FROM
THE NEW QUOZINARY
OF THE ENGLISH LANGUAGE
(WITH ILLUSTRATIVE QUOZTATIONS)

Quoz (kwŏz), n. Anything, anywhere, living or otherwise, connecting a human to existence and bringing an individual into the cosmos and integrating one with the immemorial, thereby making each life belong to creation, and so preventing the divorce of the one from the all which brought it into being.

· *The Ancient Abyssinian Book of Quests:* "Seek thee therefore the quoz of thy life that thou mayest find abundance surpassing understanding."
· *The Gospel According to the Cosmic Travailleur:* "Unto you is given potential according to the measure of the gift of curiosity through which you shall find strength. Wherefore the Cosmic Travailleur saith, Be ye alert that quoz, like stardust from which it ariseth, come unto you and grace your days."
· *A Natural History of Invisibilities:* "Upon the pintle of a quoz do our lives pivot."
· *Navigating the Gulfs of Heaven:* "A quoz is a snubbing post to hold fast the smallest coracle in the severest gale."
· *Field Guide to the Third Planet:* "Pull the cotter pin of a quoz, and watch plenitude slip away like a lost propeller in deep waters."
· *The Nodgort Manual of Diagnosis and Therapy:* "In a human spiritual anatomy, as in existence itself, quoz are ligatures conjoining the heart to the brain."

THE NEW QUOZICON
ONE-QUARTER-THOUSAND
QUOZO-NEOLOGISMS

FIRST EDITION

quozabaly	quozception	quozeration	quoziety
quozability	quozciple	quozerdotal	quozificial
quozable	quozculiar	quozery	quoziform
quozage	quozcumbent	quozescent	quozify
quozagonize	quozcurism	quozession	quozigence
quozaic	quozdantic	quozeteer	quozigentsia
quozal	quozdatic	quozeum	quozigraph
quozality	quozdelity	quozevation	quoziland
quozamic	quozdemity	quozevision	quozilation
quozanalia	quozdom	quozevotion	quozilential
quozancholia	quozdratic	quozfibber	quozilient
quozancy	quozdulgence	quozfliction	quozilious
quozarama	quozdurate	quozformation	quozilize
quozarchy	quozebration	quozfuddle	quozillance
quozardic	quozedly	quozfully	quozillion
quozarkable	quozegory	quozgestic	quoziloquence
quozastic	quozelous	quozhound	quozilusion
quozataneous	quozemia	quoziastic	quozily
quozathesia	quozemic	quozibilate	quozimate
quozation	quozemplate	quozibly	quozimatic
quozbibber	quozendary	quozicable	quoziment
quozbiquitous	quozendence	quozicant	quozimony
quozbitionist	quozendental	quozication	quozimythical
quozbolic	quozenious	quozicide	quozinarian
quozbolism	quozennium	quozicize	quozinary
quozbotic	quozentical	quozicord	quozinate
quozbrasive	quozentient	quozicular	quozinct
quozcentric	quozenuity	quozicum	quozineer

quozing	quozmania	quozonastic	quozship
quozinity	quozmanship	quozonomy	quozsome
quozinize	quozmantic	quozontal	quozsplendent
quoziosity	quozmatic	quozopedia	quoztalgia
quoziotic	quozmic	quozophile	quoztarian
quozipatetic	quozmire	quozophobe	quoztation
quozipation	quozmonious	quozopolis	quozterious
quoziptal	quozmute	quozopoly	quozterity
quozisect	quoznalysis	quozordinate	quozterminate
quozism	quoznify	quozorial	quozterpolate
quozistence	quozniscient	quozorious	quozticulous
quozistible	quoznoiter	quozorium	quoztificate
quozitality	quoznonymous	quozory	quoztility
quozitant	quozocracy	quozosive	quoztiquity
quozitary	quozodical	quozosopher	quoztiste
quozite	quozoficient	quozosophy	quoztival
quozitecture	quozographic	quozosphere	quoztraction
quozitical	quozoholic	quozotic	quoztributor
quozition	quozoid	quozotive	quoztronic
quozitis	quozolary	quozotypical	quoztropic
quozitism	quozolate	quozparate	quoztrusive
quozitive	quozologer	quozpeccable	quozuberance
quozitration	quozologic	quozpendent	quozumbent
quozitudinous	quozologist	quozphonic	quozvangelist
quoziture	quozology	quozpiration	quozvergence
quozity	quozolonious	quozplex	quozvermental
quozlery	quozolution	quozplicable	quozversary
quozless	quozomancy	quozpondent	quozversation
quozlet	quozomation	quozpostolic	quozversible
quozlibrium	quozomental	quozquence	quozvert
quozlicity	quozometer	quozquibbler	quozvocate
quozlingual	quozomics	quozquisition	quozways
quozliterate	quozompense	quozrogate	quozymoron
quozlitic	quozonaire	quozscape	quozynthesis
quozlivion	quozonasm	quozsensate	

ACKNOWLEDGMENTS

In addition to those people mentioned in the text, I want to thank Geoff Shandler, Karen Landry, Junie Dahn, Karen Andrews, Michael Pietsch, Terry Adams, Keith Hayes, Denise LaCongo, and Mary Tondorf-Dick at Little, Brown and Company. Also designer Laura Lindgren and indexer Ruth Cross. Across America, I'm indebted to:

Jess Abney
Margaret Abney
William Abney
Judy Agrelius
Ed Ailor
Susan Ailor
Kelly Archer
Stephen Archer
Steven Archer
Bill Atkins
Pam Bagnall
Brad Belk
Sarah Bishop
Carolyn and
    Darwin Britt
Julie K. Brown
Larry Brown
Matthew J. Brown
Philip A. Brown
Sandra Brown
T. Rob Brown
Roger Brunelle
Marjorie Bull
Bill Caldwell
Norman Caron
Paul Cary

Schery Case
Andy Collins
June DeWeese
Joel Dicentes
Stephen Easton
Stephen Edington
Norma Elliott
Maggie Engen
Shellie Bell Finfrock
Marlene Fry
Tim Gallagher
Andy Gardner
Tim Gay
Steve Green
Ron Hall
Deborah Harmon
Sheridan Harvey
Hilary Holladay
William Iseminger
Trebbe Johnson
T. R. Kidder
Pat Lesser
Barbara Luczkowski
Maurice Manring
Mike Mansur
Bruce McMillan

Scott Meeker
John Meffert
Galen Moyer
Patrick Muckleroy
Stanley Nelson
Bob Poepsel
Philip Rivet
Greg Robinson
Jim Ross
David Schenker
Ernie Seckinger
Bill Shansey
Joel Silver
Leslie Simpson
Jennifer Smith
Dora St. Martin
Mike Stair
Saundra Taylor
William A. Thomas
James Wallace
Doris Wardlow
Kip Welborn
Steve Weldon
Karen Witt
George Wylder

INDEX OF PLACES

ABOUT THE AUTHOR

William Least Heat-Moon, the pen name of William Trogdon, is of English, Irish, and Osage ancestry. He lives near Columbia, Missouri, on an old tobacco farm he's returning to forest.

His first book, *Blue Highways,* is a narrative of a 13,000-mile trip around America on back roads. His second work, *PrairyErth,* is a tour on foot into a small corner of the great tallgrass-prairie in eastern Kansas. *River-Horse* is an account of his four-month, sea-to-sea voyage across the United States on its rivers, lakes, and canals. His three books of travels have never been out of print. Heat-Moon is also the author of *Columbus in the Americas,* a compendium of the explorer's adventures in the New World.